The Eucharist in Pre-Norman

IRELAND

The Eucharist in Pre-Norman
IRELAND

NEIL XAVIER O'DONOGHUE

University of Notre Dame Press

Notre Dame, Indiana

Library of Congress Cataloging-in-Publication Data

O'Donoghue, Neil Xavier, 1972–
The eucharist in pre-Norman Ireland / Neil Xavier O'Donoghue.
p.   cm.
Includes bibliographical references and index.
ISBN-13: 978-0-268-03732-1 (pbk. : alk. paper)
ISBN-10: 0-268-03732-9 (pbk. : alk. paper)
1. Lord's Supper (Liturgy) 2. Liturgies, Early Christian—Ireland.
3. Liturgics—History. 4. Celts—Ireland—Religion.
5. Celtic Church.   I. Title.
BV825.5.O37   2011
264'.020360941509021—dc22
2010049969

Ó fu-rócbath a chride, mac ríg na secht noebnime,

do-rórtad fín fu roenu, fuil Críst triä geltoebu.

[The King of the seven holy heavens, when His heart was pierced, wine was spilled upon the pathways, the Blood of Christ flowing through His gleaming sides.]

Blathmac, Son of Cú Brettan

CONTENTS

ABBREVIATIONS

AFM   John O'Donovan, trans. and ed. *Annals of the Kingdom of Ireland by the Four Masters from the Earliest Period to the Year 1616.* 2nd ed. Dublin: Hodges, Smith and Co., 1856.

AI   Seán Mac Airt, trans. and ed. *The Annals of Inisfallen (Ms. Rawlinson B. 503).* Dublin: Dublin Institute for Advanced Studies, 1951.

AU   Seán Mac Airt and Gearóid Mac Niocaill, trans. and eds. *The Annals of Ulster to AD 1131.* Vol. 1: *Text and Translation.* Dublin: Dublin Institute for Advanced Studies, 1983.

CE   Charles G. Herbermann et al., eds. *The Catholic Encyclopedia.* New York: Robert Appleton Company, 1914.

DACL   Ferdinand Cabrol and Henri Leclercq, eds. *Dictionnaire d'Archéologie Chrétienne et de Liturgie.* Paris: Beauchesne, 1907–53.

DPI   Angelo Di Berardino, ed. *Diccionario Patristico y de la Antigüedad,* trans. Alfonso Ortiz García and José Manuel Guirau. Salamanca: Ediciones Sígueme, 1991.

DSAM   Charles Baumgartner, ed. *Dictionnaire de Spiritualité Ascétique et Mystique.* Paris: Beauchesne, 1953.

NCE   William J. McDonald, ed. *The New Catholic Encyclopedia.* New York: McGraw Hill, 1967.

NDL   D. Achille Sartore, M. Triacca, and Juan María Canals, eds. *Nuevo Diccionario de Liturgia.* 3rd ed. Madrid: San Pablo, 1987.

NDSW   Peter E. Fink, ed. *The New Dictionary of Sacramental Worship*. Dublin: Gill and Macmillan, 1990.

NGDM   Stanley Sadie, ed. *The New Grove Dictionary of Music and Musicians*. 2nd ed. New York: Grove Dictionaries, 2001.

PG   Jacques-Paul Migne, ed. *Patrologiae Cursus Completus: Series Graeca*. Paris: Garnier, 1857–66.

PL   Jacques-Paul Migne, ed. *Patrologiae Cursus Completus: Series Latina*. Paris: Garnier, 1844–65.

PREFACE

Pre-Norman Ireland holds a fascination for many people, scholars included, who in recent years have produced a large body of scholarship on different aspects of the history of and life in pre-Norman Ireland. Personally I come to the field of early Ireland not as a historian but as a student of Christian liturgy. I discovered that a great deal of academic work has been published on the archaeology, art, and architecture of this period, and that the place of the church in society in pre-Norman Ireland and also of various elements of church organization itself have been studied extensively. But I was surprised to learn that relatively little has been published either on the eucharistic liturgy as celebrated in the pre-Norman church or on the attitudes of the people of the day to the Eucharist.

This omission is all the more unusual given that so many of Ireland's national treasures from the pre-Norman period are directly connected with the celebration of the Eucharist (one thinks, for example, of the Ardagh Chalice, the *Book of Kells,* and Cormac's Chapel). In addition, a great deal of both the textual and archaeological sources for the study of pre-Norman Ireland and her culture in general, such as saints' lives, penitentials, monastic rules, manuscripts, eucharistic vessels, church buildings and ecclesiastical complexes, are also directly related to the celebration of the Eucharist. Many of these have been individually studied, but there has been no modern attempt at a synthesis. Indeed, apart from the publication of some new editions of contemporary texts that deal with the Eucharist, there has been minimal publication directly relating to the Eucharist in pre-Norman Ireland since the 1881 appearance of F. E. Warren's *Liturgy and Ritual of the Celtic Church.* This is all the more lamentable as such a rich ensemble of contemporary historical source material is not to be found in present-day Britain. Indeed, it could be argued that pre-Norman Ireland rivals any other region of Christendom for such a wide variety of surviving early sources of the celebration of the Eucharist.

While Warren's study remains an indispensable tool for the student of the liturgy in pre-Norman Ireland, it must be treated with a certain hesitation. He was writing in a specific time and place, and his work was conditioned by particular struggles in the Anglican Communion of his day, as well as his desire to find a non-Roman precedent for authentic British liturgy, which he thought he had found in the liturgical practices of pre-Norman Ireland. Moreover, much of the material Warren treated needs to be analyzed anew, particularly because some of the material that he presumed to be Irish (notably the *Bobbio Missal*) is no longer considered to have any direct connection with Ireland. Additionally, with the passage of more than 125 years, a number of previously unknown texts and artifacts have come to light. As well as reevaluating and supplementing the texts examined by Warren, this new study takes into consideration the social dimension of the Eucharist—its treatment in art and architecture and in the spirituality of the people of the time—placing them within the overall Western European cultural and liturgical context.

On another level I have noticed a tendency of historians to rely on older and somewhat out-of-date liturgical scholarship, and likewise a tendency on the part of many liturgical scholars to see Ireland as a peripheral region where the normal lines of Western church history supposedly do not apply. Therefore I hope that the present work can serve as a bridge between the various disciplines. In this sense I have endeavored to be particularly detailed in terms of the bibliographical information contained in the footnotes. Chapter 1 provides a historical synthesis of the period between the Christianization of Ireland and the coming of the Normans, both in terms of the history of Ireland and the general history of the Eucharist in the West. Chapter 2 analyzes the pre-Norman, Irish textual sources relating to the Eucharist. Liturgical manuscripts serve as the primary sources of information, but they are supplemented by many other contemporary texts. As many of them were not available to Warren, I hope to have provided a new synthesis of the eucharistic references from the literature of the pre-Norman period as a whole, taking advantage of the insights gained from advances made by the sciences of liturgical studies and liturgical theology since the turn of the twentieth century. These advances are particularly important in regard to the scholarly treatment of the experience of the laity in the liturgy, as the overly clerical bias of earlier liturgical studies is less prevalent in contemporary scholarship.

Chapter 3 examines the nontextual sources for understanding the Eucharist in pre-Norman Ireland, including the study of the archaeological remains of church buildings and sites where the Eucharist was celebrated. It incorporates an analysis of the relation of these elements to the ecclesiastical site as a whole and the stational dimension of the eucharistic rites celebrated there. As an appreciation of the physical objects used in the celebration is also very important for an understanding of the actual liturgical experience, those surviving artifacts associated with the celebration of the Eucharist, such as chalices and patens, chrismals, reliquaries, and so on, are also studied, as well as the iconographical sources, such as high crosses and manuscript illustrations.

Given the high quality and wealth of analysis provided by many modern editions of those early Christian texts dealt with here and the consequent difficulty in separating them into primary and secondary sources, I have elected to have a single bibliography in this book. I would like to draw the reader's attention to my use of the abbreviation "cf." which is used to indicate a disagreement between two sources or to provide an alternative interpretation to my own (when I want to draw the reader's attention to a particular reference I simply use the word "see"). In quotations from published editions of Early Irish I have elected to quote the text exactly as it is found in the published edition and have not attempted to standardize punctuations and the stylistic formalities of the original editors.

Many people graciously helped me with the research for this book; I was constantly surprised by the generosity of so many who gave of their time and provided expert opinions, bibliographies, and even prepublication copies of articles in answer to my inquiries about arcane matters of liturgy and history. It would have been impossible to write this work to the same level of detail and interdisciplinary balance without this help.

I have always loved the liturgy and the early Christian heritage of Ireland. My academic interest in the Eucharist in pre-Norman Ireland started with my thesis for a Master's of Theology at St. Vladimir's Orthodox Theological Seminary, Crestwood, New York. Doctor Paul Meyendorff directed this thesis and set me on the right path. I continued my research on early Irish eucharistic practice in writing a PhD thesis that I submitted to St. Patrick's College, Maynooth, and which formed the basis for this present book. I would like to acknowledge the work of Rev. Dr. Liam Tracey, OSM, who directed the thesis, and Dr. Colmán Etchingham of the Department of History, National University of Ireland, Maynooth, who graciously helped a nonspecialist in the field of early Irish history and saved me from making too many historical blunders. My treatment of archaeology was greatly helped by Dr. Tomás Ó Carragáin of University College Cork. I would also like to acknowledge the role of Rev. Dr. Hugh Connolly, president of St. Patrick's College, as the reader of the thesis and Rev. Dr. Paul F. Bradshaw, professor of liturgy at the University of Notre Dame, Indiana, who served as the external examiner. Among the many other people who come to mind for their help are: Ana Abarca Lyman, Michael Adams, John Baldovin, Patrick Brannon, Cormac Burke, Sean Gibney, Yitzhak Hen, Hugh P. Kennedy, Maxwell Johnson, Cardinal Theodore E. McCarrick, Bernard Meehan, Thomas F. X. Noble, Tadhg O'Keeffe, Uinseann Ó Maidín, Pádraig Ó Riain, Michael Ryan, Marina Smyth, and Robert Taft. The transformation of this work from a manuscript to the present book is a result of the care and art of the editorial and production team at University of Notre Dame Press, and I particularly must acknowledge the labors of Matthew Dowd, Wendy McMillen, and Barbara Hanrahan in seeing this book through to press.

Many priests who are sent to do further studies have no choice in the subject they study. I was very fortunate to have the support of my own archbishop, the Most Reverend John Joseph Myers, archbishop of Newark, who granted me full freedom to pursue my love of liturgy, which led to this book. This love of liturgy is the fruit of the faith that I received from my family and from the Roman Catholic Church herself, which in no small way is due to my involvement in the Neocatechumenal Way. I would like to acknowledge the love and reverence for the liturgy given to me by my catechists in the Neocatechumenal Way and in the formation that I received at Redemptoris Mater Seminary in the archdiocese of Newark. I consider myself fortunate to have studied under Canon Pedro Farnés, emeritus professor of liturgy at the Instituto Superior de Liturgia, Barcelona, who generously gave of his time to make many visits to our seminary and imparted to us a clear vision of the liturgical renewal providentially initiated by the Second Vatican Council.

Finally, a special word of thanks to my family and friends who supported me at every stage of this project, and to the staff of Redemptoris Mater Seminary who willingly covered many of my responsibilities in order to allow me to complete this book.

Go méadaí Dia a stór.

CHAPTER ONE

Historical Background

Liturgy cannot exist in a vacuum or even exclusively in texts. Unless one understands the cultural and historical background of pre-Norman Ireland's Christians (the people of the day), there is little point in studying the Eucharist of that time. Unfortunately, because of a tendency on the part of liturgical scholars to see Ireland as somewhat different from other places in Western Europe, it was thought that the normal rules of liturgical history did not apply there. Some popular works have even imagined Ireland as a forerunner of modern-day hippie colonies with typically modern ecological concerns and lack of regard for authority.[1] Although serious scholars usually shun such facile views, in the case of Ireland many have accepted the concept of a "Celtic church." In recent years, however, this very nebulous concept has been called into question, as those who propose a "Celtic church" usually have something in mind that is quite different from reality:

> They imagine that there were common beliefs, common religious practices, and common religious institutions in Celtic countries, and that these were distinct from beliefs, practice and institutions in England and on the Continent. They also imagine that the church in Celtic countries was distinctly saintly and monastic; moreover, it was individual, unorganized and the very opposite of Roman.[2]

Happily, because nowadays many historians are studying pre-Norman Ireland, a clearer picture can be painted of the church and her place in that society.

THE IRISH CHURCH FROM ITS FOUNDATION TO
THE NORMAN CONQUEST

IRELAND AND HER PLACE IN EUROPE PRIOR TO THE
COMING OF CHRISTIANITY

Older histories tend to emphasize the differences between pre-Norman and post-Norman Ireland (and, to a lesser degree, the differences between pre-Viking and post-Viking Ireland). This book does not go far into post-Norman Ireland, but this outline of the historical background will identify many points of continuity between these periods. The liturgy of the post-Norman period was indeed quite different on many levels from that of earlier times, yet the seeds of many of these differences were already present before the Normans arrived. In fact, it is possible that the Irish church would have undergone similar changes by the thirteenth-century even if the Normans hadn't come. This element of continuity will be important in understanding the liturgical evidence.

Confessional polemics arising from the post-Reformation history of Irish Christianity have also affected scholarship about the church in Ireland both before and after the Norman arrival. In this context the differences between the Irish church and her near neighbors are sometimes exaggerated. Whereas there were differences, they were not as substantial as they are often portrayed (and arguably they were no greater than the differences between any other two neighboring regions in Europe of the time).

As there are no extant insular written records for the period prior to the coming of Christianity, historians are left with writings about Ireland in classical sources and with archaeological evidence from Ireland itself. Their work is further hindered by the fact that most references to Ireland in classical authors are mainly given in the name of comprehensiveness and do not evince any real interest or knowledge about Ireland.[3] In fact, only thirty-two classical authors mention Ireland, the earliest being Rufus Festus Avienus in his *Ora Maritime*, written in the mid-fourth century BC but perhaps drawing on fifth-century material.[4] Most of these are token references in geographical descriptions of the whole known world or in side-references to Britain. Apart from the approximate geographical location of Ireland, the few other details that are learned from these sources fall more into the category of trivia than real history. Diodorus Siculus in the first century BC mentions that there are cannibals on the island of Ireland.[5] In his *Geography* (AD 19) Strabo adds that these cannibals are also incestuous, and his contemporary Pomponius Mela mentions in *De chorographia* that the island has a good climate for grain and cattle.[6] But there was little positive to be said about Ireland in these earliest written sources. Around AD 200 Solinus records that:

> *Hibernia* is inhuman in the savage rituals of its inhabitants, but on the other hand is so rich in fodder that the cattle, if not removed from the fields from time to time, would happily gorge themselves to a dangerous point. On that island there are no snakes, few birds and an unfriendly and warlike people. When the blood of killers has been drained, the victors smear it on their own faces. They treat right and wrong as the same thing. There have never been any bees there, and if anyone sprinkles dust or pebbles from there among the hives, the swarms will leave the honeycombs.[7]

A few decades before St Patrick's mission to Ireland, St Jerome (d. 420) adds the following about the Irish people:

> Why should I speak of other nations when I myself as a young man in Gaul saw the *Atticoti* (or *Scoti*), a British people, feeding on human flesh? Moreover, when they came across herds of pigs and cattle in the forests, they frequently cut off the buttocks of the shepherds and their wives, and their nipples, regarding these alone as delicacies. The nation of the *Scoti* do not have individual wives, but, as if they had read Plato's *Republic* or followed the example of Cato, no wife belongs to a particular man, but, as each desires, they indulge themselves like beasts.[8]

The archaeological record confirms the view of these texts that Ireland was not accorded much importance by the Roman world. While there have been some archaeological finds in Ireland of Roman material, these are not really very significant and not much can be inferred from them.[9] A linguistic theory (founded on a fairly complicated linguistic analysis of Latin loan-words in Early Irish) was often advanced in older works for stronger pre-Christian contact between Ireland and the Roman empire, but more recent scholarship is hesitant to read much into this.[10]

There is evidence of human settlement in Ireland from about 8000 BC.[11] These people inhabited different parts of the island and originally lived by hunting and gathering, but by about 4000 BC the practice of raising crops and rearing domesticated animals was introduced.[12] There are some impressive extant monuments from the pre-Christian period. The Stone Age passage tombs of the Boyne Valley, which probably date to the fourth millennium BC, are some of the best and most complex monuments for that period from any region in the world.[13] There was also significant metalworking, first in bronze and gold and, later, in iron. Many of these pieces were of a very high quality, as the Bronze Age (ca. 1000–700 BC) archaeological finds on display in the National Museum of Ireland bear witness. However, while great artistic skill was required to manufacture these artifacts, it would seem to have been used predominantly to provide artifacts for the elite rather than for society at large.[14] Moreover, the artifacts themselves do not really tell us much about the people who manufactured them. One of the great unanswered questions of this time period is: When did Ireland become dominated by a Celtic culture, or when did the Indo-European language that was the ancestor of modern Irish become the dominant language on the island?[15]

Once again, we are faced with a lack of written evidence. It is known that when Christianity was introduced, the Irish spoke a Celtic language. But not much else can be said. Caution must be exercised in examining the "Celticness" of early Ireland, since next to nothing is known about the culture of the Celts. True, there are some references in classical authors, but these are very biased and, for example, very little can be learned about the people of pre-Christian Ireland from Julius Caesar's comments about his Celtic adversaries in *De bello gallico*. Furthermore, even less can be said of the religious observances of the pre-Christian peoples of Ireland; most of what is "known" today about the druids is mere Victorian invention.[16]

ST PATRICK AND THE FIFTH-CENTURY ORIGINS OF
THE IRISH CHURCH

I am very much God's debtor, who gave me such great grace that many people were reborn in God through me and afterwards confirmed, and that clerics were ordained for them everywhere, for a people just coming to the faith, whom the Lord took from the utmost parts of the earth, as He once had promised through his prophets: To Thee the gentiles shall come from the ends of the earth and shall say: "How false are the idols our fathers got for themselves, and there is no profit in them"; and again: I have set Thee as a light among the gentiles, that Thou mayest be for salvation unto the utmost part of the earth.[17]

With its arrival to Ireland, Christianity had reached in the words of Patrick *ab extremis terrae*, or, as St Columbanus (d. 615) would explain to Pope Boniface in the early seventh century, the Irish were "inhabitants of the world's edge."[18] This was the first time that the Latin church expanded beyond the boundaries of the Western Roman empire.

But it was precisely in this period that the Western Roman empire supposedly collapsed, with the population of the city of Rome dropping from half a million to only 50,000 between AD 450 and 550.[19] This was the time when Rome itself was repeatedly invaded by barbarian tribes. While this "fall" of Rome is of significance, there has been a tendency to exaggerate the contrast between the Romans and the barbarians, whereas, in fact, the "fall" of Rome was not the total collapse of a civilization that is often imagined. Recent archaeological studies have pointed out that Roman influence penetrated deep into the barbarian territories, slowly inculcating aspects of Roman lifestyle and culture in these people.[20] Even from the point of view of economy, there seems to have been very little decline in the trade in the ancient world between Late Antiquity and the early Middle Ages.[21] On all the western frontiers, the barbarians became more and more Roman, while the Romans also adopted many of the barbarians' customs.

Another popular modern mistake is to see these tribes as the ancestors of modern European nations. This is simply not true, as even the tribes themselves were not ethnically defined. They were made up of fighting men (of both Roman and barbarian ancestry) and their dependents, and it was allegiance to a chief and not ethnicity that determined belonging.[22] It is too simplistic to see them as marauding hordes who were only interested in rape and pillage, even if there was a certain amount of turmoil in the West as the empire's center of gravity shifted eastward to Constantinople. It would be better to understand the barbarian tribes as being made up of people of diverse origins who were related to the Roman empire in different degrees and who, during this period, came to settle within the frontiers of what had been the Western Roman empire.[23]

For the study of early Irish Christianity, one would probably be better off starting with a study of Britain than of the Continent. Britain (a Roman colony from AD 43 to 410) was more than likely the source of the evangelization of Ireland. There may also have been some direct interaction between Ireland and the Gaulish church, although it is hard to distinguish between the churches of Britain and Gaul at this time.[24] During this period in both Gaul and Britain the church was organized along similar lines, and British bishops were in attendance at a number of early Continental councils.[25] But while there was a certain continuity of Roman civilization on the Continent after the fall of Rome, this was not as true of Roman Britain. While Roman Britain had had quite an impressive civilization with villas, walled towns, and Hadrian's Wall, this economy was largely based on the Roman military, and, when the legions left, the economy more or less collapsed.[26] Indeed, archaeological reconstruction of post-Roman Britain paints a picture of a flattened landscape;[27] many public buildings were abandoned, cultivated land may have reverted to wilderness, and there was a general fall in population.[28]

Yet this post-Roman Britain also had a significant Christian presence. In the period of Late Antiquity, after the edict of Milan in 313, the empire had been the medium for the spread of Christianity. The empire's support of the orthodox and catholic synthesis of Christianity was not simply a benevolent change of heart on the part of an establishment that had formerly persecuted Christianity; it was, rather, a pragmatic admission of the success of Christianity in converting many people throughout the empire, as well as a growing conviction that monotheism was a better medium for the promotion and, indeed, the expansion of the empire itself. This was seen particularly in the Eastern provinces that became the Byzantine empire, but it was also a factor of the development of Christendom in the West.[29]

In Britain itself, it is possible that even the bulk of the population remained pagan well into the fifth century; nonetheless, the British church survived the fall of the empire and proved vital enough to evangelize Ireland.[30] The first missionaries to Ireland, while possessing a Roman heritage, probably had a certain affinity for the cultural world they found in Ireland. Some aspects of Irish culture may have been comparable to the remnants of pre-Roman British culture.[31] Whereas in later centuries there was a tendency for the Roman-British peoples to emphasize their Britishness in contrast to the Anglo-Saxon peoples converted by the newer Augustinian mission,[32] at this stage they still considered themselves to be Romans.

These missionaries made the important decision that the introduction of Christianity into Ireland was to be accompanied by the introduction of Latin as the language of the liturgy and the scriptures.[33] This choice may further point to the "Romanness" of the first missionaries.[34] The introduction of Latin into Ireland would, in later centuries, prove to be of help in the evangelization of other nations.[35] The Irish had an advantage in the fact that Latin was never the vernacular, and whereas the various Continental groups who spoke Latin had already begun to experience an onset of regionalism that would lead to the modern Romance languages, they were unable to stand back and appreciate Latin for what it was. This use of Latin, along with the new grammars, penitentials, law collections, and other works, played an important role in the next generations in the evangelization of other non-Roman people of the West such as the missions of St Boniface (d. 755) in Germany or even the eventual evangelization of Scandinavia.[36]

The first mention of Christianity in Ireland is a cryptic line in Prosper of Aquitaine's *Chronica minora* which tells us that in 431, "Pope Celestine ordained Palladius and sent him to those Irish who were believers in Christ to be their first bishop."[37] Later on, in his encomium on Pope Celestine, Prosper (d. ca. 455) tells us that

He has been, however, no less energetic in freeing the British provinces from this same disease [the Pelagian heresy]: he removed from that hiding-place certain enemies of grace who had occupied the land of their origin; also, having ordained a bishop for the Irish, while he labours to keep the Roman island catholic, he has also made the barbarian island christian.[38]

Even allowing for some hyperbole, the claim that Celestine "kept the Roman isle catholic and made the barbarian isle christian" would indicate some success for Palladius's mission. In the mid-eighth century St Bede the Venerable (d. 735) repeats the same information[39] without adding much new. Little else is known about Palladius, and in later centuries, when Patrick was the undisputed national patron saint, Palladius's presence in the ancient histories was explained by conveniently making him a disciple of Patrick, and even the traditional 432 date for the arrival of Patrick (a mere year after Palladius's arrival) may well have been invented by later Patrician hagiographers to dispose of Palladius as quickly as possible.[40] Today it must be admitted that Palladius was a significant historical character.[41] Indeed, some modern scholars have even gone so far as to attribute papal backing to his mission.[42] Moreover, Columbanus, who in the early seventh century is much closer to Palladius's time than ourselves,[43] can speak of the Irish as having been evangelized directly by Rome:

> For all we Irish, inhabitants of the world's edge, are disciples of Saints Peter and Paul and of all the disciples who wrote the sacred canon by the Holy Ghost, and we accept nothing outside the evangelical and apostolic teaching; none that has been a heretic, none a Judaizer, none a schismatic; but the Catholic Faith, as it was delivered to you first, who are the successors of the holy apostles, is maintained unbroken.[44]

Whatever may be the case regarding Palladius (and barring some significant discovery of new evidence, there can only remain some tantalizing theories as to his exact historical role), St Patrick holds pride of place as the apostle of Ireland.

Nowadays one could almost be forgiven for dismissing St Patrick as being so distorted by popular culture as to have next to no real historical importance. But not only was Patrick a real person, he has also bequeathed his autobiography to us—the only Latin work of its kind to be composed outside the boundaries of the empire in Late Antiquity.[45] His *Confessio* tells of his being captured as a youth by Irish marauders and sent to Ireland as a slave, of his subsequent escape, and of how he eventually returned to Ireland as a missionary and established the church there.

Regardless of how much actual missionary work Patrick did, how many churches he founded and the probable existence of some Irish Christians prior to his mission (not to mention the persistence of paganism in Ireland long after his death),[46] it is very important to stress that Patrick was *recognized* by the Irish as their patron saint. Already in the seventh century there was a widespread cult of Patrick, not only in the churches he founded but also throughout the whole of Ireland.[47] Notwithstanding the difficulties of analyzing the success of Patrick's mission or even of evangelization in general in Ireland, the sixth century, coming straight after one of the traditional dates for Patrick's death (493), marks a radical change in Ireland on the level of material culture:

What caused Ireland after AD 500 to become so different from before was the new religion and with it the institution of the church. Even though many were not initially converted, the whole nature of society was transformed; the change was far more than just one of religion. Indeed, archaeologically most of the change seems to be related to settlement, subsistence agriculture and technology. The old order was completely revolutionized in all aspects of life.[48]

Traditionally this change has been attributed to acculturation associated with the arrival of technology and farming innovations that accompanied the Christianization of Ireland (with Britain being the likely source for this influence).[49] A number of causes other than Christianization have been recently posited, among them, refugees fleeing the fall of the Roman empire, slave raiders, Irish mercenaries

returning from service abroad, and bonds of kinship with Irish colo-
nists in Britain. But I think that the new worldview of Christianity is
a far more likely explanation for these changes. Material remains from
Iron Age Ireland (the seventh to the third centuries BC) already point
to a high level of technological development. Until the advent of
Christianity these techniques were mostly used to produce luxury
objects that were probably status symbols for the elite; in the early
Christian period "craft production turned away from limited, individual works to mass produced goods."[50]

EARLY RELATIONS AND POLEMICS BETWEEN THE IRISH AND ENGLISH CHURCHES

Christianity had been well implanted in Britain by 406, the year the
Roman legions withdrew from there. Although it had been introduced into Britain through the medium of the Roman empire, the
church did manage to survive without the protection of the legions.
When pagan Saxon tribes arrived in Britain, the church was not destroyed by these newcomers, but it was not strong enough to convert
them. So a new hybrid Roman British–barbarian society developed
(which was to become the nation of England) in which Christian and
Roman elements existed alongside pagan Saxon ones.[51] The natural
struggle between the Romanized Britons and the new arrivals might
help to explain the hesitancy of the newer Saxon tribes to accept
Christianity, which they considered to be the religion of their rivals.

While Ireland did not fully become even nominally Christian
until the seventh century, there was a slow but sure acceptance of
Christianity from the time of Palladius and Patrick and the other missionaries. This eventually led to the development of a new Christian
commonwealth in the British Isles. To use Brown's term, this was a
"Celtic Mediterranean" made up of the original British Christians
(the forerunners of the Welsh) and the Irish (including the inhabitants
of their Scottish territories). While these peoples held many aspects of
their culture in common, Christianity was an important part of the
glue that bound them together. Even if the Irish and the Welsh were
both Celtic peoples, speaking what are now classed as Celtic languages, these languages were probably mutually unintelligible and recourse had to be made to Latin as a common tongue.[52]

This is the context needed to understand St Augustine of Canterbury's mission. There was a strong Christian presence in Great Britain when Augustine (d. 604) arrived. But this Christianity was concentrated in the western and northern parts of the island. Mercia and Northumbria (most of present-day England) were Saxon and still pagan. However, while most of these pagans were hesitant to accept Christianity from their British or Irish neighbors, they were not as hesitant about Augustine, who represented the old order of Rome, its empire, and the prestige of the pope.[53]

Although St Bede the Venerable is a very important historical witness to this time, we cannot treat his works as one would treat those of a modern historian. Bede's main historical work is his *Ecclesiastical History of the English People*. This book, which he completed in 731,[54] is as much a work of theology as history. Bede is not simply recounting facts as they happened; he is, in fact, constructing a theological view of reality. This view is intent on justifying the superiority of the English nation[55] and their church. The work, therefore, is biased, and particularly biased against the Irish. The *Ecclesiastical History* is founded on the patristic view of history as having six ages, the sixth age being the age of the church. His *Ecclesiastical History* is set in this last age and, to Bede's understanding, the earlier ages are necessarily inferior. Concretely, this bias presents British Christianity prior to the evangelization of the Anglo-Saxons as inferior to the churches arising from the missionary work in the kingdom of Kent carried out by St Augustine and his companions who were "much worthier heralds of the truth."[56] The earlier Christian heritage is impossible to ignore and Bede cannot but admire many of the Irish missionaries, men such as Aidan (d. 651)[57] and Fursey (d. ca. 650),[58] not to mention the giant St Columba (d. 597).[59] But in the end Bede's worldview leads him to the conclusion that prior to Augustine's arrival "in Ireland, as well as in Britain, the life and profession of the people was not in accordance with church practice in many things."[60]

Basing their work on a faulty interpretation of the evidence (and particularly that of Bede), some modern authors have held that Ireland was indeed rife with Pelagianism and other lines of thought condemned by mainstream Christianity as heretical.[61] But as so little evidence exists of real heresy in early Ireland, it is hard to maintain this thesis. Yet some controversy did exist. According to Bede, St Gregory the Great (d. 604) had given Augustine very liberal prescriptions on dealing with the existing Christians in Britain.[62] Yet Augustine pushed for uniformity in church discipline and practice. There was some resistance to his program of uniformity, and this crystallized around two central points—the paschal controversy and the Celtic tonsure.[63]

The method for calculating the date of Easter is one of the problems that Christianity struggles with to this very day, as varied methods of calculation are still being used internationally. It seems that initially British and Irish Christians were using a method for this calculation different from the newer Roman method introduced among the English by St Augustine's missionaries (although, perhaps, this "Irish" method may also have been imported from Rome at an earlier date).[64]

In the conversion of the pagan tribes, prestige baptisms of the king or chieftain sometimes took place on Easter Sunday. This may well be the reason why the paschal controversy came to the fore in mid-seventh-century England where different missionaries vied for the conversion of various nobles. Very public baptisms, like that of King Edwin of Northumbria in 627, took place on Easter, and how the date of Easter was calculated betokened nearly as much as the actual fact of acceptance of the Christian faith.[65]

The tonsure controversy is closely related to the paschal controversy. Most Western monks were tonsured by shaving the hair from the top of the head. In Ireland, the tradition was to shave the front half of the head from ear to ear.[66] Tonsure in general was an important visible sign of the monk's consecration to God, particularly in an age where illiteracy was the norm and visible signs had a greater significance. By the eighth century the issue of tonsure (also fuelled by the desire for unity in practice) had become entwined with the paschal question,[67] and, for Bede at least, the Roman tonsure was a touchstone of orthodoxy. He condescendingly conceded that the mere wearing of the Irish tonsure does not guarantee that a man will be "dammed," but for Bede that man's immortal soul was in danger.[68] As would also be the case with the paschal controversy, the Irish form of tonsure eventually died out.

The paschal controversy was eventually settled at the Council of Whitby in 664. This council was not simply a matter of the Romans ganging up on the ignorant Celts. Whitby was a convent recently founded by the Anglo-Saxon princess Hilda, who had had important contacts with both parties. Indeed, it could be said that "almost everyone in Whitby had close and friendly contact with both Roman and Irish missionaries."[69] Also, all parties considered a unity of practice to be an absolute need; for them, differences in practice could only lead to differences in dogma. Everyone present at the council could have agreed with Bede's position that "those who served one God should observe one rule of life and not differ in the celebration of the heavenly sacraments, seeing that they all hoped for one kingdom in heaven."[70]

The victory of the Roman party at Whitby was a hollow one. By the time of the council the issues were already old. The problem of the two manners of calculation had already come about half a century earlier, during the lifetime of Columbanus, who had clashed with the local Gallic bishops over the date of Easter.[71] This controversy had brought the matter to the forefront in Ireland, and, by the time of Whitby, many in Ireland were already following the Roman calculation.[72]

In the aftermath of Whitby, there was no split between the Irish and English churches; rather, there occurred temporary divisions within each of the individual churches with some in both Ireland and England refusing to accept the Roman manner of calculation of Easter.[73] But in the long term even Iona and the other outspoken critics of the Roman method conformed to that usage, and, in general, a certain closeness remained between the Irish and English churches.[74]

THE CHURCH IN THE SIXTH TO EIGHTH CENTURIES

Monasticism and Church Organization
Traditionally, historians have tended to place much emphasis on the monastic characteristics of the pre-Norman Irish church, the theory being that in this period the earlier episcopal and protodiocesan structure of the church—based on each *túath*, or petty-kingdom, having its

own church under its own bishop—was replaced by a church domi-nated by monastics where the bishops were reduced to the state of chaplains. In addition, the monastic structure itself became subject to a degree of secularization with the role of the abbot often becoming a hereditary office that could be held by a lay-abbot, or *coarb*. All stud-ies dealing with the Irish church in the pre-Norman period written before the mid-1980s accept this theory, often portraying the reality in too radical terms.[75] But today's scholarship takes a more nuanced view.[76]

That said, monasticism was indeed an important dimension of the church at this time, and one might even go as far as to class the Irish church as being "unusually monastic."[77] But this monasticism did not affect its fundamental character and constitution. Christianity had taken root in Ireland during the period that monasticism was being introduced into the West in general.[78] Patrick's *Confessio* bears wit-ness to the fact that as part of his evangelization work he valued con-secrated virginity. He says that "the sons and daughters of the kings of the Irish are seen to be monks and virgins of Christ."[79] In the face of his critics, Patrick takes this as proof that an authentic church has been founded in his Irish mission. The fact that the Irish church was initially a church without martyrs caused the great monastic founders such as Columba to take the martyrs' place in popular religiosity and imagination.[80] But, even taking this veneration of monastic saints into account, there is little in Irish monastic observance that could be termed unique.[81]

In fact, there is no evidence that the bishops were in any way sidetracked at this time.[82] Likewise, earlier theories of a monastic ele-ment swamping an earlier diocesan structure with abbots usurping the bishops' governing role is to be abandoned. Indeed, the very idea of placing bishops and abbots in opposition is due more to the mis-takes of modern historians than to historical evidence.[83]

On the level of pastoral care (which will be treated in more de-tail below) there is also evidence that sacramental ministry was the domain of nonmonastic clergy.[84] The *First Synod of Patrick* protects the rights of the bishop vis-à-vis itinerant monastics: "if a new-comer joins a community, he shall not baptize, or offer the holy sacrifice, or consecrate, or build a church, until he receives permission from the bishop. One who looks to a layman for permission shall be a stranger."[85] In some of the penitentials, monks are forbidden to administer baptism. The sixth-century *Penitential of Finnian,* perhaps the oldest Irish penitential, instructs that "Monks, however, are not to baptize, nor to receive alms. Else, if they do receive alms, why shall they not baptize?"[86] In this text, alms go hand in hand with pastoral care: those who accept financial support are obliged to provide pastoral care. It is significant that this ban was reiterated over five hundred years later by Gille of Limerick (d. 1145): "it is not the task of monks to baptise, to give communion or to minister anything ecclesiastical to the laity unless, in case of necessity, they obey the command of the bishop."[87] In liturgical studies, the fact of repeated legislation against a practice is often regarded more as evidence that the condemned abuse (and not the "correct" observance) was what was actually happening.[88] However, these texts do point to an ideal model of the church whereby pastoral care (at least to those who reciprocated financially) was provided by a nonmonastic clergy under the direction of a bishop.

By the seventh century Christianity had gained cultural ascendancy in an Ireland that was "a highly inegalitarian society."[89] Although any study of pre-Christian Irish society is hampered by a lack of contemporary written texts, it would seem that Christianity did not disband the hierarchical structure of pre-Christian Irish society but rather inserted itself into and modified this preexistent structure.[90] Describing the celebration of St Brigit's feast day at her important church at Kildare in the seventh century, Cogitosus describes different physical barriers between groups of the faithful and adds that they all pray "to the omnipotent Master, differing in status, but one in spirit."[91] Ecclesiastics[92] were given high status in this society; this was undoubtedly influenced by the fact that many prominent ecclesiastics were also members of royal families. Thereby, prominence in the church became associated with prominence in society in general.[93]

On another level, it is also important to remember that the church in Ireland was not as isolated as is often thought. There was a clear consciousness throughout the West of the importance of being Roman, and this played no little part in the local church's self-understanding.[94] In the mid-seventh century, Armagh conducted a great campaign to have herself recognized as the Rome of Ireland. As she was particularly hampered by not having the mortal remains of Patrick, she placed great emphasis on the fact that she possessed relics of both Peter and Paul, the principal patrons of the Roman church.[95]

Irish Ecclesiastical Scholarship in the Sixth to Eighth Centuries
A particular feature of the early Irish church was the place it gave to learning. While there is no contemporary evidence for a pre-Christian priestly class, it is often assumed that such a class did exist and that these were the forerunners of the *filí,* or bards. The earliest evidence for the *filí* is from the seventh century and thus postdates the introduction of Christianity. In these earliest texts they are a high-class people producing vernacular learning, law, histories, and genealogies. They are fully incorporated into the now-Christian society and, like the clergy, they are subject to monogamy, thus forming a quasiclerical caste.[96] Patrick wrote in a rustic Latin,[97] but, only a few generations later, many Irishmen were fluent in the Latin language, building up great repositories of learning.[98] The masters of both clerical schools and those of the *filí* occupied one of the higher levels of society, and, while many positions did not transfer between one *túath* and another, that of the priest and *fileadh* did.[99] This allowed for a scholarly dialogue from which both benefited, and it gave the Irish ecclesiastical schools a big boost at a time when Continental Europe was at a low ebb. Bede records how the Irish opened their schools to English students:

> At this time there were many in England, both nobles and commons, who, in the days of Bishops Finan and Colman, had left their own country and retired to Ireland either for the sake of religious studies or to live a more ascetic life. In the course of time some of these devoted themselves faithfully to the monastic life, while others preferred to travel around the cells of various teachers and apply themselves to study. The Irish welcomed them all gladly, gave them their daily food, and also provided them with books to read and with instruction, without asking for any payment.[100]

Not only did the Irish monasteries open their schools to foreigners, but many monks also left the country to go to the Continent, where they were very influential in establishing new monasteries; in one reckoning, the number of monasteries in seventh-century Gaul increased from 220 to 550 mainly due to the Irish influence.[101] In the early ninth century, Irish monks and scholars, poets, astronomers, and grammarians played a major role in Charlemagne's court and in the general flourishing of learning in his kingdom,[102] although the importance of the Irish scholars seems to have been due to strength of numbers rather than exceptional scholarship.[103]

The Development of Pastoral Care in Seventh-Century Ireland
Pastoral care (*cura animarum*) is one of the principal reasons for the church's existence. The church is made up of individual believers who contribute to and avail of its pastoral services. But in scholarship this most basic of facts has often been overlooked, and both modern scholarship and ancient sources tend to concentrate on clerics, monastics, and nobles. Lack of evidence of popular religion hampers study of this subject, but one area that is a little more accessible is that of early Irish laws. These help us to glimpse a society where, "just as observance of treaty and contract were thought of as a bulwark against man-made social catastrophe, the render of dues to the church was envisaged as a quasi-contractual guarantee of divine benevolence manifested in the cosmic order."[104]

One characteristic of pastoral care in Ireland at this time is the multiplicity of church buildings. Many churches dot the landscape dating from this early period, with more than 250 known churches dating to the period prior to 800 (which is more than all of England or any comparable area on the Continent).[105] While the study of these buildings is significantly hampered by a serious lack of archaeological excavations,[106] nevertheless, the sheer volume of church buildings would suggest the physical proximity of a church building to a significant portion of society.[107]

A consideration of legal texts provides some idea as to the use made of these churches. The texts portray an ordered society with rights and obligations applying to both the church and *túath*. This mutual relationship basically says that, in return for "baptism and communion and praying for the dead and Mass from each church for all according to what is proper to their religion, with preaching of the Word of God to all who may listen to it and fulfil it," the church was entitled to "their grant, their tithe, their first fruits and their firstlings and their *audacht,* their *imnae.*"[108]

For the church, the principal concern is that the *túath* provide it with enough contributions and tithes to be able to continue its mission,[109] which involved not simply the support of the clerics and ecclesiastical properties, but also involved the care of the poor in society. For the *túath,* there is a concern for pastoral care; the *Ríagail Pátraic,* a law text probably originally written in the eighth century, is most significant for the study of this subject. It testifies to the basic concept of the *túath* as the center of pastoral care, and so mandates the ordination of a bishop for each *túath.*[110] It is his duty to ensure the physical structure of the diocese so that "each church [is] to have its oratory and its burial ground purified, and that the altar has its proper fittings always in readiness for the ordained."[111]

Perhaps the idea of the altar having the proper fittings "in readiness for the ordained" might imply that the Eucharist was not regularly celebrated in these churches; but later on, the *Ríagail Pátraic* mandates that the bishop make sure that there "be an offering of the body of Christ on each altar."[112] This mandate for pastoral care goes hand in hand with the collection of tithes, so that "any church in which there is no service to *manach* tenants for baptism and communion and the singing of the intercession; it is not entitled to tithes or to the heriot cow or to a third of [each] bequest."[113] A little further on it outlines the service due the *manaig,*[114] along with the cleric's other responsibilities:

> He selects a surety on their behalf from the *manaig* of each church which is his responsibility, with respect to a proper stipend, comprising price of baptism and the due of communion and [of?] chanting the requiem of all the *manaig,* with respect to the living and the dead and mass every Sunday and every chief solemnity and every chief festival and celebration of every canonical hour and singing the three fifties every canonical hour, unless instruction or spiritual direction, i.e. unction and baptism, prevent him.

If indeed it be on account of the scarcity of ordained men in the *túatha* [it is lawful?] that there be three churches or four in the care of each ordained man, provided he can offer communion and baptism there for the souls of all and mass on solemn days and feast-days on their altars.

These are the counter-obligations to the ordained man, i.e., a worthy day's ploughing each year with its seed and land and a half measure of clothing as a mantle, or a shirt or a tunic. A meal for four at Christmas and Easter and Pentecost.[115]

In this text the eucharistic celebration and the reception of Communion are indeed mentioned, and the priest must sing the liturgy of the hours (although it is not clear whether he does this alone or with the laity in attendance); baptism, care of the dying, and spiritual direction are also considered to be necessary. Here the concern is more with a regular sacramental and prayer life being carried out by the priest (who was perhaps alone or accompanied by only a few people) rather than the reception of Communion by a large segment of the population: mention of Communion being "offered" does not necessarily imply that everybody present actually received Communion and still less that everybody in the locality attended.[116]

It is also worth nothing that, while having the presence of a functioning church was important to the *túath*, this called perhaps for more priests than were available and may have contributed to a clergy shortage. The provisions for one priest to be responsible for as many as four churches implies that at least sometimes a church may have been left without any pastoral care.[117] Yet this provision of pastoral care was a serious obligation of the priest, who "was to do penance if he was absent on one Sunday, and to be degraded if he missed two or three."[118]

The picture painted by the *Ríagail Pátraic* is borne out in other documents. The *Bretha Nemed Toísech* (composed in Munster in roughly the second quarter of the eighth century, and written in Old Irish) lists the faults that disqualify a church so that it reverts to its original donor:

What are the disqualifications debasing a church? It is not difficult: being without baptism, without communion [*chomnai*], without mass [*oifrend*], without praying for the dead, without preaching, without penitents, without the active life, without the contemplative life; water through it onto the altar, driving guests away from it; disobedience, misappropriation, private property, complaining, providing for clients; an ex-layman tending it, a young boy in its stewardship, a nun announcing its canonical hours; reddening it with blood, putting it under a lord, going to it after plundering, its being diminished through supporting women, increasing debts on it, wearing it away with sin, giving it as payment to a lord or a kin.[119]

Once again the presence of a priest who prays for the dead and offers the other elements of pastoral care is stressed, and, if the church doesn't provide this, the church building reverts to its original donor.

While all of these documents point to a church with a structure in place to provide the necessary pastoral care, it could also be inferred that the great attention to detail in the matters of tithes and offerings, as well as the fact that there was somewhat of a shortage of parochial clergy, suggests a church that had some difficulty in providing all the pastoral care necessary.[120] Some law texts even resort to curses to encourage a more diligent provision of pastoral care:

For no soul will dwell in heaven which has not been baptized with a lawful baptism before everything, so that for that reason it is an obligation incumbent on all the souls of the men of Ireland together with their rulers and their nobles and the heads of churches that there should be baptism and communion and the singing of prayers for the dead in every church for proper monks (*manaig*). For an unmitigated curse and malediction will be directed from Patrick and all the saints of Ireland against every ruler and against every monk who does not enforce upon his own particular church that there be within it baptism and communion and singing of prayers for the dead.[121]

These nuances would somewhat modify Sharpe's enthusiastic vision of Ireland as having "the most comprehensive pastoral organizations in northern Europe."[122] The evidence seems to point to two groups within the laity: those within territories with strong connections to the church who received some pastoral care; and those who lived in other territories—and who may well have received very little pastoral care of any type.

> The idea that the church depended on the goodwill of secular lords for the wider levy of ecclesiastical dues is perfectly consistent with the . . . thesis . . . that what evidence there is relating to regular pastoral care and dues suggests that, while in theory bearing on the populace at large, they are likely to have applied consistently only to those over whom the church exercised direct authority, namely its *manach*-tenants. The corollary, hinted at in the Tallaght documents and elsewhere, is that much of society was regarded as almost beyond redemption and not a part of the truly Christian elite. It therefore seems quite possible that the complaints of Giraldus Cambrensis and Bernard of Clairvaux . . . represent more than the rhetoric of those with an axe to grind.[123]

Another factor in the study of pastoral care is the general lack of fervor. In the texts that do speak of the Eucharist, the emphasis is not on reception of the Eucharist by the laity but on making sure that the eucharistic celebration was offered. A man who became a priest was embarking on a dangerous career. It was terrifying to approach the altar and pronounce the fearful prayer, and, judging by the evidence of the penitentials, some of the clergy were far from being pillars of virtue.[124] Their bad example, combined with this fear, may help explain the shortage of priests that some areas experienced. The other important element of pastoral care had to do with the end of life: viaticum was more important than a life spent in regular reception of Communion.[125]

THE IRISH CHURCH IN THE NINTH AND TENTH CENTURIES AND THE VIKING RAIDS

Coming from present-day Scandinavia and having never formed part of the Roman empire, the Vikings were still pagan. They were to have a huge impact on the history of Europe in the ninth and the tenth centuries. Their small bands of fierce warriors played a major role in the battles and wars of Continental Europe that eventually led to the fall of the Carolingian empire.[126] During the ninth century they began incursions into Ireland. At this time the monasteries of Ireland provided the best targets due to the absence of large centers of population in the country. Some monasteries were also quite wealthy, and, due to the lack of a good road system, they tended to be located close to the sea or rivers. Viking raiders in search of rich pickings needed to go no further than the monasteries. The first reference to the Vikings in the annals tells how:

> A naval force of the Norsemen sixty ships strong was on the Bóinn, and another one of sixty ships on the river Life. Those two forces plundered the plain of Life and the plain of Brega, including churches, forts and dwellings.[127]

From the beginning of the ninth century the annals contain many reports of attacks on monasteries. However, some historians today point out an earlier tendency to overemphasize the Viking destruction through a somewhat simplistic use of annals.[128] Not every raid and destruction of a monastery in this time reported by the annals can be attributed to the Viking raiders. There are also many unidentified raids and burnings by the Irish themselves: "where actual churches are mentioned [as being burned], 43 were perpetrated by the Irish, 14 by Scandinavians and there are four cases of both being involved. There are a further 6 cases of violence where no information is given about the perpetrators."[129]

While the earliest Viking raids may have been indiscriminate attacks on any monasteries that they happened to find, it would seem that by the mid-ninth century the raiders, unsurprisingly, tended to select more powerful and therefore richer monasteries. Through that century, Vikings became less likely to actually burn the church buildings and seem to be more interested in plundering than destroying (they may even have developed a reluctance to burning, perhaps so as to allow the monastery to rebuild and restock in preparation for a later raid).[130] While the Vikings may have stolen artifacts from Irish monasteries and churches, Irish liturgical vessels were more marked by excellence in workmanship and intricacy of programming and design than by the actual value of the precious metal used. Indeed, some of the most valuable of the Irish objects may have been next to worthless as scrap metal. As a result of this, fragments of highly decorated Irish workmanship on liturgical objects were sometimes reused as jewelry by the Vikings. There is even some archaeological evidence that the Vikings may have been importing silver into Ireland in the late ninth and early tenth centuries.[131] Here, also, it needs to be remembered that many of the monasteries' most prized possessions were in the form of relics and had basically no monetary value (although there are also cases of Vikings taking such items and holding them for ransom). The other items that were of interest to the raiders were slaves and livestock.[132]

After about a generation of these raids, which resulted in a great deal of destruction of monasteries and their possessions,[133] the Vikings changed their tactics. They began to base themselves in Ireland itself and to build fortified towns, from where they could mount their raids. Aside from any religious impact, these towns were to have a monumental effect on Irish history. Up until that time Ireland had no true towns or cities, and the Vikings introduced a new form of society. They founded the modern Irish cities of Dublin, Waterford, and Limerick, and introduced into Ireland a new model of coastal, trade-oriented settlement.[134]

The new Viking presence arrived at a time when the native Irish kingdoms were at war with each other. It must be remembered that while Ireland (and the Irish colonies in Scotland) were a cultural whole, a religious whole, and more or less operated under a common legal code, they were not a single political whole. Society was made up of many petty-kingdoms, where some kings were more powerful than others and exercised a kind of jurisdiction over these lesser rulers. But while sometimes a king could claim to be high king over all Ireland, in reality his power remained quite tenuous. The Viking presence added a new element to the political make-up of Ireland, thus upsetting the fragile coexistence that had existed among these Irish kingdoms.[135]

While (as modern historians point out) the Irish church and society received obvious benefits from their contact with the Vikings, on a number of levels the Irish church suffered from it. The Christianization of a nation is never complete, and undoubtedly there are many examples of un-Christian behavior in Ireland prior to contact with the Vikings; but it is still true that by the ninth century a certain Christianization had indeed taken place and the church was having a calming influence on Irish society as a whole.[136] The Christianization of Ireland had meant a gradual purification of morals and a transformation of society as a whole. The evangelization took place over an extended period; but the Viking invasions led to a notable coarsening of Ireland's Christian values.[137]

While there may have been cultural benefits from contact with the Vikings, there was also cultural destruction. Alfred Smyth points out that it only needed a single Viking raider "to torch an undefended monastic library which had taken two and a half centuries to accumulate, or to slay a monastic scholar who carried that accumulated wisdom in his or her head."[138] Another negative effect of the Viking incursions on Ireland (often overlooked) is that prior to their coming the Irish area was much bigger. The Irish saw themselves as living *ab extremis terrae*,[139] at the end of the world. While it would be wrong to imagine an Irish empire, there was a significant Irish presence outside Ireland—not only in Scotland and the Isle of Man, but also in the Scottish islands and other islands in the North Sea. The monk Diucul (d. ca. 835) can mention Irish monks living in the island of Thule six days sail to the north of Britain where "not only at the summer solstice, but in the days round about it, the sun setting in the evening hides itself as though behind a small hill in such a way that there was no darkness in that very small space of time, and a man could do whatever he wished as though the sun were there, even remove lice from his shirt."[140] He also mentions that two days sail from Britain "there is another set of small islands, nearly all separated by narrow stretches of water; in these for nearly a hundred years hermits sailing from our country, Ireland, have lived. But just as they were always deserted from the beginning of the world, so now because of the Northman pirates they are emptied of anchorites."[141] Archaeological remains of Irish monastic settlements have been found as far away as Iceland.[142] This was the world of Brendan the Navigator (d. 575), who embarked on a mythical voyage to a far-off land at the world's end, only to discover that this land was already inhabited by Irish monks. Here the significance is not whether an Irishman managed to beat a Viking to the title of the first European to set foot in the new world, nor indeed the size of these Irish presences abroad: the central point is that world's end belonged to the Irish and that the Vikings changed this. The psychological loss of this supremacy as the Vikings displaced these remote Irish outposts was probably a cruel blow to the pride of the Irish religious psyche.

On other, more tangible, levels, the Irish benefited from Viking war techniques and adopted Viking armaments and ships. The Irish kings often regarded each other as bigger threats than the Vikings and would even enlist Viking allies in their battles against each other (although they tended to drop these alliances as soon as the battle was over).[143] On a cultural level, Viking metalworking skills and design were combined with the native Irish to produce such masterpieces as the Cross of Cong, and Viking decorative animal heads became a distinctive feature of the Hiberno-Romanesque architectural style.[144] By the battle of Clontarf, in 1014, both sides were using the same armaments, and while the Vikings left many permanent marks on Irish society, culture, art, and even language, in the end these were only marks and not an abiding cultural influence, for the Vikings who settled in Ireland were gradually Christianized and their settlements absorbed into the broader Irish society.[145]

It would be untrue to suggest that the Viking invasion led to the downfall of traditional Irish society. If anything, it was an impulse to reform. Irish kings fell in battles against the Vikings, but their kingdoms continued to exist. Many Irish monasteries were burned and pillaged, yet monasticism continued in Ireland, even in the areas that were occupied by the Vikings.[146] At this time the presence of the Irish missionaries on the Continent and among men of learning in the royal courts of Europe was at its high point, with such individuals as Sedulius Scottus (d. ca. 860) and Johannes Eriugena (d. ca. 877) actively involved in Charlemagne's ecclesiastical reforms. Church organization and hierarchy did not suffer from these troublesome times, but again showed themselves capable of adapting to the situation.

FROM THE ELEVENTH CENTURY TO THE COMING OF THE NORMANS

Contact with Canterbury

By the mid-eleventh century (if not a century earlier), the Vikings no longer posed a threat to the Irish church or to society as a whole. They contributed to the development of urban life and introduced some technical advances in craftwork and warfare. This time period is often eclipsed by the Norman invasion of Ireland and has been seen simplistically as a time of ferment that preceded the invasion and which served as a historical parenthesis during which time little of importance happened. But Irish society had by now progressed towards the concept of unitary kingship, that is, having the whole island subject to one high king, and it even developed a native form of feudalism (though both these developments remained somewhat conceptual as no single individual or family managed to successfully remain as high king).[147]

Before invading Ireland, the Normans first undertook the conquest of England in 1066. This was to have a significant effect on Ireland also, as it marked a distancing from the English church. After the Norman William the Conqueror became king of England in 1066, he quickly established a Norman hold on the upper levels of the English church.[148] Notably he brought Lanfranc (d. 1089), who as abbot of Bec had already been very close to him, to act as archbishop of Canterbury and bring the English church in line with Norman practice.[149] Many other top ecclesiastical posts were filled by Normans, and this all happened at a time when England had become richer and more populated than Ireland. As England assumed its place in the new European order, the older insular "micro-Christendom" of the British Isles no longer had the same significance, and hence Irish churchmen and the Irish church itself were less esteemed and, indeed, less understood in England.[150] Yet as contacts between Ireland and England declined, new bonds with the English church were being forged by the churchmen and leaders of the Hiberno-Viking settlements.

The Hiberno-Vikings of Dublin may well have decided to retain their relationship with the see of Canterbury partly due to their past activities in that part of England and partly because they were operating somewhat outside the ecclesiastical organization of Gaelic Ireland and would have found it easier to turn to Canterbury than to present their candidates for episcopal ordination in Ireland.[151] In 1074, when the Hiberno-Viking city of Dublin needed to consecrate a monk called Patrick to succeed their dead bishop, they contacted Lanfranc at Canterbury.[152] When Lanfranc received their petition, he was happy to oblige. However, he required their candidate to take an oath of obedience to himself and his successors as bishops of Canterbury, and had him take this oath as the man who was to succeed "the church of Dublin which is the metropolitan see of the island of Ireland" (*ecclesia Dublinensis quae Hiberniae insulae metropolis est*).[153] The idea of Dublin as the metropolitan see seems to have been a novelty invented by Lanfranc to further Canterbury's claims in Ireland.

In 1096 St Anselm (d. 1109), Lanfranc's successor, proved less demanding than his predecessor when asked to consecrate Bishop Samuel for the see of Dublin and Bishop Malchas for the Viking see of Waterford; he used the title of *totius Britanniae primas*, which was designed not to give offence to the Irish bishops.[154] But Anselm was unable to achieve any further influence in Ireland due to his own difficulties with the Norman politics of England, which drove him into exile in France. While he was away, Bishop Samuel began to assert his independence from any metropolitan authority of Canterbury. In 1101, upon his return to Canterbury, Anselm wrote to Samuel accusing him of a number of abuses: Samuel had given away vestments, ornaments, and books, probably missals, that Lanfranc had given to his predecessor; he had driven away a community of Benedictine monks who had been serving in his cathedral; and Samuel had had his cross carried before him in procession on his journeys (this worried Anselm because it was the prerogative of an archbishop who had received a pallium from the pope).[155] However, the influence of the archbishop of Canterbury on twelfth-century Ireland was by no means absolute. When Gille was ordained bishop of the Hiberno-Viking city of Limerick, he was not consecrated by Anselm, even though he had probably become a personal friend of Anselm while he was studying in France.[156]

Irish Renewal Movements

In the eleventh and twelfth centuries a number of reforming synods were held in Ireland.[157] While many details about these remain somewhat unclear, there certainly existed parallel impulses for reform coming from both outside and inside Ireland.[158] Unfortunately, even though quite a bit was written by Irishmen in these centuries, they were more interested in dealing with their past rather than their present.[159] So it is not surprising that history has tended to neglect this reform movement. Yet, even if history and their own contemporaries have neglected them, there was still an important reform movement in twelfth-century Ireland, and, thanks to chance preservation and the interest shown by their foreign contemporaries, something is known about its leaders.[160]

In 1073 the papacy inaugurated a new office of "permanent legates, resident in the transalpine countries."[161] Even though all six legates appointed to Ireland in the twelfth century were, in fact, Irishmen already ministering as diocesan bishops in Ireland, nonetheless, they helped give an international papal dimension to the Irish synods and provided a focal point around which reform-minded factions could rally.[162] This was not the only contact between Ireland and Rome at this time; in fact, there are thirteen separate references to pilgrimages to Rome in the annals between 927 and 1175.[163] It even seems that there was an Irish monastery in Rome itself, for the *Annals of Inisfallen* in 1095 note the death of "Eógan, head of the monks of the Gaedil in Rome."[164] These contacts would have provided an opportunity for churchmen that were so inclined to have contact with the policies and customs being observed in the Eternal City.

One of the major goals of this reform was the establishment of diocesan boundaries.[165] As secular power became more centralized, a need was seen for church organization to mirror the social and political reality. Indeed, contrary to the understanding of earlier historians, the reformers were not facing a church with too few bishops, but rather a church that had too many.[166]

The first important synod is that of Cashel held in 1101.[167] As with the other synods, evidence of what actually took place here remains somewhat sketchy. It seems that this synod did not tackle the issue of the reorganization of diocesan boundaries, but rather dealt more with the protection of the church's rights against secular powers' demands for tax and tribute; an attempt to regulate marriage laws; and the struggle against simony when dealing with ecclesiastical appointments.[168] But perhaps the main significance of this synod was the fact that it was to be the first in a series in which the Irish hierarchy decided that reform was necessary and that they, together with the papal legate, ought to achieve this reform by themselves. Their actual reforms seem to be in accordance with the recommendations of Lanfranc a quarter of a century earlier, yet they made no appeal to Anselm, the illustrious incumbent on the throne of Canterbury. As Anselm had expressed an interest in Irish affairs, this seems to point to a deliberate exclusion of Canterbury from this reform program.[169]

The next important synod was that of Ráth Bresail (near Cashel) in 1111. By this time Bishop Gille was the papal legate, and his work at this synod did result in some liturgical provisions, which will be examined in chapter 2.[170] In an interesting development the Synod of Ráth Bresail was presided over by Cellach Ua Sínaig, the lay-abbot of Armagh and the *comarba Pátraic,* or heir of St Patrick. He had been influenced by the general reforming mentality and was himself ordained a bishop. This was a very important step, as laymen had held this post for generations. We lack detailed information about this synod, but the lists of the dioceses recognized at it survive: it split Ireland into two provinces, with Armagh having primacy over the thirteen sees in the north and Cashel over the twelve in the south.[171]

In 1024 the young Máel Maedóc, better known as St Malachy of Armagh (d. 1148), succeeded Cellach as archbishop of Armagh. Malachy, a member of the Uí Sínaig family that had supplied the *comarba Pátraic* for generations, entered the ancient monastery of Armagh in his youth; although he was formed there in the traditional Irish monastic traditions, he was to become a zealous proponent of Continental Christianity. During his time in office he traveled widely throughout Ireland reforming the church. One of his most significant contributions is that he introduced the Cistercian observance of the *Rule of St Benedict* to Ireland. He had met St Bernard of Clairvaux

(d. 1153) on one of his trips to Rome, and the two became very close friends. Malachy himself desired to enter Clairvaux as a Cistercian, but Bernard refused to accept him as he considered his mission in Ireland to be too important. Malachy left four of his own monks from Armagh at Clairvaux; these, with eight French Cistercians, founded the first Irish Cistercian monastery at Mellifont, Co. Louth, in 1142. Cistercian foundations spread like wildfire throughout Ireland, and this could be seen as the beginning of the end of traditional Irish monasticism.

Although not as well known historically, the Augustinian Order of Arrouaise was also introduced by Malachy.[172] These Augustinians were perhaps even more influential than the Cistercians.[173] New Augustinian foundations often replaced older native foundations. This happened so often that one could legitimately ask whether existing monasteries adopted the newer Augustinian rule as a type of juridical fiction that allowed them to continue as before, albeit with a new rule or charter.[174] If an existing group of monastics adopted the rule of Augustine, this could represent the best of both worlds, given that "the Rule carried the authority of a man of great sanctity, an intellectual heavyweight and one of Christendom's most revered figures, but, as it was not the written word of Augustine himself, a certain latitude was permissible in the practice of it."[175]

On the internal level of the Irish church, the Augustinians may have been more important than the Cistercians, particularly for the preservation of traditional Irish monastic practices, and the Cistercians were to become allied with the Anglo-Norman faction of the church in the following centuries.[176] Bernard's friendship with and esteem for Malachy were to have their own historical importance: this friendship led Bernard to compose the most famous work on Ireland and her church in the twelfth century, the *Vita Sancti Malachiae*.[177] In this panegyric for his friend, however, Bernard paints a very bleak picture of religious life in Ireland. He informs the world that:

> Once he had begun to exercise his office the man of God realized that he had been sent not to men but to beasts. Never had he known such men, so steeped in barbarism; never had he found people so wanton

in their way of life, so cruel in superstition, so heedless of faith, law-less, dead set against discipline, so foul in their life-style; Christians in name, yet pagans at heart. They gave no tithes, no first-fruits; they did not contract legitimate marriage nor make confession; there was nei-ther penitent nor confessor to be found. There were few to minister at the altar. But what need was there of more where the small showing among the laity was practically idle? There was no hope of a harvest they might reap among so good-for-nothing a people. In the churches there was heard neither the preacher's voice nor the singer's chant.[178]

It would be unfair to claim that Bernard had no knowledge of af-fairs in Ireland; he did know Malachy and must have had some knowl-edge of the local Irish affairs from him. He also had lived with the four Irish monks that Malachy left with him for training as Cistercians. However, Bernard never visited Ireland himself, and there would be a natural tendency to exaggerate the situation in Ireland so as to paint his friend in the best light—showing how Malachy introduced the "customs of the Holy Roman church" into Ireland.[179] Furthermore, he needed to support nascent Cistercian foundations in Ireland which faced many difficulties in their first years (for example, the French monks sent to found Mellifont returned to France: as one modern historian, who also happened to be an Augustinian friar, pointed out, "Cistercian asceticism had its limits!").[180] But regardless of its truth, the *Vita Sancti Malachiae* was widely read, especially in the Norman circles of Nicholas Breakspear (the future Pope Adrian IV, d. 1159) and others who would promote the Anglo-Norman invasion of Ire-land partly in a desire to reform Christianity there.[181]

Although St Malachy died in 1148, the Synod of Kells in 1152 could be said to be the culmination of his life's work. There had been a lot of political maneuvering since the Synod of Ráth Bresail and the twenty-five-see division was enlarged to thirty-six. This included both the reestablishment of some sees suppressed by the earlier synod, and the erection of some new small sees. The campaigns for the eleva-tion of certain churches to diocesan status included a liberal patronage of the arts.[182] Four archdioceses were formed, with Dublin and Tuam joining Armagh and Cashel.[183] Cardinal Paparo (the first nonnative papal legate to Ireland), who was at the synod, presented the four new Irish archbishops with their *pallia* as a sign of their authority from the pope. One notable achievement of this synod was the successful integration of the Hiberno-Viking sees with the Irish.[184]

THE TWELFTH-CENTURY CONQUEST OF IRELAND BY THE ANGLO-NORMANS

Unlike the later haphazard invasion of Ireland, William the Conqueror's invasion of England in 1066 was carried out in a very ordered way, enlisting recruits from France, Germany, and other parts of Europe.[185] However, in spite of all the organization, the invasion of England had not been an easy matter. William did manage to subdue the local rulers, but a generation after the Conquest the majority of the people living in England were Britons, Anglo-Saxons, and Vikings—not Normans. When William died, he was succeeded by his son Henry I, on whose death in 1135 the English crown was contested. Henry II eventually won the crown, but not without aid. Among his allies was an Irish king, Diarmait Mac Murchada (d. 1171), whose kingdom was centered on Ferns, Co. Wexford, along with the Hiberno-Vikings of Dublin, who joined the coalition under Mac Murchada's influence.[186]

Mac Murchada had enemies in Ireland, in particular Tiernán O'Rourke of Breifne (who was not only Mac Murchada's political enemy, but perhaps also a bitter personal foe, as O'Rourke's wife, Dervorgilla, is said to have eloped with him). In 1166 O'Rourke managed to outmaneuver Mac Murchada, and Mac Murchada fled into exile to Bristol. He eventually contacted his erstwhile ally Henry II and asked him for help. Even though Henry was in France and actually spent little time in the English part of his domain (he also ruled huge tracts of present-day France), he had already shown interest in Ireland.[187] In 1155 he had obtained the bull *Laudabiliter* from Pope Adrian IV but had been unable to act on it. This bull granted Henry permission to enter Ireland on his behalf:

> [We] are well pleased that you should enter that island, for the enlargement of the boundaries of the church, for the restraining of vice,

for the correction of morals and the planting of virtues, for the growth of the Christian religion. [You should] accomplish there the things that look to the honor of God and to that land's own salvation. And may the people of that land receive you with honor, and venerate you as their lord.[188]

On one level this was surprising, as the Synod of Kells had a mere three years earlier confirmed the Irish church on a good path towards a fuller integration in the current renewal of the Western church. This synod had been attended by Cardinal Paparo, who would have brought a favorable report to Rome.[189] But the role of various churchmen in this whole enterprise is somewhat ambiguous. It is not clear to what degree Adrian IV was influenced in his decision to promulgate *Laudabiliter*.[190] While Henry himself did not reject the pope's commission, it would seem that he did not ask for it. The bull may have been written at the instigation of the archbishop of Canterbury, who had been denied any role in the Irish reforming synods and whose secretary was part of the English delegation that traveled to Rome to congratulate the new pope and who were charged with the delivery of the bull to Henry on their return to England.[191]

Mac Murchada swore fealty to Henry II in return for the latter's help in regaining his kingdom. Henry was not really in a position to help him directly, but promised that he would help him in the future. He also gave him letters urging his subjects in England to go to the aid of Mac Murchada. No allies were forthcoming in England, but Mac Murchada was lucky enough to recruit some helpers in Wales. Principal among these was Richard FitzGilbert de Clare (d. 1176), better known as Strongbow, one of the most powerful Norman leaders in Wales.[192] These were Cambro-Normans, descended from Norman warriors who had taken local Welsh wives. Many in Wales had supported the other claimant to the throne against Henry II and, although they had subsequently given their loyalty to Henry, they were still held in suspicion by the king.[193] They saw the Irish adventure as their chance to redeem themselves. Mac Murchada also promised them the town of Wexford, which was not his to give but whose Hiberno-Viking inhabitants had supported his enemies in their attacks against him.[194]

In 1167 Mac Murchada returned to Ireland with 300 Norman warriors. With their help he managed to retake his own kingdom. A second group arrived in 1169 and conquered Wexford; then the other Irish kings made peace with Mac Murchada, allowing him to form the kingdom of Leinster to the south of Dublin on the condition that he would send away his Norman allies. Instead, a new wave of Normans arrived under Strongbow a few months later, and this army succeeded in conquering Waterford and Dublin, confirming Mac Murchada as one of the most powerful kings of Ireland; in return, Mac Murchada gave Strongbow his daughter's hand in marriage and designated him his heir.[195] Ruaidrí Ua Conchobair, high king at the time, besieged Strongbow and his garrison in Dublin in 1171. But Strongbow managed to break the siege and defeat Ruaidrí's army. This was a very significant defeat, as the high king had humiliatingly failed to assert his lordship over Strongbow.[196]

While Henry II may have been happy to let some of his minor lords risk their lives in a precarious mission in Ireland, once they had established the beginnings of a potentially strong kingdom in Ireland, he came to Ireland in person in 1171 to remind them where their loyalties ultimately ought to lie. This trip was a triumph for Henry, as not only the Normans, but also the Irish and the Hiberno-Vikings, did him homage.[197] Regardless of the importance that would be given to this act in later times, it is not known what significance these Irish nobles gave to it, nor whether they saw it as legally binding on themselves or their successors; nor is it clear what was understood by Henry himself.[198] However, on his return to England Henry entered negotiations with Ruaidrí Ua Conchobair, who, although he had met with Henry in his trip to Ireland, had refused to swear loyalty to him then. These negotiations culminated in their signing the treaty of Windsor in 1175, in which Ua Conchobair swore loyalty to Henry and promised to collect tribute for him in Gaelic Ireland. In return Henry recognized Ua Conchobair as high king of Ireland (that is, the part of Ireland that had not been occupied by the Normans) and undertook that the Normans would take no more territory from the Irish.[199] This treaty probably expressed the intentions of both parties, but it did not have any lasting impact. Ua Conchobair had a tenuous grip on the high-kingship and was unable to pass on his high-kingship to an heir or to collect the tribute due to Henry.[200] Not only was Henry unable to prevent individual Normans in Ireland from carving out new territories for themselves, he continued to grant his followers lands in the Gaelic territories. This relentless occupation continued so that by 1250, a mere eighty years after the first arrival of the Normans, over three-quarters of Ireland was under Norman domination.[201]

CHURCH REFORM IN EARLY NORMAN IRELAND

Perhaps it is significant that, in his 1171 visit to Ireland, one of Henry's first acts was a prolonged visit with Bishop Christian of Lismore. Christian was the papal legate, had been the abbot of the Cistercian abbey of Mellifont, and was one of the monks that Malachy had left at Clairvaux to be trained by Bernard. He had been appointed legate by Pope Eugene III (d. 1151), some twenty years earlier (both Christian and Eugene had served as novices together in Clairvaux under St Bernard).[202] Many other Irish bishops endorsed Henry when he arrived in Ireland and swore oaths of loyalty to him in the council at Cashel in 1172 (perhaps in the hope that his intervention would foster a good climate for ecclesiastical reform). This endorsement came at an important time for Henry, who was still held in low esteem by the pope since his implication in the murder of Thomas Becket. It was also to the advantage of Pope Alexander III (d. 1181), who in 1159 had succeeded Adrian IV, and who was also in a precarious position due to the challenge of an antipope backed by the German emperor Frederick Barbarossa (d. 1190), one of the most powerful leaders in the West. Alexander needed to be able to reconcile with Henry so as to avoid Henry uniting with Fredrick against him. Henry's trip to Ireland provided an opportunity for mutually potential benefit for himself, Alexander, and the Irish bishops. Whether or not the Irish bishops benefited from this in the long run is still open to debate.[203]

The influence of the new religious orders was not a negligible feature of the church in Ireland in the period following the Norman invasion. As these new bodies were founded around the same time as this invasion, obviously they had not been a feature of the church in pre-Norman Ireland. St Dominic died in 1221, and the Dominicans reached Ireland by 1224. St Francis died in 1226, and the Franciscan order reached Ireland by 1231. Both of these orders came to Ireland from England, although the Franciscans enjoyed more autonomy whereas the Dominicans were part of the English province. This period proved to be a fruitful time for monastic life in Ireland because, despite the destruction of some Irish monasteries in the upheavals following the invasions of Ireland, the new Norman landowners founded more religious houses than had been destroyed.[204] A notable feature of Christianity in both the Norman and Gaelic sections of Ireland in the thirteenth century was the very high number of religious houses belonging to these new religious orders that were founded:

> By 1230 the number of religious houses for men, of all orders, in Ireland was about two hundred of which one hundred and twenty were of Irish foundation and eighty, Anglo-French. Comparable figures for Scotland and Wales were forty-six and thirty-three respectively. The comparison no doubt reflects differences in respective sizes of population. But it certainly indicates how substantial had been the progress of the reform movement in Ireland.[205]

The Dominican and Franciscan friars carried on the Cistercian tradition by bringing Irish pastoral practice into line with that on the Continent. The friars widespread distribution throughout both Norman and Gaelic Ireland, and the fact that, unlike the Cistercians, they concentrated on pastoral work, meant that they had a great influence on the religious practices of the population at large. It is to be assumed that the Franciscan friars played the same role in Ireland as they did elsewhere in Europe in the spread of a standardized form of the Roman rite in the liturgy.[206]

Another element in the gradual assimilation of the Irish church into a more Continental model was the anglicization of the episcopate. By 1254 almost one third of the dioceses were occupied by foreign-born prelates, and sixteen of the twenty-three native-born bishops were to some degree beholden to the English crown for their episcopal nomination.[207] Nevertheless this assimilation was never complete, and tensions did arise in Ireland between Gaelic and Anglo-Norman factions in the church. In what is usually called the "Conspiracy of Mellifont," some of the Irish Cistercian houses broke away from obedience to the Norman center of the order in France in the first half of the thirteenth century.[208] There was also a more scandalous event in the general chapter of the Irish Franciscans held in Cork in 1291. Here the Irish friars felt discriminated against by their Anglo-Irish brethren, and a vicious fight broke out in which at least sixteen people were killed.[209]

But the church did continue in Ireland, and despite the above-mentioned difficulties the church managed to successfully adapt to the new sociopolitical situation. While divisions remained it would likewise be false to portray this period as having two separate ethnic churches and not a single Irish church, a member of the Western church.[210]

THE EUCHARIST IN THE WEST UNTIL THE TWELFTH CENTURY

Having presented the historical background, I shall now examine the study of the Eucharist in pre-Norman Ireland in the context of the liturgical history of the West during this time. By the fifth century and the evangelization of Ireland, a certain common "shape" of the eucharistic liturgy had developed, so that the general structure of the rite was common throughout virtually all of Christendom. The concrete application of that "shape" was different in different areas, and these regional variations, usually centered on a preeminent see, came to be known as rites.[211] Most traditional studies of the liturgy in the pre-Carolingian West presume the existence of a number of Latin rites: Roman, Ambrosian, Gallican, Hispanic (or Mozarabic), North African, and Celtic. In the nineteenth century, in particular, it was supposed that a Celtic liturgy existed in Ireland and other areas under Celtic influence. In 1881 F. E. Warren published the definitive work on the subject, *The Liturgy and Ritual of the Celtic Church,* an exceptionally well researched volume and even today, over one hundred years later, yet to be surpassed. But, for all his scholarly acumen,

Warren had a major ideological shortcoming: he approached the study of early Irish liturgy with the "desire to find a catholic church-life and order [in the British Isles] which were nevertheless independent of Roman control and centralizing."[212]

This desire to "find" a type of proto-Anglicanism in early Ireland colored Warren's work. He was by no means the only one to "discover" an ancient Celtic liturgy that reflected a church ordered in the way he thought best; most scholars of the period saw in the early Irish either proto-Anglicans or an early example of ultramontane Roman Catholics,[213] and there was a fairly general agreement that the early church in Ireland had its own rite and that this Celtic rite was different from the other Western liturgical rites.[214]

But more modern studies tend to see far fewer Western rites; writing shortly after World War II, Jungmann divided Western liturgy into two groups, the Roman/African and the Gallican. He then divided the Gallican into four subgroups: pure Gallican (Franco-German), Celtic, Mozarabic, and Ambrosian.[215] Today, modern scholarship would tend to agree with his fundamental intuition; I go along with this division of liturgical rites and argue that the church in early Ireland was using the Gallican rite, albeit with some local variations.

THE DEVELOPMENT OF THE SHAPE OF THE EUCHARIST

Throughout the first millennium all Christians traced their eucharistic practice back to the person of Jesus Christ and the Last Supper, which he celebrated with his disciples "on the night before he was betrayed" (1 Cor 11:23).[216] The first modern students of liturgy in the eighteenth century therefore tried to get back to the ritual of that night. When faced with the present variety of eucharistic rites, the presumption was made that these had developed from a single common eucharistic liturgy of apostolic times.[217] By the beginning of the twentieth century when scholars realized that it was, in fact, impossible to reach a common apostolic text of the eucharistic liturgy, this caused somewhat of a crisis in scholarship. Dom Gregory Dix, an Anglican Benedictine, stepped in to fill this gap with his very influential book, *The Shape of the Liturgy*. While Dix rejected the idea of a common apostolic text, he replaced this with a proposed apostolic "shape" of the eucharistic liturgy that would have been common to all of the earliest Christians. There is, he said, "even good reason to think that this outline—the Shape—of the Liturgy is of genuinely apostolic tradition." He assumed that the first part of the eucharistic liturgy, which centered on scripture readings, was imported into early Christian liturgy from the Jewish synagogue service, with which the apostles would have been familiar. In Dix's understanding, this liturgy of the Word was followed by a eucharistic celebration. He analyzed the actions of Jesus in the Last Supper and saw that he carried out seven actions and that these soon became a universal fourfold eucharistic rite that was common to all Christians: "(1) the offertory; bread and wine are "taken" and placed on the table together. (2) The prayer; the president gives thanks to God over the bread and wine together. (3) The fraction; the bread is broken. (4) The communion; the bread and wine are distributed together."[218]

Most studies from the mid-twentieth century onwards accept this structure as proposed by Dix, and a linear model of development of the eucharistic rite is generally presumed.[219] When exceptions to this development are found (such as the prayer in the *Didache* which today is generally accepted as being a eucharistic prayer, but which lacks reference to the Last Supper and deals with the cup before the bread), earlier studies thought of them as being aberrations or eccentricities of individual churches that bore little relation to this linear development.[220]

Today most liturgical scholars do not fully agree with Dix's theories, placing a greater emphasis on the evidence that is not consistent with his shape, and therefore many propose a more heterogeneous liturgical practice among the first Christians.[221] Nevertheless, while there is debate about the apostolic origins of Dix's proposed "shape," all scholars would admit that this shape is clearly defined by the time of the Council of Nicea (325). Indeed, although Dix's theories are no longer universally held, many early eucharistic liturgies fit into his pattern quite well. The *Apologia* of St Justin (d. ca. 165), composed around the year 155, provides the Roman emperor Antoninus Pius with a description of a Christian eucharistic celebration.[222] This description is one of the most significant early Christian descriptions of the Eucharist and is fully consistent with Dix's proposed shape.

While the critiques of modern scholars ought to be duly taken into consideration and while it would be a mistake to try to "situate all extant examples of later Christian rites and prayers within a single line of development,"[223] nonetheless I disagree with the overly cautious view of many contemporary liturgical scholars. In all of the polemics there seems to be a fascination in proving that we can say little or nothing about early liturgy. Although many variants do exist and it is impossible to fit every scrap of the evidence into a very neat progression, nonetheless "it is certainly true that the liturgical skeleton provided by Justin is discernable in every Christian tradition thereafter."[224]

While the most ancient eucharistic prayers may lack some elements that were later considered indispensable, such as the *sanctus* or, perhaps, even the institution narrative, these elements seem to have soon come to be included in most eucharistic prayers;[225] it looks like the structure and basic content of the eucharistic prayers developed in different places in a more or less parallel fashion. Undoubtedly there were real differences, and maybe even radical differences, in the ways that the eucharistic prayer was structured in different churches (and maybe even between different celebrants in the same church). But I agree with Bouley when he speaks of a "basic unanimity" in this period. Even though the celebrant was not tied to a text, there was a definite commonality to most of the prayers so that it could be said in general about any eucharistic prayer that "its *animus*, its spirit, fundamental direction and most basic content were one."[226]

THE SOLIDIFICATION OF THE SHAPE OF THE EUCHARIST IN
THE FOURTH AND FIFTH CENTURIES

The general acceptance of Christianity after the edict of Milan in 313 was also to profoundly influence the liturgy.[227] In these centuries "the basic structure of the eucharistic liturgy developed in a remarkably similar fashion throughout the Christian world."[228] There was also a great push for uniformity in the liturgy in the fourth century, leading to what has been called the "fourth-century homogenization" of Christian liturgy.[229] There were a number of causes for this, not least of them the start of pilgrimages to Jerusalem where pilgrims from various regions came together. As a result, various liturgical practices spread to different places from Jerusalem itself, and many others passed from one local church through Jerusalem to other local churches. Another major factor in the standardization of liturgical practices was the struggle to define and defend orthodoxy against the new heresies. This was the period of the great councils, which provided a forum for bishops to exchange ideas on the liturgy and liturgical practices. The councils also were instrumental in the abandonment of freer forms of expression in liturgical prayers so that the presider would not be accused of heresy (the earlier, freer versions of prayers may have been open to a number of interpretations). In this period there was also a marked professionalization of the clergy, who dominated the liturgy as it increasingly became a social affair.[230]

As history is never neat, this process of "homogenization" also carried within it the beginnings of the differentiation of the various liturgical families.[231] In other words, as the liturgy developed a common form in most churches, the creative juices did not stop there. There was also a desire to fill in the blank spaces, leaving no quiet moments in the rite. This eventually led to some older and more important elements being eliminated or cut down in favor of these newer elements; but perhaps more significantly these modifications differed from church to church and led to a partial obscuring of the shape of the eucharistic celebration. The most important of the Western modifications was the introduction of the offertory procession.[232]

It is probably worth emphasizing that, despite the emergence of a clear "shape" and of a homogenization of the liturgy, the liturgy was still far from identical in each and every church in a given region. A certain orality remained in the celebration of the liturgy in all of its various settings.[233] It has been pointed out that the many examples from the High Middle Ages of ordination and novitiate requirements of memorization of substantial passages of scriptural and euchological texts—when considered together with the records of episcopal visitations to rural parishes, which often lament the lack of liturgical texts in a given parish—would lead one to the conclusion that often the Eucharist was celebrated by "illiterate rural clergy using only a small number of memorized texts."[234]

THE DEVELOPMENT OF THE GALLICAN RITE AND ITS
PROBABLE USE IN IRELAND

In the Latin West, there was a certain plurality of liturgical rites, but most of the West celebrated the Eucharist using some form of the Gallican rite.[235] Due in particular to the fact that no hymnographical texts have survived, it would be almost impossible to reconstruct a full "Gallican" liturgy from the extant manuscripts. The Gallican rite was the rite used in the area of present-day Europe composed by France, Germany, and the Low Countries, as well as Britain and, I would hold, Ireland. The greatest period of liturgical creativity of the Gallican rite took place during the end of the fifth and the beginning of the sixth centuries.[236] But the rite would not survive in the long term probably due to the fact that, apart from Rome, no single metropolitan see was able to command a lasting liturgical influence over this area.[237]

It is likely that the Hispanic (or Mozarabic) rite of Spain had a common origin with the Gallican rite, namely, some liturgical traditions from the East and Italy but especially North Africa.[238] However, the Hispanic rite was to have a more sustained and stronger development, perhaps due to its later development in the sixth and seventh centuries and, unlike the Gallican rite, the existence of strong metropolitan sees on which it was centered.[239] The common origin of the Gallican and Hispanic rites is important for our considerations.[240] The theory of a common origin is fairly modern; earlier authors tended to see these rites as being independent. But the presence of some common characteristics in liturgy in Ireland and Spain (regions that were supposedly separated by Gaul, which was using a different rite) has led to some interesting theories being formulated to explain this commonality.[241] Edmund Bishop, one of the pioneers of modern liturgical scholarship, has famously pointed out the existence of certain "Spanish symptoms" in Irish liturgical material.[242] The most important example of this is the presence of the Creed in the *Stowe Missal*. This has led scholars to trace the use of the Creed in the Roman Mass from the East to Spain through Ireland to Alcuin and Charlemagne.[243] But it is probably futile to look for direct liturgical connections between Ireland and Spain. It is quite possible that some Irish ecclesiastic did find his way to Spain and back or vice versa, but this was hardly the basis for major liturgical exchanges. It is far more probable that these Spanish symptoms can be explained in a different way—namely, a shared basis of the Gallican and Hispanic rites. As there is only fragmentary evidence for the Gallican rite, it is quite possible that some Gallican elements are preserved only in Spanish and Irish material, but that this is due to a common origin and not any particular Spanish elements in Irish practice.[244]

Perhaps the most notable characteristic of the Gallican rite was its flexibility. Together with the Hispanic rite, it shared the tendency to "compose the eucharistic prayer from variable euchological texts." This meant that the Gallican rite "was largely composed of variables, with a small number of fixed formulas," so that while the general shape of the eucharistic rite would have been fairly common throughout the Gallican region, "there would have been considerable variations in the different provinces."[245] However, the Hispanic rite perfected this technique, whereas the Gallican rite remained at an earlier level of development, lacking the sophistication of the Hispanic synthesis.[246] Due to its unfinished state, the Gallican rite never managed to become codified in its liturgical books.[247] It is interesting that Alan Bouley in his work extolling the improvisation of the early church's euchological traditions, and given his preference for the "freedom" of the early church over the "formula" of later ages, has to admit defeat when dealing with the Gallican liturgical tradition. He sees how the Gallican eucharistic texts remain "unfinished" and lacking in "vigor."[248] This rite was eventually to give way to the Roman rite. But while the later forms of the Roman and Byzantine rites can be described as "mongrels" in their development,[249] the Gallican rite was probably never celebrated in a "pure" form.

An actual celebration of the Eucharist according to the Gallican rite probably lasted between one and two hours,[250] while its structure or shape looked something like this:

- The three scriptural readings (Old Testament, Epistle, and Gospel);
- Chants and prayers (including a Psalm; and in Gaul the *Benedictus,* also known as the Canticle of Zechariah, or in Spain the *Gloria;* the *Trisagion* and a triple *Kyrie;* the *Benedicite,* also known as the Song of the Three Young Men; and sometimes a diaconal litany)
- A homily
- The dismissal of the catechumens and penitents
- The eucharistic synaxis, which was composed of about ten variable prayers, including
  - the *Praefatio missa*
  - *Oratio communis*
  - *Collectio*
  - the diptyches (or *nomina*) and their prayer (the *Post-nomina*)
  - the prayer of the *Pax*
  - the eucharistic prayer: the *Contestatio* (or *Immolatio*) and the *Sanctus*
  - the *Post sanctus* prayer (or the *Vere sanctus*) and the institution narrative (the *Qui pridie*)
  - The *Post mysterium*
- The *Pater* (with its introduction and embolism)
- The *Sancta sanctis* (at an early stage)
- A lengthy episcopal blessing of those who would receive Communion
- The two post-Communion prayers (*Oratio* and *Collectio*)
- *Dimissio*[251]

A central problem for our consideration is whether this was the rite that was brought to Ireland in the fifth century. This cannot be easily answered, as only a few liturgical manuscripts survive from ancient Ireland. An additional difficulty in the study of liturgy in early Ireland, particularly in the earlier centuries, is that, if there is scant manuscript evidence for Irish liturgical practices in the pre-Norman period, there is virtually no extant manuscript evidence for British liturgy in the same period.[252] However, as was outlined above, there is every possibility that the early church in Ireland was very close to the British church in its character, and therefore we presume that Irish liturgical practice would have had a lot in common with British practice and that both would have been very similar to the other Gallican areas.[253]

At this time in Ireland (or for that matter in any given region) one would not find liturgical books that were identical to those in use in any other part of Europe.[254] A church used the books that it had, and even if there were more up-to-date versions available, it is likely that the old version would have been retained because most churches found it very expensive to acquire new manuscripts. We must remember that books were extremely important and very expensive; the vellum used was difficult to manufacture, and expensive to the degree of making it almost impossible for a private individual to own a book. The lives of the Irish saints tell many stories of how the saint miraculously saved a book after it had fallen in water;[255] and some attribute St Columba's founding of Iona as being due to a penance imposed on him after he caused a war over a copy of the Psalter, a liturgical book.[256]

Only very rarely and for a very good reason would a book be discarded. If a book was found wanting, it might be slightly altered or recycled as a palimpsest. At the same time, the Irish had no problem in making modifications to the liturgy and adding material that they found interesting. While Bishop's label of "the Irish eclectic, or tinkering, method in liturgy"[257] might be a bit harsh, there is some evidence of an admixture of liturgical materials.[258] Regarding the adoption of Roman elements in particular, history shows that the Gallican area as a whole was apt to dabble in this "Irish eclectic method."[259]

But what position ought we to take today as regards the Celtic rite as proposed by many scholars of bygone ages? In my opinion, the most persuasive piece of evidence for the nonexistence of a separate Celtic rite is the controversy over the *Bobbio Missal*. This missal (now in Paris, Bibliothèque Nationale de France, *Codex latini* 13246)[260] was formerly to be found in the library of the north Italian monastery of Bobbio, founded by St Columbanus.[261] It is an interesting manuscript, which may have been written as early as the seventh century, and it combines the functions of sacramentary and lectionary as well as containing a "plethora of miscellaneous material."[262] While most earlier authors tend to classify this manuscript as belonging to the so-called Celtic rite,[263] more recent authors classify it as Gallican;[264] but the best solution to defining the liturgy of this missal is to see in it an example of the Gallican rite that at an early date was becoming Romanized.[265]

I believe that the probability of this manuscript (which was often pointed to as being a prime example of the Celtic rite) having no contact with Ireland shakes the very foundations of the existence of a separate and identifiable Celtic rite.

Paradoxically, while the *Bobbio Missal* was definitely not written in Ireland or, for that matter, is probably not very indebted to Ireland in any way, the fact that it was typical for the Gallican liturgy implies that similar books could well have been in use in Ireland. In the next chapter the various Irish evidence will be studied, and it will be seen how the Irish *Palimpsest Sacramentary* of Munich can be considered among the best examples of the early Gallican liturgy[266] and the *Stowe Missal* as a perfect example of a later Gallican type of missal that had accepted many Roman elements including the Roman Canon.[267]

THE JOURNEY OF THE ROMAN RITE OVER THE ALPS AND THE NEW LITURGICAL SYNTHESIS

As the Gallican rite flourished throughout much of the West, it is worth noting two factors of Roman liturgical history—the Roman Canon and ritual splendor. The Roman Canon or eucharistic prayer of Rome was to have extraordinary success being imported wholesale into most other Western liturgies.[268] New studies on the origins of the Roman Canon need to be undertaken because, despite its great popularity and widespread diffusion, specialists remain somewhat baffled as to the origins of this enigmatic text that shows little textual relationship to any other classical eucharistic prayer or liturgical family.[269]

The other element of Roman liturgy that impressed Northern Europeans and visitors from the Gallican area was the ritual splendor of the Roman church. The legalization of Christianity came in the fourth century at exactly the same period as the Roman empire was shifting its center to the new and purpose-built capital city of Constantinople.[270] As the empire gradually became more concerned with the Eastern provinces, the bishop of Rome (and Western bishops in general) took on some of the civil and judicial roles that formerly were reserved for the emperor. It is not surprising that elements of court ceremonials were to enter the liturgy. In Rome, in particular, the papal liturgy was to become quite ceremonialized,[271] often developing into stational liturgy whereby the liturgical celebration is not confined to the church building but "spills over" into the environs.[272]

The papal Mass as celebrated in Rome was extremely influential in the West. Pilgrims and visitors to Rome were impressed by the intricate ceremonial, which led to the creation of a new type of liturgical document: the *Ordines Romani*.[273] Other liturgical texts contained very little instruction but were mainly made up of prayer texts. The *ordines* were composed as descriptions of the ceremonies of the rite as opposed to the texts and were to be used either by a master of ceremonies or as a text to train clerics. The different *ordines* describe different liturgical rites and were initially compiled in Rome, starting around the year 700. Almost immediately these texts were copied and taken back across the Alps to the Gallican area by visiting ecclesiastics. Once there, the various *ordines* were gradually collated to form collections that described a number of different rites.[274]

While the *ordines* are very important for the history of Roman liturgy, in fact none of the extant manuscripts was written in Rome itself. As no other local church in the West could celebrate the same type of stational liturgy as Rome with her multiplicity of churches and sacred sites, all of these collections, to a greater or lesser degree, were adapted to different local circumstances.[275] These documents bear witness to a complicated papal liturgy that was imitated throughout the West, and while not exactly replicated in every parish church (or even in the great monastic and cathedral churches) it was nonetheless the goal to which they aspired.[276] The adoption of a Roman ceremonial, albeit in a modified form, along with the gradual adoption of the Roman Canon are the preeminent ways in which the Roman liturgy traveled north of the Alps. In all likelihood, these Gallicanized forms of Roman ritual[277] were also influential in Ireland. They would have come both directly from Rome itself (which some Irish ecclesiastics did visit) and from the various Frankish or Gallican adaptations of the Roman ritual that these ecclesiastics would have met on their journey to Rome (as well as the traditions that Irish ecclesiastics would have met in their journeys to the Continent).[278]

In the late eighth and early ninth centuries many significant elements of the Roman rite were gradually and voluntarily adopted throughout the local churches using the Gallican rite in what was to

become the Holy Roman Empire. Charlemagne seems to have offi-
cially encouraged this adoption as he considered liturgical correctness
desirable because it could encourage a sense of stability in society in
general, as well as the "creation of a better Christian society, whose
salvation is assured, and thereby ensures the salvation of the king."[279]
Two of his advisers in particular were to have a great influence in liturgical matters, Alcuin of York (d. 804) and Theodulf of Orleans
(d. 820); they helped Charlemagne to reform the liturgical practices of
his domain.[280] As part of this policy, he requested a typical Roman
sacramentary from Pope Hadrian (d. 795), which was thought to have
been composed by Gregory the Great. The pope, after a delay of a
number of years, sent a Roman sacramentary commonly known as
the *Hadrianum*.[281] However, this sacramentary was not from the time
of Gregory (it was probably from the reign of Pope Honorius I,
d. 638) and it proved to be very unsuitable because its usages reflected
the papal stational liturgy of Rome, and it lacked a lot of material necessary for cathedral and parish worship. To render it usable for non-
papal liturgies, St Benedict of Aniane (d. 821) composed a *Supplement*
to the *Hadrianum*.[282] To do this he used material from sources already
in use in the Frankish territories. The resulting liturgy was "an amalgam of late eighth-century Roman material, older practices thought
to be Roman, and indigenous Frankish-Gallican prayers."[283]

Traditionally scholars have said that Charlemagne imposed this
new amalgam of Roman and Gallican elements on his entire realm.[284]
However, Hen has recently challenged this view, pointing out that we
have no record that Charlemagne ever imposed the use of this sacramentary. The project seems to have been given a cold shoulder by Alcuin, Charlemagne's chief liturgist. There is no record that Benedict
of Aniane received a royal commission to write his *Supplement,* and
there is abundant evidence of the continued use and copying of older
sacramentaries throughout Charlemagne's reign even in ecclesiastic
centers that were clearly linked with his liturgical reforms.[285]

However, whether or not the traditional view is to be held, in one
form or other the Roman and Gallican rites fused in the areas to the
north of the Alps. Most ecclesiastics thought that they were using
pure Roman liturgy, but their adaptation of the Roman books for use

in these areas actually necessitated the retention of many prayers of the older Gallican books. So, while the shape of the rite may have been Roman, and the Roman Canon became the exclusive eucharistic prayer of these areas, quite a number of prayers, chants, feast days, and other Gallican usages prevailed.[286] These prayers in particular were markedly different from the Roman ones, as the Roman prayers tended to be of a very simple and elegant structure, whereas the Gallican prayers were of a much more complex and wordy structure.[287]

Then, as time progressed, Rome fell on hard times, the city decayed, the population plummeted, and the bishop of Rome was sometimes not of the highest moral character. This led to a decline in the Roman church as a whole, including the nature and quality of the liturgical celebrations.[288] Thus Rome was herself influenced by some new Cluniac monasteries staffed by diligent foreign monks who celebrated an elaborate liturgy using the books from their native homes to the north of the Alps. This, along with the patronage of the church of Rome by Frankish and Saxon leaders, which included the physical importation of French liturgical manuscripts to Rome, led to the adoption of a Gallicanized Roman rite even within the city of Rome itself.[289] So by the year 1000 the liturgy of the church of Rome would have resembled the liturgy in much of the West. Even so a number of the elements of a stational liturgy were to persist in Rome until the period of the Avignon papacy in the fourteenth century.

Many of the eleventh-century popes desired to reform the church, which led to what has been called the Second Gregorian Reform of Pope Gregory VII (d. 1085). This had been prepared by Leo IX (d. 1054) and Nicholas II (d. 1061). Gregory took back into his hands the Roman liturgy from the rulers and bishops from north of the Alps. Although he was able only to work minor changes, he urged bishops to follow the customs of Rome in a rigorous way. His work was important for the foundations it laid for future reforms: the reforms by which Ireland was brought even more fully into line with English and Continental practice. He promoted the view that Western Christianity as a whole should follow the uses of the papal see as opposed to a particular diocese, religious order, or secular order promoting this same ideal for its own purposes.[290]

So while the Norman invasion of Ireland was to have clear consequences in the field of liturgy with the adoption of books and practices common to English dioceses, this was not as radical a change as
has often been thought. Irish churchmen had already for centuries
been moving towards the adoption of Roman liturgical practices. The
gradual supplanting of the native monastic foundations and rules and
St Malachy's introduction of the Cistercians and the Augustinians
into Ireland as part of the eleventh-century reform were to affect the
liturgy as celebrated in Ireland, making it more in line with the new
Gallicanized Roman rite used in the rest of Europe.

THE PARTICIPATION OF THE LAITY IN THE EUCHARIST

One of the first facts that needs to be noted about the laity's participation in the Eucharist is the role of language in the liturgy. The introduction of Latin into the liturgy of the church in North Africa and
later on in Gaul and Rome itself was carried out in order that people
(or at least the presiders) could understand the language of the liturgy,
as the use of Greek in the West was in decline.[291] But while the faithful
in Italy and Iberia continued to understand some Latin for a long
time, already by the sixth century Latin was unintelligible in France;
and many Christians coming from the barbarian tribes, as well as the
first Irish Christians, would never have understood Latin. In general,
by the ninth century throughout the West, Latin was a language belonging exclusively to the clerical and educated classes.[292] This contributed to the Eucharist becoming more and more the realm of
clerics, as little by little even the language of the liturgy became foreign to the ears of the laity. In fact, the various reform movements
with their emphasis on a correct usage of Latin tended to make the
language of the liturgy even more incomprehensible to the laity.[293]

When people could no longer understand the words of the liturgy, their spirituality was necessarily affected. To add to this problem, between the seventh and the ninth centuries in the West (and
even earlier in the East), the eucharistic prayer became inaudible. First
of all, celebrants began to whisper the prayer so that only the other
clergy could hear it, and then later on it came to be whispered inau-

dibly so that nobody could hear it. Perhaps this took place to preserve the mystery of the Eucharist from being profaned by the unclean ears of the laity, although historically there is no contemporary evidence of anyone giving a clear reason for the adoption of the practice.[294] The net result was that, even if someone in the assembly did happen to understand Latin, it would have been of little use as he would have been unable to hear the central prayer of the Eucharist.

This necessitated a shift in the understanding of the function of the liturgy and led to a greater emphasis on allegorical interpretations of the liturgy. In the early church, the actions of the liturgy were nearly all pragmatic and functional. While the priest may have held the bread and the cup at different points of the celebration, this was either because the liturgical action demanded that he physically move them or to give emphasis to some part of the prayers. But, starting in the fourth century, an important shift in the understanding of the Eucharist was introduced whereby the original significance of the Eucharist as a meal was replaced by an allegorical explanation centered on the bread and wine representing Christ's passion and cross for the noncommunicating laity.[295]

These works applied a hermeneutic of interpretation to the liturgy that earlier generations of Christians had used to interpret the Bible. While different allegorical interpretations of the liturgy can be found in the fathers of the church, they gradually gained more popularity with the *Expositiones Missae,* explanations of the Mass produced for devotion and catechetical purposes partly as a consequence of the Carolingian reform.[296] As there was a more or less standard shape of the celebration of the rites of the Eucharist, it was possible to provide a common interpretation of these rites so as to "make people consider the events of the history of salvation by the rites" of the Eucharist.[297] Amalarius of Metz (d. 850), a member of Charlemagne's court and a fan of a particularly allegorical form of interpretation, was the most popular proponent of this method of interpretation (perhaps he learned of this method on his journey to Byzantium as part of an embassy in 813–14). Using Amalarius's method, the whole liturgy becomes a "drama that encompasses the life of Christ and, indeed, the whole history of salvation, from the Garden of Eden to the death of

Christ on the Cross and his burial."[298] In this new form of interpretation (which was controversial during Amalarius's lifetime but proved very popular afterwards), every action of the celebration of the Mass had a meaning and no movement could be understood simply at face value. In this, Amalarius did not simply carry on the patristic tradition of allegorical interpretation; he turned the traditional interpretation of the Eucharist on its head, because "whereas the Fathers see the Old Testament fulfilled in New Testament worship, [he] finds in Christian worship, not a fulfillment of Old Testament worship, but allusions to it."[299] The rites of the Mass are no longer "mysteries" in and of themselves, but they rather now point to the divine mysteries.[300] Yet another hermeneutical issue is that for Amalarius, and those who followed him, the key to understanding the Mass is no longer the paschal mystery of Christ's death and resurrection: now they concentrate solely on Christ's passion and death.[301]

Another aspect of this shift has been described as a "Germanization" of the liturgy. According to this theory, the evangelization of the Germanic peoples in the fourth to the ninth centuries resulted not only in their adoption of Christianity but also in a transformation of the spiritual fabric of Western Christianity.[302] There was a great sense of the majesty of Christ in these regions partly because of their concept of kingship and partly due to the emphasis placed on Christ's divinity. A number of the Germanic tribes passed to the Western church by way of Arianism, and as Arianism had denied the divinity of Christ, this divinity tended to be emphasized by the church to the degree that Jesus was often referred to as "Christ our God."[303] This was combined with a culture heavily influenced by a warrior elite that naturally saw Christ as a warrior chieftain.[304] Hence Christ was seen as deserving honor as a warrior lord. In this milieu the importance of the liturgy was that it provided the locus to honor God. Naturally the Eucharist was reinterpreted in the light of this new emphasis. Indeed, this missionary work among the Germanic tribes may have been one of the impulses behind the eucharistic controversies that laid the foundation for the scholastic treatment of the Eucharist that was to have a great importance in the history of the Eucharist in the West up until the present day.[305]

This shift in interpretation also contributed to the decline in the Communion of the faithful as the value of the eucharistic celebration was considered independent of the people's reception of Communion (or of their participation or, for that matter, their very presence). Participation in the liturgical action of the Eucharist eventually became something that was quite separate from the daily life of regular Christians. It was an affair of the clergy; the laity could only watch the celebration. Indeed, most of the Carolingian reforms were centered on reform of clergy. Not only was the use of correct Latin recommended, but complicated specialized pieces of music were introduced to the liturgy, which contributed even more to the liturgy becoming the preserve of a specialized clerical and monastic elite. The Eucharist was no longer an assembly participating in the saving mysteries, but people came to look upon a saving drama and the cultivation of a mystical consciousness. It was also a time of an individualistic spirituality and, with the introduction of private Masses and the multiplication of votive Masses, people felt that the priest could act on their behalf.[306] In the Carolingian period, alongside the adoption of Roman usage we also begin to see a multiplication of private prayers being said by the priest during the Mass. Normally prayed in the singular, these prayers are often penitential in tone and sometimes even directly address Christ present in the eucharistic species. Jungmann points to the introduction of the *Agnus Dei* into the Roman Eucharist by Pope Sergius I (d. 701) as the first instance of this practice of addressing Christ in the eucharistic species.[307] The rite of the Eucharist was gradually filled with these apologies, with as many as seventy-five of them being prayed in a single celebration.[308] Indeed, far from valuing the communal participation in the eucharistic liturgy, Western Christians generally felt that they could reap more spiritual benefit from a Mass that a priest had agreed to celebrate for their intentions to the exclusion of everyone else.[309]

As with many other developments this "principle of multiplying Masses arose without real theological reflection and was regarded as indubitably correct."[310] While not all of the root causes of this multiplication of Masses are known, the extant evidence indicates a strong monastic dimension to the multiplication of private Masses at the end of the sixth and start of the seventh centuries.[311] At its birth, monasticism did not have a strong priestly dimension (the monks often attended the local parish church with other Christians on Sundays for the celebration of the Eucharist).[312] But in the Middle Ages, Benedictine monasteries became places where monks performed the liturgy on behalf of the laity, but also very clearly apart from the laity. This was emphasized by the monastic renewal of Benedict of Aniane, who is credited with providing Benedictine monasticism with the liturgical emphasis that characterizes it to this day.[313] The Mass came to be seen as the *opus bonum par excellence* whereby it takes pride of place "among the other exercises through which the religious sanctify themselves."[314] In this context it is interesting to note that by the year 800, 23 to 32 percent of all monks were priests and by the tenth century 55 percent of monks were priests.[315]

From the eighth century onwards, patronage for monasteries often entailed a repayment from the monks in the form of Masses celebrated for the donor's intentions, and by the ninth century there are many instances of monasteries undertaking Masses numbered in the thousands for their royal patrons.[316] One of the most significant church buildings in the twelfth century was that of the abbey church of Saint-Denis. Abbot Suger, the man who masterminded its construction, has left an account of its consecration in 1144. The high point of the celebration was a harmonized celebration of the Mass by the nineteen consecrating bishops, each celebrating on a separate altar, placed in a semicircle on two levels around the high altar. Suger tells us:

> After the consecration of the altars all these [dignitaries] performed a solemn celebration of Masses, both in the upper choir and in the crypt, so festively, so solemnly, so different and yet so concordantly, so close [to one another] and so joyfully that their song, delightful by its consonance and unified harmony, was deemed a symphony angelic rather than human.[317]

While Dekkers may be correct in pointing out that in its origins monasticism was not always liturgical, in Abbot Suger's world St Benedict's pristine balance of *ora et labora* had been replaced with a specialized monastic elite, the majority of whom were ordained priests, whose work was the liturgy (the physical work of the monastery was often carried out by lay brothers who worked to support their ordained brethren). His new abbey church was to be the cradle of the Gothic style. St Bernard of Clairvaux did try to start a new, simple style of monasticism, and this renewal was to be of great importance in Ireland. But despite the objections of St Bernard, and the weight of his sanctity and the influence of the Cistercian order, "within a half-century of Bernard of Clairvaux's death, the Gothic style and its accompanying liturgical glitter could be found throughout the length and breadth of France; by the end of the thirteenth century, it had been replicated all over Europe."[318]

While economic reasons and an individualistic spirituality definitely played their parts in the multiplication of Masses, there were other reasons as well. The stational liturgy of the city of Rome (whereby the liturgy was celebrated in different places on different days with great emphasis being placed on processions and solemnity)[319] perhaps also played its part in the development of the liturgy to the north of the Alps. But while on one level this was an imperfect copy of the Roman model, probably only directly affecting some feast days,[320] this desire to replicate the religious topography of Rome may have had a profound influence on the introduction of many altars in the monastic and cathedral churches of the Carolingian empire.[321]

The ninth century also marked the emergence of the first catechisms for the instruction of the laity. These catechisms deal with the reception of Communion. First of all, they encourage the laity to receive Communion more often than the three times a year that seem to have been the norm. The catechisms are free from the eucharistic controversies that had begun to occupy the learned, and in this time most parish priests and laity would have been ignorant of these controversies.[322] But it is also true that by this time the Mass was often seen principally as a special prayer that is very powerful. In the *Liber manualis* written in the early 840s by the Aquitaine noblewoman Dhouda for her eldest son, she recommends that her son take advantage of going to Mass to pray for his dead father. She also recommends that he have Masses offered for him:

You should see to it that the solemnities of Masses and sacrifices are frequently offered for him and for all the faithful departed. There is no better prayer.... It is said of the incomparable Judas [Maccabeus]: It is a holy and pious thought to pray for the dead, and to offer sacrifices for them so that they may be freed from their sins.[323]

The practice of praying for the dead in Masses blossomed into a veritable industry in the ninth century, with many monasteries earning their economic well-being by having their monks offer Masses for the departed loved ones of the rich.

FREQUENCY OF COMMUNION

Another fundamental element in the consideration of lay participation in the Eucharist is the actual reception of the eucharistic species. In the first three centuries it seems that the faithful received Communion every time they attended the Eucharist. The third century seems to be the high point of frequent Communion: the faithful received Communion every Sunday and on any feast days that fell during the week; even infants received Communion, and there was also the custom of bringing Communion home in order to receive it on the days before the next eucharistic celebration.[324] This practice became common in both East and West. But while vestiges of this practice persisted for quite some time in the East, it soon died out in the West in general.[325]

In later centuries, the manner of reception of Communion would come to be on the tongue. But this was not yet the case; in fact, throughout Eastern and Western Christendom until the end of Late Antiquity everyone received Communion standing, first the eucharistic bread on their hands and then drinking from the chalice (in a manner very close to the practice of many post–Vatican II Roman Catholics).[326]

But in the fourth and fifth centuries, although the Eucharist was still considered to be very important, nonetheless the faithful lost some of their closeness to it. In this period, pastors insisted more and more on the fasting required in order to prepare for Communion, and this, combined with the long penances, provoked a reluctance on the part of the faithful to approach the altar. In addition to this, many late-fourth- and early-fifth-century bishops insisted that the faithful show reverence to the eucharistic species at the moment of Communion.[327] These bishops did not invent this practice: for example, St Cyprian (d. 258), bishop of Carthage, preached of unworthy reception of the Eucharist in a frightening way. Speaking of those who had lapsed in persecutions, he gives a number of examples of those whose sin was not public and yet God himself manifested these sins as they approached Communion. Among these is the example of a woman who had the Eucharist in her house and when she "tried with unclean hands to open her box in which was the holy [body] of the Lord, thereupon she was deterred by rising fire to touch it."[328] These later bishops, however, often also had to scold their congregations for not receiving Communion, but, in general, this type of preaching often had the exact opposite effect to that intended.[329]

With the passage of time, pastors were no longer interested that their flocks receive Communion every week: for them it was too high an aspiration for simple lay folk to possibly attain. In earlier centuries, to receive Communion the Christian had to be free from grave sin (usually meaning adultery, murder, or apostasy).[330] However, as it became more common for people to receive Communion only rarely, at specific times and feasts, a greater emphasis was placed on preparation for the reception of Communion. Taking advantage of the penitential seasons of Lent and Advent, pastors used these times of conversion to prepare their people for the reception of Communion.[331] But in certain regions, many Christians (and ecclesiastics in particular) did continue the practice of daily Communion.

The fifth and sixth centuries were not periods of particular religious crisis. Yet perhaps the masses of new converts who were entering the church at this time (many belonging to the barbarian tribes or non-Roman people of the new Europe, entering the church after having first passed through Arianism) often entered the Catholic church for political or social motives. The church reacted to Arianism by emphasizing the divinity of Christ, which probably also contributed to the fear of receiving Communion.[332] Because of the gradual breakdown of the catechumenate and other forms of catechesis and formation, many of these new converts could never appreciate the early church's understanding of the Eucharist.[333] In this new mentality the reception of Communion became a sacred obligation, but an obligation that people were so afraid of fulfilling that the church eventually had to threaten them with excommunication.[334] Time and again the injunction for the faithful to receive Communion is found in the local councils of this time.[335]

As time went by, the custom of receiving Communion under both species became less and less common in the West. It is true that from the earliest times it was possible to receive just the eucharistic bread, but this was generally out of convenience when one had to bring the Eucharist to a sick person or when it was brought to a house for Home Communion, not when receiving Communion during the eucharistic liturgy.[336] However, after the patristic period the chalice gradually came to be denied to the people. There were undoubtedly many factors contributing to this, but one of the most important seems to have been the custom of daily Communion outside of the eucharistic celebration. The monk or devout layperson would have brought the eucharistic bread home with him and every day (until the next liturgy) would have received Communion before eating his midday meal. This in turn contributed to the custom of receiving only the eucharistic bread in the actual liturgical celebration.[337] But by the time of St Leo the Great and St Gregory the Great, the incidental evidence from all parts of the West points to the fact that the laity rarely received from the chalice.

By the ninth and tenth centuries this gradual denial of the chalice to the laity had become complete throughout most of the West. Only the hands of the priest who had been anointed were considered worthy to handle the Eucharist; therefore the laity were expected to receive Communion directly in the mouth.[338] This in turn necessitated that the faithful also kneel to receive Communion, initially for practical purposes as this made it easier for the priest to administer Communion.[339] By the eleventh century the use of bread in the form of wafer-like hosts had also become common in the West; these were often prepared by monks or nuns who took great care for ritual purity in the process. This new form of bread, however, bore little resemblance to people's everyday experience of bread from their own houses and tables.[340] A further development was that the faithful could now only receive Communion after the celebration and not during the liturgy itself so as not to "interrupt" the eucharistic liturgy.[341]

Although evidence for popular devotion to the eucharistic species in the first millennium is quite scarce,[342] there is plentiful evidence that the cult of relics played an important role in the early church. It is likely that later devotion to the eucharistic species developed from this initial devotion to the relics of the martyrs.[343] The first Christian altars would not have contained any relics, and in the pre-Nicene period it is likely that in most churches the Eucharist would only have been celebrated on Sundays.[344] But in the age of the martyrs, as their cult started, it became customary for Christians to gather around their tomb on their *dies natalis* (the anniversary of their death) and to celebrate the Eucharist in close proximity to the tomb. After the edict of Milan it became practical to do this in a more public way, and soon Christians started to build *martyria*, or little chapels, enclosing these tombs. The altar was often fashioned on the actual tomb or placed directly over it. The next step was to move the tomb inside the city and to place the relics of the martyr (or saint) within an altar there.[345] Initially, these would only have been in some churches (particularly in those churches that were able to obtain the relics of a famous local saint), but eventually relics came to be placed in every altar.[346]

Gradually the use of relics spread, particularly as the dismemberment of the saint's mortal remains became a legitimate practice, thus allowing for a single saint's mortal remains to be placed under any number of altars. By the Carolingian period, most churches in the vicinity of the city of Rome had acquired their own relics, and the placement of these relics in the altar had become an integral part of the liturgical rite of consecration of a church.[347] This was a feasible practice in Rome where, due to the drastic fall in population and the various barbarian invasions, the catacombs were being emptied of the bones of the saints interred therein (most probably along with many other bones of dubious origins). But in the lands of the Carolingian domain, where there were far fewer local martyrs and saints, new foundations had trouble finding enough relics to meet their needs.[348] In this context, the eucharistic species were sometimes seen as a "relic" of Jesus Christ, and a relic of Christ could trump any saint's relic. While there are some examples of the eucharistic species being used as a relic in the dedication of altars, it was never an approved liturgical practice.[349] But less extreme versions of this tendency also developed. In earlier times, the altar itself was the preeminent symbol of Christ in the church building, but gradually the eucharistic species became associated with the altar outside of the celebration itself. In the eighth century the practice of the eucharistic doves developed, whereby the eucharistic bread was placed in a hollow metallic "dove" that was suspended above the altar.[350] In addition, the forerunners of tabernacles were developing in which the eucharistic species were being reserved on the altar itself.[351] As time passed, this practice became more and more common, and eventually the altar became intimately associated with the reservation of the Eucharist.

By the end of the twelfth century the eucharistic species had become divorced from the liturgical celebration of the Eucharist. People only rarely received Communion, and the language of the liturgy had become unintelligible. At the same time a very realistic eucharistic theology became popular. This led the faithful to a particular devotion to the host as the locus of the humanity of Christ so that by gazing on the host they were able to participate in ocular communion.[352] So even on the level of popular devotion the Eucharist remained central: though the laity no longer received Communion with any frequency, it was still the privileged place of encounter with Christ.[353] Their devotional life was centered on eucharistic devotion, particularly on prayer in front of the tabernacle on the altar of churches, processions with the eucharistic species, and eucharistic exposition.[354] In the minds of all eleventh and twelfth-century Christians, "The holy mystery of the Lord's body" was the greatest of all the benefits granted to mankind, "because the entire salvation of the world consists in this mystery."[355]

CHAPTER TWO

Written Sources

The written sources for the Eucharist in pre-Norman Ireland are sparse, and even the discovery of another one or two liturgical manuscripts could totally transform our current understanding. However, there is an inappropriate tendency to lament this paucity of evidence and not realize that what we do have is an amazing corpus of evidence from a time in liturgical history when a few surviving manuscripts have been said to constitute a "tsunami of information."[1] The *Stowe Missal,* the most important surviving source, is a complete manuscript and can tell us quite a bit; this picture can be supplemented by the *Palimpsest Sacramentary,* a partially reconstructed palimpsest manuscript of early Irish provenance currently in Munich. Some material found in the *Antiphonary of Bangor,* the *Irish Liber Hymnorum,* and various rites of Communion of the sick and viaticum can further supplement these liturgical texts. The first part of this chapter examines these texts.

They are not the only documentary sources of the Eucharist. While not as informative as liturgical texts, monastic rules and penitentials bear witness to elements of eucharistic practice. Irish saints' lives (some of which are quite early) and devotional material along with other incidental texts such as annalistic entries are also important sources. The second part of this chapter examines these texts to see what light they shed on eucharistic practice in pre-Norman Ireland. As most of this material is far from systematic in its treatment of the Eucharist, some organization is needed when dealing with these documents; therefore I have arranged the texts into different categories.

However, due to the lack of clear-cut divisions in the material, some of the written sources have been dealt with in other chapters. Chapter 1 examined the texts directly pertinent to pastoral care, and chapter 3 will examine the texts that deal with the physical dimensions of the Eucharist (church buildings, eucharistic vessels, bread and wine, and so forth).

LITURGICAL TEXTS

THE *STOWE MISSAL*

The *Stowe Missal* is without doubt the most famous Irish liturgical manuscript.[2] This small manuscript (15 cm by 12 cm) has survived more or less intact to the present day. While scholarly opinion is somewhat divided as to its date, Warner's opinion that the missal seems to have been originally written shortly after the year 800 is accepted as a conservative estimate today.[3] The name Stowe derives from the fact that the missal was located for a time in the duke of Buckingham's house at Stowe, England (today it can be found in the library of the Royal Irish Academy in Dublin). Traditionally the missal has been associated with the Céli Dé movement.[4] However, this attribution is largely based on the fact that in the Canon, or eucharistic prayer, mention is made of St Maelruin, one of the founders of the Céli Dé.[5]

After the manuscript ceased to be used as a liturgical book, it was considered to be a relic and was encased in a valuable reliquary. Ó Riain has studied this reliquary and reaches the conclusion that it was made to enshrine the missal sometime between 1026 and 1033 under the patronage of "Mathgamáin grandson of Cathal" at Lorrha (Co. Tipperary) and that it remained there at least until the fourteenth century when a new face was made for the shrine. Therefore, the *Stowe Missal* has no connection with Terryglass or any Céli Dé center between these dates. Ó Riain also plausibly points out that, if the *Stowe Missal* was important enough to be considered as a relic in Lorrha in the tenth century, it must already have been in that church for some time prior to this.[6] So it is quite possible that the only connection between the *Stowe Missal* and the Céli Dé is that made by modern scholars.

The missal itself contains an order of the eucharistic liturgy and three "common" Masses—one for saints, one for penitents, and one for the dead. It also contains texts for baptism and the visitation of the sick and a tract on the meaning of the eucharistic liturgy written in Early Irish (the present manuscript contains a copy of the Gospel of John, but this seems to have been bound into the liturgical section at a later date).[7] In the greater European context the *Stowe Missal* is quite significant as it contains all the texts necessary for the celebration of the Eucharist, and is therefore perhaps the first book anywhere in the West to which the title "missal" can be attributed (as opposed to the sacramentaries which contain only the presiding priest's prayers and do not contain the other ministers' prayers).[8] Additionally, the missal is one of the earliest witnesses of the Roman Canon. When Dom Botte deals with the textual history of the Roman Canon, the *Stowe Missal* (along with the earlier canon of the *Bobbio Missal,* which scholars no longer believe to have any Irish connection) is one of the first two sources he lists, noting that the "famille irlandaise" is very important for any attempt to reconstruct the text.[9] In a comprehensive series of articles Bernard Capelle has placed the *Stowe Missal* in the center of his analysis of the history of certain aspects of the Roman Mass. While Capelle should not be faulted for his examination of the evidence, it must be noted that at the time when he was writing scholars dealt with the scattered manuscripts—which had survived in various corners of Europe and coming from different times and places—as if they constituted a single body of similar material. Therefore, in his reconstruction of a linear model of liturgical development it is perhaps simplistic to treat the simple liturgical vade mecum of a humble Irish cleric on the same level as some books that may have been used in papal liturgies. This being said, Capelle helps to show, once again, how the Irish liturgical evidence is more mainstream than it is often thought to be.[10]

The small size of the book, together with the variety of the "pastoral mix" it contains, would suggest that this book would have been a sort of vade mecum that a priest would have used as he made his rounds to the different churches that depended on his pastoral services.[11] In its original form it seems that the *Stowe Missal* contained no rubrics. This makes it hard to interpret the manuscript, as prayers adjacent to each other may have been alternatives or it could be that they were all prayed in each and every celebration. There is no direction for the preparation of the altar or for the exchange of peace.[12] But the fact that the manuscript more probably originates in a parochial context in contrast to early liturgical manuscripts that come from the high liturgy of cathedrals and great abbey churches adds to the importance of the *Stowe Missal* as more typical of the experience that common people had.

Another important fact concerning the *Stowe Missal* is that, shortly after its completion, a man named Móel Cáich revised the manuscript. We have no idea who he was, but he inserted many *"postprimam manum* alterations"[13] including rubrics and additional euchological texts. Many scholars find his work infuriating because at times he obscured the original text, and it is often difficult to work out whether in a given instance he was simply adding rubrics or whether he also changed some of the wording of the prayers. It is generally held that he altered the missal to be more in line with current Continental Gallican practices.[14] But this modification shows that at this stage (prior to becoming a relic) the *Stowe Missal* was a manuscript that was actually used in the liturgy and considered worth updating, and also that the changes deemed necessary by Móel Cáich were mostly in the Gallican tradition.[15]

An analysis of the original edition of the *Stowe Missal* shows that it was quite Roman in its structure:

This first edition of the Stowe rite is a heavily Romanized Rite: most of the prayers are in the concise Roman collect form, the Old Testament lesson has been dropped, the eucharistic prayer is the Roman Canon, and the peace has probably been moved to the Roman position after the breaking of the bread. This rite is very close kin to the *Missa Romansis cotidiana* of the Bobbio Missal. Yet a number of Gallican features have been retained: the apparently normative use of a canticle in the entrance rite, the Creed, the chant after the gospel and Creed, the *Post nomina* and *Ad pacem* prayers, the place of the Lord's Prayer, and the *Consummacio.* Other features normal in a Roman Rite at this point in time are missing: introit, *Kyrie,* psalm at the offertory, and *Agnus Dei.* The rite also has several unusual, if not unique, features: the inclusion of prayers for use after (or possibly during) epistle, gradual, and Alleluia; the place of the litany between epistle and gospel; texts related to the offering between epistle and gospel; use of *N.* to indicate a place to insert names; and commemoration of Old Testament worthies within the eucharistic prayer. It contains relatively early forms of the *Gloria in excelsis,* the Nicene Creed, and the Roman Canon.[16]

The *Stowe Missal* is probably a typical witness to its period where the Gallican liturgy was adopting many Roman elements. Indeed, it is probable that these Roman elements came to Ireland from another Gallican region (such as present-day France) as the forms and variations of the Roman prayers have parallels to other Gallican books as opposed to the pure Roman forms.[17] Although written at a time when the Gallican rite in general was becoming more and more Roman in content, Móel Cáich's changes and additions to the manuscript were more Gallican than the original missal. While it may be tempting to look to a traditionalist tendency or interchurch liturgical feuds as reasons behind the reworking of the manuscript, there is simply not enough evidence to be able to give any interpretation to the *post-primam manum* alterations other than to say that Móel Cáich decided that the missal would be of more use with the alterations.[18] And it also needs to be remembered that the amended version of the text was the version that was actually used prior to the missal's enshrinement.

Here is not the place to carry out an in-depth analysis of the euchology (or prayer texts) of the *Stowe Missal.*[19] All I shall do is signal the places where the *Stowe Missal* differs from contemporary Continental missals. Basically there are three major differences worth noting; these take the form of three texts without exact parallel elsewhere: (1) the eucharistic celebration begins with a long litany; (2) a hymn for the *fractio panis,* or the breaking of the bread during the eucharistic liturgy; and (3) a Communion chant of a type that we do not find elsewhere.[20] The first of these differences is the long litany:

We have sinned, O Lord, we have sinned: Spare us from our sins. Save us. You who guided Noah over the waters of the flood. Hear us. You who called back Jonah from the abyss with a word: deliver us. You who stretched out your hand to Peter as he sank: help us O Christ. O Son of God you showed the wonderful works of the Lord to our ancestors, be merciful to us in our times: put forth your hand from on high and deliver us.

Christ hear us.	[Christ graciously hear us].
Christ hear us.	[Christ graciously hear us].
Christ hear us.	[Christ graciously hear us].
Kyrie eleison,	[Kyrie eleison, Kyrie eleison.
Christe eleison,	Christe eleison, Christe eleison.
Kyrie eleison,	Kyrie eleison, Kyrie eleison].
Saint Mary,	[Pray for us].
Saint Peter,	[Pray for us].
Saint Paul,	[Pray for us].
Saint Andrew,	[Pray for us].
Saint James,	[Pray for us].
Saint Bartholomew,	[Pray for us].
Saint Thomas,	[Pray for us].
Saint Matthew,	[Pray for us].
Saint James,	[Pray for us].
Saint Thaddeus,	[Pray for us].
Saint Matthias,	[Pray for us].
Saint Mark,	[Pray for us].
Saint Luke,	[Pray for us].
[*] Saint Stephen,	Pray for us.
Saint Martin,	Pray for us.
Saint Jerome,	Pray for us.
Saint Augustine,	Pray for us.
Saint Gregory,	Pray for us.
Saint Hilary,	Pray for us.
Saint Patrick,	Pray for us.
Saint Ailbe,	Pray for us.
Saint Finian,	Pray for us.
Saint Finian,	Pray for us.
Saint Ciaran,	Pray for us.
Saint Ciaran,	Pray for us.

Saint Brendan,	Pray for us.
Saint Brendan,	Pray for us.
Saint Columba,	Pray for us.
Saint Columba,	Pray for us.
Saint Comgall,	Pray for us.
Saint Cainnech,	Pray for us.
Saint Finbar,	Pray for us.
Saint Nessan,	Pray for us.
Saint Fachtna,	Pray for us.
Saint Lugaid,	Pray for us.
Saint Lachtain,	Pray for us.
Saint Ruadán,	Pray for us.
Saint Carthach,	Pray for us.
Saint Kevin,	Pray for us.
Saint Mochonne,	Pray for us.
Saint Brigid,	Pray for us.
Saint Ita,	Pray for us.
Saint Scetha,	Pray for us.
Saint Sínech,	Pray for us.
Saint Samthann,	Pray for us.
O [all] you saints,	Pray for us.
Be merciful to us,	Spare us.
O Lord be merciful to us,	Deliver us O Lord.
from every evil,	Deliver us O Lord.
Through your cross,	Deliver us O Lord.
Sinners,	We ask you to hear us.
O Son of God,	We ask you to hear us.
That you might give us peace,	We ask you to hear us.
Lamb of God who takes away the sins of the world, have mercy on us.	
Christ hear us!	[Christ graciously hear us].
Christ hear us!	[Christ graciously hear us].
Christ hear us!	[Christ graciously hear us].[21]

What is significant about the *Stowe Missal*'s initial litany is not simply the fact that the eucharistic celebration starts with a litany, as litanies of one form or another (particularly variations of the *Kyrie*) were common in other places.[22] What marks out the *Stowe Missal* is the sheer length of the litany. It seems that the original version of the *Stowe Missal* contained a shorter form and that the second section (containing the Irish saints) was added by Móel Cáich.[23] Irish devotional texts have many examples of litanies and litanic forms of prayer,[24] but here is an example that seems to be properly liturgical.[25] The original list of saints mentions only our Lady, the apostles, and the evangelists. The additions also contain saints of the universal church (such as Martin of Tours and Augustine of Hippo). While Patrick and Columba are mentioned, the list does seem to concentrate on saints venerated particularly in Leinster and north Munster. This may in fact be consistent with the earlier Céli Dé identification of the *Stowe Missal,* but it could also be significant that no mention is made of the Archangel Michael, who was particularly venerated in texts associated with Tallaght and other Céli Dé centers.[26] Whatever else may be understood from the litany, it is clear that the Eucharist is seen as a communion with the saints in heaven. The saints are also very present in the Canon—over one hundred saints of both Old and New Testament along with many Irish and some non-Irish saints.[27] Because local saints were seen as heavenly patrons and defenders of local churches in early Ireland, this long list of saints may be related to the early Christian custom of reading the diptychs during the eucharistic liturgy, to show the churches with which the particular church was in communion,[28] the names of neighboring bishops being replaced with their saintly counterparts.

The second important element of the *Stowe Missal* is the chant used at the *fractio panis:*

> They knew it was the Lord, Alleluia;
> in the breaking up of the bread, Alleluia.
> The bread we break is the body of Jesus Christ, our Lord, Alleluia;
> the chalice we bless is the blood of Jesus Christ, our Lord, Alleluia.
> For the remission of our sins, Alleluia.
> Lord, let your mercy rest upon us, Alleluia;
> who put all our confidence in you, Alleluia.
> They knew it was the Lord, Alleluia;
> in the breaking up of the bread, Alleluia.

O Lord, we believe that in this breaking of your body and pouring
  out of your blood we become your redeemed people;
We confess that in taking the gifts of this pledge here, we lay hold in
  hope of enjoying its true fruit in the heavenly places.[29]

The original text of this prayer has been changed by Móel Cáich,
who has erased the last six lines to replace them with the current ending. Here we find a catena of scripture verses dealing with the reception of Christ in Communion. This text was said or sung as the priest
broke the bread. In the next section of this chapter we will examine
the *Mass Tract* of the *Stowe Missal*, which tells how the eucharistic
bread was sometimes broken into as many as sixty-five pieces. While
the recitation of this prayer would give enough time to break the
bread on less solemn occasions when there were few communicants,
it is doubtful that the priest could have accomplished the intricate
fraction rite as described in the *Mass Tract* during the available time. It
is possible that the text may have been repeated as needs dictated,[30] or
if it was sung it would have taken longer. While it does ask for forgiveness, the actual prayer is centered on the presence of the Lord and
the timbre of the prayer is one of closeness to God, which is achieved
by the actual reception of the eucharistic elements.

The third distinctive feature of the *Stowe Missal* is the presence of
a very long series of prayers for use during Communion that could be
called a "Communion antiphon":

My peace I give you, Alleluia;
my peace I leave you.
Those who love your law have great peace, Alleluia;
they do not stumble, Alleluia.
[Bless] the King of Heaven [who comes] with peace Alleluia;
full of the odour of life, Alleluia.
O sing him a new song, Alleluia;
come, all his saints, Alleluia.
Come, eat of my bread, Alleluia;
and drink the wine I have mixed for you, Alleluia.
Psalm 23 is recited.

He who eats my body, Alleluia;
and drinks my blood, Alleluia;
abides in me and I in him, Alleluia.
Psalm 24 is recited.

This is the living bread come down from heaven, Alleluia;
he who eats of it shall live forever, Alleluia.
Psalm 25 is recited.

The Lord fed them with bread from heaven, Alleluia;
men ate the bread of angels, Alleluia.
Psalm 43 is recited.

Eat, O friends, Alleluia;
and drink deeply, O beloved ones, Alleluia.
This is the sacred body of our Lord, [Alleluia];
the blood of our Saviour, Alleluia;
feast, all of you, on it for eternal life, Alleluia.
Let my lips declare your praise, Alleluia;
because you teach me your commandments, Alleluia.
I will bless the Lord at all times, Alleluia;
his praise always on my lips, Alleluia.
Taste and see, Alleluia;
how sweet is the Lord, Alleluia.
Where I am, Alleluia;
there shall my servant be, Alleluia.
Let the children come to me, Alleluia;
and do not stop them, Alleluia;
for to such belongs the kingdom of God, Alleluia.
Repent, Alleluia;
for the Kingdom of heaven is at hand, Alleluia.
The Kingdom of heaven has suffered violence, Alleluia;
and violent men have taken it by force, Alleluia.
Come O blessed of my Father, inherit the kingdom, Alleluia;
prepared for you before the foundation of the world, Alleluia.
Glory be to the Father [and to the Son and to the Holy Spirit];

come O blessed of my Father, inherit the kingdom;
as it was in the beginning, [is now, and ever shall be, world
without end];
come O blessed of my Father, Amen, Alleluia.[31]

If we are correct in assuming that the entire texts of the four
psalms are recited (only the incipit of each psalm is actually given in
the missal but it is probable that at that time the reader would understand that to mean that the whole psalm, which most clerics knew by
heart, was to be recited), then this rite would have lasted a long time.
It would have given time for the assembly to receive the Eucharist.
The text of this chant is very much based on the physical consumption
of the eucharistic elements. The length and content of these chants
would imply that many people communicated and not that they remained as spectators. Also the euchology is fully consistent with the
full assembly's actually receiving Communion (presuming that an assembly was present). However, it is also possible that this text would
have been used on those feast days when there were many communicants and that some shorter version would be used on other days.

THE *OLD IRISH MASS TRACT* OF THE *STOWE MISSAL*

True to its nature as a vade mecum, the *Stowe Missal* contains other
material in additional to the euchological texts for the celebration of
the Eucharist.[32] These include a vernacular Mass tract, a rite for baptism, a rite for the Communion of the sick, and even some spells.[33]
The most famous of these texts is a document that is often referred to
as the *Old Irish Mass Tract* of the *Stowe Missal.* It is an allegorical
interpretation of the eucharistic liturgy. While the version of this text
in the *Stowe Missal* is available in a number of translations and mentioned by many authors, it is not often noticed that another version of
this text is to be found in the *Leabhar Breac.*[34] The fact that two versions exist gives weight to the possibility that this text enjoyed some
popularity.[35] Moreover, it provides a fascinating insight into how the
Eucharist was considered by the Irish in this period.

As the text is quite long, and there are various differences between the versions, a parallel of them is included as an appendix to
this volume. The fact that it is in Old Irish may imply that the text
was used in the instruction of the laity or at the very least as homily
preparation material for the priest (the fact that it was bound to the
Stowe Missal, which may have formed a clerical vade mecum, lends
weight to this theory). However, as vernacular learning and literature
were also popular in clerical circles, it is also possible that this was
simply for the instruction or personal edification of clerics.[36]

The *Mass Tract* is very clearly within the lines of allegorical interpretation of the eucharistic liturgy as examined in chapter 1. These interpretations see the eucharistic celebration as making the whole of
salvation history and especially the death of Christ present again on
the altar. These interpretations also give precedence to the actions of
the celebrant over and above the actual words. However, while the
interpretations that the *Mass Tract* gives do bear the hallmark of the
medieval allegorical method in line with Amalarius of Metz, they also
retain some individual traits.

The *Mass Tract* sees the Eucharist through a penitential lens common to the West in general. Godel (in one of the few scholarly treatments on early Irish spirituality) sees the prayers of the *Mass Tract* as
being characteristic of Irish spirituality of the time emphasizing sinfulness.[37] Many different episodes of salvation history and the life of
Christ are mentioned, but the weight of these references is to the Crucifixion and to sufferings in general. In the *Stowe Missal* version, the
opening words are "the altar, a figure of the persecution that was inflicted."[38] The *Leabhar Breac* version is generally longer and has an
introduction: "the church that shelters the people and the altar, a figure of the shelter of the Godhead divine, of which was said: you guard
me under the shelter of your wings."[39] This version seems to imply
that the people were in the church during the celebration, adding to
the evidence against the theory of the laity having to wait outside the
church while only the clerics entered (this theory will be discussed
more fully in chapter 3). Section 5 of the *Stowe Missal* version, which
has no parallel in the *Leabhar Breac,* mentions the Eucharist being
above or on the altar seemingly at the start of the celebration.[40] Mac-

Carthy translates this as "the oblation upon the altar." Stokes, however, interprets it to mean "the Host, then, *super altare,* i.e. the turtle-dove," thus perhaps referring to the possibility that it means a eucharistic dove containing a form of eucharistic reservation before the eucharistic liturgy.[41]

Reference is made to various examples of the private prayers that the priest would have said, generally of a penitential nature. We are told that water is first added to the chalice with the prayer, "I ask you, O Father; I beseech you, O Son; I implore you, O Holy Spirit."[42] Later on as the wine is placed into the chalice on top of the water, another private prayer is cited, "May the Father forgive; may the Son be indulgent; may the Holy Spirit have mercy."[43] The *Leabhar Breac Tract* specifies that there are three drops ("banna") of both water and wine; this describes a liturgy where only a little wine was used (to which an equal amount of water may have been added).

The consecration (which probably refers to the institution narrative) seems to be very important. The *Leabhar Breac Tract* says that:

> The time, now, *Accepit Jesus panem, stans in medio discipulorum suorum* is chanted, the priests bow thrice for sorrow for the sins they did, and they offer to God, and they chant all this psalm: Have mercy on me, O God; and no sound is sent forth by them (the people) then, that the priest be not disturbed, for what is meet is that his mind separate not from God, even in one vocable, at this prayer: for it is guilty of the spiritual order and of bad reception from God, unless it is like that it is done; wherefore it is from this that the name of this prayer is *Periculosa Oratio.*[44]

The penitentials (which will be examined below) also speak of the *periculosa oratio.* This is very significant for a number of reasons. Firstly, it does seem that Ireland is ahead of many other regions in assigning the consecration to this particular moment of the liturgy. This is in keeping with the theory of the development of a eucharistic theology centered on these words as proposed by Jungmann, who sees "a very lively sentiment in the Irish-Celtic tradition for a definitive meaning of the words of institution" at a time before so clear a doctrine developed in the West in general.[45] In verse 11 of the *Tract* the congregation is portrayed as being prostrate on the floor (*Stowe*), after having sung Psalm 50 (*Leabhar Breac*). While this seems strange to modern sensibilities, it shows that the assembly had some idea as to what was happening in the eucharistic prayer and that they were present in the church and may even have been able to hear this section. But the actual prayer has nearly a magical quality, as even the mispronunciation of a single syllable is seen as a serious offence.

The most important part of the *Mass Tract* is the elaborate description of the *fractio panis,* or rite of breaking of the bread prior to Communion. The *Stowe Missal* version gives much more detail of this rite. The fact that the *Stowe Missal* itself (being bound in the same manuscript, but originally separate) has a very long antiphon to accompany this rite may be significant. This description in the *Mass Tract* recounts that:

> There are seven kinds upon the Fraction: that is, five parts of the common Host, in figure of the five senses of the soul. Seven of the Host of Saints and Virgins, except the chief ones, in figure of the seven gifts of the Holy Spirit. Eight of the Host of Martyrs, in figure of the octonary New Testament. Nine of the Host of Sunday, in figure of the nine folks of heaven and of the nine grades of the church. Eleven of the Host of Apostles, in figure of the imperfect number of Apostles after the scandal of Judas. Twelve of the Host of the calends [of January, that is, Circumcision] and of [Last] Supper day, in remembrance of the perfect number of Apostles. Thirteen of the Host of little Easter [Low Sunday] and of the feast of Ascension—at first, although they were distributed more minutely afterwards, in going to communion—in figure of Christ with his twelve Apostles.
>
> The five, and the seven, and the eight, and the nine, and the eleven, and the twelve, and the thirteen—they are five [and] sixty together; and that is the number of parts which is wont to be in the Host of Easter, and of the Nativity, and of Pentecost; for all that is contained in Christ.[46]

A number of points can be seen from this complicated description. First of all, mention is made of a common host (*obli choitchinn*). This could imply a smaller, simpler host was used for daily eucharistic celebrations, or even for regular Sunday eucharistic celebration, when there would have been fewer communicants, as opposed to the feast days with the greater numbers. It also lists a few important feast days—the Circumcision, Holy Thursday, the Ascension, Low Sunday, Easter, Christmas, and Pentecost, as well as some feasts of (unnamed) saints. These seem to be days when there were more communicants than normal. But it is on Easter, Christmas, and Pentecost that the host is broken into sixty-five pieces, a greater number than any other day. This would lend weight to the theory that many people only received Communion on a few select feast days. But even if more did receive on these days, the number of sixty-five cannot be seen as a great number especially when compared to the "numberless people" mentioned as attending a feast day in seventh-century Kildare.[47] The relatively small number may be due to the *Stowe Missal*'s use in a parish setting.

The passage then continues with this complicated description:

> And it is all arranged in the form of a cross upon the paten; and on the incline is the upper part on the left hand, as hath been said: Inclining his head He handed over His Spirit.
>
> The arrangement of the Fraction of Easter and of the Nativity—thirteen [fourteen] parts in the tree of the crosses; nine [fourteen] in their cross-piece; twenty parts in the circuit-wheel (five parts of each angle); sixteen between the circuit and the body of the crosses (that is, four of each portion).
>
> The middle part, that is the one to which the celebrant goes [partakes of]: namely, a figure of the breast with the mysteries.
>
> What is from there upwards of the tree to bishops.
>
> The thwart-piece on the left-hand to the priests.
>
> The portion [athwart] on the right hand, to all undergrades.
>
> The portion from the thwart-piece downwards, to anchorites of . . . penance.

The portion that is in the upper left-hand angel, to true clerical students.

The upper right-hand (portion), to innocent youths.

The lower left-hand (portion), to folk of penance.

The lower right-hand (portion), to folk of lawful wedlock and to folk who have not gone to hand [that is, to Communion] before.[48]

The elaborate nature of the *fractio panis* continues in this section. It can thus be deduced that this rite was of some special importance. It also gives the impression of a very ordered and hierarchical assembly. Not only do the different groups receive Communion by rank, they also receive from a different part of the host. Prior to the distribution the pieces of the eucharistic bread are arranged on the paten in the form of a cross with a circuit wheel (*cuairtroth*) around it.[49] This is sometimes taken to be a literary reference to a circle superimposed upon a cross as in the very famous high cross examples.[50] If this interpretation is accepted, it would be unique, as no other contemporary text mentions the use of a shape similar to the high crosses (keeping in mind, however, that the *Mass Tract* does not make explicit reference to the high crosses). While it is quite conceivable that larger hosts would have been prepared when more communicants were expected, it is hard to believe that the exact number of communicants could be determined with complete accuracy before the celebration. It may, however, have been the case that this passage's numerological information would give the celebrant the possibility of calculating an acceptable numerical interpretation for whichever number he needed to break. But regardless of the actual number of pieces broken for a particular celebration, the significance of the *fractio panis* cannot be denied in this text.[51] This importance is echoed in the Derrynaflan Paten and the high cross iconography of the *fractio panis* that will be examined in chapter 3.

The *Mass Tract* finishes with a description of the reception of Communion, where Communion is to be taken simply without consuming it too quickly or slowly and in all probability under both species:

Now the effect of this is (to cause) a meaning to be in [these?] figures and that this be your meaning, as if the part that you receive of
the Host were a member of Christ from off His Cross; and as if it
were this Cross whence runs upon each one his own draught [lit.
run], since it is united to the crucified Body.

It is not proper to swallow it, the part, without tasting it; as it is
not proper to pause in tasting the mysteries of God.

It is not proper to have it go under back teeth; in figure that it is
not proper to dwell overmuch upon the mysteries of God, that hearsay be not forwarded thereby.[52]

THE *PALIMPSEST SACRAMENTARY*

This important manuscript (Der Staatsbibliothek München, *codices
latini monacenses 14429*), having been published only in 1964, is a
relatively new element that can aid a modern understanding of pre-
Norman Irish eucharistic liturgy. The fact that it was not known to
Warren means that much secondary literature makes no reference to
it. Although in a fragmentary state, it is an extremely important source
for our knowledge for the liturgy of early Ireland. This manuscript,
now to be found in Munich, was taken to the Continent at some time
in the first millennium and ended up in Reichenau. Unfortunately this
vellum manuscript was recycled as a palimpsest in the second half of
the ninth century when the original text was scraped off and a glos-
sary (also in an Irish hand) was written on it. Through the labors of
Dold and Eizenhöfer the text of the original sacramentary has been
partly reconstructed. David Wright has made a contribution to the
critical edition by analyzing the handwriting and giving his opinion
that the sacramentary had been written in Ireland (or possibly in Northumbria) in the third quarter of the seventh century.[53]

The approximate date of 650 AD means that it was written more
than one hundred years before the *Stowe Missal.* However, due to the
manuscript's re use as a palimpsest, it is not complete. Exasperatingly,
besides the manuscript's incomplete state, an earlier attempt to restore
the original text by removing the newer text with acid actually destroyed some portions of the original (including a lot of material

around Easter) that the more modern deciphering techniques using ul-
traviolet images would probably have been able to read. Of the still
extant pages, 158 fragments have been deciphered. These are from 31
different Masses: "15 de Tempore, 14 de Sanctis, one unknown and
one for the dead."[54] Of these, 29 have parallels in the (Gallican) *Missale Gothicum* and another 15 in various Spanish libres missarum.[55]
The parallels with the *Missale Gothicum* are not "confined to some
scattered formulae, for there are whole sets of parallel formulae in
both of these books."[56] Unlike the *Stowe Missal* or other later works
that contain a variety of material, what remains of the *Palimpsest Sacramentary* is actually a list of Masses for various feasts of the liturgical
year along with a fairly extensive sanctoral.[57] Other than some small
fragments of material for the liturgy of the hours for Christmas, the
Epiphany, and Easter, all the texts belong to the Order of Mass. The
sacramentary does not contain any noneuchological texts or vernacular material; the only element other than euchology is the presence of headings that describe where the prayer is used in the liturgy.
With these keys it is possible to reconstruct a eucharistic liturgy "of
the Gallican type with the Praefatio missae, Collectio, Post nomina
recitata, Collectio (ad pacem), Immolatio missae, Post sanctus, Post
secreta (consisting of two formulae), Antae orationem dominicam,
Prefatio post eucharistiam and Collectio post eucharistiam."[58] It is
true that there is some Roman material, but this seems to be more in
the form of individual borrowings of useful texts rather than representing the beginnings of the merging of the Gallican and Roman rites:

> Roman influence is clearly indicated by the Preface for Peter and
> Paul, Nr. 108 which is Nr. 285 in the Leonianum. There are some
> other small pieces of our texts identical with Roman expressions, also
> of the canon of the Mass. But the Roman Canon is not presupposed
> as the norm, as it is in the Stowe Missal or in the Bobbio Missal, for
> the sanctus is followed in Clm 14429 by a Vere sanctus which is al-
> ways changing. Our Sacramentary is not romanized like the others.[59]

Perhaps the greatest significance of this manuscript is the strong
parallels that it has to (other) Gallican missals, adding to the weight of
evidence that denies the existence of an individual Celtic rite.[60] How-

ever, another contribution of the *Palimpsest Sacramentary* concerns the debate as to whether there was a sanctoral in early Irish liturgy. Hennig maintained that the absence of a sanctoral was a very important characteristic of "Celtic" liturgy.[61] While the abundant evidence in the lives of the saints and the annals could not dissuade him, there is unequivocal evidence of the existence of a sanctoral in the *Palimpsest Sacramentary*. Although this manuscript has been somewhat of an unwanted child of scholars of ancient Ireland,[62] it cannot be denied that not only is it "amongst the oldest preserved books of Irish script and decoration and is a particular treasure of Old Ireland,"[63] but, for our purposes, it is the oldest surviving liturgical manuscript with strong Irish connections pointing to Ireland as being one with most of Western Europe in using a form of the Gallican rite.

RITES OF THE SICK

Many commentators have noted that the church in pre-Norman Ireland was especially concerned with pastoral care at the moment of death.[64] Whether by chance preservation or due to the importance given them, more rites for the sick survive than any other ritual of the early Irish church.[65] While we really have only one complete order of Mass, we have four rites for the sick.[66] The *Stowe Missal* contains a rite of visitation of the sick. Along with this we have surviving examples in the Scottish *Book of Deer,*[67] the *Book of Dimma,* and the *Book of Mulling* (the witness from penitentials and saints' lives will be examined below). Exactly how much can be read into this fact is hard to say. The survival of four rites of the sick in and of itself does not necessarily mean that this rite had a particular importance in Ireland and could be simply due to the vagaries of manuscript survival. However, given the other evidence of the esteem in which this rite was held, perhaps it is significant that more manuscript versions of this liturgical rite survive than any other type of liturgical text. Additionally, if it is accepted that this rite was of particular importance in pre-Norman Ireland, it could also be significant that there is a good deal of similarity between the forms of this rite in the four manuscripts, which bears witness to a certain common format to this rite throughout this period.[68]

Examining these rituals side by side, Jenner divided them into ten sections: (1) blessing of water; (2) *Prefatio,* a Gallican-type prayer for the sick person; (3) scripture readings (from Mt 22:23, 29–33; 24:29–31 and, only in *Dimma,* 1 Cor 15:19–22);[69] (4) anointing either preceded by a profession of faith in the Trinity or followed by the Creed; (5) the Our Father; (6) prayers for the sick person; (7) *Pax;* (8) Communion; (9) thanksgiving; and (10) final blessing. While helpful, this schema is not perfect: none of the four examples exactly conforms to this pattern.[70]

As these rites are similar (and all conveniently accessible in Warren) here we will simply look at the text of the *Book of Mulling* and note the significant differences offered by the other three:

The beginning of the prayer of Communion for the sick
Let us pray, dear brothers, for the spirit of our dearly beloved .n., who according to the flesh is suffering discomfort, that the Lord may have present the revelation of present pains, may grant him life and may fill him with every saving good thing in repayment for his good works, through [our] Lord.

Beginning of the preface of Communion
Let us pray, dear brothers, for our brother .n. who is vexed by the suffering of the flesh and discomfort, that the Lord may have mercy by the heavenly medicine of the angels may [deign to] visit and strengthen, through [our] Lord.

Father all powerful, keep your servant, .n., who has been sanctified and redeemed by the great price of your blood, for ever and ever.

BLESSING OF WATER
Let us pray to and beseech the almighty Lord, that he might deign to bless and sanctify this font with his heavenly spirit, through [our] Lord.

BLESSING OF MAN
May the Lord bless and keep you, may the Lord always enlighten you with his face and have mercy upon you, may he turn his countenance towards you, and give you his peace and healing. May n. d. a. have mercy.

While he anoints him with oil

I anoint you with the oil of salvation in the name of God the Father, and the Son and the Holy Spirit, that you may have health in the name of the Holy Trinity.

At the same time [the following] is sung.

I believe in God the Father.

While he says this that all may be sent away

COLLECT OF THE LORD'S PRAYER

Creator of all nature, God, and Father of everything in heaven and the origin of everything on earth, let the religious prayers of the people of the Trinity be accepted before the throne of light, and be clearly listened to together with the cherubim and seraphim who tirelessly stand around praising [you].

Our Father.

Now the collect follows.

Free us from evil, Lord Jesus Christ, and guard us in every good work, author of all good, reigning and remaining for ever and ever. Amen.

Then he receives the Body and the Blood

May the Body with the Blood of our Lord Jesus Christ be health for you unto eternal life.

Prayer after the reception of the Eucharist

Guard within us, O Lord, the glory of your gift, that the Eucharist that we have partaken of may keep us strong against all the evils of the present time, through our Lord.

Alleluia.

Let them offer sacrifices of praise, and announce his deeds in songs of joy, alleluia.

I will take up the chalice of salvation and call on the name of the Lord. Refreshed by the Body and Blood of Christ, let us always say, alleluia, unto you, O Lord.

Let all men praise the Lord.

Glory [be to the Father].

Offer a sacrifice of praise and hope in the Lord.

O God, we give you thanks, through the holy mysteries we have celebrated, and the gift of holiness we have received, through our Lord Jesus Christ, your Son, to him be glory for ever and ever.[71]

In the care of the sick and dying, the reception of Communion was important. It is not administered by itself but is given as the climax of a rite that has other elements. In the Mulling example, there are *benedictio super aquam* and the *benedictio hominis,* but the prayers in *Stowe* and *Dimma* mirror these with the opening euchology and the biblical readings. The fact that three of the rites have the Creed or a creedal formula prior to the reception of Communion is also important, and this will later make its way into the Roman rite of the Eucharist a number of centuries after these rituals were composed. The Creed was not originally part of the eucharistic liturgy in the Roman rite. It was only to make its way into the Roman Mass in the year 1014 when Henry II of Germany (d. 1024) visited in Rome to be crowned Holy Roman emperor by Pope Benedict VIII (d. 1024) and insisted that the Creed be sung. From here it passed into common usage for all solemn Roman Masses (although it is not usually recited in weekday Masses).[72] The fact that all of these rituals of Communion, along with the eucharistic liturgy of the *Stowe Missal,* contain the Creed (or a creedal formula) is historically significant because it may indicate some Irish influence in the eventual adoption of the Creed in the Roman Mass.[73]

The formula for the administration of Communion is very similar in each of the rites:

Stowe: "Corpus et sanguis domini nostri ihesu christi fili Dei uiui altissimi." [The Body and the Blood of our Lord Jesus Christ, Son of the most high and living God.]

Dimma: "Corpus et sanguis domini nostri ihesu christi fili Dei uiui conservat animam tuam in vitam aeternam." [May the Body and the Blood of our Lord Jesus Christ guard your soul unto eternal life.]

Mulling: "Corpus cum sanguine domini nostri ihesu Christi sanitas sit tibi in uitam eternam." [May the Body with the Blood of our Lord Jesus Christ be health for you unto eternal life.]

Deer: "Corpus cum sanguine domini nostri ihesu Christi sanitas sit tibi in uitam perpetuam et eternam." [May the Body with the Blood of our Lord Jesus Christ be health for you unto perpetual and eternal life.][74]

Thus the reception of Communion is the center of this rite of the sick. But rather than there being anything particularly special about this rite, other than the importance and emphasis given it by contemporary Irish Christians (which will be examined below when dealing with saints' lives), it seems to have been a fairly normal ritual of pastoral care of the sick, and it compares with similar rituals of visitation, Communion, and the viaticum throughout the West. Also, the formulae for the actual administration of Communion are typical of general Western practice.[75]

LITURGICAL MUSIC IN PRE-NORMAN IRELAND

There are many difficulties in studying the role of music in the liturgy of pre-Norman Ireland. Not least is the fact that it is virtually impossible to reconstruct musical practice in this period because prior to the year AD 800 there is no type of musical notation—manuscripts give only the texts of the sung parts of the liturgy—rudimentary pitch notation only appears around the year 1000, and the rhythmic notation necessary to fully reconstruct the music finally appears around the year 1200.[76] This has led many to hold that apart from being able to believe that music was important in the early Irish church, nothing further can be said about it.[77] While few particulars of music in the early Irish liturgy can be known, it is probable that the music used in the liturgy would not have been very different from other Western liturgical music that would have come to Ireland with the other elements of the liturgical rites. In practice, then, the first Irish liturgical chant would probably have resembled old Gallican chant as used in Britain and the Frankish domains. In turn, these practices would have had their roots in the early church.[78] However, very little is actually known about the music being used in the eucharistic celebrations throughout the West in the first millennium. While there may well have been a common origin for some musical chants, melodies, or styles of singing, the diversity of later evidence makes it hard to assert a single origin for later Western practices.[79]

In the period of Late Antiquity, ecclesiastics were struggling with problems associated with the integration of musical styles and practices into Christian liturgy.[80] While the festive and emotional elements of music were never done away with, these tended to value music as a means to an end: the main goal of music was to transmit a text. At this time liturgical ministers and ministries tended to become more specialized. The liturgical role of a cantor, whose function was specifically to sing texts (as opposed to proclaiming them), developed.[81] Initially these cantors sung certain parts of the chants, while the assembly sung the refrains. In Rome a *schola cantorum*, traditionally associated with Gregory the Great, also began to develop, gradually taking on the same role. But with the loss of comprehension of Latin in the West, these singers became fully professional (singing all of a piece without any participation of the assembly), and the music was now alien to the people.[82]

Although the liturgical singing of (biblical) psalms is a clear characteristic of the musical practice of later Latin Christianity and the Roman rite in particular, the pre-Nicene church seems not to have used the psalms themselves for worship, preferring to compose new hymn texts.[83] However, it happened that many of the early Christian composers of hymns were later judged to have been heterodox,[84] which eventually led to a general hesitancy towards the acceptance of nonbiblical hymns and even to canonical legislation prohibiting their use.[85] In the East, St Ephrem the Syrian rehabilitated the use of nonscriptural hymnography. With his hymns he met the heretical composers on their own ground, using theologically orthodox lyrics to counteract his opponents' heretical ones.[86]

In the West, apart from some ancient hymns such as the *Te Deum* and the *Gloria in excelsis*, hymns remained somewhat questionable.[87] Nonpsalmic hymns were still frowned upon, despite the rehabilitation of Western hymnography under Hilary and Ambrose in the fourth century.[88] Indeed, Western hymnography was for the most part relegated to the liturgy of the hours and not very welcome in the celebration of the Eucharist.[89]

Whereas I argued in chapter 1 that the Irish church was basically Gallican regarding its celebration of the Eucharist, a particular regional variation in Ireland seems to be that (unlike their Gallican or Roman brethren) Irish Christians took delight in the composition of distinctive hymns in the second half of the first millennium. Examples can be found in the *Antiphonary of Bangor,* the Irish *Liber Hymnarum,*[90] and the distinctive hymns in the *Stowe Missal.* All of these show creative genius at work in the composers. There are very clear parallels particularly to Spanish and also to Ambrosian and Gallican material, but the hymns are unique for two reasons. First of all, at a time when hymnography was just regaining its standing in the West in general with the use of the so-called *Old Hymnal,* a small standard collection of hymns, the Irish took the liberty of supplementing (or perhaps even replacing) this with a collection of their own using the hymns of the *Old Hymnal* as models.[91] The second interesting point is that the Irish abandoned the traditional metrical quality of Latin hymnography: using the traditional forms of the iambic diameter but reinterpreting these forms as *syllabic* meters, thus breaking with established tradition in favor of innovation and allowing for compositions not based on meter but on rhyme.[92]

But these hymns, while significant, survive only as texts, and there are very real difficulties when trying to analyze the music used in the eucharistic celebrations in pre-Norman Ireland. However, recent scholarship has illuminated a number of points in this field. What is clear is that music did play an important role in the liturgy. From an iconographic vantage point we have quite a large corpus of manuscript illustration, details of metal reliquaries, and carvings on high crosses; these show monastic choirs and various characters playing harps, lyres, and horns.[93] From written sources, it would seem probable that these were clerics.[94] It is also quite possible that there would have been instrumental accompaniment to at least some of the sung parts of the Eucharist.[95] We know from the *Stowe Missal* that many parts of the Eucharist would be sung.

A close look at some post-Norman sources can also possibly cast some light on previous practices. Stephen of Lexington came to Ireland in 1228 to make a visitation of the Irish Cistercian monasteries. At the time, simplicity was one of the hallmarks of Cistercian liturgy, and this extended to singing. He has this conclusion to make:

> It is decreed that the rules of the Order in chanting and psalmody shall be followed according to the writing of Blessed Bernard. No one

shall attempt to sing with duplicated tones [vocibus duplicatis] against the simplicity of the Order. Otherwise anyone who transgresses in this, and the keepers of the chant unless they immediately restrain the aforesaid disobedient persons, shall be on bread and water on the day following and shall be flogged in chapter without dispensation for as often as he does so.[96]

Patrick Bannon sees this reference to "vocibus duplicatis" as possibly being a reference to the persistence of a pre-Norman tradition of harmony and notes that it "may be one of the earliest known references to liturgical polyphony in medieval Ireland."[97]

Another area that is only beginning to be studied is that of the later Irish medieval manuscripts. In general, these follow Anglo-Norman practices, but when dealing with the musical texts for the feast days of Irish saints, they have no Anglo-Norman prototypes and so it is quite probable that they retain earlier Irish musical traditions. To these Irish texts, the vast body of offices of Irish saints from Continental sources can be added. An initial study of the material hints at a native style of chant (which, however, would be indistinguishable from Roman or Gallican chant to the untrained modern ear), but a lot of work still needs to be carried out in this area.[98]

THE *ANTIPHONARY OF BANGOR*

The *Antiphonary of Bangor* is a very important source for the study of the liturgy of the hours as prayed by the Irish in particular.[99] This manuscript, from the monastic center of Bangor, Co. Down, and written between 680 and 691, at first glance would seem to be simply an antiphonary and so have little to do with the Eucharist. However, it contains an important hymn for use in the eucharistic celebration. Given that we have so little evidence of the use of hymnography in the Eucharist at this stage, scholars would have been quite happy to assign all the texts in the *Antiphonary* to use in the liturgy of the hours, albeit with the eucharistic resonances in this particular hymn. However, this hymn has a specific title: "The hymn to be sung while the priests receive Communion." This clearly marks the hymn out as being used in the celebration of the Eucharist,[100] and therefore as a eucharistic hymn it is unprecedented in the whole of the West in the seventh century.[101]

The hymn to be sung while the priests receive Communion

Come, you holy ones, receive the body of Christ,
drinking the holy Blood by which you were redeemed.

You who were saved by the Body and Blood of Christ,
let us praise God, by whom we are made anew.

By this sacrament of the body and blood,
all have escaped from the jaws of hell.

Giver of salvation, Christ, the Son of God,
has saved the world by his Cross and Blood.

The Lord has been sacrificed for all,
Himself both priest and victim.

The law commanded the sacrifice of victims,
foreshadowing the mysteries divine.

Bestower of light and Saviour of all,
He granted most noble grace to His holy people.

Let all draw near with pure and faithful minds,
let all receive the protection of eternal salvation.

Guardian of the saints, you are leader, O Lord,
and dispenser of life eternal to those who believe.

He gives heavenly bread to the hungry,
and to the thirsty water from the living spring.

Christ the Lord himself comes, who is Alpha and Omega.
He shall come again to judge us all.[102]

Curran dates the hymn to the sixth century,[103] and, in keeping with this age, it is a catena of biblical verses.[104] Once again we see the themes of holy fear, a eucharistic piety centered on the Passion of Christ, and the Eucharist as being a protection from the Last Judgment. The importance of the actual reception of Communion is self-evident, although the rubric that it is for use as the priests receive Communion would once again point to the possibility that the laity did not receive the Eucharist on a frequent basis. The Blood of Christ has a prominent place in the hymn, appearing four times, as opposed to the Body of Christ, which appears only three times. Also "heavenly bread" is juxtaposed to "water from the living spring," which is probably a reference to the Blood and Water that flowed from the side of the crucified Christ.

Another very significant aspect of this hymn is that there is a reference to its use in another early Irish source. The seventh-century hymn *Audite omnes amantes,* which tells some stories of St Patrick's ministry in verse form, makes an interesting reference to *Sancti venite:*

> As Patrick and Sechnall were walking around the churchyard, they heard a choir of angels singing around the eucharist in the church. They were singing the hymn which begins "Come, you saints, to the body of Christ," that is why that hymn has been sung ever since in Ireland at the time of approaching the body of Christ.[105]

Having a second reference to the liturgical use of this same text is important.[106] While it may not be possible to attribute a universal usage of *Sancti venite,* it is at least plausible to postulate that a number of Irish centers used it. Another incidental question posed by *Audite omnes amantes* is why Patrick and Sechnall were "walking around the churchyard" while a Eucharist was being celebrated in the church. It could be that this account of the eucharistic celebration is just the setting for the vision of angels granted to the saints. But this story could be understood as hinting at a private Mass, or at least at a eucharistic celebration for a small group that would not have been attended by everyone in the ecclesiastical center.

THE *CORPUS MISSAL* AND OTHER IRISH LITURGICAL MANUSCRIPTS

While there are relatively few liturgical texts from the pre-Norman period, there are a number of texts from the period around the Norman arrival. These texts were generally thought to be of the English Sarum use and therefore have been little studied.[107] They include three missals—the *Corpus Missal,* the *Drummond Missal,* and the *Rosslyn Missal.*[108] Perhaps the most significant of these is the *Corpus Missal.* This missal was written in Ireland and is clearly decorated in traditional style.[109] This has been dated variously from the ninth to the fourteenth century,[110] although most scholars have followed Gwynn, who dated it to the decade 1120–30 on the basis of French studies on the style of its illumination.[111] But Gwynn also proposes that the missal may be the copy of an earlier Irish missal and may in fact reflect Irish liturgical practice in the early eleventh century, thus making it a pre-Norman source. He points to the fact that the *Corpus Missal* contains a pre-tenth-century form of the *Memento* for the living (f. 2v). He also sees a strong connection between the liturgy in Ireland and that at Winchester, pointing to strong textual similarities in a litany of Holy Saturday between the *Corpus Missal* and the *Winchester Troper,* which can clearly be dated to the reign of King Aetheldred (978–1016). This was a time when scholars from the south of Ireland, from the domain of Brian Boru, may have brought back to Ireland missals from the early Sarum tradition. So, according to Gwynn, this missal may well preserve a form of liturgy used in Ireland in the early eleventh century.[112]

A recent article that approaches the problems of dating the *Corpus Missal* from a different angle comes to similar conclusions. Analyzing it from the standpoint of euchology, a number of elements are found to date to the early eleventh century: "first, the two concluding prayers from the *ordo baptismi;* second, the influence of the Gelasian and eighth-century Gelasian rites on the *ordo sponsalium;* and third, the occurrence of a non-Vulgate variant in both the epistle and gradual of the Mass for the feast day of the Holy Cross."[113]

While some present-day scholars place these missals within the pre-Norman period, others still hold the older view that they are post-Norman, and more critical work needs still to be done before we can date them with certainty. However, if these newer theories prove true, then this would be quite significant for showing how the eucharistic liturgy in Ireland was quite similar to that of other parts of Europe in the early eleventh century. Indeed, the very fact that these missals could conceivably be attributed both to periods before and after the Norman arrival points to a far greater continuity of eucharistic practice than once theorized.[114] Apart from perhaps some pieces of chant for the feasts of Irish saints, there is little unusual in these missals when compared to contemporary English missals.[115] A final point worth noting is that in the Ireland of the eleventh and twelfth centuries, the texts of the Eucharist gradually came to be celebrated in an environment very similar to that of the Continent. This transformation would not be complete until the new religious orders, first the Cistercians and later the Franciscans, arrived in Ireland. Therefore, as the setting became closer to that of the rest of Western Europe (church architecture will be examined in chapter 3), even if the odd feast or rubric were slightly different or the odd antiphon bore some traces of pre-Norman Irish musical tradition, the overall effect of the liturgy was very close to that found in the rest of the West.

OTHER WRITTEN SOURCES

THE PENITENTIALS

In liturgical textbooks, the penitentials are usually only mentioned when dealing with the history of the sacrament of Penance.[116] Popular works on "Celtic" spirituality tend to give the penitentials short shrift, as their view of human sinfulness that has to be combated with mortification and sexual abstinence does not agree with the attempt of many of these works to find proof-texts for their politically correct version of early Irish Christianity.[117] While many scholars today would propose that this form of literary genre developed in the

British (or Welsh) church after the fourth century, the nascent Irish church adopted the style prior to the late sixth century. They then took this form of literature, developed it, and popularized it in England and the Continent.[118]

From the sixth to the eighth centuries various penitentials were composed in Ireland and in those places under Irish influence. It would be a mistake to think of the penitentials as compendia of detailed prescriptions, even though at times they do contain a lot of detail. Their goal was not to cover every possible situation but, rather, to form a corpus of guidelines for the abbot or confessor to use in the pastoral care of souls. Some, like the famous *Penitential of Cummean*,[119] systematically treat each of Cassian's eight vices and prescribe remedies based on the contrary virtue (*contraria contraries curare*); most of the Irish penitentials, however, take the form of less systematically structured collections.[120] Obviously, we do not find a systematic treatment of the Eucharist in this literature. Nevertheless, many of the penitentials do mention the Eucharist. Here we are provided with valuable information about some of the attitudes towards the Eucharist in the church in Ireland at this time.

By far the most frequent treatments of the Eucharist in the penitential literature are texts dealing with penances for particular sins involving the mistreatment of the eucharistic species. The word "*sacrificium*," often used by the penitentials to refer to the eucharistic bread or host, is itself evidence of a strong emphasis on the sacrificial dimension of the Eucharist.[121] The most basic offences deal with the consumption of the *sacrificium*. This means that at least in the circles governed by these texts, some people actually received the Eucharist, even if at times they did so unworthily.[122]

Not surprisingly, the first category of sin that is common to many of the texts is the case of a sinner receiving Communion unworthily. This is generally condemned, as one has to have expiated one's sins prior to receiving Communion.

> A boy who communicates in the sacrament although he has sinned with a beast, shall do penance for a hundred days on bread and water.[123]

But the penitentials clearly see the reception of Communion as a necessary part of Christian life. It is true that sometimes they prescribe a
long time of penance without the reception of Communion, but these
times of abstinence are always temporary.[124] There is a clear concern
that if a penitent is in danger of death that he has to be given Communion as the viaticum,[125] and that the norm is that the penitent be
eventually joined to the altar once more:

> If any man or woman is nigh unto death, although he (or she) has
> been a sinner, and asks for the communion of Christ, we say that it is
> not to be denied to such a person if that person promise God to take
> the vow, and do well and be received by Him. If he is restored to this
> world, let him fulfill the vow which he vowed to God, (the conse-
> quences) will be on his own head, and we will not refuse what we owe
> to him: we are not to cease to snatch prey from the mouth of the lion
> or the dragon, that is of the devil, who ceases not to snatch at the prey
> of the souls, even though we may have to follow up and strive (for his
> soul) at the very end of a man's life.
>
>   If one of the laity is converted from his evil-doing unto the Lord,
> and if he has wrought an evil deed, by committing fornication, that is,
> shedding blood, he shall do penance for three years and go unarmed
> except for a staff in his hand, and he shall not live with his wife, but in
> the first year he shall fast on an allowance of bread and water and salt
> and not live with his wife; after a penance of three years he shall give
> money for the redemption of his soul and the fruit of his penance into
> the hand of the priest and make a feast for the servants of God, and in
> the feast (his penance) shall be ended and he shall be received to com-
> munion; he may then resume relations with his wife after his entire
> and complete penance, and if it is so decided he shall be joined to the
> altar.[126]

Here the Eucharist itself is presented as something that in and of
itself formed part of the cure of the penitent. The *Preface of Gildas on
Penance* in its very first article mentions the case of a cleric who has
committed fornication or sodomy. He is given three years' penance,
but it then stipulates that at the halfway point:

After a year and a half he may receive the Eucharist and come for the kiss of peace and sing the psalms with his brethren, lest his soul perish utterly from lacking so long a time the celestial medicine.[127]

Unworthiness for reception is balanced with the theme of the Eucharist as "celestial medicine." It is important that the penitent receive it on occasion as part of the healing process, thereby conveying both the need for holiness of life to receive Communion and the Eucharist as being the source of this holiness. This tension is paralleled in other sections of the penitential literature. The *Second Synod of Patrick* goes so far as to mandate that even those who are in penance must receive the Eucharist at Easter:

OF TAKING THE EUCHARIST AFTER A FALL
After a proving of the flesh it is to be taken, but especially on the eve of Easter; for he who does not communicate at that time is not a believer. Therefore short and strict are the seasons (of penance) in their ranks, lest the faithful soul perish, by abstaining from the medicine for so long a time, for the Lord saith: *Except you eat the flesh of the Son of Man, you shall not have life in you.*[128]

A further proof that the medieval mind and theological interest is distinct from our own is provided by the emphasis given to another abuse in the penitential literature: the sin of vomiting of the *sacrificium.*

He who vomits the host because of greediness, forty days. But if with the excuse of unusual and too rich food, and from the fault not of over-saturation but of the stomach, thirty (days). If it is by reason of infirmity, he shall do penance for twenty (days). Another (authority) says differently: If by reason of infirmity, seven days; if he injects it into the fire, he shall sing one hundred psalms; if a dog licks up the vomit, he who has vomited shall do penance for one hundred days.[129]

While far from a developed theology of eucharistic presence, the fact that this was seen as a sin portrays the belief that the *sacrificium* ought to be considered as sacred. The presence lasts longer than the actual liturgy, and the *sacrificium* preserves its sacred character even if it is regurgitated. It is also worth noting the difference in penance for vomiting the *sacrificium* into the fire where it was burned up (one hundred psalms) and when dogs licked up the *sacrificium* (one hundred days penance). This again points to a eucharistic presence that lasts, and it is far preferable that the regurgitated *sacrificium* be consumed by fire than by a dog.

Another abuse that also appears in the penitentials is the loss of the *sacrificium*.

He who fails to guard the host carefully, and a mouse eats it, shall do penance for forty days. But he who loses it in the church, that is so that a part falls and is not found, twenty days. But he who loses his chrismal or only the host in what place soever, and it cannot be found, three forty-day periods or a year. One who pours anything from the chalice upon the altar when the linen is being removed shall do penance for seven days; or if he has spilled it rather freely, he shall do penance with special fasts for seven days. If the host falls from one's hand on the straw, he shall do penance from the time of the accident. He who pours out the chalice at the end of solemn Mass, shall do penance for forty days.

One who vomits the host because his stomach is overloaded with food, and if he casts it into the fire, twenty days, but if not forty, if however, dogs consume this vomit, one hundred. But if it is with pain and he cast it into the fire, he shall sing one hundred psalms.

If anyone neglects to receive the host and does not ask for it, and if no other reason exists to excuse him, he shall keep a special fast; and he who having been polluted in sleep during one night, accepts the host, shall do penance likewise.

A deacon who forgets to bring the oblation until the linen is removed when the names of the departed are recited shall do penance likewise.

. . . He who acts with negligence towards the host, so that it dries up and is consumed by worms until it comes to nothing, shall do penance for three forty-day periods on bread and water. If it is entire, but if a worm is found in it, it shall be burned and the ashes shall be concealed beneath the altar, and he who neglected it shall make good his negligence with forty days (of penance). If the host loses its taste and is discoloured, he shall keep a fast for twenty days; if it is stuck together, for seven days.

He who wets the host shall forthwith drink the water that was in the chrismal; and he shall take the host and shall amend his fault for ten days. If the host falls from the hands of the celebrant to the ground and is not found, everything that is found in the place in which it fell shall be burned and the ashes concealed as above. If the host is found, the place shall be cleaned up with a broom, and the straw, as we have said above, burned with fire, and the priest shall do penance for twenty days. If it is only slipped to the altar, he shall keep a special fast. If the chalice drips upon the altar the minister shall suck up the drop and do penance for three days, and the linens which the drop has touched he shall wash three times, the chalice being placed beneath, and he shall drink the water used in washing. If the chalice drips when it is washed inside, the first twelve psalms shall be sung by the minister.

If the minister stammers over the Sunday prayer which is called "the perilous" ["*periculosa*"], if once, he shall be cleansed with fifty strokes; if a second time, with one hundred; if a third time, he shall keep a special fast.[130]

This seventh-century text contains the most detailed treatment of the Eucharist in the Irish penitential literature.[131] There is little unique to this text: most of the themes are treated in other penitentials. Cummean's value is that it gathers much of the material into a single section entitled "Of questions concerning the *sacrificii*" (*De questionibus sacrificii*). He treats two different kinds of sin—abuses of the *sacrificium* and mistakes within the eucharistic liturgy itself.

Again there is an explicit expectation that the Eucharist is to be received. Initially, the text seems to deal with the reception of Communion during the eucharistic celebration. If someone "neglects to receive the host and does not ask for it," he has to do penance. So here it is seen as sinful not to receive Communion; however, one might be forgiven for asking whether the reason for not receiving was always "negligence" (*neglexerit*) and not perhaps a feeling of unworthiness.

In addition, the text (and its parallels) show that there was a practice of taking the *sacrificium* and keeping it outside of the context of the liturgy. When it refers to a mouse eating the *sacrificium,* this presumably is referring to an abuse outside of the liturgy (one would hope that the celebrant would stop a mouse eating the *sacrificium* as he was celebrating Mass). Gildas mentions someone "by mishap through carelessness [losing] a host, leaving it for beasts and birds to devour."[132] Again, this is hardly a case of an abuse during the liturgy. Perhaps this refers to a continuation of the patristic practice of Home Communion. However, while it is unlikely that a daily celebration of the Eucharist was common at the time these texts were written, it is likewise unlikely that Home Communion was practiced in Ireland at this time,[133] and Home Communion was the only reason that the eucharistic species were reserved by individuals in the first four centuries of the Christian era. The text mentions that the *sacrificium* was kept in a "chrismal." While we are not sure exactly what an Irish chrismal looked like, scholars tend to think that it was a small reliquary-like pyx that was worn around the neck. The fact that the text mentions that the *sacrificium* might be eaten up by worms, dried up, lose its color, or stick together would seem to suggest that, even in the damp Irish conditions, we are dealing with a time period of somewhat more than the maximum of a week between eucharistic liturgies. Once again these penances for abuses point to a clear belief in some sort of a perduring presence in the eucharistic elements.

The list of abuses at Mass is also significant. Referring to "the Sunday prayer which is called 'the perilous'" ("oratione dominica quae dicitur periculosa") points to an element of fear and dread in the Eucharist.[134] Given that stumbling over a word of this prayer in particular was considered sinful, it can be taken that this prayer was understood to be more important than the rest of the liturgy. As was seen above when dealing with the *Mass Tract,* this probably refers to the institution narrative.

It is worth noting that the abuses to the Eucharist could be to either species. The eucharistic wine was just as important as the *sacrificium.* Care is to be taken not to spill anything during the celebration, but again a presence is perceived to remain even after the end of the celebration. Even the cloths that had soaked in a "drop" from the chalice had to be purified and the water used in washing them had to be drunk. As wine is much harder to store than bread and was therefore not reserved to the same degree, we have no material in the penitentials dealing with the eucharistic wine after the liturgy.

This passage also provides evidence of prayer for the dead during the Eucharist. The practice of reading the diptyches after the offertory might be alluded to when it mentions the part of the celebration "when the names of the departed are recited."[135] The concept of a priest offering a Mass for a particular intention is also foreseen in the penitentials:

> For good rulers we ought to offer the sacrifice, for bad ones on no account. Presbyters are indeed not forbidden to offer for their bishops.[136]

There is also an instance where offering Mass for a victim of suicide is forbidden:

> Anyone who kills himself while insane, prayers are to be said for him, and alms are given for his soul, if he was previously pious. If anyone has killed himself in despair or for any other cause, he must be left to the judgement of God, for men dare not offer prayers for him—that is a Mass—unless it be some other prayer, and almsgiving to the poor and miserable.[137]

Indeed, the whole concept of offering Mass for a particular intention seems to have been partly born in the Irish milieu. In Irish society, honor was very important, and a king who could no longer command this honor, as for example a king who had been physically disfigured in a war, had to be deposed.[138] But due honor and respect had to be paid to kings who were in power, and, by transference, the celebration of the Eucharist came to be seen as a way to honor God, the supreme high-king.[139] Paxton proposes that the practice of offering Mass for the dead in particular spread from Irish missionaries, and that the Irish influenced English missionaries to the Franks, and from the

Franks to the whole Continental church.[140] There may be an element of truth to this, but the importance of gift-giving was seen to be important in both early Irish and Germanic societies,[141] and it would be hard to trace the influence directly from Ireland to the rest of the West.

In later medieval Europe the practice was common of having Masses offered for one's intentions in order to fulfill penances. Some scholars think that this too started in Ireland,[142] and indeed there is one example of this "substitution" of Mass for a penance that survives in the literature:

> A commutation of seven years' strict penance consisting of expiatory prayers in order to rescue a soul from the pain of hell: a hundred Masses, a hundred and fifty psalms, a hundred *Beati*, a hundred genuflections with each *Beati*, a hundred Credos, a hundred Paters, a hundred soul hymns.[143]

Here the goal of the Eucharist is to remit sin and is much easier than seven years of penance; but this is an isolated instance, and it seems that this practice did not originate in Ireland nor was it ever popular there (although Irish ecclesiastics on the Continent may well have encouraged these practices there). Vogel has examined the texts of all the penitentials (of both Continental and Irish origins) with reference to Masses being celebrated to commute penances. He notes that the vast majority of such cases come from the Continental penitentials and that, while there is abundant British and Continental evidence, there is very little evidence in the Irish material for this practice.[144] It would therefore seem that the Irish were at the forefront in popularizing the penitential genre and also in offering the celebration of the Eucharist for a particular intention, but they did not start either of these practices and were not generally in favor of substituting the offering of Mass for penance.

MONASTIC RULES

The picture of the Eucharist in the various monastic rules is comparable to the penitentials. While these rules are perhaps of more importance liturgically for describing the liturgy of the hours as celebrated in the monasteries, once again the Eucharist does figure in them. These various rules are spread over a number of centuries and they should be seen as guidelines for an abbot who will modify them to best suit his monastery and the temperament of the individual monks. The *Rule of the Céli Dé,* which is in the *Leabhar Breac,* may be as early as the ninth century.[145] It contains a very interesting picture of the formation of novices regarding the reception of Communion:

> Someone who attends the midnight liturgy for the first time receives the Body of Christ but not the chalice. He is not allowed to receive again until the end of the next year.
>
> The second year he receives at the midnight liturgy and also at the *Corpus paschae* on the following day. The third year he will receive at midnight, Easter and Christmas. The fourth year he may receive at Christmas, Easter Sunday, Low Sunday (the two Easters), and Pentecost. The fifth year at the solemn festivals and at the end of the forty nights. After six years he is allowed to receive every month, and in the seventh year every two weeks. On the completion of the seven years he is allowed to receive every Sunday, saying *Pater Sair* and "O God come to my aid, Lord make haste to help me" while holding both hands extended towards heaven. Afterwards he makes the sign of the cross with the right hand in every direction, thus + down and up.
>
> They regard this as the shrine of devotion, but the cross-vigil must precede it. It is called the "Breastplate of Devotion."
>
> When a monk does not receive Communion [*teit do láim*][146] on Sunday, he may do so on the following Thursday; otherwise, were he to wait until the following Sunday, the interval would be too long for one accustomed to receive weekly. These two days are celebrated in a special way at Mass.[147]

The main conclusion that can be drawn from this text is that ideally the monk was initiated into weekly Communion.[148] This initiation took seven years, and in the first year he only received the eucharistic bread at a midnight liturgy that may well have been the Paschal Vigil.[149] According to this rule the monks attended a community Eucharist on Sundays and Thursdays. It was preferable to receive

Communion at the Sunday Eucharist, but the monk could choose to wait until Thursday. This is paralleled by a prescription in the ninth-century *Rule of St Carthage* that also recommends a Sunday and Thursday community Eucharist. But it adds that this is a minimum when the Eucharist is not celebrated "on every day, so that all evil might be banished."[150] Later on the *Rule of St Carthage* mentions that every monk must go about his work every day between the prayers of terce and none, specifying that during this time "those in holy orders go to prayer or to celebrate Mass as is right."[151] For the regular monks, not surprisingly, one of the rules mentions that they must be spiritually prepared to receive Communion:

> When each person goes to Mass, what a wonderful gift we offer; we should have compunction of heart, the shedding of tears, and the raising of the hands to God, without hilarity, without whispering, but with gentleness, in silence, and with forgiveness of all past, present and future evils. When you go to communion [*tam tiager do láim*] you should go with great fear, confessing your sins, and in peace with all your neighbours. . . The Body you approach is pure, so must you be holy when you receive it.[152]

A document known as *The Monastery of Tallaght* coming from Céli Dé circles also gives some details of the Eucharist.[153] Once again, the emphasis is on the actual celebration of the Eucharist rather than on having a lot of people attend:

> It is all one whether one person or a number is present at the *Beati* or the Mass; for there is no less efficacy in his prayer than if it be appropriated to himself alone—just as the light of the sun is no greater for one man only than for a number.
>
> He makes much of going the thousand paces, or more, to visit the tenantry on Sunday; and the thousand paces have been left as an ordinance for watching a sick man, and for administering the communion to him, and to the young, and to the laity who are under spiritual direction who come to wait for the Mass, and to hear preaching, and for urgent matters besides, etc.[154]

The *Rule of the Céli Dé,* which is related to *the Monastery of Tallaght,* has another important section on the Eucharist. Follett thinks that both documents are later derivatives of a document now lost, which he names *Tecosc Máilruain.* He identifies the *Rule of the Céli Dé* as being a tenth-century recension of earlier material.[155] This rule gives the following information on the different aspects of the payment of tithes and the Eucharist:

A church is not entitled to the tenth cow or the third part of the revenue payable by another church, nor has it any right to the other dues payable to its monks, unless it is faithful to its obligation. These duties are the administration of baptism, the distribution of Holy Communion, and prayers which are offered by the monks for both the living and the dead. The rightly established church should be properly furnished with altars, and Mass should be celebrated on those altars each Sunday and solemnity. Any church lacking any of these essentials is not entitled to the full tribute payable to the church of God, and is to be regarded by Christians as a den of thieves and robbers.

A priest of the class of the laity, no matter what church he may be attached to, is not entitled to the dues payable to the priestly order. These dues consist of a house, garden, and bed, all of which are to be as good as the church can provide. In addition, he is to have a sack of meal and its condiment, a milch cow every quarter, together with all his just requests. In return he is to provide baptism and communion, that is, the Eucharist; he is to make intercession for the living and the dead; and on Sundays, solemnities, and other major feasts, he is to offer Mass. He is to celebrate all the daily hours of prayer, chanting one hundred and fifty psalms each day unless instruction or spiritual direction prevents him from doing so. Any ordained man, then, who is ignorant of the law and unable to carry out the functions of his office, who is unable to chant the hour of prayer, or to offer the Eucharist in the presence of king or bishop, is not entitled to his rank in the eyes of church or state.

. . . The person with whom a lad consecrated to God and Patrick studies is entitled to recognition and reward at the proper times. He is to be given a milch cow when he has taught the one hundred and fifty psalms together with the hymns, canticles and readings, and also the correct method of administering Baptism and Communion, the manner in which the intercessions are to be sung, and in general everything pertaining to the priesthood, until such time as the student is ready to receive holy orders. Each year by way of reward for these blessings he is to be paid a calf, a pig, three sacks of malted meal, and one sack of grain together with a reasonable supply of clothing and food. The milch cow is to be handed over as soon as the psalms and hymns have been taught, while the remainder are paid when the obligations of holy orders have been explained. The sage or bishop before whom the psalms are recited by the young man is entitled to a supper, of food and beer, for a party of five that night.[156]

If a church does not provide a bare minimum of pastoral care it is not entitled to receive any tithes or financial support. This vision of pastoral care is very similar to that outlined in the documents examined in chapter 1. An important element of this is providing Communion (perhaps referring to the viaticum) and celebrating the Eucharist on Sundays and feast days. If this is not fulfilled then the priest has no right to a living from the church. The section on the preparation of a candidate for ordination is also interesting. While it practically repeats the requirements for a parish priest, it is significant as it is the only text I have found dealing with the liturgical formation of ministers in pre-Norman Ireland. The great emphasis on memorization is noteworthy. If the candidate had to memorize all 150 psalms, it would not have been particularly difficult to learn some basic eucharistic liturgies by heart. There is no actual requirement that he understand the Latin of the prayers he memorizes. So it is possible that these priests trained in apprenticeship to an older priest may have performed the liturgy quite poorly, only copying what had been taught to them and never actually understanding the ritual.

SAINTS' LIVES

Saints' lives are one of the most important sources for the study of pre-Norman Ireland; today there survive some one hundred Irish saints' lives in Latin and fifty in Irish that were written mainly in the Middle Ages.[157] However, this form of hagiography is not the same as modern historic biography,[158] and the saints' lives are usually more important as sources for the times they were written rather than when the saint they portray was active.[159] In general, the medieval saint's life could be described as "a response to the present in terms of the past,"[160] and there is often a greater desire to establish a "tradition" of ownership of a particular property or of the rights of a particular local church or monastery rather than revealing liturgical practices. Regarding the study of the Eucharist in particular, many saints' lives provide absolutely no details whatsoever on eucharistic practice even though it is most probable that the Eucharist would have occupied a significant place in the historical life of the saint portrayed.

So, while there are many saints' lives, most of these were written after the arrival of the Normans. Indeed, there was an intense burst of hagiographical activity in the fifty years after the Normans arrived. This can perhaps be best interpreted as the attempts of the local Gaelic ecclesiastics and rulers to establish their rights when faced with the challenges posed by the Normans. Conversely, there is little evidence that earlier reform movements, such as the Céli Dé, produced any hagiographical material at the time of their reforms;[161] the biographers of Malachy and Laurence O'Toole, the two most important biographies of twelfth-century Irish ecclesiastics, were not written in Ireland but in France by St Bernard of Clairvaux and an anonymous canon of Eu.[162] Nonetheless, there is some very valuable material pertinent to the study of the Eucharist, particularly in the earlier hagiographical material, which will be studied in this section.

St Adomnán of Iona's Life of St Columba

In the last years of the seventh century, St Adomnán, the ninth abbot of Iona and a descendent of St Columba's grandfather, wrote the *Life of St Columba*.[163] This is one of the most important works of Irish hagiography, and, besides providing some important references to the Eucharist, the work is an extremely important source for the history of Ireland, Scotland, and England in this time. Once again we find many references to the practice of celebrating the Eucharist in the morning. It seems that the Eucharist was not celebrated on every morning but only on Sundays and feast days, and occasionally upon receiving news of the death of a friend.[164]

Two particular passages are cited frequently in the secondary literature. One interesting story is often used to explain the small size of some early Irish churches:

> When the sacred mysteries of the Eucharist were to take place, with one accord they chose St Columba to act as celebrant. He obeyed their command, and with them he entered the church as usual on the Lord's day after the Gospel had been read. There, while the sacrament of the mass was celebrated, St Brendan moccu Altae saw a radiant ball of fire shining very brightly from St Columba's head as he stood in front of the altar and consecrated the sacred oblation. It shone upwards like a column of light and lasted until the mysteries were completed.[165]

As Columba is said to enter the church to celebrate the Eucharist *post euangelii lectionem,* this is taken to mean that the Liturgy of the Word was celebrated outside the church, and then for the liturgy of the Eucharist only the clerics went inside.[166] Undoubtedly, this is an attractive theory and there may well be some truth in it; however, it would be rash to build a universal theory for all eucharistic liturgies celebrated in pre-Norman Ireland on a single text that is not even very clear on the point in question. Furthermore, it must be noted that this is a very special celebration, and St Columba is accompanied by a number of other monastic founder saints. Perhaps such an august assembly of saints would have inspired a larger than average number of people at that liturgy. It could be that at such a special occasion they decided to hold the start of the celebration outside as an exception to the normal practice for pastoral reasons. If in the future more texts come to light on the practice of the laity attending outside, then this text could accompany them, but until then it has to remain as a tantalizing passage on which little can be built.

Another section from this work that is cited by virtually every author who deals with Irish liturgy is about the *fractio panis:*

Once there came to the saint a stranger from the province of Munster who, so far as he was able, concealed his identity out of humility, for he did not want people to know that he was a bishop. But such a thing could not be hidden from St Columba, for on the Lord's day, when he was bidden by the saint to perform the sacrament of the body of Christ, he called on the saint that as two priests they should together break the Lord's bread. As Columba approached the altar, he suddenly saw into the man's face and spoke to him thus, "Christ's blessing on you, my brother. Break this bread alone according to the rite of a bishop. For now we know that this is what you are. But to what end did you try to conceal your identity until now, so that you have not had from us the reverence due to you?" The humble pilgrim was much surprised by the saint's words, and reverenced Christ in him, while all present were struck with wonder and glorified God.[167]

Some have interpreted this passage to mean that in Columban circles it was the practice for two priests to break the bread, except when a bishop was a celebrant, in which case he broke the bread by himself.[168] Again this is *an* interpretation, but it is not the only possible interpretation. We do know that the *fractio panis* was most likely a particularly important moment in the popular understanding of the eucharistic liturgy in pre-Norman Ireland. The fact that Columba tells him to do the breaking *episcopali ritu* is significant. But once again, just how much can be read into these two words? It is unlikely that if a given Eucharist had only a limited number of communicants in attendance that two priests would have performed the breaking.[169] However, if large crowds were in attendance, which would be consistent with many people only receiving on a particular holy day or while on pilgrimage, there could well have been work for more than one priest. While it may be the case that there was a special episcopal form of the eucharistic liturgy, this story could just as likely be understood that Columba is surprised to see the illustrious bishop's humility and steps back from the altar so that all can appreciate just who it is that had joined them.

Another interesting reference to the Eucharist deals with Librán, a noble penitent who comes to Columba for penance. He has murdered a man and then escaped from his brother, who had bailed him out of jail where he was awaiting execution on the understanding that Librán would become a slave to this brother. Columba gives him a seven-year penance and tells him, "When a term of seven years is completed, you shall come to me here during Lent so that at the Easter festival you may approach the altar and receive the sacrament."[170] After completing his penance, receiving the Eucharist and going home to be reconciled with his brother, he comes back to Columba who receives his profession as a monk. This text, taken with the penitentials and some of the monastic rules that were examined above, lends weight to the theory that a lot of pastoral care was actually centered on the social elite of the laity, as presented by Etchingham. Many of these elites entered a quasi-monastic state at the end of their lives where, after a period of penitence and monastic formation, they had frequent recourse to the sacraments, including the reception of Communion.[171]

It is also possible to see a reference to the Eucharist in another section from the *Life of St Columba*. Here Columba comes to learn of a plague-bearing rain that is moving through the east of Ireland around the river Delvin. He sends his monk Silnán there to cure the people and livestock. He instructs him as follows:

> You shall take from here the bread that I have blessed in the name of God, you shall dip this bread in water and then sprinkle that water over both people and livestock, and they will soon recover health.[172]

Silnán carries out his master's instructions bringing the "healing bread" (*salubri pane*), dipping it in water to create the "water of blessing" (*aqua benedictionis*), and the cure is granted as promised.[173] While this is a significant text, the bread is not presented as being the bread of the Eucharist. Nonetheless, this passage does have eucharistic overtones and it probably refers to the practice of the *eulogia*. This involved bringing to the altar more bread than is necessary for the communicants at a given eucharistic celebration. The celebrant says the offertory prayers over all the bread, but removes some of it prior to the eucharistic prayer for consumption during a meal that will take place at a later time. In this way, the *eulogia* joins the following meal to the Eucharist, allowing those who did not receive the Eucharist itself at that celebration to participate in a lesser, but still tactile and gustatory, way (there could also be some residual memory of earlier times when Christians took Communion home for later consumption).[174] Sometimes, in the West in general, there is confusion between the blessed bread and the eucharistic bread. This is partly due to the lack of precision in distinguishing between what we now refer to as sacraments and sacramentals, but it is probable that these texts refer to the *eulogia*.[175]

There is another mention of the *eulogia* a little later in the book. Adomnán tells of St Cainnech at Aghaboe who saves St Columba and some monks who are caught at sea in a storm.

> Nones was already over and the saint was beginning to break the bread of the blessing [*eulogiam*] in the refectory. But he instantly left the table and ran to the church, one shoe on his foot and the other left behind in his hurry. "We cannot have dinner at this time," he said, "for St Columba's boat is even now in peril on the sea."[176]

It is important to note that the bread spoken of here is specifically called "*eulogia.*" A third parallel passage in the *Life of Columba* speaks of Columba sending a "blessing" [*benedictio*] to Mogain to cure her broken hip: "When Lugaid was ready to set out, Columba handed him a little pinewood box with a blessing inside it, and said: 'When you arrive to visit Mogain, the blessing contained in this box should be dipped in a jar of water and then the water of blessing should be poured over her hip. Then call on the name of God and at once her hipbone will be joined and knit together and her full health will be restored.'"[177]

Here we are even less sure exactly what the saint placed in the box, but as it immediately follows the account of the blessed bread curing the plague it is at least possible that here also the *eulogia* was used. If this is the case, the little pinewood box (*capsella*) carved by Columba could be related to the chrismals that will be examined below.

Cogitosus's Vita Brigitae

Because the *Vita Brigitae* has been dated to the seventh century, it is of great importance. It is one of only four hagiographical texts from this time (alongside Adomnán's *Vita Columbae*, Tírechán's *Collectanea* on St Patrick, and Muirchú's *Vita Particii*), and it may well be the earliest of these documents.[178] One of the main themes of this work is to use the life of Brigit to support the ambitions of the see of Kildare for supremacy against the see of Armagh. Cogitosus informs his readers that Kildare "is the head of almost all the Irish churches with supremacy over all the monasteries of the Irish and its *paruchia* extends over the whole land of Ireland, reaching from sea to sea."[179]

In common with most of the saints' lives, this work only makes a few incidental references to the Eucharist. Perhaps the most important passage for our purpose deals with the cathedral of Kildare (this text will be examined in chapter 3). While St Brigit is portrayed as a monastic foundress *par excellence,* and while she has a great deal of prestige and authority, there is no suggestion that she could preside over a eucharistic celebration.[180] In fact she is portrayed as having a bishop as her personal chaplain:

> And by her wise administration she made provision in every detail for the souls of her people according to the rule, as she vigilantly watched over the churches attached to her in many provinces and as she reflected that she could not be without a high priest to consecrate churches and confer ecclesiastical orders in them, she sent for Conleth, a famous man and a hermit endowed with every good disposition through whom God wrought many miracles, and calling him from the wilderness and his life of solitude, she set out to meet him, in order that he might govern the church with her in the office of bishop and that her churches might lack nothing as regards priestly orders.[181]

From a later story we learn that this Conleth owned some foreign vestments which he used when presiding the Eucharist:

Once, she generously gave away to the poor the foreign vestments from overseas belonging to his distinguished eminence Bishop Conleth, which he was wont to use on the solemnities of the Lord and on the vigils of the Apostles, when offering the sacred mysteries on the altar and in the sanctuary.[182]

Vita Prima Sanctae Brigitae

The *Vita Prima Sanctae Brigitae* is another very early document that is related to Cogitosus's *Vita Brigitae*. It probably comes from the middle of the eighth century.[183] It provides yet more details about the Eucharist. In a parallel to Cogitosus, St Patrick himself is said to assign Brigit a priest chaplain after she converts a pagan who had refused to convert for Patrick:

> Next day Patrick said to Brigit, "From this day on you may not travel without a priest. Your charioteer is always to be a priest." So he ordained a priest named Nathfroích who was Brigit's charioteer all his life.[184]

Once St Brigit goes on a journey with some of her nuns to look for corn during a famine. She meets the bishop St Ibor who offers them hospitality. However, due to the famine, he has no corn to give them but only dry bread and pork. Two of St Brigit's nuns refuse to eat the meal due to their scruples regarding the Lenten fast regulations, and their portions were turned into serpents. When she hears of this, St Brigit reprimands them and sends them out to fast and pray. Then St Brigit and St Ibor also go out to fast and pray with them:

> And so they did, and the two serpents were changed into two hosts of the purest and whitest bread and one host was given to bishop Ibor and the other was offered to saint Brigit, and they were the hosts for the Eucharist and Christmas.[185]

The mention of Christmas and Easter could just mean that this miraculous bread was preserved for these two special feasts as highpoints in the liturgical year. But as these days are mentioned as possible days for the Communion of the faithful, this could be a reference to the use of a larger host on those days because more people would receive Communion.

In another story, St Brigit blesses a big bucket of water for two men, they later drop it on its side, and none of the water escapes and so: "St Patrick ordered the water to be kept and shared out among all the churches of that part of the country that it might be used for the Eucharist of the blood of Christ and that the sick might be sprinkled with it to make them well."[186] Presumably this refers to the water mixed with the wine in the chalice. It is an interesting reference as usually wine is the important element in the eucharistic chalice, but if in Ireland there was a high percentage of water in the mix than perhaps this was an indication of the importance of the water in the popular mind. The fact that the author of the *Vita Prima* felt no need to have Brigit change water into wine (as Christ did in the miracle of Cana) might be taken as a hint that wine was not terribly hard to come by at this time.

On one of her journeys an angel warns St Brigit at night to evacuate the building she is in because it is about to burn down. Her nuns later question her as to whether the angel normally speaks to her. St Brigit admits that the angel is normally at her side and she says that, among the other things he does, it is "thanks to him too I can hear the masses of holy men which they celebrate to the Lord in distant lands as if they were close by."[187] St Brigit's experience of these celebrations leads to her desire to introduce Roman practice to Ireland:

"I heard masses in Rome at the tombs of Sts. Peter and Paul and it is my earnest wish that the order of this mass and of the universal rule be brought to me." Then saint Brigit sent experts to Rome and from there they brought the masses and the rule. Again after some time she said to the men, "I discern that certain things have been changed in the mass in Rome since you have returned from there. Go back again." And they went and brought it back as they had found it.[188]

Whether or not an Irish envoy went to Rome at Brigit's bidding is not what is important here: there is no historical proof one way or the other, although during the paschal controversy various Irish ecclesiastics made the journey to Rome and back.[189] What is important is that the Roman form of eucharistic liturgy was significant for the eighth-century author. The author is not perturbed by the fact that the Roman Mass changed at this time, as this is simply fixed by an envoy returning there to bring back the updated version. It is also interesting that Brigit sees it as a special favor to be able to *hear* Masses in Rome as opposed to actually attending and receiving Communion at these celebrations.

The *Vita Prima* also bears unequivocal witness to a nonordained person (albeit of the exalted status of Brigit) receiving the eucharistic wine directly from the chalice:

> After that saint Brigit went to stay in the territory of the Connacht-men with two bishops who accompanied her and they lived there in Mar Aí.
>
> So one day she approached the altar to receive the eucharist from the hand of the bishop and as she gazed down into the chalice she saw in it a hideous monster, that is, she saw the outline of a goat in the chalice, for one of the bishop's attendants was holding the chalice.
>
> Then Brigit refused to drink from the chalice and the bishop said to her, "Why aren't you drinking from the chalice?" Brigit disclosed what she had seen.
>
> Whereat the bishop said to the attendant, "What have you done? *Confess to God.*" The attendant confessed that he had committed a theft against the goatherd and killed one of his goats and eaten part of its meat.
>
> The bishop said to him, "Repent and shed tears of sorrow." And the attendant obeyed his orders and repented.
>
> On a second invitation Brigit came to the chalice and this time saw no trace of the goat in the chalice, for the tears had atoned for the fault.[190]

In a parallel to Cogitosus's story, the *Vita Prima*'s story of Con-láed's vestments adds some details.

Another time saint Brigit gave Bishop Conláed's Mass vestments to the poor because she had nothing else to give them. And just at the time of the sacrifice Conláed asked for them and said, "I won't offer up the body and blood of Christ without my vestments."

Thereupon at Brigit's prayer God provided similar vestments and all who were witnesses gave glory to God.

Another time too saint Brigit put vestments on the sea in a shrine that they might go a very long distance over the sea to Bishop Senán who was living on another sea-girt island and as the Holy Spirit revealed it to him he said to his brethren, "Go as fast as you can to the sea and bring here with you whatever you find." They went and found the shrine containing the vestments as we have said.

When he saw it Senán gave thanks to God and Brigit, for where human beings cannot go without the greatest difficulty, the shrine went by itself with God to guide it.[191]

While this text bears witness to the use of vestments to celebrate, and Conláed refuses to celebrate without them, it could be asked whether he was being cantankerous or if there is something more to the story. The value of these vestments could simply be that they came from abroad. But it could also be that at this period vestments (or at least similar vestments) were not in normal use.[192] Likewise, the story about Senán could simply mean that these vestments were now a relic and therefore may have been used only on special occasions, but it could have been possible that his church did not have vestments. While it may have been the case that the occasional Irish cleric didn't use vestments in this early period, the practice was wide-spread by the end of the pre-Norman period, as the testimony of Gille of Limerick (below) shows.

The Bethu Brigte

This vernacular life of Brigit probably dates to the early ninth century.[193] Part of the life deals with an Easter Week (the week beginning on Easter Sunday) when having first miraculously produced eighteen vatfuls of ale from a single sack of malt, Brigit and her nuns start to celebrate Easter Week with "no lack of feasting."[194] There is no actual mention of a Eucharist on Easter Sunday itself, but the account continues with the rest of Easter Week:

> On the following day, Monday, Mel came to Brigit to preach and say mass for her between the two Easters. A cow had been brought to her on that day also and it was given to Mel the bishop, the other cows having been taken. Ague assails one of Brigit's maidens and she was given Communion. "Is there anything else you might desire?" said Brigit. "There is," said she. "If I do not get some fresh milk, I shall die *at once.*" Brigit calls a maiden and *said:* "Bring me my own mug, out of which I drink, full of water. Bring it without anyone seeing it." It was brought to her then, and she blessed it so that it became warm new milk, and *the maiden* was *immediately* completely cured *when she tasted of it.* So that those are two miracles *simultaneously, i.e. the changing of water to milk and the cure of the maiden.*[195]

It is difficult to draw definite conclusions from this text. We are told that Bishop Mel celebrates the Eucharist and that the sick sister received Communion. What it does not tell us is whether the other sisters received or whether she received because she was sick and perhaps dying. It is also interesting that what cures her is not the Eucharist but Brigit's miraculous milk. The passage continues:

> On the following day, Tuesday, there was a good man nearby who was related to Brigit. He had been a full year ailing. "Take for me today," said he, "the best cow in my byre to Brigit, and let her pray to God for me, to see if I shall be cured." The cow was brought, and Brigit said to those who brought it: "Take it immediately to Mel." They brought it *back* to their house and exchanged it for another cow unknown to the sick man. That was related to Brigit, who was very angry at the deceit practiced on her. "Between a short time from now and the morning," said Brigit, "wolves shall eat the good cow which was given into my possession and which was not brought to you," said she to Mel, "and they shall eat seven oxen in addition to it." That was related to the sick man. "Go," said he, "take to her seven of the choice of the byre." It

was done thus, "*thanks be to God,*" said Brigit. "Let them be taken to Mel for his church. He has been preaching and saying Mass for us these seven days between the two Easters; a cow each day to him for his labour, it is not greater than what he has given; and take a blessing with all eight, a blessing on him from whom they were brought," said Brigid. When she said that he was healed immediately.

. . . Low Sunday approached. "I do not think it fortunate *now,*" said Brigit to her maidens, "not to have ale on Low Sunday for the bishop who will preach and say Mass." As soon as she said that, two maidens went to the water to bring in water and they had a large churn for the purpose, and Brigit was not aware of this. When they came back again, Brigit saw them there, "*Thanks be to God,*" said Brigit. "*God has given us beer for our bishop.*" The nuns became frightened then. "May God help us, O maiden." "Whatever foolish thing I have said, I have not said anything evil, O nuns." "The water which was brought inside, God did what you desired and *immediately* it was changed into ale with the smell of wine from it, and better ale was never set to brew in the [whole] world." The one churn was sufficient [for them] with their guests and the bishop.[196]

Once again this passage does not deal exclusively with the Eucharist. But what it does tell us is that the Eucharist was celebrated seven times between Easter Sunday and Low Sunday and that each of these liturgies included preaching. It also tells how Brigit gave a cow to Mel for each Eucharist. While this might seem like an excessive stipend today, Brigit thinks that she has gotten a good deal for this price is "not greater than what he has given." Brigit turns water into beer on Low Sunday so that the bishop, the guests, and the nuns can feast. However, there is no mention of Brigit or any of her sisters, other than the sick sister, actually receiving Communion.

This passage could lead one to ask exactly how usual daily Mass was. Is Brigit generous because of her devotion or holiness, or would a bishop or priest have required a substantial payment to go to a given church to celebrate there? Other documents speak about a cow being given to a church every quarter, which may be related to the periodic days of Communion.[197] This could lead to an interpretation of this passage in which Brigit was so much more pious than normal Christians that, rather than having a solemn Eucharist with the possibility of Communion of the faithful celebrated every few months, she actually had a bishop celebrate it every day during Easter week and even went so far as to give him the customary quarterly payment of a cow every day.

The Book of Armagh

This manuscript today preserved in Trinity College Dublin has been described as "the most important historical manuscript of Ireland prior to the twelfth century."[198] The present manuscript was assembled at an early date from a number of other texts including some material on St Patrick, the *Life of St Martin* by Sulpicius Servus, and some books of the New Testament. What is of interest here is the Patrician material, and this section of the manuscript has been dated to the year 807.[199] Like the Brigit material, these texts mainly concern the cult of St Patrick in the context of the struggle for ecclesial primacy. It is of a great importance for historical study of this time period in general, but it also provides some additional material for the study of the Eucharist in early Ireland.

When describing Patrick's preparation for return to Ireland as a missionary, Muirchú tells how he went to Rome to learn the "holy mysteries":

> [Patrick] set out to visit and honour the apostolic see, the head, that is, of all the churches in the whole world, in order to learn and understand and practice the divine wisdom and the holy mysteries to which God had called him, and in order to preach and bring divine grace to peoples beyond the Empire, converting them to belief in Christ.[200]

Once again, the text is more important for showing pre-ninth-century concern for learning the Roman way to celebrate the Eucharist than for any historical value vis-à-vis the actual clerical training of Patrick.[201]

Tírechán, the author of another section of this manuscript, mentions some more details. He gives a reference to the inventory needed for a typical new church to function: "Patrick took with him across the Shannon fifty bells, fifty patens, fifty chalices, altar-stones, books of the law, books of the Gospels, and left them in the new places."[202] When recounting how once Patrick ministered at the well of Stringell, he tells how the people there "received the Mass of Patrick."[203] But rather than implying that the Mass of Patrick was different from that of Rome or another liturgical rite, this probably is in contrast to pagan practices.

The *Sayings of St Patrick* are to be found as part of a short addition to Tírechán's memoir in one manuscript.[204] They contain an interesting passage that might be dealing with the Eucharist:

> The church of the Irish, which is indeed that of the Romans; if you would be Christians, then be as the Romans, and let that the song of praise be sung among yourselves at every hour of prayer: Lord have mercy, Christ have mercy. Every church that follows me, let it sing: Lord have mercy, Christ have mercy, Thanks be to God.[205]

Obviously this dictum has been much used on the Roman Catholic part of post-Reformation polemics. But what interests us here is that this refers to an early Western use of the *Kyrie* as a liturgical formula. However, care must be taken in assuming that this automatically refers to the use of the *Kyrie* in the eucharistic liturgy. The inclusion of this invocation in the eucharistic liturgy of the West is famously attributed to Pope Gelasius (d. 496) during the last decade of the fifth century.[206] But prior to this it was to be found in various euchological formulae of the liturgy of the hours, and there is no reason to believe that this text is referring to anything other than its use in such a context.[207]

The Navigatio *of St Brendan*

The *Navigatio* of St Brendan is an important work of Irish hagiography. It was very popular in the Middle Ages: not only do we possess 116 Latin manuscripts, but it was translated into at least seven vernacular languages.[208] This miraculous travel log of a voyage purportedly made by St Brendan (d. 575) was probably written in the late ninth or early tenth century.[209] It is still very readable today and is also the basis of the claim that St Brendan actually was the first European to discover America.

There are many examples of the Eucharist as viaticum in the *Navigatio*. Each time before one of his monks is about to die, St Brendan has a supernatural foreknowledge of the monk's sudden impending death. He invariably advises the monk to receive the Eucharist as viaticum (the fact that there is no mention of the celebration of the Eucharist in these episodes could indicate that some members of his monastic party carried the eucharistic bread on their person using a chrismal):

> Turning to the monk, Brendan said, "You must receive the Body and Blood of the Lord, for your body and soul are soon to part company. You will be buried here." . . . The monk received Communion, his soul left his body and was borne heavenwards by angels of light, as the brethren stood looking on. Brendan buried him where he had died.[210]

There are also references to the celebration of the Eucharist, including unambiguous testimony to the practice of private Mass:

> When morning came, he told the monks who were priests each to say his own Mass, and this they did. After Brendan had sung Mass in the boat, the monks took out of the coracle joints of raw meat and fish which they had brought with them from the other island, and sprinkled them with salt.[211]

It is also interesting to note that Brendan sings his own Mass in the boat. In another place, when they are at sea and being chased by a monstrous fish, the monks go to beg St Brendan not to sing so loudly.

> St Peter's Day was celebrated by St Brendan at sea, and the water was so clear that the monks could see every movement of life beneath the boat; so clear, indeed, that the animals on the ocean bed seemed near enough to touch. If the monks looked down into the deep, they could see many different kinds of creatures lying on the sandy bottom like

flocks at pasture, so numerous that, lying head to tail, and moving gently with the swell, they looked like a city on the march. The monks urged their master to say mass silently lest the fish hearing his voice, might rise up and attack them: "I am surprised at your foolishness. What—are you afraid of these creatures? Have you not several times landed on the monarch of the deep, the beast who eats all other sea creatures? Why, you have sat down on his back and sung psalms, have even gathered sticks, lighted a fire and cooked food—and all this without showing fear. Then how can you be afraid of these? Is not our Lord Jesus Christ the Lord of Creation? Can he not make all creatures docile?" Brendan sang at the top of his voice, causing the brethren to cast an anxious eye in the direction of the fish, but at the sound of singing the fish rose up from the sea bed and swam round and round the coracle. There was nothing to be seen but crowds of swimming forms. They did not come close but, keeping their distance, swam back and forth till mass was over.[212]

St Brendan was the only one to celebrate Mass on the boat on this occasion (although the next chapter of the *Navigatio* states that a number of Masses were celebrated on the next day). In contrast to some tendencies to say the eucharistic prayer silently, he sings "at the top of his voice." While there is evidence of private Masses in the *Navigatio*, it is also the case that St Brendan's Mass is more important than the private Masses of the other monks. On another occasion, St Brendan's Mass is referred to as the "community Mass," which all the monks, ordained or not, attend.[213] It is possible that the other monks celebrated private Masses after that of Brendan or on feast days. The loudly sung Mass is on the feast of St Peter, the "community Mass" is on the feast of Pentecost, and for the Paschal Vigil it seems that only one Mass is sung.[214] Therefore it is likely that Mass was celebrated by Brendan, and on other days when Mass was celebrated everyone who could celebrated a private Mass (the text is far from clear as to whether Mass was celebrated on every ferial day).

The *Navigatio* is more an epic myth than an actual ship's log, and it makes reference to mysterious episodes and details that obviously do not relate to real practice.[215] At one point they find a crystal church with altars, chalices, and patens made of crystal or glass.[216] Some scholars will point to this as evidence of the use of glass chalices in Ireland.[217] There is also an interesting reinterpretation of the meeting of Paul and Antony from St Jerome's *Life of St Paul, the First Monk*. Here Brendan takes the place of Antony and St Paul the Hermit is actually a disciple of Patrick. In this meeting the sharing of a mystical water is a symbol of the Eucharist.[218]

The Viaticum in the Saints' Lives and the Annals

Earlier in this chapter rites for the viaticum and Communion of the sick were examined; here we concentrate on the hagiographical material. On the one hand, an emphasis on the Eucharist as viaticum (or "food for the journey" to the next world) is perfectly normal and keeping with Western liturgical tradition. On the other hand, it should be noted that the many cases of viaticum in the Irish material suggests that this reception of the Eucharist at the end of the Christian's life received even more prominence in Ireland than elsewhere. Muirchú's early-ninth-century life of Patrick tells how "when the hour of [Patrick's] death was approaching he received the sacrament from the hands of the bishop Tassach for his journey to a blessed life."[219] In this and virtually every other text that mentions death in an ecclesial context the reception of the Eucharist is almost an indispensable element of Christian death.

The most important surviving Céli Dé text gives great importance to the viaticum with an interesting combination of Old Testament imagery. While the viaticum is important, the priest needs to depart from the house before the actual moment of death so as not to become ritually unclean.

> Now, to eat a meal with a dead man (though saintly) in the house is forbidden; but instead there are to be prayers and psalm-singing on such occasions. Even one in orders who brings the sacrament to a sick man is obliged to go out of the house at once thereafter, that the sick man may not die in his presence; for if he be present in the house at the death, it would not be allowable for him to perform the sacrifice until a bishop should consecrate him. It happened once upon a time

to Diarmait and to Blathmac mac Flaind that it was in their hands that Curui expired. When he died, they were about to perform the sacrifice thereafter, without being reconsecrated, till Colchu hindered them from doing so. The authority is Leviticus; and Diarmait also, the Abbot of Iona, was with him on that occasion.[220]

In a later text, when St Brendan of Clonfert foresees in a vision that he is about to be martyred (by mice), he is told in the vision, "Arise and take the body and blood of Christ, and depart to eternal life, for I hear the song of angels calling to thee."[221] This is like a refrain in the Irish hagiographical literature. In one instance when King Brandub is suddenly murdered and dies without the benefit of the Eucharist, St Maedoc temporarily resurrects him so that he can receive the Eucharist and he can die again and "go to heaven forthwith."[222]

Starting in the tenth century, notices of death given in the annals sometimes add the detail that the individual concerned died having first received the viaticum. The first reference to this in the *Annals of Ulster* for 974 reads:

> Murchad son of Flaithbertach went on a foray in Cenél Conaill and took a great spoil; and one dart struck him, and he died thereof at Dún Clóitige, with communion and penance.[223]

The fact that the annals do not mention the viaticum earlier does not necessarily mean that the practice only started in the tenth century: the later annalistic entries tend to be more detailed than the earlier ones. While one ought to be wary of reading too much into these annalistic entries, it may be significant that not every death mentioned has this detail. The *Annals of Inisfallen* recount simply that "Céile son of Donnocán, the most pious man in Ireland, rested in Christ in Glenn dá Locha."[224] A little further on, an entry reads, "Sadb, daughter of Ua Conchobuir Chiarraige, rested in Les Mór after a victory of pilgrimage and penance."[225]

While so many kings die "after victory of penance," or "having received the sacrifice," and some prominent ecclesiastics are simply recorded as dying, could this point to nobles, having first lived their secular life in the world, ending their days in a semi-monastic state as proposed by Staincliffe?[226] There are many parallels to this concept of dying in the later Middle Ages, with many Continental nobles receiving a monastic habit prior to death.[227] Also in this vein, in the twelfth-century *Irish Life of Colum Cille* one of the blessings Columba imparts on King Domnall mac Aodh is that "a year and a half would be the duration of his final illness, and he would receive the body of Christ every Sunday during that time."[228]

If this hypothesis is correct, at least in the higher levels of society great hope was placed in repentance with the reception of the Eucharist at the moment of death, and thus the emphasis on the viaticum in pre-Norman Ireland is understandable. While the reception of the Eucharist may not have been a regular event (and one might even ask whether prior to their last years of repentance these nobles received Communion on those few recommended days of Communion throughout the year), it was nonetheless the crown of each individual Christian's spiritual life.

Chrismals in the Saints' Lives

The use of a chrismal to carry the Eucharist on one's person is a peculiarity to pre-Norman Ireland.[229] The lives of the Irish saints and other written sources provide many instances of the use of a chrismal, which is paralleled by some material in the penitential literature which has been treated above, while the physical remains of chrismals will be examined in chapter 3. The chrismal in an Irish context was a small vessel that was used to carry a portion of eucharistic bread on one's person, as opposed to the more general use of the term for a container holding the oil of chrism used in the anointings associated with Christian initiation, ordination, and the consecration of churches.[230] From still extant chrismals in Continental holdings, we can see that the chrismal was a small box that was carried around the neck. Being made of worthy materials, these chrismals had a certain monetary value, and, judging by the saints' lives, sometimes these chrismals were, in fact, stolen for their economic worth.[231]

Another important piece of evidence for the use of the chrismal comes from a tenth-century copy of the *Pontifical of Egbert* (Egbert was archbishop of York from 732 to 766) now in the Imperial Library of Paris (No. 138).[232] This text contains two blessing formulae for a chrismal:

> Chrismal Preface
> Let us pray, most beloved and dearest brothers, that almighty God may deign to accomplish this ministry of the bodies of his Son, our Lord Jesus Christ, in the bearer by the blessing of holiness, the safety of protection praying for us. Through the same.
> Or
> Almighty God, inseparable Trinity pour into our hands the riches of your blessing so that by our blessing this small vessel may be sanctified and a new tomb of the Body of Christ may be accomplished by the grace of the Holy Spirit. Through.[233]

It is clear that these prayers are not speaking of a chrismal in the normal sense (the oil of chrism is not mentioned), but both versions of the prayer make explicit reference to the Body of Christ. It is also significant that these prayers request "the blessing of holiness, the safety of protection" for the bearer of the chrismal, which is in keeping with the concept of the chrismal offering its bearer divine protection.

The *Vita Prima* of St Brigit, one of our earliest Christian texts from Ireland, mentions pagans "wearing sinister amulets."[234] There is no formal connection between this and the Irish practice of wearing a chrismal. But today it is hard not to see the chrismal as having a talismanic association, which might provide some explanation as to the origins of the practice.[235] Later on in this document we are given one of the first mentions of a chrismal:

> The holy bishop Brón returned to his part of the country and took with him a chrismal from saint Brigit. Now he lived by the sea.
>
> One day the bishop was working on the shore and a boy with him. And this chrismal was left on a rock on the shore and the tide came in up to high water mark.

Then the boy remembered the chrismal and began to cry. But the bishop said, "Don't cry. I'm confident that saint Brigit's chrismal won't get lost."

And so it turned out. For the chrismal was on the rock dry and had not been shifted by the waves of the sea and when the tide went out they found it just as it had been left.[236]

In general, two possible purposes for the reservation of the sacrament can be discerned. The first one is to be able to receive the viaticum, which was of particular importance in Ireland.[237] The saints' lives seem to imply that the viaticum was taken from the chrismal that was ordinarily on the person of the saint, and that it was not necessary to fetch the sacrament from the church. When St Comgall is dying, he is visited by the abbot Fiachra. When Fiachra realizes that Comgall is dying, he is able to give him the viaticum on the spot—"dedit statim communionem dominicam."[238] In another instance St Molua, who *thought* he was about to die, was able to ask St Cronan to give him the viaticum, and St Cronan, who was with him, was able to give him Communion, again on the spot.[239] In the slightly later life of St Laurence O'Toole, archbishop of Dublin (d. 1180), we are told that bandits once attacked him while he was on a journey and desecrated the host he carried on his person "as *viaticum* and as a safe guide on the journey, as was then the custom."[240]

The main reason for ecclesiastics to carry the chrismal, however, seems to have been to provide them with divine protection; the possibility of administering the viaticum was a secondary motive.[241] Much like a relic, or an image of the cross or a saint, the chrismal was carried on one's person in an almost talismanic way.[242] We can see this use of the chrismal in another incident in the life of St Comgall.

One day, while Saint Comgall was working by himself in a field, he placed his chrismal upon his cloak. On that same day a band of Pictish bandits came to that locality, to capture everything there, be they men or sheep. When the pagans came upon Saint Comgall as he worked outside, and they saw his chrismal as it lay upon his cloak,

they considered this to be the God of Saint Comgall; and these bandits were unable to touch him due to the fear of his God that filled
them.[243]

In a story in the life of St Mochoemog, a young monk is murdered
and St Kynnecus objects to his being buried in the hallowed ground
of the monastery. Mochoemog agrees but has his chrismal (and his
staff) buried with the young monk who is thus assured of salvation.[244]
From these stories we can deduce that the Eucharist was seen as something powerful. It was a great protector in the moment of death. But,
as we saw above, the Eucharist was somehow "fearful," and for this
reason it was carried as a *coimge conaire*, a path-protector.[245] The reason the *chrismal* can grant protection is precisely because it contains
the awesome majesty of God.

HOMILETIC MATERIAL

Homilies were very important in transmitting an understanding of
the Eucharist to the laity at large. Many of the texts on pastoral care
and the rights and responsibilities of a particular church stress the importance of preaching.[246] However, very few Irish homilies from the
early medieval period have survived.[247] Perhaps this could be explained culturally, as memorization of legal texts and poetry played a
great role in secular society and therefore Irish priests may have been
more likely than their Continental brethren to commit their sermons
to memory. In any case, it appears from the surviving homilies that
Irish homilists tended, unsurprisingly, to be relatively mainstream.[248]

St Columbanus's *Sermon on the Eucharist* is one of the few homiletic texts on the Eucharist connected with Ireland, and although Columbanus was ministering far from Ireland when he composed his
sermons, his collection is perhaps the most important of the few remaining relics of Irish sermons still extant.[249] This series of thirteen
sermons was probably preached by St Columbanus in Milan or Lom-
bardy between late in 612 and his death in 615.[250] At this time he was
attempting to promote "practical religion" and a general religious formation as part of his struggle with the Arians at the Lombard court.[251]
The last sermon, which is the high point of the collection, deals with

the Eucharist. It is true that these sermons were preached outside Ireland, and may well be somewhat influenced by Continental concerns. However, St Columbanus was of the opinion that his duty was to bring Continental Christians back to true Christianity and to fight against any hint of laxity, and so the sermons are permeated with the spirituality (and view of the Eucharist) that St Columbanus learned as a young man in Ireland.[252]

Here in this last sermon we do not see any rigorism. Instead we see St Columbanus exhorting his listeners to find in the Eucharist a remedy for their spiritual thirst. In this beautiful sermon, the stress is on the Eucharist as the "fountain" that the Christian must approach. It is unusual that he speaks of the Eucharist as being the Body of Christ and the fountain where the faithful may quench their thirst and omits any mention of the chalice or the Blood of Christ.[253] Nonetheless, this sermon is still an eloquent appeal to Christians to approach Christ in the Eucharist:

> Observe whence that Fountain flows; for it flows from that place whence also the Bread came down; since He is the same Who is Bread and Fountain, the only Son, our God Christ the Lord, for Whom we should ever hunger. For though we eat Him in loving, though we feast on Him in desiring, let us still as hungering desire Him. Likewise as the Fountain, let us ever drink of Him with overflow of love, let us ever drink of Him with fullness of longing, and let us be gladdened by some pleasure of His loveliness. For the Lord is lovely and pleasant; though we eat and drink of Him, yet let us ever hunger and thirst, since our food and drink can never be consumed and drained entire; for though He is eaten He is not consumed, though He is drunk He is not lessened, since our Bread is eternal, and our Fountain is perennial, our Fountain is sweet.[254]

The other important homiletic treatment of the Eucharist comes from the collection of homilies in the *Leabhar Breac.* These homilies, composed in Early Irish but with extensive passages in Latin, probably date to the eleventh century.[255] They are very similar to Continental material and so are not important for any new evidence of independent traditions and theologies of the Eucharist in pre-Norman

Ireland; rather, their significance is in showing how mainstream the Irish were. If these homilies were destined for use in vernacular preaching to the faithful or as formational materials for clerics, then they would have helped to nourish and foster a fairly typical attitude towards the Eucharist.

From these homilies a mainstream vision of the Eucharist as a representation of the Passion of Christ emerges:

> Jesus Christ, the Son of the King of Heaven and Earth, the Third Person of the Trinity, is coeval and coequal with the Father and the Holy Ghost, true God and true Man, the High Priest and High Bishop, who offered Himself on the altar of the cross to redeem and ransom the human race; it is He who, on the night before His crucifixion, offered up His blood and body, and gave them to His apostles to partake thereof. And He left with those Apostles, and with His whole church, to the end of time, the custom of making the same oblation to commemorate the first oblation when He subjected Himself to the cross and to death in obedience to the Heavenly Father, and to fulfil His will.
>
> This is the oblation in which is the full satisfying of God and the appeasing of His anger against the accurst seed of Adam; for in it was the full-growth of humility and lowliness, the full-growth of charity and heart-pity, and perfect sympathy for the wretchedness of the human race in general.[256]

The idea here that the Eucharist is to be received in a penitential manner is perhaps an Irish trait, for this is paralleled in the penitential dimension of other Irish material:

> Every person, then, who desires life perennial, let him take part in this oblation, and partake of the heavenly food faithfully, opportunely, penitentially. For everyone who partakes of it with penance and tears, and with steadiness of faith, and with reverence for it in his heart, will be the abode and consecrated temple of God; but it (the Eucharist) will be lasting destruction to every one who shall partake of it unworthily, that is, without repentance of his sins, and without having a firm conviction that it is the true body and true blood of the Saviour that

he partakes of, and without due honour to Him in his heart, merely taking it as any other food.[257]

But there are traces of another eucharistic theology. In a later section the homilist sees the Eucharist as a heavenly food that has the role of bringing the faithful to heaven. The one who will go to heaven with Christ is the one who "partakes of his body and blood, or has an earnest desire to partake thereof if he could get [it]."[258] There is also an interesting instance of what has been classed as an *inverted* eucharistic theology, when it says that God "could convert His Body and Blood into bread and wine."[259] The role of the priest is again mainstream:

> For the universal Royal Priest, Jesus Christ Himself at first offered up that sacrifice for mankind, so every priest of His race, by the virtue and power of words offers up that oblation. Not the same is what He did before them, and what He instructed them to do; but yet indeed in truth it is Jesus Christ Himself, the real Priest, who, though invisible, is blessing and sanctifying the oblation every day, though the other priest be ministering as His deputy.[260]

The homilist (again in a fully mainstream Western manner) outlines that the holiness and efficacy of the Eucharist does not depend on the priest or the recipient. It is valid and efficacious in and of itself due to the grace of Christ:

> Not inferior is the little part to the great part of this body of Christ; neither is its part less than its totality, for the perfect whole and entire of the body of Christ is in each particle thereof; and the full virtue and power of the healing and saving of every man abides in them. Not better, then, nor worse, one than another, O man, that pure mystery of the body of Christ and of His blood, for man's sin cannot defile it or make it bad; it is not by the goodness of any man, or on account of his holiness, that its good and sanctification grows greater, since it is it that makes good and sanctifies every one, both lay and clerical.[261]

Finally, there is another striking eucharistic image that emerges from these homilies. In its treatment of the birth of Christ, the beasts in the grotto of Bethlehem realize that the baby Jesus is the Creator of the universe who will later give himself to mankind as food in the Eucharist. Therefore they lick him in adoration:

> Then was filled the cave with a very great fragrance as is (exhaled) from a (precious) ointment, and from wine, and from the true-perfume of the whole world; the cave was filled (with it), so that all were satisfied therefrom for a long time; and the very great and conspicuous star was seen above the cave from morning till evening, and its like was not seen before or after, nor (aught) that was equal to it. Mary set her Son to rest thereafter with (swaddling) clothes of white linen about Him in the stall of the ass and the young ox for no other place was to be found for Him in the guest-house. And the irrational creatures then recognised their Creator, for they were licking Him and adoring Him, both the ass and the young ox, He being in the middle between them. Then was fulfilled what the prophets said of old, namely, Esaias, son of Amos.[262]

THE *TRACT ON THE REAL PRESENCE*

The *Tract on the Real Presence,* written in Early Irish, comes from the end of our period, when the Irish church was increasingly coming into contact with Continental spirituality and the second Gregorian reform.[263] According to St Bernard of Clairvaux, Ireland experienced controversies over the real presence that were comparable to the more famous eucharistic controversies of the early Middle Ages. In his *Vita Sancti Malachiae* he tells us about "a certain cleric in Lismore, good in character, they say, but not in his faith":

> In his own eyes a knowledgeable man, he had the presumption to say that in the Eucharist there is only the sacrament and not the *res sacramenti,* that it is only the sanctification and not the true presence of the Body. He had often been called up on this by St Malachy in secret, but to no purpose. Then he was summoned into the open and the lay people were excluded, so that if possible he could be cured of this malady rather than be confuted. So it was that in an assembly of clerics the man was given the opportunity to defend his own viewpoint.

Although he attempted to set forth and defend his error with every point of ingenuity—which he was not unskilled in, with Malachy arguing against and refuting him, he was worsted in everyone's opinion.[264]

When the cleric refused to listen to any admonition of St Malachy or anyone else, he was excommunicated and declared a heretic. He then decided to leave his monastery and on his way was struck down with a sickness, came to his senses, and returned to St Malachy.

He confessed that he had been wrong and was absolved. Then he asked for the *Viaticum* and reconciliation was effected. At practically the same moment that his lips renounced all his faithless wrong-doing he was dissolved by death.[265]

This probably took place in the 1140s.[266] While we cannot know the content of St Malachy's argumentation, we do possess the contemporary *Tract on the Real Presence*. This document was composed by one Echtgus Ua Cuanáin, who can possibly be identified as Bishop Isaac Ua Cuanáin of Ros Cré (d. 1161).[267] The *Tract* has been dated on linguistic grounds to around the year 1090, which (give or take a few years) would allow this attribution of authorship.[268] Apart from this biographical information, we know little else about the reasons behind the authorship of the *Tract*. However, if it wasn't composed in response to the controversy that St Bernard mentions, it would most likely have had its origin in a similar context.

The *Tract* consists of eighty-six paragraphs in Early Irish opening with the invitation:

O you who do not have true belief regarding the feast you enjoy at the altar will be subject to a severe and painful judgment. Woe to the one who gave birth to you.[269]

The *Tract* then goes on to outline what exactly true belief is; this is done mainly by making reference to scriptural passages. Not only are the typical New Testament accounts of the Last Supper referred to, the *Tract* also makes ample use of the Old Testament:

If God, out of nothing, created all there is in heaven and on earth, surely he will make body and blood of the bread and wine. Just as God turned the rod of Moses into a real serpent, and as he immediately made a rod of that serpent.[270]

The *Tract* is very scriptural in its content, but it is a far cry from the exhaustive treatment of Scholastic theology. Time and again, it reiterates that the bread and wine become the Body and Blood of Christ, "the King of Heaven."[271] Mention is made of the fact that the unworthiness of the minister has no effect on the validity of the sacrament and even "if Judas, though he was an evil priest, had given the body of Christ to a devout man who believed and who had repented of his sins, it would have been an absolutely pure sacrifice."[272] The *Tract* is very pastoral in tone, warning against unworthiness of the minister and of the one who receives, yet inviting the faithful to take the Eucharist seriously.

There are some elements characteristic of later eucharistic piety in the *Tract*. For example, mention is made of Bishop Flagellus who sees the Christ-child in the host (this parallels the many stories of visions granted to unbelieving priests from both East and West).[273] There is also a preoccupation with the possibility of dividing the host without at the same time dividing the Body of the risen Lord.[274]

The *Tract* sees the wine as representing Christ, and the water added to the wine as sinful mankind. Then it says how good this wine is: it is beautiful, for it represents Christ and therefore it must be "sweet."[275] While it does still mention the *fractio panis,* it says that there can be "many hosts on the paten."[276] Perhaps this signals the end of large patens such as the Derrynaflan example. The *Tract* finishes on an eschatological note warning that "the outcome of the reception of that body is beyond all question: eternal judgment will mean either heaven or cold stormy hell."[277]

THE *CÁIN DOMNAIG*

In the early church, Sunday was understood to be the Lord's Day, as opposed to being simply the Christian Sabbath: Christ himself was understood to be the Christian Sabbath, and Sunday was the day to celebrate his resurrection. However, as time went by, other themes were introduced into the popular Western understanding of Sunday so that it did, in fact, gradually become the Christian Sabbath.[278] By the sixth century this concept was widespread, and pentateuchal legislation forbidding work on Sunday was commonly issued.[279] In Ireland in particular the idea of Sunday as Sabbath implied that the Old Testament laws of the Sabbath rest were applied to Sunday.[280] This leads many Irish texts to mention that Christians are forbidden to work on Sunday. In his *Life of Patrick,* Muirchú puts a curse on pagans working on Sunday.[281] Patrick himself, when he is on a journey, will not travel "from the evening of the Lord's night (that is, Saturday night) until Monday morning," so he spends the night in a field when a great rain storm comes, but he is miraculously kept dry.[282]

The *Cáin Domnaig* is an Irish adaptation of a famous apocryphal work, the *Carta Dominica,* a document that many believed to have been written by the glorious Christ in heaven and dropped down to one of the famous centers of Christianity (there were a number of candidates for exactly which city it was). This document mandated a strict observance of the pentateuchal legislation.[283] A version of the *Carta Dominica* is found in Irish: the *Epistil Ísu* (Epistle of Jesus), which forms part of a larger Irish work, the *Cáin Domnaig* (the Law of Sunday).[284] The *Annals of Ulster* for the year 886 tell us how "a letter, with the 'Law of Sunday' and other good instructions, came to Ireland with the Pilgrim."[285] However, the actual text for the *Cáin Domnaig,* written in Old Irish, is probably earlier and dates from the beginning of the eighth century. It lays down rules for Sunday, imposing fines on those who do not obey:

Now these are the fines for transgressing Sunday: An ounce of silver on a man who travels with a load on that day, and his clothes to be burned, and his load to be forfeited. A half-ounce on a man traveling without a burden on that day, and his clothes to be burned. Whosoever rides a horse on Sunday shall forfeit his horse and his clothes. Grinding in a mill on Sunday after the swearing of the law, if it be a mill of the laity, an ounce of silver [is the fine on the first occasion] for it, and five *seds* from that out. If, however, it be a church mill, a *cumhal* is the fine for grinding in it on Sunday. Whatsoever quern is ground with on Sunday shall be broken, and a half-ounce of silver [imposed] on the man or woman who grinds with it. If it be a man-servant or woman-servant who grinds with it, his clothes shall be burned, and he himself driven out of the place.[286]

Strangely enough, there is no mention of the institution of the Eucharist in the document. There are whole lists of important Old Testament events that are said to have taken place on Sunday as well as many of the New Testament miracles, including the manna and the multiplication of the loaves, but the institution of the Eucharist is missing.

The Céli Dé are often credited with the introduction of sabbatarianism into Ireland.[287] But while they probably were influenced by this type of spirituality, they were simply continuing earlier traditions and understandings, as sabbatarianism predates them by at least a generation.[288] This said, the *Monastery of Tallaght* does contain some texts of clearly sabbatarian vein:

A herb that is cut on Sunday, or kale that is cooked, or bread that is baked, or blackberries or nuts that are plucked on a Sunday, it is not his [Maelruain] practice, nor the practice of true clerics, to eat these things.

. . . Now the gathering of apples on a Sunday or lifting a single apple form the ground is not allowed among them.[289]

While there are many texts forbidding the most trivial works on Sunday, it is not known if Mass attendance was mandatory in Ireland. In his penitential, St Columbanus requires that the monks be present in the church, but the porter and cook are excused:

But before the sermon on the Lord's Day let all, except for fixed requirements, be gathered together, so that none is lacking to the number of those who hear the exhortation, except the cook and the porter who themselves also, if they can, are to try to be present, when the gospel bell is heard.[290]

In the Irish penitential literature and the monastic rules there is only one text that prescribes a penance for missing the Eucharist:

> Someone who is unfaithful to the Sunday Mass is to chant fifty psalms standing behind closed doors and with eyes shut. This is the price of the Mass, and he shall also make one hundred genuflections and cross-vigils with the *Beati*.[291]

From these texts it can be seen that Sunday was indeed important. The legal texts show that the priest was expected to celebrate the Eucharist on Sundays, and the fact that he celebrated in their church and mentioned their need and their dead does seem to have been important to the people of the time. However, it might also be true that clerics considered it more important that Christians rested in an Old Testament sense than actually going to church on Sundays. Indeed, while it is preferable for the cook and the porter to go to the eucharistic celebration, they are permitted to miss it for their duties (which, at least in the case of the cook, are presumably not strictly a matter of life or death).

THE POEMS OF BLATHMAC, SON OF CÚ BRETTAN

The poems of Blathmac, son of Cú Brettan, are preserved in a single seventeenth-century manuscript now in the National Library of Ireland. While the manuscript is very late, it seems to be the work of an antiquarian who copied it from an early manuscript no longer extant.[292] Carney is of the opinion that the scribe copied this manuscript from the *Book of Glendalough*, a now lost twelfth-century codex.[293] Unable to place Blathmac's genealogy, Carney simply proposes that he was probably a cleric, perhaps involved in the Céli Dé, working, at the latest, sometime between 750 and 770.[294] However, others have connected Blathmac to the Fir Rois and possibly to their territories in Co. Louth.[295]

The poems are in Early Irish and place a lot of emphasis on Marian devotion and devotion to the Passion of Christ. Various biblical scenes from the life of Christ and Old Testament prefigurations are recounted in verse. They contain no account of the institution of the Eucharist, but there is an interesting interplay between blood and wine in the poem.

> The King of the seven holy heavens, when his heart was pierced, wine [*fín*] was spilled upon the pathways, the blood [*fuil*] of Christ flowing through his gleaming sides.
> The flowing blood from the body of the dear Lord baptised the head of Adam, for the shaft of the cross of Christ had aimed at his mouth.
> By the same blood (it was a fair occasion!) quickly did he cure the fully blind man who, openly with his two hands, was plying the lance.[296]

In another place Blathmac speaks of *fínfolo* or "wine-like blood."[297] This occurs where the Gospel texts are dealing with the physical blood of Jesus shed on the cross; the eucharistic blood is not mentioned. It would be normal to use blood and wine interchangeably when dealing with the Last Supper, but the fact that this text is dealing with the Crucifixion, and that Blathmac mentions wine, could show how important the eucharistic wine was for him.[298] Later on, he deals with the eucharistic wine itself. Here the emphasis is also on the blood as the source of the Eucharist's efficacy and forgiveness, and, indeed, the blood is portrayed as that which gives life to the human body of clay that Christ takes:

> It is your Son's body that comes to us when one goes to the Sacrament [*sacarfaic*]; the pure wine [*fírfín*] has been transmuted for us into the blood of the Son of the King.
> It is your Son's body (well that it came!) from which comes an eternal kingdom, eternally happy; and without doubt it is in his blood that every saint washes his bright garment.
> The blood of the Son of the King reddens a body of clay in the brightness of gore; the blood of your Son, the Son of the living God, from it is made its (i.e. the body's) resplendence.[299]

While this is poetry and does not give a literal description of the eucharistic liturgy or say whether anybody other than the presiding

cleric received from the chalice, it is still important for its communication of the attitudes surrounding the Eucharist. The fact that it is in
the vernacular and not Latin could also mean that it is closer to lay
spirituality, even though many clerical texts were also composed in
the vernacular. In addition, the very fact that the poems are in the
form of a written text would remove it from the population at large.
The strong emphasis on the wine-blood of Christ in this poetry, however, is yet another isolated piece of evidence that lends support to the
view that the eucharistic cup held a special place in pre-Norman Irish
spirituality.

GILLE OF LIMERICK'S *DE STATU ECCLESIAE*

Gille of Limerick (d. 1145) was an important churchman of the
twelfth-century reform in Ireland. And although a significant treatise
of his has survived, until recently it has received little attention. A
new critical edition of this work has lately been published,[300] and this,
combined with a new understanding of this period in Irish ecclesiastical history, probably means that Gille will receive more attention in
the future. We know little of Gille's early life; even his name displays
great variety in the different sources. The first definite reference to
him is his 1106 letter to Anselm of Canterbury, where he presents
himself as the newly ordained bishop of the Hiberno-Viking city of
Limerick; from the tone of the letter and of Anselm's reply, it seems
that they had personally known each other in Normandy.[301] However, in a time when some of his contemporaries were traveling to
England for episcopal ordination from Canterbury, Gille had not followed suit, despite the fact that he was at least an acquaintance if not
an actual friend of the current incumbent at Canterbury. Perhaps this
signaled a rejection of Canterbury's attempt to exercise jurisdiction in
Ireland even on the part of those Irish reformers closest to the Continental Gregorian reforms. By the time of the Synod of Ráth Bresail in
1111, Gille had also become papal legate in Ireland, a role that Malachy of Armagh was to inherit in 1138. Earlier editions of Gille's work
attribute two treatises to him: *De Usu Ecclesiastico* and *De Statu Ecclesiae*. But originally these two treatises formed parts of a single treatise that were separated by a diagram of the structure of the church;

when they were copied into manuscripts and early printed versions that did not contain the diagram, they came to be considered as two distinct treatises. It is possible that this treatise may have been presented by Gille at the Synod of Ráth Bresail.[302]

Gille was a reformer of the church and labored to implement a Continental model of the church in Ireland, so in this canonical treatise he is more interested in proposing the current Continental models of the Eucharist than in preserving the older traits of liturgy (be they Irish or otherwise). There is no way of knowing how widespread an influence Gille's directives on the eucharistic liturgy had, nor even if they were actually observed anywhere. But the very fact that he had to legislate on liturgical matters would seem to imply that the liturgy was not always celebrated in a way Gille considered to be correct.[303] However, once again, it is hard to discern whether he was combating against what he considered to be wrong ritual practices inherited from the former liturgical traditions or simply legislating against poorly performed liturgy.

Gille presents a very organized liturgy. He speaks of the roles of porters, lectors, exorcists, acolytes, subdeacons, deacons, priests, and bishops. There is a church building that is guarded by the porter, whose job it is "to ensure that no Jew, pagan, or catechumen may be in the church during the hour of sacrifice, that a dog or anyone unclean or stained with blood may not enter, and to exclude the excommunicated."[304] The acolyte must "light and extinguish the candles at certain hours."[305] The church is a sacred place, a number of whose elements must be dedicated by the bishop, namely, "the porch, the sanctuary, the altar and the table of the altar." The bishop also has to consecrate the things used in the church, including "the ciborium, that is the canopy over the altar, the cross and the bell."[306]

Not surprisingly, Gille provides us with more details about the priest than anyone else: "it is his duty to offer; to sacrifice bread and wine with water each day . . . before the Sacrifice he is to incense above and around the altar and sacrifice. However, before the gospel the deacon should incense the altar."[307] He goes on to provide a detailed description of the priest's vestments and the elements necessary for the celebration of the Eucharist:

Just as there are seven steps by which a priest is elevated so also there are seven vestments in which he is ordained; his everyday clothes, an amice, alb, cincture, maniple, stole and chasuble. Otherwise the offices can be performed without a chasuble and sometimes only with a stole. Each day at Mass he wears at least the following four vestments: a linen gown, a tunic, breeches and shoes. The Romans wear boots. Amalarius says that the priest should wear sandals and a dalmatic but among us only pontiffs use these.

. . . A priest should use the sprinkler for holy water, the book of the holy Gospels, the Psalter, the missal, the book of hours, the manual and the book of the synod. He should have the veil, the candelabra and candles, a wardrobe of vestments, a pyx with the offering and their irons, a flask for wine and a bottle for water, a basin and a towel for washing hands, a tree trunk or a carved stone into which the water used for washing sacred things may be poured away, the concealed base for a candle and a lectern for the lectionary.[308]

Subdeacons and deacons also wear vestments; the subdeacons read the epistle and "pour water and wine into the chalice,"[309] and it "is the duty of deacons to say: 'Let those who are not in communion leave,' 'Bow down for the blessing,' 'Bow your heads to God,' 'Go, it is ended,' 'Let us bless the Lord,' to read and proclaim the Gospel, to place the sacrifice on the corporal, and to minister to the priest."[310]

Gille also recommends when the priest should give Communion to the faithful:

He ought to give communion to the baptised immediately and to all the faithful three times a year, at Easter, at Pentecost and at Christmas and to those near death if they should seek it by word or by sign or if in the evidence of a faithful witness they have already sought it. Praying, he ought to commend the souls of the faithful as they leave their bodies and celebrate their memory at Mass and in prayer.[311]

Here is yet another text, this time from the end of our period, that recommends that the laity receive Communion on only a few of the major feasts, as well as the ever-present viaticum. He also recommends that the reception of the Eucharist accompany the rite of baptism.[312]

GERALD OF WALES'S *THE HISTORY AND TOPOGRAPHY OF IRELAND*

Gerald of Wales was a Cambro-Norman ecclesiastic who visited Ireland in 1183. While his is most definitely a post-Norman text, it was written before the Anglo-Norman and Gaelic traditions had had much chance to interact. He wrote a treatise describing this visit partly as a work of propaganda to defend the Norman mission in Ireland. Although it is very derogatory of the Irish and is full of fantastic tales, it is valuable as it provides the impressions of an educated foreigner of the ecclesiastical situation in Ireland. Moreover, it mentions the Eucharist a few times.[313]

Gerald relays a number of stories about the Eucharist. The first of these is about the island monastery that is commonly identified as Skellig Michael:

> In the South of Munster near Cork there is a certain island which has within it a church of Saint Michael, revered for its holiness from ancient times. There is a certain stone there outside of, but almost touching, the door of the church on the right-hand side. In a hollow of the upper part of this stone there is found every morning through the merits of the saints of the place as much wine as is necessary for the celebration of as many Masses as there are priests to say Mass on that day there.[314]

If we accept that Gerald did not invent this story (and there is little reason for him to have done so), it gives a number of clues about the Eucharist (although it would be dangerous to build a whole theory on Gerald). First, not surprisingly, it shows that wine was somehow hard to come by (even today Skellig Michael is an isolated place that can be impossible to reach in bad weather). Even if it were possible to procure wine by normal means, it is an appreciated miracle to be given it without anyone having to bring it onto the island. This passage also recounts that one Mass per priest was celebrated there every day which would, again, point to private Masses, which is in agreement with the archaeological record: the Skellig Michael monastery was a relatively small monastery, and yet the site contains a number of churches.[315]

In another passage (which is probably not historical) he mentions the use of a chrismal while speaking by a priest giving the viaticum to a dying woman who had been changed by a curse into a wolf:

> She then received from the priest all the last rites duly performed up to the last communion. This too she eagerly requested, and implored him to complete his good act by giving her the viaticum. The priest insisted that he did not have it with him, but the wolf, who in the meantime, had gone a little distance away, came back again and pointed out to him a little wallet containing a manual and some consecrated hosts, which the priest according to the custom of his country carried about with him, hanging from his neck, on his travels.[316]

The value of this passage is that it is an independent witness to the use of the chrismal as a particularly Irish practice. Although he does not use the word "chrismal" but refers to a little wallet ("perulam"), the fact that he says that this was carried "according to the custom of his country" and not that the priest was going to bring viaticum or Communion to someone else shows that in all likelihood this refers to the use of the chrismal.

Two other stories in *The History and Topography of Ireland* deal with the Eucharist. These stories do not really add anything to our knowledge. Both portray the Irish as being very superstitious regarding the Eucharist. It is probably true that Gerald needs to portray the Irish in a bad light for the political purposes of supporting the Norman invasion, but it is also probably the case that Ireland had its fair share of superstitious practices on the borders of the official form of Christianity:

> There is a well in Munster, and if one touches or even looks at it, the whole province is deluged with rain. The rain will not cease until a priest who is a virgin both in mind and body and specially chosen for the purpose, celebrates Mass in a chapel not far from the well and

known to have been erected with this end in view, and appeases the well with a sprinkling of holy water and the milk of a cow of one colour. This is certainly a barbarous rite, without rime or reason.

Among the many other tricks devised in their guile, there is this one which serves as a particular good proof of their treachery. Under the guise of religion and peace they assemble at some holy place with him whom they wish to kill. First they make a treaty on the basis of their common fathers. Then in turn they go around the church three times. They enter the church and, swearing a great variety of oaths before the relics of saints placed on the altar, at last with the celebration of Mass and the prayers of the priests they make an indissoluble treaty as if it were a kind of betrothal. For the greater confirmation of their friendship and completion of their settlement, each in conclusion drinks the blood of the other which has willingly been drawn especially for the purpose.[317]

Despite such fantastic stories, it would seem from all these texts that Gerald of Wales found little unusual in the attitude towards and celebration of the Eucharist in Ireland. He does not lament unusual liturgical practices, and while he notes that the priests carry the host on their persons, he does not single out this difference for criticism. The last story is the only place where the Eucharist is seen in a negative light, and even here there is no real liturgical abnormality as the priests only administer oaths and celebrate the Eucharist: the more unsavory aspects of this pact could well have taken place without any involvement of the clergy.

INFANT COMMUNION

In the early church, reception of the Eucharist often accompanied baptism. It is probable that infants received baptism in many geographic regions since the beginnings of Christianity, and quite possible that they received Communion as part of the baptismal rite (either in the form of a tiny piece of the eucharistic bread or a drop from the chalice). After this they may even have continued to receive Communion on a regular basis with their parents. Our first explicit testimony to infant Communion is St Cyprian of Carthage (d. 258). In *De lapsis* 9 he speaks of infants being carried to the idolatrous sacrificial meal in their parents' arms during the Decian persecution. After they have died and are sent to Hell, they protest, "We have done nothing; we have not abandoned the Lord's bread and cup and of our own accord hastened to profane contaminations. The perfidy of others has ruined us."[318] Here "abandoning the Lord's bread and cup" can probably be interpreted as proof that the infants had already received Communion prior to their being taken to the pagan sacrifice in their parents' arms.[319] Later on in the same work, Cyprian writes of a young girl who was abandoned by her parents during the same persecution. Her wet-nurse took her to partake in the pagan sacrifice, where she was given bread and wine as she was too young to consume meat. Less than eighteen months later, still before the little girl had learned to speak, after the persecution had ended and she had been found again by her parents, she was taken to Communion by her mother, who was unaware of what had happened to her daughter.[320] Cyprian, who was presiding the Eucharist himself, describes the scene:

> But when the solemnities were completed and the deacon began to offer the cup to those present, and when as the rest were receiving, her turn came, the little girl with an instinct of divine majesty turned her face away, compressed her mouth with tightened lips, and refused the cup. The deacon, however, persisted and poured into the mouth of the child, although resisting, of the sacrament of the cup. Then there followed sobbing and vomiting. In the body and mouth which had been violated the Eucharist could not remain; the draft consecrated in the blood of the Lord burst forth from the polluted vitals.[321]

St Augustine of Hippo (d. 430), also writing in North Africa, seems to state categorically that infants need to receive Communion to enter eternal life.[322] But it needs to be remembered that the rite of baptism to which he was accustomed considered Communion to be a constitutive part of the rite, and it was unthinkable for a child to have received the water of baptism without being given Communion also.

In any case, Augustine posed a problem that he himself struggled to answer, and, today, scholars are unsure as to what exactly Augustine taught.[323]

The perception of the need for the newly baptized infant to receive the Eucharist as being almost indispensable traveled from Augustine in North Africa to other regions, and it received important encouragement from Pope Gelasius at the end of the fifth century. [324] A description of baptism in *Ordo Romanus* XI[325] says that after baptism "they go in to Mass and all the infants receive Communion. Care is to be taken lest after they have been baptized they receive any food or suckling before they communicate."[326]

It is probable that the custom of including the reception of Communion as part of the baptismal rite was introduced at the earliest stage of the evangelization of Ireland. One of the earliest witnesses to this practice is from the early 800s when *Tírechán* tells the story of how Patrick baptized the two daughters of King Loíguire:

> And Patrick said: "Do you believe that through baptism you cast off the sin of your father and mother?" They answered: "We believe." "Do you believe in penance after sin?" "We believe." "Do you believe in life after death? Do you believe in the resurrection on the day of judgement?" "We believe." "Do you believe in the unity of the church?" "We believe." And they were baptized, with a white garment over their heads. And they demanded to see the face of Christ, and the holy man said to them: "Unless you taste death you cannot see the face of Christ, and unless you receive the sacrament." And they answered: "Give us the sacrament so that we may see the Son, our bridegroom," and they received the eucharist of God and fell asleep in death, and their friends placed them on one bed and covered them with their garments, and made a great lament and great keening.[327]

This is a very early Irish text that refers to the practice of giving Communion with baptism. However, given the details of this particular story, it might also be that the author considers this Communion to be the viaticum and not part of the baptismal rite.

The next important source is the rite of baptism in the *Stowe Missal*. Here the Communion of the infants forms part of the rite of baptism. Immediately after the *Pedilavium*,[328] *Stowe* continues:

> The Body and Blood of our Lord Jesus Christ: may it avail to you unto eternal life.
>
> Refreshed with spiritual food, restored with the heavenly food of the Body and Blood of the Lord, let us give due praise and thanks to our Lord Jesus Christ, and ask his unwearied mercy that we may possess the sacrament of the divine gift unto the increase of faith and the advancement of eternal salvation. Through . . .[329]

Here it is clear that the Eucharist is an integral part of baptism; indeed coming at the end of the rite, it could be interpreted to be the crowning moment of the ceremony. And, indeed, based on the fact that at this time baptism was normally administered to infants, it is clear that this rite foresees infants receiving Communion.[330]

The *Mass Tract* of the *Stowe Missal* also mentions children receiving Communion. The instructions for the breaking of the host say: "the upper right-hand [portion], to innocent youths."[331] Centuries later, Gille of Limerick recommends that the priest "ought to give communion to the baptised immediately."[332]

But eventually this developed into a theological problem. On the one hand, the Communion of infants was gradually removed from the rite of baptism;[333] on the other hand, some theologians maintained that, if a baptized child died without having received Communion, that child could not enter heaven.[334] There are traces of this discussion in Ireland. The *Corpus Missal* contains a rite of baptism that has no trace of the infant's receiving Communion.[335]

It seems that this Communion of infants was not suddenly omitted from baptismal rituals in Ireland, but that the gradual omission caused some discussion (perhaps between the Gaelic-Irish and the Hiberno-Vikings, who may have been closer to English practice). In 1080/81 Lanfranc answers a question on this matter posed by Bishop Domhnall Ua hÉnna:

You may be assured that it is absolutely beyond question that neither the continental churches nor we English hold the view that you think we hold concerning infants. We do all universally believe that it is of great benefit to the people of all ages to fortify themselves by receiving the body and blood of the Lord during their lives and when they are dying. But should it happen that baptized infants leave this world at once, before they receive the body and blood of Christ, we do not in any sense believe—God forbid!—that on this account they are lost for eternity. Were that so, the Truth would be untrue in saying, "He who has believed and been baptized shall be saved." And according to the prophet, "I shall pour water upon you and you will be cleansed from all your filthiness." All the commentators on this passage are unanimous in maintaining that it refers to baptism. The Apostle Peter says, "Now baptism, which follows a similar pattern, saves you also." The Apostle Paul says, "As many of you as have been baptised in Christ have put on Christ." To "put on Christ" is to have God dwelling in you through the remission of sins. For that text which the Lord utters in the Gospel, "Unless you shall eat the flesh of the Son of Man and drink his blood, you will not have life in you," cannot be applied to all men universally in the sense of eating in the mouth. Many of the holy martyrs, racked by various tortures, departed from the body without even being baptized. Yet the church reckons them to be saved, following the Lord's assurance that "He who shall confess me before men, him will I confess also before my father who is in heaven." Again canon law directs that an unbaptised infant at the point of death be baptized by a lay believer if no priest is available; nor does it cut him off from the community of the faithful if he dies immediately after. Therefore the Lord's saying must be understood in this way. Let every believer who can understand what is a divine mystery eat and drink the flesh and blood of Christ not only with his physical mouth but also with a tender and loving heart: that is to say, with love and in the purity of a good conscience rejoicing that Christ took on flesh for our salvation, hung on the cross, rose and ascended; and following Christ's example and sharing in his suffering so far as human weakness can bear it and divine grace deigns to allow him.[336]

Here it seems that the practice of not including Communion was causing some doubts in Ireland. Lanfranc gives a very reasonable answer, and, while he certainly does not condemn the practice of infants receiving Communion, neither does he recommend that this practice be adopted where it has already been omitted.

This is one of the few cases for which we have a Scottish parallel. A letter survives from Pope Paschal II to Bishop Turgot of the Scots. Here Paschal answers a number of questions asked at the request of King Alexander, including one about infant Communion. The letter probably dates to about 1112–14. It was originally a cover letter accompanying a (now lost) book. Speaking on infant Communion, Pope Paschal says:

> From ancient times the Roman church has given the Body and Blood to those capable of receiving them. To those not capable [of receiving them] an infusion of the Blood alone is given to revive and conserve them. Therefore what the Lord said in the Gospel, "unless you eat my flesh and drink my blood you do not have life within you," applies only to those who are capable [of receiving them].[337]

Here the pope seems to advocate that infants be given Communion in the form of a drop from the chalice as they were "not capable" of receiving in the normal way (that is, the eucharistic bread).[338]

CHAPTER THREE

Archaeological and
Iconographic Sources

It would be easy to reduce the study of the Eucharist in pre-Norman Ireland to a study of those surviving texts that deal with the Eucharist. Obviously texts are of primary importance, but even different eucharistic liturgies celebrated using the same ritual text can be vastly different. As an illustration of this, we can note that the four hundred years after the liturgical renewal of the Council of Trent was the period in the church's history that saw the least change and greatest uniformity in the liturgical texts dealing with the celebration of the Eucharist. Yet one recent history of the liturgy in this time has as its central historical thesis "that the worship life of Roman Catholicism was in constant transition during this period despite the intransigence of liturgical texts."[1]

Today, any study of the Eucharist in pre-Norman Ireland can, and indeed must, benefit from the multitude of studies being carried out in the fields of archaeology, the history of architecture, and art history that have flourished in recent years. This chapter surveys the vast corpus of work being carried out in these fields and relates it directly to the eucharistic practice of the pre-Norman Irish church. As the physical setting of the liturgy is of such great importance, we will start by looking at the church buildings in use in Ireland in this period and then give an introduction to the stational dimension of the eucharistic liturgy in pre-Norman Ireland. The second part of the chapter examines surviving eucharistic vessels and other physical objects associated with the eucharistic liturgy and devotion. Obviously it is impossible to make a clear-cut distinction between textual and physical sources, so I have reserved textual treatment of church buildings for this chapter. Also, once again, the closer one gets to the Norman arrival, the more physical evidence pertaining to eucharistic practice remains.

THE ARCHITECTURAL SETTING FOR THE CELEBRATION OF THE EUCHARIST IN PRE-NORMAN IRELAND

CHURCH CONSTRUCTION

The principal function of a church is to be a building where the Eucharist may be celebrated (although throughout this period it was also common for the liturgy of the hours to be celebrated in churches). Within the Roman empire, church buildings had taken on the form of existing buildings: houses and temples were converted into Christian churches, and finally the basilica was adopted for Christian use.[2] But Ireland was not part of this empire, and it is hard to say much about the architectural setting of the first eucharistic liturgies celebrated during the evangelization of Ireland.[3] While, particularly in recent years, many new investigations have been carried out on early Irish churches, nonetheless it is still the case that much study needs to be done.[4]

In his *Irish Churches and Monastic Buildings*, the erstwhile standard work on Irish ecclesiastical architecture, Leask states that the principal characteristic of early Irish ecclesiastical construction is the "well-authenticated tradition that timber was the material normally used for several centuries by the Irish in church building."[5] Stone churches were typically seen by Leask (and the many scholars who follow his theories) as a particular adaptation made by those building on the "exposed and treeless coast lands of Ireland, remote from the woodlands of the interior."[6] But this view is not completely accurate: although wooden churches were to remain the majority throughout the pre-Norman period, there are also many examples of stone churches, and the annals give examples of stone being used for construction of churches even in places with no shortage of wood.[7] By the tenth and eleventh centuries (well before the Norman period), there was a wide distribution of stone churches even in areas where wood was plentiful.[8]

Nonetheless, timber and a type of wattle were the materials used in secular construction in Ireland,[9] and this style of construction was to be predominantly used in the construction of churches in pre-Norman Ireland.[10] Typically, a building was outlined with wooden posts; these were joined together by woven reeds, and the result was probably plastered in clay. Due to the perishable nature of the materials little remains today of these structures.[11] It is unclear whether churches were built using wooden posts and reeds, wooden boards, or, more likely, a combination of both styles; perhaps more important churches were built of boards while lesser ones of posts and reeds. Archaeology has not been able to add much light to this problem: post holes are the predominant remaining trace of these buildings, and excavations have not been able to discover if these posts had been joined together with reeds and plaster or whether boards were attached to the posts. Additionally, even though some of the ancient texts do mention the use of tree trunks and boards, the textual evidence is far from clear. Because it has little bearing on our subject, I use the traditional designation of "wooden churches" to refer to both possibilities.

In pre-Christian Ireland, houses were normally round, unlike houses in contemporary Britain, Scandinavia, and the Continent. The first churches were always rectangular, however, and this new form eventually took root in most domestic architecture.[12] The adoption of the rectangular shape may have been a positive decision on the part of the first Christian missionaries in Ireland to use the form to which they were accustomed or may have been a more negative decision to reject the round shape used in Irish construction, which may have held some pagan associations.

From a textual point of view, there are two significant literary witnesses to wooden churches being a typical Irish practice. The first of these is from Bede:

[Finan] constructed a church on the Island of Lindisfarne suitable for an episcopal see, building it after the Irish method, not of stone, but of hewn oak, thatching with reeds; later on the most reverend Archbishop Theodore consecrated it in honour of the blessed Apostle Peter. It was Eadbert, who was Bishop of Lindisfarne, who removed the thatch and had the whole of it, both roof and walls, covered with sheets of lead.[13]

In a later period St Bernard applauds the young St Malachy, who built a church of "polished boards, firmly and tightly fastened together— an Irish work finely wrought."[14] However, further on in the same work Bernard reports how Malachy ran afoul of his monastic community at Bangor, who reacted to his proposal to build a stone church with the rejoinder that they were "Irishmen not Frenchmen."[15]

It may be worth noting that the two main textual references to wood being the typical Irish construction material come from the English Bede and the French Bernard, both of whom need to portray elements of Irish ecclesial practice as suspect to further their own theological goals. While we don't know why the Irish retained the use of wood in the construction of their churches, it is certain that the reason was not because pre-Norman Irish church-builders were incapable of building elaborate stone buildings.[16] The practice of wooden churches probably started with the initial Christian missionaries in Ireland who, mainly for logistical reasons, would have been hard pressed to secure the construction of churches in any other material. The general retention of wood in later centuries may be attributed to a number of factors, including simple inertia. The traditional construction methods were easier and cheaper than using stone. Perhaps the slow adoption of stone churches was influenced by the fact that, as we have seen earlier, the pastoral care of a number of churches was occasionally provided by a single cleric and the celebration of the Eucharist was sometimes considered more important than the physical attendance of the laity at that service. If few people actually attended the Eucharist, there would have been less of an impetus to build stone churches, as the traditional wooden churches were cheaper to construct. Moreover, it is also probable that the continued use of wood was a matter of tradition in at least some centers: desiring to preserve the spirit of the earlier generations of founding saints, later ecclesiastics continued to use wood as a construction material. Indeed, when earlier churches were replaced by stone structures, there was an evident concern to maintain the form and original outlines of the earlier structures.[17] Archaeologists have found at least "five instances where traces of wooden structures have been uncovered beneath stone churches."[18]

While there are some early stone churches, the incidence of stone churches becomes greater the nearer one gets to the Norman arrival. Again, this is probably attributable to a variety of factors. Undoubtedly there was a desire on the part of some ecclesiastics to follow Continental models. On a practical level, although stone is a more expensive material, it is also more durable,[19] and the building of a stone church could have sent a message to others in the competitive struggles between ecclesiastical and civil leaders: as we saw in chapter 1, the construction of churches played a role in the ecclesiastical politics of the eleventh and twelfth centuries. Another possible factor that contributed to the adoption of stone churches might be a pragmatic response to a scarcity of large oaks at the beginning of the tenth century, as recent studies in dendrochronology have shown.[20]

Although there are few archaeological remains of Irish wooden churches, we do have some textual evidence of them (although, unlike the texts seen above, these attribute no particular significance to the use of wood). An oft-quoted seventh-century text from Cogitosus's *Life of St Brigit* describing the cathedral church of Kildare is of the greatest importance:

> Neither should one pass over in silence the miracle wrought in the repairing of the church in which the glorious bodies of both—namely Archbishop Conleth and our most flourishing virgin Brigit—are laid on the right and left of the ornate altar and rest in tombs adorned with a refined profusion of gold, silver, gems and precious stones with gold and silver chandeliers hanging from above and different images presenting a variety of carvings and colours.

Thus, on account of the growing number of the faithful of both sexes, a new reality is born in an age-old setting, that is a church with its spacious site and its awesome height towering upwards. It is adorned with painted pictures and inside there are three chapels which are spacious and divided by board walls under the single roof of the cathedral church. The first of these walls, which is painted with pictures and covered with wall hangings, stretches width wise in the east part of the church from one wall to the other. In it there are two doors, one at either end, and through the door situated on the right, one enters the sanctuary to the altar where the archbishop offers the Lord's sacrifice together with his monastic chapter and those appointed to the sacred mysteries. Through the other door, situated on the left side of the aforesaid cross-wall, only the abbess and her nuns and faithful widows enter to partake of the banquet of the body and blood of Jesus Christ.

The second of these walls divides the floor of the building into two equal parts and stretches from the west wall to the wall running across the church. This church contains many windows and one finely wrought portal on the right side through which the priests and the faithful of the male sex enter the church, and a second portal on the left side through which the nuns and congregation of women faithful are accustomed to enter. And so, in one vast basilica, a large congregation of people of varying status, rank, sex and local origin, with partitions placed between them, prays to the omnipotent Master, differing in status, but one in spirit.[21]

Although this may be the most complete literary description of a pre-Norman Irish church, it needs to be noted that this was not a typical church. It was a major cathedral church, and the description comes from a time when Kildare was competing with Armagh for primacy of the whole Irish church. Cogitosus composed his *Vita Brigitae* as part of this campaign. Unfortunately today there are no archaeological remains of the church described by Cogitosus (a Church of Ireland cathedral now stands on the traditional site). While there was an obvious interest on Cogitosus's part to emphasize the grandeur of the cathedral of Kildare, he was probably correct in his description of the extending and modification of the monastic church to accommodate the great number of the faithful and to house the relics of the two saints. These relics were particularly important in contrast to Armagh, which did not possess the body of Patrick.[22] It is likewise very important to consider whether this church in Kildare was thronged with multitudes of local lay folk on every Sunday and feast day or whether such crowds traveled to Kildare on the feast of St Brigit (as described in this text) only to participate in a pilgrimage and a type of stational liturgy culminating in one of their periodic but rare receptions of Communion.

Another textual description of an early wooden church comes from the *Hisperica Famina*. This is a very complicated work that still poses many unanswered questions. It seems that it comes from an Irish milieu and was probably a text associated with a Christian school. It contains many obscure words and may have had its value as a compilation of difficult words and phrases for the student to master. It seems to have been written some time between the mid-sixth to the mid-seventh century.[23] The text does not form a coherent whole, but rather is made up of individual pieces. One of these deals with a church:

> This wooden oratory is fashioned out of candle-shaped beams;
> it has sides joined by four-fold fastenings;
> the square foundations of the said temple give it stability,
> from which springs a solid beamwork of massive enclosure;
> it has a vaulted roof above;
> square beams are placed in the ornamented roof.
> It has a holy altar in the centre,
> on which the assembled priests celebrate the Mass.
> It has a single entrance from the western boundary,
> which is closed by a wooden door that seals the warmth.
> An assembly of planks comprises the extensive portico;
> there are four steeples at the top.
> The chapel contains innumerable objects,
> which I shall not struggle to unroll from my wheel of words.[24]

While this is an interesting text, it is hard to interpret, and other than giving clear testimony to the use of wood as a building material, it adds little to our knowledge. Herren's translation would suggest a large wooden building with the altar in the "center" and having four steeples. However, this is not the only interpretation. Niall Brady points out that center need not be the "geometrical center" but could refer, rather, "to anywhere on the central axis."[25] He also posits that the building may be on the same scale as the cathedral in Kildare and that the four "steeples" would be better understood as the *finials* which are at the terminals of some stone churches and in some representations of churches, such as the illustration of the Temptation of Christ in the *Book of Kells* (fol. 202v) where the Jewish Temple in Jerusalem seems to be modeled after a contemporary Irish wooden church (figure 2).[26]

Churches are often mentioned in the annals, the four main words being used in them are *oratorium, dairthech, damliac,* and *teampall* (the first two usually refer to a wooden church and the second two to stone churches).[27] Unfortunately most English translations of the annals mistranslate some of these words; in particular *dairthech* is translated as "oratory," which gives the false impression that these were small structures, which was not necessarily the case. In his analysis of these references in the annals, Conleth Manning reaches the conclusion that prior to 1060 the majority of churches mentioned were wooden whereas from 1060 to 1170 most were made of stone.[28] Care needs to be taken, however, in assigning too rigid an interpretation to these terms over the centuries. It could well be the case, for example, that *dairthech* might have lost its wooden connotation in later texts and may well simply mean church.

The entry for the year 850 in the *Annals of Ulster* provides a significant literary reference to a large wooden church:

> Cinaed son of Conaing, king of Cianacht, rebelled against Mael Sechnaill with the support of the foreigners, and plundered the Uí Néill from the Sinann to the sea, both churches and states, and he deceitfully sacked the island of Loch Gabor, levelling it to the ground, and the oratory of Treóit, with two hundred and sixty people in it, was burned by him.[29]

In order to fit 260 people in the church, even if they were huddled together so that the church would have been fuller than at a normal eucharistic celebration, the church "must have measured at least 12 meters by 8 meters, and probably much more."[30] While there is little archaeological evidence for the size of the wooden churches, a Middle Irish manuscript, probably dating to the end of our period when stone churches were more common, "establishes a rate of payment for construction of a *dairthech* or wooden church based on its width, starting with a base design of 10 feet working up to a large church, defined as more than 15 feet wide."[31] No matter how we interpret these texts, they do give the impression that an early Irish wooden church could be something bigger than is often imagined.[32]

As virtually no trace remains of the pre-Norman wooden structures, archaeological inquiry has concentrated on the stone churches. The early single-celled churches seem to have exhibited very little variety in their construction so that "most stone churches of the pre-Romanesque age must have looked remarkably similar,"[33] being built as single-chambered structures, oftentimes with a length to breath ratio of between 1:1.4 and 1:1.7 (and very occasionally of 1.5:1).[34] A famous example of this type of church built in the corbelling technique is Gallarus Oratory on the Dingle Peninsula, Co. Kerry (figure 1). While it is hard to know about the interior decoration of pre-Romanesque Irish churches, there is no early evidence of internal stone sculpture.[35]

The most famous and, incidentally, the largest surviving church from early Ireland is the so-called cathedral of Clonmacnoise, Co. Offaly. The present structure is a simple rectangular church, with internal measurements of 18.8 meters by 8.7 meters, and with a sacristy on the south side.[36] The church has been rebuilt on a number of occasions, and it seems that the original church was slightly wider than the modern one so that the west doorway would not have been off-center as it is today.[37] Due to the absence of surviving features, it is hard to give it any definite date. Documentary sources point to the early tenth century.[38] This building is large enough for a fair-sized congregation, and the structure would not have been very out of place on the Continent. It has been recently estimated that another early medieval church located at Lorrha, Co. Tipperary (figure 18), could have comfortably held a congregation of two hundred people.[39]

When looking at the remains of Irish churches from this period, there is a danger of, almost unconsciously, comparing the present-day remains with those of England or the Continent and being unduly influenced by the fact that the Irish remains are usually smaller than these others.[40] But a typical sub-Roman church in western Britain or Gaul would not have been very different from a typical Irish church, which would have mirrored both the size and simplicity of the sub-Roman examples.[41] This is, in fact, supported by an analysis of the actual Irish church buildings that remain from this period, whose dimensions are typical of contemporary England.[42] The main differences perceptible by today's visitors can be attributed to the fact that many of the Irish churches are older than the ecclesiastical sites—both in Britain and on the Continent—that remained in active use for centuries longer than the Irish ones and were enlarged and modified after the twelfth century.

It could also be pointed out that churches that later became parish churches tended to be bigger than those that eventually fell out of use, and that, on average, the remains of stone churches on islands off the Irish coast and in lakes are half the size of those on the mainland, again pointing to the factor of pastoral use increasing the size of the structure.[43] Although we have already nuanced Sharpe's view of Ireland as having "the most comprehensive pastoral organizations in Northern Europe,"[44] nonetheless he is to be credited with drawing attention to the fact that there were a good number of churches in use throughout this period. These preexisting buildings would have discouraged newer constructions. It is also unclear whether the early churches could be classed as parish churches in the later sense that the entire local populace was required to actually attend the Sunday eucharistic celebration.[45] The textual evidence examined earlier paints a picture of little popular attendance at the typical Sunday eucharistic celebration juxtaposed with a strong desire in the legal texts for the physical presence of a church with a priest carrying out the required liturgies in each *túath*. This desire for a local religious center where the liturgy was celebrated, combined with a low population density and a lack of towns, could also have discouraged the construction of newer, bigger churches as was happening in other parts of the West.

In contrast, later on in the late eleventh and early twelfth centuries many churches with coeval naves and chancels were built, and at this time chancels were also added to older churches.[46] The fact that earlier churches did not have a separate chancel was not due to any architectural problems in their construction. Their introduction at this time was for some other reason and may have been influenced by a desire to bring the spatial setting of the liturgy more into line with Continental practices; it could also be symptomatic of a new emphasis of actual regular attendance to the Eucharist by the laity.[47] It is not my contention that prior to the construction of bicameral churches that the laity remained outside the church. I propose that when they did attend they were present inside the single-celled church building along with the clerics. However, in the normal course of events few laity attended (the *Old Irish Mass Tract* of the *Stowe Missal* gives a maximum of sixty-five communicants at important eucharistic celebrations). The advent of bicameral churches could signify a number of things: it is quite possible that more of the laity were now attending the Sunday Eucharist; perhaps it indicates a new concept of division between the clerics and laity (coming from Continental practice) whereby the laity could no longer stand close to the altar, which meant a physical restructuring of the liturgical space; or it could indicate a different use of liturgical space and the transfer of stational liturgical processions from outside the church to within; and it is more than likely that it was due to some combination of all of these factors.

A major change in Irish church architecture prior to the Norman arrival was the introduction of the Romanesque style. "Romanesque" is a concept developed about two hundred years ago to describe the work of Western European artists and masons in the eleventh and twelfth centuries.[48] Irish Romanesque is not a homogeneous style but rather comprises a combination of stylistic elements from Hiberno-Viking, English, and Continental Romanesque, as well as older native traditions.[49] There was a building boom in twelfth-century Ireland making use of this style, perhaps given its impetus by the Synod of Kells (1152).[50] Until recently most commentators, following Leask and Henry, believed that Cormac's Chapel on the Rock of Cashel was the source of the Irish Romanesque style and that German, or German-trained, masons built something so radically different from everything else that it served as the single exemplar for the Irish Romanesque style. Today this earlier theory is no longer accepted, and Cormac's Chapel is seen as being more of an oddity rather than a typical church for the period. A number of other theories have been advanced about the origins of Irish Romanesque that trace it to contacts with the English North Country or France.[51]

O'Keeffe points out the connection between the emergence of this style and the struggles surrounding the solidification of the twelfth-century diocesan structure.[52] These new churches were in stone and not wood, and often built on a grander scale than earlier churches—although this grandeur tended to be more in style and embellishments, as the actual dimensions of many Hiberno-Romanesque churches were more or less the same as their predecessors.[53] One of the notable characteristics of the Irish Romanesque style is the importance that it places on doorways and portals, so that often there is a very ornate doorway on a plain wall (the best among many examples is Clonfert cathedral).[54]

While these embellished portals might have been installed during the interchurch struggles to support claims for diocesan status in the eleventh and twelfth centuries, it would be too limited a view to consider this style to be simply an architectural folly created for power-hungry kings and ecclesiastics who desired that their own *túath* have an episcopal see for sociopolitical and economic reasons. Although these were undoubtedly factors in Irish Romanesque church construction, once again it must be pointed out that these churches were built to be churches and not just show pieces: their primary purpose remained to have the Eucharist celebrated in them. The grandeur of the rites celebrated in them was reflected in the architectural style. In this time, the liminal boundaries were transferred to the church itself. The low earthen or stone walls that enclose the earlier ecclesiastical sites are sometimes absent from this style, and the portal assumes a clearer iconic role as the focus for processions, perhaps incorporating some processional dimension of the liturgy within the church building as opposed to an earlier use of stational movement throughout the ecclesiastical complex. The Irish Romanesque churches are generally bicameral structures with highly decorated archways separating the sanctuary from the nave. This style probably emphasized a liminal eucharistic boundary between the clerics and laity.

Despite the similarities, Continental and English churchmen coming to Ireland in the twelfth century were struck by the differences in architecture in general and not just ecclesiastical architecture.[55] The Cistercians, arriving in Ireland a few decades before the Norman invasion, constituted a type of religious colonization. They did not simply introduce a new style of architecture or the *Rule of St Benedict,* but a complete way of living monastic life.[56] On the level of architectural style, the Cistercians were by far the most significant innovators in Ireland. They introduced churches, cloisters, and monasteries that were much more in keeping with Continental and English Cistercian style. The fact that St Bernard sent the French monk Robert to oversee the construction of the new monastery at Mellifont is an important indicator of the importance that the Cistercians placed on architectural unity. It is, perhaps, no coincidence that Mellifont, the first Cistercian foundation in Ireland, came to be known as *an Mainistir Mór,* or the Great Monastery.[57] This church contained at least nine side altars: in its account of the consecration of the church of Mellifont, the *Annals of the Four Masters* tell that Derbforgaill "the wife of O'Ruairc, the daughter of Ua Maeleachlainn, gave as much more, and a chalice of gold on the altar of Mary, and cloth for each of the nine other altars that were in that church."[58] Irish Cistercian style developed some of its own characteristics, partly due to local conditions and economic constraints, but also due to a less than rigorous concern for a strict interpretation of the Cistercian architectural canon.[59] Indeed, on the architectural level this Cistercian form of monasticism was not always successful, and not everybody was impressed by the magnificence of the Cistercian monasteries. One of the abuses that Stephen of Lexington encountered in his 1228 visitation of the Irish Cistercian monasteries was that "few [of the monks] are living in community, but they live in miserable huts outside the cloister in groups of threes or fours."[60] While on occasion he complains against this abuse, he himself seems to have been convinced of the appropriateness of it in some cases and recommended dispensation for certain monks to live outside the monastery.[61]

On the other hand, the *Rule of St Augustine,* also introduced into Ireland by St Malachy, brought something of mainstream Western religious life without the colonial cultural package.[62] While many of these monasteries were established (or native communities were re-established as Augustinian canons), there was no particular architectural importation, and the earliest surviving Augustinian churches do not have any set architectural identity.[63] But stress must be laid on the importance given to continuity by all those who founded new monastic and other ecclesiastical sites in the post-Norman period. Tadhg O'Keeffe points out that "of some 160 buildings or building fragments known to me, 13 per cent were cathedrals, another 13 per cent were associated with reformed monastic orders other than the Cistercians, and virtually all (95 per cent) are on sites with histories of Christian use stretching back before the twelfth century."[64]

Later on, the twelfth-century reform would usher in the construction of bigger churches (along with city living, a higher population density, and a new emphasis on actual church attendance). Whatever arguments are made for earlier Irish churches being bigger than is often credited, it is undeniable that after the twelfth century church size did increase, in some cases dramatically so. Apart from the abbeys of the newly introduced Cistercian order, recent studies have also pointed out the possibility of a Viking influence in the increase in church size, as late eleventh-century examples of churches in the Hiberno-Viking port towns tend to be bigger than the native Irish counterparts.[65]

ROUND TOWERS

Many early Irish ecclesiastical sites possess a round tower (for an example, see figure 20). To this day many still stand in various states of repair and, counting both extant and documented round towers, we know that at least one hundred once existed in Ireland.[66] Unfortunately, the early sources do not say much about these buildings and their function. The documentary sources tell us that they were built during a three-hundred-year period from the start of the tenth to the end of the twelfth centuries (therefore straddling the Irish Romanesque period). This form seems to be uniquely Irish as, apart from two Scottish examples and one on the Isle of Man (both areas under a heavy Irish influence), there exist no such buildings anywhere else.[67] There is no indication where the first round tower was built, but it is possible that a prestigious exemplar existed in one of the famous monasteries and that the form was copied from there.[68] As the round towers are by far the tallest buildings from pre-Norman Ireland, and had they been built to even half the height they would still have been comparatively much higher than everything else, it would seem that the average height of 97 feet (29.53 m) of the still-complete towers might suggest a desire to reach 100 feet as a symbolic number. The fact that the round tower at Glendalough is exactly 100 feet tall and has a circumference of 50 feet 2 inches is unlikely to be a coincidence.[69]

Round towers have always evoked the fascination of scholars, and in the nineteenth century a number of bizarre theories for their function were advanced, including the theory that they were actually remnants of sun temples from the druids where a perpetual fire was kept burning to the sun god.[70] But since the work of George Petrie in the mid-nineteenth century there has been a more rational approach to the study of round towers. Petrie showed how these buildings had an ecclesiastical origin and proposed that they were bell-towers based on their designation in the annals as *cloigtheach,* or bell-house.[71]

The annals are the main contemporary source for information on the round towers: they contain twenty-five references to events relating to the round towers.[72] But these remain silent as to their exact function. They record the destruction or other tragedies associated with towers, along with notes on the construction and dedication of others. The following entry is typical:

> The bell-house of Sláine was burned by the foreigners of Áth Cliath. The founder's episcopal staff, and the best of all bells, the lector Caenachair and a large number with him, were *all* burned.[73]

Announcements like this, combined with the fact that the round towers made their debut at roughly the same time as the first activity of

the Vikings in Ireland, led many scholars to make a connection between them. The theory was that the Irish monasteries devised the
round tower as a variant on the Continental bell-tower in answer to
raids by marauding Vikings. These towers were purportedly used as
watchtowers with a sentry positioned with a bell. When he saw the
approaching Viking longships, he would ring the bell. The monks
then would take refuge in the tower along with their most precious
treasures. The Vikings who could only stay a limited time away from
their ships would be unable to get into the tower as the door was
raised from the ground.[74]

If this is the case, then there is only a marginal connection between
the round towers and the Eucharist. Today, however, there are some
challenges to the accepted theory. The first problem is with the bells
themselves: while we possess over seventy bells from the period
of the early Irish church, and hagiography and sculpture point out that
these are essential elements for an Irish monastic founder, these bells
have never been associated with bell-ringing activities in the round
towers. The extant bells were made before the towers were built, they
are very small for conceivable use at the top of a round tower, and, indeed, they bear little marks of any use at all. Stalley has claimed that
perhaps the towers had hanging bells.[75] While this is possible, and there
is probably some relationship between the round towers and bells
based on the etymological root of *cloigtheach,* O'Keeffe points out
that there is no textual, architectural, nor archaeological evidence that
supports the traditional theory or Stalley's variation thereof.[76]

O'Keeffe proposes that these towers were used as a part of the
ritual space of major ecclesiastical sites. These towers appear first in
the early tenth century and seem usually to have two associations:
royalty and relics. We are told of kings being killed in these towers
and of relics being destroyed there. This information fits well with the
traditional view of these towers as defense sites. However, it is also
possible that the towers were in fact a type of church or shrine that
were used as part of the stational liturgy where the relics could have
been displayed.[77] The position of the towers is often in relation to
the main church in some ecclesiastical complexes, and they probably
were used in some form of stational liturgy.[78] The towers, then, could

have been a place of legal sanctuary rather than actual fortification. This would offer an alternative explanation for both the destruction of relics and the killing of people in the various raids: rather than providing physical refuge, they provided legal and spiritual sanctuary (albeit unsuccessfully in the incidents noted in the annals).[79]

The idea of the round tower as a church may seem strange at first sight. Most dwellings in pre-Christian Ireland, whether of the rich in crannogs or ringforts, or of the poor in palisaded or open settlements, were in the form of round houses.[80] We have seen above how the first Irish churches rejected the traditional round shape in favor of a rectangular form. But by the tenth century when the first round towers were being built it could well be that whatever cultural problems suggested by the use of round buildings for the eucharistic liturgy were no longer an issue in the programming of a new type of ecclesial building.[81]

O'Keeffe has suggested that the Eucharist may have been celebrated at the summit of the round towers.[82] A possible parallel can be found in the contemporary church of St Gall in France, where there are records of two round towers with altars to the archangels St Michael and St Gabriel. While the form of these towers bears no resemblance to the Irish round towers, and there is no known connection between these towers and Ireland, nonetheless, this does show that in other parts of the Christian West the idea of altars in towers did occur.[83] Still, while this is an attractive theory, and the round towers may well have played a role in a stational liturgy at early church sites, the possibility that the Eucharist was celebrated in them remains a tentative theory, and it would be premature to accept this theory of O'Keeffe while rejecting the majority opinion of the round towers being a variant on the belfry.[84]

ALTARS

The altar is the central, and indeed often the only, furnishing in the typical church. The first Christian altars were probably small, and they may well have been portable. The earliest iconography often portrays the altar as a very small, three-legged table barely big enough to hold the bread and chalice. But it seems that stone altars were to re-place these earlier structures (which were made of wood or metal) very soon after the edict of Milan. The use of stone altars may have come from the cult of the martyrs: there is archaeological evidence that the tomb of St Peter in the Vatican had a stone altar as early as the third century. As the church was to emerge triumphantly in the fourth century, the tombs of the martyrs became focuses of popular devo-tion, and relatively small stone altars became part of the shrines built over these tombs. In the fifth century, the custom of having stone al-tars was transferred to the church, often accompanied by the transfer of the actual body of the martyr, or with the development of a church over the tomb. In the sixth century, the altar began to occupy a defi-nite place in the spirituality of Christians as being the most sacred part of the church; and in the churches that were built at this time, the altar began to become physically distant from the faithful.[85]

In Ireland it is probable that, in common with the churches that housed them, the first altars would have been simple affairs. The earli-est examples may have been made entirely of wood or have only had a small altar stone integrated into a wooden altar. During the fifth and sixth centuries, as Christianity was being introduced into Ireland, some of the more important Continental churches had developed elaborate frontals to give the altar grandeur,[86] but it is unlikely that style would initially have been possible in Ireland. Nonetheless, later on, given the elaborate eucharistic vessels and manuscripts in use in pre-Norman Ireland, it is not impossible that there would have been similarly elaborate altar frontals.[87] Another phenomenon that was probably present in Ireland was the use of the portable altar.[88] When archaeologists examined the tomb of St Cuthbert in England, they discovered a small, portable, seventh-century altar that had been cov-ered in silver in the mid-eighth century, as it was now a relic of the saint and was later placed in his tomb. The altar itself was small, wooden, and inscribed on top with five crosses, one in the center and one at each corner. Along one side ran the inscription "In honour of St Peter."[89] One would imagine that the earliest Irish portable altars would have resembled this.[90]

While wooden altars were common enough until the Carolingian period throughout Europe, it would seem that the use of wooden altars continued in Ireland longer than it did in other areas. At the very end of our period, John Cumin, the first Norman archbishop of Dublin, held a diocesan synod there in 1186.[91] Evidence suggests that wooden altars were still in use in Dublin in the late twelfth century. The first canon

> Prohibits priests from celebrating Mass on wooden tables, according to the usage of Ireland; and enjoins that in all monasteries and baptismal churches altars should be made of stone; and if a stone of a sufficient size to cover the whole surface of the altar cannot be had; that in such a case a square entire and polished stone be fixed in the middle of the altar, where Christ's body is consecrated, of a compass broad enough to contain five crosses and the foot of the largest chalice. But in chapels, chantries or oratories if they are necessarily obliged to use wooden altars, let the Mass be celebrated on plates of stone, of the before-mentioned size, firmly fixed in the wood.[92]

It is interesting to note that a description of St Brigit's consecration as a virgin, written in the seventh century, makes reference to an altar remarkably similar to the one mandated for poorer churches by the 1186 synod: "Kneeling humbly before God and the bishop as well as before the altar and offering her virginal crown to almighty God, she touched the wooden base on which the altar rested."[93] In the parallel, mid-eighth-century *Vita Prima* of St Brigit, Brigit tells her nuns, "When I was a little girl, I made a stone altar as a child's game and the angel came and perforated the stone at the four corners and put four wooden legs under it."[94]

The *Leabhar Breac* contains a tractate on the consecration of a church that was probably composed in the present form in the eleventh or twelfth century.[95] Here the consecration of an altar is described:

> The first subdivision of the consecration of the Altar is this: the Host, the water and the wine are mixed together in one vessel, and consecrated according to the rite of consecration in the Bishop's Book. The reason why those three things are consecrated at first is because they are offered continually at the Mass.

The second subdivision that grows out of the Altar is the consecration of the Table of the Altar itself. The Bishop himself marks four
crosses with his knife on the four corners of the Altar, and he marks
three crosses over the middle of the Altar, namely, a cross over the
middle on the east at its edge, and a cross over the middle on the west
at its edge, and a cross over the middle on the west at its edge [*sic*], and
a cross over the centre. And he washes the Table of the Altar down
with the water and with the wine and with the Host. And he spills
what remains of the water round the base, and wipes the Altar with
his small linen cloth until it is dry, and he kindles incense in the small
vessel on the Altar, and he sings, "Let my prayer be set forth in thy
sight as the incense" down to "evening sacrifice," as it enumerates in
the Bishop's Book, and he anoints with consecrated oil the seven
crosses which he marked on the Altar and says [the prayer entitled]
"Anointing the Altar with holy oil," with the form which follows it in
the Bishop's Book.[96]

This is an interesting text, but it is not very clear. Some authors have
interpreted the use of a knife as proof that the altars were made of
wood.[97] However, if the altar was of stone, the bishop could be using
the knife to symbolically trace over the already existing grooves. Indeed, even if the altar was of wood (as may well have been the case)
it is unlikely that such an important feature would be chiseled out
by an untrained bishop during a complicated rite, rather than by an
expert carpenter either before or after the consecration. It is likewise
unclear whether the bread and wine used in the consecration of the
altar had themselves been previously consecrated in an earlier eucharistic celebration or whether they had been simply blessed. Finally,
this is the only pre-Norman Irish text that makes unambiguous reference to the use of incense.[98]

It is hard to say much more about Irish altars throughout this
period. One would imagine that the majority were fairly simple affairs inscribed by a number of crosses. Some priests may have brought
portable altars on their travels similar to that of St Cuthbert. But it
may also be the case that judging by the opulence of the contemporary eucharistic vessels and shrines some Irish altars may have been
covered with intricate decorated altar frontals. No metal ones survive

(if indeed, they ever existed), but there are at least five examples of decorated altar fronts from the Isle of Man, including the magnificent carving of the Calf of Man Crucifixion (figure 17).[99] These make present the cross of Christ as the central decoration of the altar, in tune with the medieval Western understanding of the Eucharist, which emphasizes the sacrifice of Christ on Calvary.

While there are no published findings of original altars within any pre-Norman Irish churches, recent archaeological work by Tomás Ó Carragáin claims that there may be some outdoor altars still in place. He gives a number of examples, the most important of which is the Ballydarrig example.

> In Ballydarrig townland near a now disused route to [Knockatober] summit is a massive, flat-topped, cross-inscribed boulder, which is best interpreted as an outdoor altar. The design on its upper surface is simple but meaningful. . . . In particular the line dividing the lower left-hand quadrant of the main cross-head into two segments may be a reference to the Eucharist, for the Stowe Missal specifies that before breaking the host for communion the priest must first break a piece from its lower left-hand quadrant in order to recall the wounding of Christ's side with a lance on Calvary.[100]

He also lists another nearby example:

> A parallel for the Ballydarrig boulder occurs in Drom West on the Dingle Peninsula. This massive boulder is (like Ballydarrig) not directly associated with a church settlement but it may have had a role in the Mt. Brandon pilgrimage, for it is quite near Cloghane church where the eastern pilgrimage route to the mountain's summit began. The rather crude design that occurs on one of its broad sides may represent an altar inscribed with the requisite central crosslet surrounded by four corner crosslets. A larger ringed cross seems to surmount the altar proper and its design is similar to that of the processional cross depicted on the base of the north cross at Aheny. It is tempting to see the seven small irregular shapes at the base of this cross and the eleven at the base of the design as representing particles of the host after the fraction.[101]

Assuming that these identifications are accurate, it is probable that these altars were used in connection with the pilgrimages to Mount Brandon and Knockatober. This identification would show that stone altars were used in Ireland and that the etching of crosses on these altars would be in keeping with typical practice elsewhere. A textual source that points to the practice of outdoor altars can be found in the *Book of Armagh:* when Patrick ordains Ailbe as a priest he "pointed out to him a marvellous stone altar on the mountain of the Uí Ailello, because he was among the Uí Ailello."[102] Perhaps this pre-ninth-century text is simply telling of the miraculous appearance of an altar. But it might also point to the use of ready-made boulders as outdoor altars. While intriguing, these altars are more than likely for exceptional use and would only have been used when a group of pilgrims was participating in a liturgy held to mark a special event such as the pilgrimage to various sites like Croagh Patrick and Mount Brandon on the last Sunday in July.[103]

MONASTIC "CITIES" AND STATIONAL LITURGY

In the first three centuries while Christianity remained an underground, albeit often tolerated, religion, there would have been few public manifestations of Christian worship. After the edict of Milan, however, pilgrimages to Jerusalem became popular, and crowds of Christians traveled there from all corners of the world. Many monastic communities developed there so that Christians could spend the rest of their days in the Holy Land. This led to the development of a particular style of liturgy whereby the holy places associated with the earthly life of Jesus became the stage for the liturgy. The liturgy of the day was celebrated in the particular holy place that was associated with that day's liturgical memorial so that the liturgy and its setting was always "suitable, appropriate, and relevant to what is being done."[104] This form of liturgy soon passed to Rome and Constantinople. The many shrines and tombs of saints and martyrs in these cities allowed the liturgy to "spill over" from the church building into the environs; thus by the seventh century the whole city of Rome was the "theatre du déploiement" for the liturgy.[105] This style of liturgy also allowed for a certain amount of unity in the diocese: there were many churches in Rome and it was impossible for all the Christians to gather at one place, so a sense of diocesan unity was fostered by the fact that on different set days the pope presided at these stational liturgies that took place at individual churches (or "stations").[106]

Little work has been done on stational liturgy apart from Baldovin's work on Rome, Jerusalem, and Constantinople. This way of celebrating the liturgy is important for the Irish context as it is probable that Irish ecclesiastics and returning pilgrims brought some elements of this liturgical style back to Ireland.[107] But it was not so simple as importing some liturgical texts from Rome because the practices of Roman stational liturgy envisioned a rich variety of major relics at the various stational churches and, more importantly, represented a particular type of urban religion that would not have been applicable in the sparsely populated pre-Norman Ireland. But the consideration of stational liturgy in Ireland may help to solve a problem in the study of this period: the case of "monastic cities." On the one hand, one finds occasional reference to monasteries as possible monastic cities in secondary literature; yet, on the other, this identification needs to be treated with care as none of the monastic centers has been able to provide documentary or archaeological evidence for its consideration as a city (or town, or big village) as would normally be understood.[108] In the early Middle Ages most people in Ireland lived in ring-forts and not in urban centers; indeed, prior to the arrival of the Vikings, there is no evidence of urban living in Ireland (and when the Vikings did found some settlements that were to grow into cities, Irishmen of the time were in no hurry to copy this style of living). I propose that the possibility of a stational liturgy in Ireland may provide a way to make sense of the sometimes-conflicting evidence regarding monastic cities and help in our understanding of the larger ecclesiastic sites.

Baldovin has pointed out that the Carolingian liturgy of Northern Europe was heavily influenced by hagiopolite and Roman practices and liturgical geography. And of all the various features of Roman liturgy the feature that was most impressive to Northern Europeans was "the centrality to it of processional movement." He also says that the structure of many medieval monastic churches with the multiplication of side-altars was, paradoxically, based on Roman stational liturgy, showing that the public liturgy *par excellence* was eventually transformed into the custom of private Masses.[109] But this particular development was not precsiely mirrored in Ireland, as massive churches were not constructed prior to the arrival of the Cistercians. Many of these sites do, however, contain a number of churches and other features that can be explained by thinking that the liturgy used to "spill out" of the bounds of the churches in a local form of stational liturgy. Given that Irish monks and scholars were involved in the Carolingian reform and that Adomnán wrote a famous account on the holy places, it is hardly any surprise to find evidence of a stational liturgy in Ireland adapted to the particular needs of that time and place.[110] We know that Rome, and its elaborate stational liturgy, also held its own appeal to some Irish ecclesiastics; for example, the *Vita Prima* of St Brigit states that St Brigit sent envoys to Rome to see how the Eucharist was celebrated there.[111] We know that some Irish ecclesiastics did travel to Rome, such as the delegation from the Synod of Mágh Léine, who were in Rome on Easter, 631, to have the decrees of the synod confirmed by the pope.[112]

When people visit an early Irish ecclesiastical site today, they are often impressed by the number of small churches and think this to be a particular Irish feature. But this is not true, because many contemporary English and Continental ecclesiastical centers would have also contained a multiplicity of smaller churches. The striking feature of the Irish examples is not their existence but that, unlike those foreign examples, they were not consolidated into a single large church with various side altars.[113] To understand these sites, it is first of all important to note that their layout is often influenced by the claim of some association with a founding saint. Although very little can be historically said of these saints, most are reputed to have lived in the fifth and sixth centuries. Excavations at church sites in Ireland, Wales, and Celtic Britain have shown that initially special graves of the founding saints were marked by early Christian inscribed stones. Prior to the Norman period, there was a reluctance in Wales to disturb the graves of the saints. This was not the case in Ireland, where by the seventh century saints' bodies were already being removed from their original graves and being treated as relics (at more or less the same time as the practice occurred in Rome).[114] But while the founders' graves may have been disturbed, there was, as has been seen above, a marked reverence for the physical structure of the churches.

The cult of the martyrs in particular had played an important role in the Christianization of the former Roman Empire. Martyrs took the place of the secular *patronus* but conferred spiritual rather than physical sustenance and protection.[115] In Ireland this experience was transferred to the founding saints of particular churches where, even after centuries, the head of that church's authority lay in the fact that he was the founder's *comarba,* or successor. Initially there is little evidence for local pilgrimages, but from the ninth century onwards the Irish church began to encourage local pilgrimages to places associated with the cult of important local saints.[116]

As these pilgrimages became popular, the commemoration of particular incidents in the lives of saints made up another important element in the sacred geography of ecclesiastical sites. The setting of the earthly life of the saint and his miracles became the focus for those who wished to obtain divine benefits from him in later times.[117] A twelfth-century vernacular life of St Columba provides a good example of the importance that the physical presence of the remains of holy founders had for an ecclesiastical site.

> The Colum Cille said to his company: "It would benefit us if our roots were put down into the ground here," and he said to them: "Someone among you should go down into the soil of the island to consecrate it." Then the obedient Odrán rose up and said: "If I be taken, I am prepared for it," said he. "Odrán," said Colum Cille, "you will be rewarded for it. No one will be granted his request at my own grave, unless he first seek it of you." Then Odrán went to heaven.[118]

These churches are scattered over a site in a seemingly random way, but in some cases the cell of the founder may have had a small oratory built over it,[119] and sometimes a special church for women was built a little apart from the other churches.[120] But it is hard to draw many conclusions as to the actual appearance of these sites, as the majority of the structures were built of perishable materials (and were never rebuilt in stone) and hence little evidence remains of them.[121]

Another way to approach an understanding of these centers is to look at the physical boundaries within the sites. Many early ecclesiastical sites are surrounded by a wall or earthen barrier that played an important liminal role in the sacred geography of these sites, as often these walls were too low to provide any real protection from attack.[122] In an archaeological survey of the Dingle Peninsula, a remote area in the southwestern corner of Ireland where there are many remains of early ecclesiastical sites, thirty such sites were identified where the church was surrounded by a wall or *termon* ranging between 30 meters and 70 meters in maximum dimension.[123] This evidence from the Dingle Peninsula is supported by a more general study of the larger ecclesiastical sites in early medieval Ireland.[124] Also, an analysis of modern aerial photography confirms this form of a church surrounded by a double enclosure (one around the church, the other around the site as a whole) and found "a marked consistency in dimension, layout, structures and features" in these sites.[125]

Looking at the smaller of the enclosures in many ecclesiastical sites, some scholars have proposed that the early unicameral churches may in fact have served as a sanctuary into which only the clerics entered while the laity attended the eucharistic celebration outside within the first wall.[126] While this theory might be intriguing, there is little hard evidence to back it up.[127] There may have been cases when the congregation was larger than the church could hold, and at such time some may have had to stay outside. This may have been the case in the text from Adomnán, for example, where the great Columba is celebrating in the company of three other founding saints, and more people may well have come than was normal.[128] This might also have been the case when the Eucharist was celebrated in the small chapels over the founder's grave on particular anniversaries. It may also have happened at larger churches on the occasion of popular pilgrimages for particular feast days when many people may have been present. But these are exceptional cases that still occur to this day;[129] I would maintain that the famous illustration of the Temptation of Christ of the *Book of Kells* (fol. 202v, shown in figure 2, and a detail of which is shown on the cover of this book) would portray such an exceptional instance where crowds of people are on either side of the church door as the priest comes out.

The study of the symbolic and special organization of these church sites is hampered by a lack of evidence. A recent work by Nicholas Aitchison has proposed a cosmological interpretation of these centers. However, his analysis tends to read a lot back into the pre-Christian past and posits a great symbolic role to the ancient division of Ireland into five provinces, claiming that this division is reflected in the architectural programming of Armagh in particular as well as other major sites. No matter how interesting these theories are, they are hard to sustain due to lack of clear evidence. Nonetheless, it may well be that in his analysis of the division of church sites, Aitchison is correct in attributing symbolic divisions to the enclosures and other features of the monasteries, such as high crosses and Cogitosus's literary references to the divisions of the church in Kildare.[130]

But the main reason that the sites boast more than one church is probably so that more than one Eucharist could be celebrated per day. Ancient tradition held that only one eucharistic liturgy could be celebrated per day on each altar,[131] and yet by the seventh and eighth centuries in the West many more monks were ordained to the priesthood so as to be able to meet the spiritual demands for more eucharistic celebrations.[132] The multiple Irish churches could be understood in this Western context. By the Carolingian period bigger churches were being built in Continental centers, yet in Ireland the tradition of several small churches remained, probably due to the veneration given to preserving the dimensions of the historic churches on sites that, by this stage, were associated with events of the founding saint's life.[133] An example of this is borne out by Skellig Michael, where a small monastic community built a number of churches that far exceeded their material needs for buildings to celebrate the Eucharist; given the inaccessibility of the island it is unlikely that large crowds of pilgrims were able to journey there even on particular holy days.[134]

Pilgrimage is another important point to be considered. Just because a site is large and we have records of large numbers of people attending the Eucharist there on some particular day does not necessarily mean that these people normally lived there. Cogitosus's mid-seventh-century description of St Brigit's monastery in Kildare is often used as an example of a monastic city:

> And who can express in words the exceeding beauty of this church and the countless wonders of the monastic city we are speaking of, if one may call it a city since it is not encircled by a surrounding wall.
>
> And yet, since numberless people assemble within it and since a city gets its name from the fact that many people congregate there, it is a vast and metropolitan city. In its suburbs, which saint Brigit had marked out by a definite boundary, no human foe or enemy attack is feared; on the contrary, together with all its outlaying suburbs it is the safest city of refuge in the whole land of the Irish for all its fugitives, and the treasures of kings are kept there; moreover it is looked upon as the most outstanding on account of its illustrious supremacy.
>
> And who can count the different crowds and numberless peoples flocking from all the provinces—some for the abundant feasting, others for the healing of their afflictions, others to watch the pageant of the crowds, others with great gifts and offerings—to join in the solemn celebration of the feast of saint Brigit who, freed from care, cast off the burden of the flesh and followed the lamb of God into the heavenly mansions, having fallen asleep on the first day of the month of February.[135]

Even allowing for a certain amount of hyperbole, it might seem that Cogitosus is describing a large settlement in Kildare at this time. However, a close reading of the text shows that he is not describing a normal Sunday assembly. He is describing the crowds that came on the first of February, the feast day of St Brigit.

In early Ireland, travel was a complex business as most people lost their legal rights as soon as they left their *túath*, or native place. But pilgrimage (along with military service and attending a fair) was one of the few opportunities to maintain their rights while traveling.[136] So, it is quite possible that these people came on pilgrimage from a great distance to participate in the celebration of a feast day and did not normally live there. Smyth has noted that Viking raiders preferred to raid certain monasteries on particular feast days, when they could be sure of taking large numbers of slaves.[137] Harbison has identified the many *clochauns* (stone huts) at the base of Mount Brandon on the Dingle Peninsula as the remains of shelter for pilgrims who came there for some particular feast day.[138]

If we accept the textual evidence as pointing to lay people receiving Communion only on a few feast days every year, it could well be that one of these receptions was on the occasion of a pilgrimage to a particular center for a feast day. The various churches, round towers, high crosses, and so on, could have provided the context for a stational liturgy that culminated in one of the three or four annual receptions of Communion. Thus a possible solution to the debate on monastic cities is provided: there existed substantial groups of buildings in the various important ecclesial centers that were inhabited by large numbers of people only during a few annual pilgrimages. The secondary church buildings may have been used in connection with these pilgrimages, but also may have served as the locus of private Masses, given that the altar in the main church may have served exclusively for the religious superior and the community Mass. In the smaller sites, perhaps some of the altars were only used in connection with the periodic pilgrimages. In this context Ó Carragáin has detected the remains of many outdoor altars on Inishmurray. These could have been used on the days of pilgrimage when there were many more communicants than normal and where the stational liturgy may have needed a number of eucharistic celebrations in different places associated with the life of the founding saint and the pilgrimage. In his overall analysis of the site he proposes that this

> suggests that some early medieval outdoor ritual involved formal eucharistic celebrations of a sort not normally characteristic of the modern pilgrimage rounds. While the official mass of the day was probably celebrated at the high altar of Temple Molaise, the main congregational church in the cashel, the various *leachta* may have been used for

private masses to mark saints' feastdays and votive masses for the sick and the dead.[139]

THE PHYSICAL OBJECTS ASSOCIATED WITH THE EUCHARIST IN PRE-NORMAN IRELAND AND THEIR EUCHARISTIC ICONOGRAPHY

EUCHARISTIC VESSELS

It is most fortuitous that two of Ireland's most important national treasures are magnificent chalices, one from the eighth century and the other from, at the latest, the tenth. These chalices are now exhibited in the National Museum of Ireland in Dublin. It seems that both of these chalices were deliberately hidden in the Middle Ages, only to be discovered nearly a millennium later.

The Ardagh hoard was found near the village of Ardagh, Co. Limerick, in 1868. It contained an important silver chalice, now known as the Ardagh Chalice, a plain bronze chalice, which was damaged during the discovery of the hoard, and four brooches (the brooches are the easiest items in the hoard to date and the various brooches date from the eighth to the tenth centuries).[140] The Ardagh Chalice (figure 3) is a handled chalice 17.8 cm high and 19.5 cm in diameter (excluding the handles) at the rim, and this chalice represents a highpoint in Irish metalwork that to this day has not been surpassed.[141] The chalice probably dates to the second half of the eighth century (this date is based on comparisons to contemporary brooches). It is made up of more than three hundred individual pieces assembled around a central bronze pin. The main body of the chalice is of beaten silver. It is decorated with cast glass "jewels" and some very high-quality filigree ornaments. The beauty of the chalice was achieved by the judicious use of material of the highest quality as opposed to the use of great quantities of these precious materials. The chalice bears fine engraving, including a band below the rim with the names of the twelve apostles.

The Derrynaflan hoard (figure 4) was found in 1980 at Doire na bhFlann, Co. Tipperary. While the hoard would indicate an impor-

Figure 1. Gallarus Oratory, Dingle Peninsula, Co. Kerry. Photograph by Peter Zoeller.

Figure 2. The *Book of Kells*, folio 202v, The Temptation. Image courtesy of the Board of Trinity College Dublin.

Figure 3. The Ardagh Chalice. Image courtesy of the National Museum of Ireland.

Figure 4. The Derrynaflan hoard. Image courtesy of the National Museum of Ireland.

Figure 5. The Derrynaflan Chalice. Image courtesy of the National Museum of Ireland.

Figure 6. The Derrynaflan Paten. Image courtesy of the National Museum of Ireland.

Figure 7. The Derrynaflan Paten reconstructed as mounted on its stand. Image courtesy of the National Museum of Ireland.

Figure 8. Lough Kinale Chalice. Image courtesy of the National Museum of Ireland.

Figure 9. Picture of author and high cross of Moone, Co. Kildare. Photograph by author.

Figure 10. High cross at Moone: The Loaves and Fishes. Photograph by author.

Figure 11. Detail of the *Book of Kells*, folio 48r, cat chasing mouse or rat holding the host in its mouth. Image courtesy of the Board of Trinity College Dublin.

(below)
Figure 12. Detail of the *Book of Kells*, folio 34r, two mice or rats holding the host in their mouths. Image courtesy of the Board of Trinity College Dublin.

(right)
Figure 13. Detail of the *Book of Kells*, folio 29r, eucharistic host in the mouth of a lion. Image courtesy of the Board of Trinity College Dublin.

Figure 14. Eucharistic chrismal in the cathedral treasury of Chur. Picture credit: Archäologischer Dienst Graubünden.

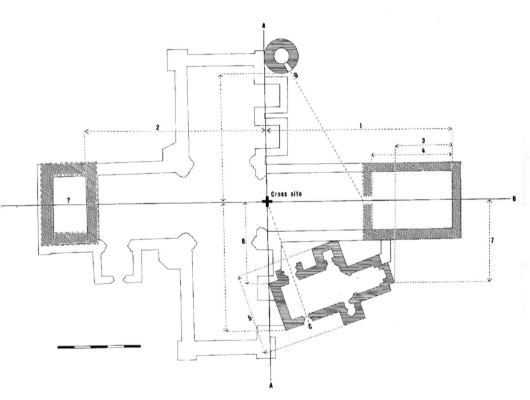

Figure 15. Suggested reconstruction of the Rock of Cashel in the early twelfth-century. Image courtesy of Tadhg O'Keeffe, from his *Romanesque Ireland*, plate 69 on page 137.

N

0   cm   10

Figure 16. Inscribed area on upper surface of a boulder in Ballydarrig
townland, Iveragh. Image courtesy of Tomás Ó Carragáin, from his "A
Landscape Converted," fig. 9.3 on page 134.

Figure 17. Cross of Mann altar frontal. Photograph courtesy of Manx National Heritage.

Figure 18. Church of Lorrha, Co. Tipperary. Photograph by author.

Figure 19. Sculpture of a *flabellum* from a standing stone at Caherlehillian on the Iveragh Peninsula, Co. Kerry. Photograph by author.

Figure 20. Round tower on Devenish Island, Co. Fermanagh. Photograph by author.

tant ecclesiastical site, in fact there is little or no contemporary mention of a monastery at this place.[142] This hoard had been concealed in the tenth century and contained a silver chalice, a paten, a silver hoop (which probably functioned as a paten stand), a bronze basin, and a bronze strainer.[143]

The Derrynaflan Chalice (figure 5) is slightly higher and wider (19.2 cm by 21 cm) than the Ardagh Chalice. On first look its form is quite similar to the Ardagh Chalice and is also built of about three hundred pieces assembled around a bronze pin. But, whereas the Ardagh Chalice had to be reinforced, the Derrynaflan Chalice is of a much solider construction. The chalice uses amber rather than glass "jewels," and has more decoration, filigrees, and so on, but they tend to be of a lesser quality than the Ardagh Chalice. Again, by comparison to contemporary brooches, it seems to have been made in the ninth century, and it had very little use prior to its being hidden.

Both of these chalices have two handles, which may, perhaps, have been modeled after the Holy Grail (the chalice supposedly used by Christ himself in the Last Supper). In his *De Locis Sanctis* Adomnán mentions the Holy Grail, saying that "the chalice is silver, has the measure of a Gaulish pint, and has two handles fashioned on either side."[144] But while the design of both chalices undoubtedly draw from similar sources, it is unlikely that the Derrynaflan Chalice was directly influenced by the earlier Ardagh Chalice.[145]

Three other chalices are still extant from approximately the same period. The Lough Kinale Chalice from Co. Longford (figure 8) is significantly smaller and plainer than the bigger chalices, measuring only 7.6 cm by 6.5 cm. However, plain as it is, it was constructed in a very similar fashion to its larger cousins. It was found with a badly decomposed footed copper paten. The second, smaller, bronze chalice from the Ardagh hoard was damaged in the discovery. After reconstruction it seems to have been originally the same size as the Lough Kinale Chalice, although of inferior workmanship. Another chalice, the River Bann Chalice, has also been dated to around the same period, and, although it bears no markings, it is assumed (from its form alone) that it was a eucharistic chalice. This cup has approximately the same dimensions as the Lough Kinale Chalice, but it would have had a much shorter stem in comparison to the others.[146]

A question that can never be fully answered is how typical were the Ardagh and Derrynaflan Chalices. Was it by a pure quirk of fate that, of the five remaining pre-Norman Irish eucharistic chalices, two belong to a very small group of show-pieces? In comparison with other contemporary chalices, the two great Irish chalices stand on their own. In proportions they resemble Byzantine chalices,[147] but while Byzantine chalices were not unknown in the West (sometimes being introduced in the form of gifts from the Byzantine emperors to the pope), no direct influence of these can be traced to the Irish chalices.[148] While no Byzantine chalices may have reached Ireland, it could be that the Ardagh and Derrynaflan chalices are examples of an Irish subgroup of chalice style inspired by Irish ecclesiastics' pilgrimages to important Continental centers.

It is likewise very probable that other eucharistic vessels on a par with the Ardagh and Derrynaflan examples would have once existed. One place to look for traces of these is in the collections of the various Scandinavian museums. But while these have a lot of material originating in pre-Norman Irish ecclesial centers, as yet no complete eucharistic vessels have been identified.[149] This is due to the fact that the value of the luxury Irish eucharistic vessels (and other ecclesial metalwork such as reliquaries) was in their intricate detail and workmanship rather than the actual value of the metal and stones used. There are many examples of decorative elements of Irish ecclesiastical metalwork being reworked into secular Viking contexts.[150] And while no actual eucharistic vessels have been identified in the Scandinavian collections, the remains of a Viking raiding party's loot were found in Shanmullagh, Co. Armagh, and are now in the Ulster Museum. Among the dismembered elements, archaeologists have identified remnants of a set of eucharistic vessels, including a bronze strainer and parts of a chalice and paten that have been compared to the Derrynaflan hoard.[151]

Occasional references to archaeological finds of glass chalices in Ireland can be found in earlier works. However, these are not sufficiently well documented to be accepted: the sources are somewhat vague, and, as the finds mysteriously disappeared again in the nineteenth century, they cannot be credited with any real historical value.[152] Some saints' lives do mention glass chalices, but these are usually associated with miraculous visions,[153] and, given that there is no evidence of glass production in early Ireland (all glass objects were likely made from imported glass and the glass was often used in very small fragments to form jewels in decorative elements), it is not likely that glass chalices were used in pre-Norman Ireland.[154]

In a recent article Cormac Bourke examines two twelfth-century Irish handbells that have been preserved as relics. He proposes that they may originally have been chalices that were refashioned as bells, perhaps because bells were a very typical relic of Irish founder saints. It is significant that the artifacts are of a half-ovoid form and, if further study proves this identification, would add some examples of more typical chalice style into the corpus of Irish eucharistic chalices. The fact that both examples were originally cast in the twelfth century also add further weight to the evidence of the Irish church moving to closer to conformity with Continental eucharistic practice at the end of our period.[155]

Useful analysis of early Irish eucharistic vessels has been carried out in recent years, particularly the work of Michael Ryan, but it is still difficult to analyze this information. First of all, while the corpus of Irish chalices has been well studied using X-rays and other modern technologies, few of even the most famous of the Continental finds from the same period have been studied with the same scientific methods.[156] Another problem is the general lack of evidence. In the whole of Western Europe (including Ireland) prior to the twelfth century, only fifty-three eucharistic chalices are extant, and this includes ministerial chalices, votive chalices, chalices for travel, chalices for daily use, and grave chalices.[157]

Nonetheless, simply by analyzing the evidence that is available, it is possible to see some clear outlines in the Irish chalices that make up about 10 percent of the total Western examples of chalices. The Irish chalices do seem to have a particular style, being more "squat" than their Continental counterparts; they are nearly hemispherical whereas the Continental examples are predominately half-ovoid in form. Another stylistic characteristic of the Irish chalices is the form of the foot which is large in relation to the cup.[158] Yet another element is the fact that the two luxury Irish chalices are assembled from hundreds of individual pieces: the Irish artisans were unable to cast or produce large pieces and so painstakingly assembled them from a multitude of small pieces, paying a great deal of attention both to the individual pieces and to the whole. Ryan is also of the opinion that both the Derrynaflan and the Ardagh Chalices and the Derrynaflan Paten may have been votive offerings. This might explain why they received so little use prior to being hidden, and he suggests that even if they had not been lost it is possible that they would have been used only on great feast days. Indeed, he proposes that, of the three luxury vessels, only the Derrynaflan Chalice may have been used for the actual distribution of Communion. He proposes that other, less ornate vessels would have been used normally for the celebration of the Eucharist outside of the highest holy days. Even on these rare occasions of use, the ornate vessels may have played a symbolic and not a practical function.[159] As the Blood of Christ had a special place in Irish devotional and iconographical sources, these beautiful chalices might have been made to help people appreciate the liturgical presence of this Blood.[160] The liturgical vessels use to great effect the chipcarving technique, whereby the myriad of facets would have reflected the little light present in early Irish churches so that these vessels would have seemed to sparkle in the semi-darkness in which the eucharistic liturgy was performed.[161] It is even possible that precisely because people did not often receive Communion that these large chalices could have functioned as a focus for devotion to the Blood of Christ in a similar way that the monstrance would focus attention on the host in the High Middle Ages.

Later on, in Ireland as in the rest of Western Europe, the chalice was gradually denied to the laity.[162] By the end of our period, as the Irish church was gradually conforming more and more to general Western trends in eucharistic practice, the style of chalice preferred by clerics would not have been immune to these changes, and the newer type of chalice styled as a small beaker on a tall stem became more popular. It is quite probable that any surviving chalices of the old style would have been melted down to be recast as newer, "modern" vessels.

While the chalices are the most striking eucharistic vessels from pre-Norman Ireland, we also have two other vessels from the Derrynaflan hoard. The Derrynaflan Paten is also very big, between 35.6 cm and 36.8 cm in diameter (figure 6). It is the only intact surviving Irish paten from the pre-Norman period.[163] It is very heavily decorated and elaborately constructed from over three hundred separate pieces and was designed to stand on its own, perhaps being attached to the stand at one time (figure 7). The main body of the paten is a shallow beaten silver dish (which was probably spun on a lathe to polish it); the dish was then stitched on the edges for decoration and soldered to a bronze rim.[164] As with the chalices, the center of the paten is void of decoration, whereas the edge and sides are heavily decorated.[165] Coincidentally, the Derrynaflan Paten seems to be of the same period and style as the Ardagh Chalice and, indeed, may have originated in the same workshop.[166] Documentary references point to both large and small patens on the Continent, but, apart from the Derrynaflan Paten, no Western examples have been preserved of what may once have been a quite popular style of large patens.[167] However, as the general design of the Derrynaflan Paten entailed its complex assembly from many pieces, this might again suggest an attempt to reproduce under local Irish artistic and technological constraints a style of eucharistic vessel seen in some great Continental ecclesiastical center.[168]

Another interesting possibility is that the programming of the Derrynaflan Paten may be influenced by the rite of the *fractio panis* in the Eucharist as we have already examined in chapter 2: the different markings on the rim of the paten may have functioned as markers to aid the priest in placing the pieces of eucharistic bread in intricate arrangements such as those described in the *Mass Tract* of the *Stowe Missal.*[169] Once again it is probable that other similar patens once existed in Ireland, but as the *fractio panis* became less important, and as small precut hosts for the faithful were adopted and the reception of Communion was postponed until the eucharistic liturgy was finished so as not to "interrupt" the flow of the liturgy, smaller patens more in line with Continental practice would have been adopted in Ireland.

The final vessel is the Derrynaflan Strainer, a bronze ladle 38 cm long with a deep bowl 11.5 cm in diameter.[170] It is paralleled by the remains of a similar strainer found in the Shanmullagh hoard.[171] These vessels were used to purify the altar wine, by pouring the wine into one side of the strainer and then out of the other. This would almost definitely have been a symbolic procedure: not only would it have been more practical to strain the impurities from the wine before the liturgy began,[172] but the strainers are of a particularly awkward form and badly designed to gracefully accomplish the actual work of straining.[173] It is true that strainers did form part of the liturgy in some important Continental centers.[174] Indeed, *Ordo Romanus Primus* also makes reference to the use of a strainer at the papal Eucharist: "when the altar is ready, the archdeacon takes a flask from the oblationary sub-deacon and pours it through a strainer into the chalice, and then the deacons' flasks."[175] But here we seem to be dealing with the reuse of a particular vessel in a new context. The form of the Derrynaflan strainer is clearly inspired by pre-Christian secular Irish ladles, which have been discovered in a number of contexts.[176] The modification of the ladle was achieved by the simple addition of a perforated plate in the center of the bowl through which the wine would have been poured to remove impurities. While the original use of these vessels is unclear, it would seem that they were adopted in the liturgical context, as these two examples witness. Some high cross iconography, as well as the image at the beginning of the Gospel of Luke in the *Book of Kells* (fol. 188r), shows a figure pouring wine into a chalice using a handled ladle. This practice was probably not universal as it is hard to reconcile the use of liturgical strainers with the description of putting "drops" of water and wine into the chalice as described in the *Mass Tract* of the *Stowe Missal.* So the strainer hints at an element of particular Irish eucharistic practice that took advantage of a preexisting vessel to add to the ceremony of the eucharistic rite. As there are no textual references to the liturgical use of the strainer (although some monastic rules refer to the monks' food and drink being distributed in ladles)[177] it is difficult to infer much more than the fact that strainers were occasionally used in the preparation of the chalice in the eucharistic liturgy, and that this action was probably more symbolic than functional, perhaps building symbolically on whatever secular use the ladle might have had.

WINE

The study of liturgical chalices needs to be complemented by the study of their primary use: a vessel to contain grape wine. Today the climate of Ireland is not very suitable to the growing of grapes. While it is hard to say with certainty whether or not grapes were cultivated in pre-Norman Ireland, wine seems to have been fairly readily available throughout the period. In this vein it is perhaps worth noting that, although there is some evidence of liturgical problems concerning the omission of various liturgical anointings of chrism, which was made with olive oil and was definitely not produced locally, there is no mention of liturgical abuses caused by a lack of wine in early Irish sources.[178] There are a number of stories in the saints' lives where water is changed into wine so that the Eucharist can be celebrated,[179] but this is not necessarily proof that wine was particularly hard to come by: there are many more instances in the saints' lives where the saint changes water into beer, which presumably could have been produced locally. Wine was produced in England at this time, and Bede mentions in his *Ecclesiastical History* that Ireland "abounds in milk and honey, nor does it lack vines, fish and birds."[180] Four hundred years later Gerald of Wales, who, unlike Bede, had personally visited Ireland, takes it on himself to explicitly refute this passage of Bede:

> The island is rich in pastures and meadows, honey and milk, and wine, but not vineyards. Bede, however, among his other praises of the island says that it is not altogether without vineyards. On the other hand, Solinus says that it has no bees. But if I may be pardoned by both, it would have been more true if each of them said the opposite: it has no vineyards, and it is not altogether without bees. For the island has not, and never had, vines and their cultivators. Imported wines, however, conveyed in the ordinary commercial way, are so abundant that you would scarcely notice that the vine was neither cultivated nor gave its fruit there.[181]

From a climatological and horticultural point of view it was probably possible to grow grapes in Ireland throughout the pre-Norman period.[182] But Fergus Kelly tends more towards the view of Gerald, maintaining the possibility of there having been small-scale cultivation of grapes in the early Christian period in Ireland.[183] Nonetheless, there is no archaeological evidence for domestic wine production in pre-Norman Ireland. In both monastic and secular texts mention is made of the consumption of wine as a festive and high-class drink,[184] although this does not necessarily mean that it was not produced locally, given that the type of flour for the production of eucharistic bread was produced locally and was also a luxury item.

While grape cultivation may have been feasible, it is also true that wine was imported into Britain and Ireland and, though still needing scholarly work and comparison with (the largely uncatalogued) Continental finds, the archaeological remains of pottery at Irish sites of the first millennium bear witness to the importation of wine.[185] There are also textual references to the importation of wine:

> There must have been regular imports of the wine required for the celebration of the Eucharist, and also featured as a luxury drink at feasts. The lost Old Irish law-text *Muirbretha* "sea-judgments" evidently referred to the wine-trade, as Cormac states in his *Glossary* that the phrase *escop fína* "wine-jar" occurs in this text. He explains it as "a vessel for measuring wine among Gaulish and Frankish traders" (*escra tomais fína la ceandaighaib Gall ⁊ Franc*). The importance of the wine-trade is also indicated by the prominence of Bordeaux (Latin *Burdigala*)—the centre of the wine-trade in early Irish texts. The name of this town was borrowed into Irish in the form *bordgal* and is used in the eighth-century *Félire Óengusso* in the meaning "meeting-place, city."[186]

Any attempt to analyze how often wine was distributed in the Eucharist, exactly who received, and how much wine was used is, once again, hampered by a lack of evidence. There are a number of texts dealing with eucharistic wine, but these are often unclear, and it is difficult to know whether they refer to ecclesiastics, a special assembly, or the lay community at large. Columbanus assigned a penance to a monk who bites the chalice with his teeth,[187] although as this is a monastic rule it is probable that here he is dealing with monks and not regular lay Christians (and given that monks could not be trusted not to bite the chalice, it would be even less likely that the chalice would be entrusted to nonmonastics). The *Rule of the Céli Dé* from the *Leabhar Breac* speaks of the gradual initiation of monks for receiving Communion and foresees that after seven years they might receive from the chalice every Sunday.[188] In another parallel text it is stated that those who have undergone penance for shedding blood may eventually receive the Body of Christ once more but may never again receive the chalice, thus further proof both of the possibility of reception of the chalice by the laity (prior to such a crime) and the high regard in which the chalice was held.[189] The *Vita Prima* of St Brigit also explicitly refers to Brigit going to receive Communion first from the hand of the bishop and then approaching the bishop's attendant, who administered the chalice to her.[190]

In all likelihood it would have been an economic challenge for everybody to receive from the chalice at each and every eucharistic celebration. On the other hand, the fact that wine was used by the nobles in their feasts means that quantities of wine far greater than necessary for the distribution of the Eucharist under both species were theoretically available. In conclusion, perhaps the question of the use of wine can be solved if one accepts that the laity did not receive Communion each and every Sunday or holy day: on the few annual occasions that they did receive Communion, they may well have received from the chalice. The tithes that were paid at those times of the year may have helped cover the cost of the wine for the celebration. At regular occasions when only the priest received, as little as a symbolic drop of wine may have sufficed for the priest's Communion. On this note, the *Leabhar Breac Mass Tract* 6 specifies that there are three drops (*banna*) of both water and wine in the chalice. Depending on the size of each drop, this could be quite a little amount of wine that was mixed with an equal part of water.[191] On a similar note, Canon 5 of Bishop Cumin's 1186 Dublin Synod forbids that "the wine in the Sacrament be so tampered with water, that it be deprived either of the natural taste or colour,"[192] indicating a tendency to celebrate the Eucharist using highly diluted wine.

Bread is the other element needed for the celebration of the Eucharist. In pre-Norman Ireland eucharistic bread was made from *cruithnecht* (bread-wheat, or *triticum aestivum,* subspecies *vulgare*). This element was definitely available locally in pre-Norman Ireland; however, wheat was grown less than other cereals, had a high status in society, and was a luxury foodstuff, as well as having religious and political symbolism. This was probably because refining wheat into quality flour required a lot of work, so even nobles often used wheat as a part of a gruel rather than as bread.[193] Not only was it difficult to refine, it was also difficult to grow due to the dampness of the Irish climate.[194] Sometimes saints performed miracles of transforming lesser grains into wheat.[195]

As to the actual form that the eucharistic bread took, early Ireland probably used a round loaf of bread for the Eucharist. The high cross of Moone clearly shows round bread, and the illustrations of the *Book of Kells* (which will be treated below) also show round bread (see figures 10–13). The question is whether or not this bread was leavened. In general, most Christians used leavened bread in the first millennium, although at the end of the ninth century many Western churches began to use unleavened bread.[196] But usually the fact of the bread being leavened or not was not an issue before the eleventh-century controversies between Eastern and Western Christians.

Even though there would be little difference to modern eyes and taste buds between what constituted leavened bread and what constituted unleavened bread in the early medieval world (the modern distinction between Western unleavened precut bleached wafers and the leavened bread used by the Eastern churches is much more evident), it is likely that the bread used in pre-Norman Ireland was unleavened. From a horticultural point of view, the climate in Ireland would naturally have produced a wheat not very given to rising. From a technological point of view, suitable ovens for leavened bread seem to have been first introduced on a widespread basis by the mendicant orders that arrived in the wake of the Normans.[197] There is one textual reference that Sexton cites as evidence of the use of unleavened bread in the Eucharist: the *Penitential of Cummean* prescribes that "if the host loses its taste and is discoloured, he shall keep a fast for twenty days; if it is stuck together, for seven days."[198] Sexton interprets the deterioration of the host as being more typical of a host made from unleavened rather than leavened bread.[199]

CHRISMALS

We have examined the textual evidence for chrismals and the importance of the viaticum in pre-Norman Ireland in chapter 2; here we will deal with the archaeological evidence. While there exist no examples of chrismals of undisputed Irish provenance, there are a number in England, including a "cast copper-alloy two-handled vessel with a rounded base" from East Clandon in Surrey, which has been dated to "before 1200."[200] This type of chrismal must also have been familiar in Ireland. Indeed, a small (5 cm by 6.35 cm) "cast bronze vessel of 11th-century date from Ballypriormore, Islandmagee, Co. Antrim,"[201] which is today in the Ulster Museum, may have been a chrismal used for storing chrism, given that its dimensions would be more suited to a liquid than a solid.[202]

The carrying of the Eucharist on one's person as a devotional practice (as opposed to simply transporting it for later domestic reception) was uncommon outside the Irish milieu. However, the carrying of relics of the saints on one's person did take place. Bede tells us that the Gaulish bishop Germanus of Auxerre carried a bag of relics around his neck, a "little bag which hung down close to his side, containing relics of the saints."[203] Gregory of Tours in sixth-century Gaul tells how his father always carried a gold medallion filled with relics of saints as protection.[204] On the other hand, there are some pyxes from this date in different parts of Western Europe. These were usually in the form of ivory and, later, metal cylindrical boxes, along the lines of earlier pagan boxes.[205] From the textual evidence it seems that the Irish chrismals were more akin to the Continental *encolpia* than pyxes.[206]

While no Irish chrismals have yet been identified, both Irish and non-Irish reliquaries still exist from this period. Some of these Irish reliquaries were designed to hang around the neck.[207] The chrismal probably resembled this. King also notes that two eucharistic chrismals survive on the Continent. One of them is a "leather chrismal overlaid with gold dating from the seventh or eighth centuries in the cathedral church of Chur in Switzerland"[208] (figure 14). The other is the Mortain Chrismal, which dates from the eighth century. It is in the form of a house-shaped reliquary made of copper alloy and gilding over a beechwood base with dimensions of 13.5 cm by 11.5 cm by 5 cm and had rings on the sides so that it could be carried around the neck by chains.[209] The iconography of the chrismal, featuring Christ, the archangels, seraphim, and birds, bears many similarities to the *Book of Kells* and the high cross of Moone;[210] the work also bears similarities to some Anglo-Saxon art, and the fact that it bears a runic inscription in Old English definitively marks this out as an Anglo-Saxon, and not Irish, object.[211]

While the Chur Chrismal is of unproven provenance and the Mortain Chrismal is probably of Anglo-Saxon origin, they do provide some idea as to what an Irish chrismal may have looked like.[212] Therefore I would make bold to suggest that some Irish artifacts that have up until now been classified as reliquaries may instead have been chrismals, and that their reexamination in the light of the plentiful Irish testimony to the uses of chrismals may result in their identification as chrismals. In particular I think the tiny house-shaped shrines resembling an early Irish church, which were worn around the neck and are peculiar to Ireland, may possibly be chrismals and not reliquaries.[213]

FLABELLA

Another eucharistic symbol of the *Book of Kells* is the presence of illustrations of liturgical fans, or *flabella*. Today the *flabellum* is used exclusively in the Eastern rites. While Byzantine liturgical commentaries now spiritualize its usage,[214] originally the *flabellum* was an ancient form of fly swatter. Our earliest secular representations of *flabella* are in the ancient Egyptian carvings of the pharaoh accompanied by slaves carrying *flabella* to protect him from insects.[215] They are also mentioned by the classical Greek and Roman authors as something carried by slaves to help their master or mistress.[216]

It is possible that the *flabellum* came to be used in eucharistic liturgy along with other elements that had their roots in fourth-century court etiquette, such as incense and candles.[217] Particularly in warmer climates, however, they may have been more than simple decorative status symbols, but were put to a practical use in the celebration. Indeed, the first explicit reference to a liturgical usage of *flabella* is in the *Apostolic Constitutions,* a composite church order generally held to have been written in Syria towards the end of the fourth century.[218] Here the *flabellum* is seen precisely as an aid to protecting the chalice from flies:

> When this is done, let the deacons bring the gifts to the bishop at the altar; and let the presbyters stand on his right hand and on his left, as disciples standing before their master. But let two of the deacons, on each side of the altar, each hold a fan, of thin membranes, or of feathers of the peacock, or of fine cloth, and let them silently drive away the flying insects, that they may not come near the cups.[219]

While the *flabellum* was more prevalent in the East, it is possible to find some references to it also in the West. The earliest Western reference to a liturgical *flabellum* is in 837 at the abbey of Cysoing in Hainaut,[220] and the eleventh-century *Customs of Cluny* instructs that the *flabellum* is to be used in a way similar to that described in the *Apostolic Constitutions.*[221] However, *flabella* were never widely used in the West and eventually they were dropped from use altogether. Today a few extant *flabella* are to be found in some Western museums, cathedral sacristies, and so on. They seem to have formed two main groups. A more primitive group are made of light materials and actually would be suitable for keeping flies away from the altar (only four of this type survive in the West, one in France and three in Italy). A later and much more numerous group are made of metal disks surmounted by a cross, and were used, often in pairs, as processional crosses or altar crosses.[222]

In an Irish context, the earliest literary reference to a *flabellum* is in a mid-ninth-century gloss on the Karlsruhe *Soliloquia* of St Augustine.[223] It is worth noting that this reference is contemporary with the earliest Western occurrence of 837. It may also be significant that Early Irish has its own translation for *flabellum: cuilebad.* This is not a loan-word but derives from the words *cuil* (fly) and *bath* (destruction or death).[224] The etymology of *cuilebad* places it firmly within the earlier practical usage of the *flabellum.*

Unfortunately, we are not in possession of any extant *flabellum* connected with Ireland.[225] Apart from the illuminations of the *Book of Kells,* our main literary reference is to the relic *Cuilebad Coluim Cille,* or "*flabellum* of St Columba," which is first mentioned in the *Annals of Ulster* in 1034. There are a number of literary references to this relic from the ninth to the eleventh centuries and many of them are connected with the Columban foundation of Kells.[226] But as the annals tell us, this relic was lost:

> Maicinia ua hUchtáin, lector of Cenannas, was drowned coming from Scotland, and Colum Cille's fan [*cuilebad*] and three relics of Patrick and thirty men [were lost] as well.[227]

The annals also provide us with another intriguing reference to a *cuilebad:*

> A detestable and unpredicted deed of evil consequence, that merited the curse of the men of Ireland, both laity and clergy, [and] of which, the like was not previously found in Ireland, was committed by Tigernán ua Ruairc and the Uí Briúin, i.e. the successor of Patrick was insulted to his face, that is, his company was robbed and some of them killed, and a young cleric who was under a *cuilebadh* was killed there. The aftermath that came of that misdeed is that there exists in Ireland no protection that is secure for anyone henceforth until that evil deed is avenged by God and man. The insult offered to the successor of Patrick is an insult to the Lord, for the Lord Himself said in the Gospel: "He who despiseth you despiseth me, He who despiseth me despiseth Him who sent me."[228]

It seems that the *Comarba,* or successor, of Patrick and his retinue were attacked as they were on their way to make a visitation. A young cleric was killed, and the crime was considered more grievous as he had been carrying the *Comarba's flabellum*. Although the text is somewhat obscure, it offers a number of points worth noting. Firstly it is textual evidence for a *flabellum* from a non-Columban source. It also would seem to suggest that the *flabellum* was in use in the twelfth century. Perhaps it formed part of the episcopal insignia of the archbishop of Armagh as he made his visitations. It may also have been considered as an object of honor that an attacker would have been afraid to violate (not, unfortunately for the young cleric, in this case). Maybe this was an ancient relic, although the annals make no reference to this, or perhaps it was a Continental import given to the reform-minded archbishop who was the immediate predecessor of St Malachy.

On the iconographic level, the most significant depictions are to be found in some of the picture pages in the *Book of Kells*. In the *Madonna and Child* (fol. 7v) and the *Symbols of the Four Evangelists* (fol. 129v), as well as in the various evangelist pages, angels hold *flabella* in the background.[229] Once again these depictions form a very early Western witness and seem to portray the more primitive type of *flabellum*. Again, their connection to the Columban foundation of Kells must be noted. There are also a number of depictions of *flabella* on standing stones.[230] The most famous of these is to be found at Carndonagh, Co. Donegal, which is, yet again, a site associated with the cult of St Columba.[231]

Some scholars have pointed to this evidence as proof that the early Irish church used *flabella* as a regular part of the eucharistic liturgy.[232] Although there is a body of evidence for *flabella* in an Irish context, it can be noted that many of the references (the *Book of Kells*, the annals, and the standing stone of Carndonagh) have a connection with Columba and his foundations. It could be that the proportionally high number of references to St Columba's *flabellum* is only a coincidence.[233] But it might also be true that St Columba may well have owned a *flabellum* that constituted an exotic novelty in the Irish context, so much so that it became somewhat of an emblem of the saint. Indeed, this famous *flabellum* may well have been presented to St Columba by a returning pilgrim as a prestige item obtained on pilgrimage to Gaul or Italy, and thus may not be indicative of any liturgical link with the East. If this is the case, we are not dealing with a widespread element in Irish liturgical practice but some peculiar local liturgical uses. However, these variations had a symbolic value and remained in the popular imagination of artistic programmers where, much like the later Byzantine commentators, the *flabellum* came to signify the heavenly dimension of the liturgy.

EUCHARISTIC ICONOGRAPHY ON THE HIGH CROSSES

Like the round towers, high crosses are a typical feature of early Irish ecclesiastical sites and from the point of view of art history constitute a very important portion of early Irish iconography. Today the remains of about two hundred of these early medieval sculpted stone crosses are to be found throughout Ireland.[234] Built with a great effort at a time when stone carving was not widely practiced on the Continent, even today these high crosses are recognized as a distinctive characteristic of the early Irish church. In general, the high cross is composed of a base stone, with the shaft of the cross being fitted into it (although the base stone is usually bigger than would be necessary to simply support the cross). The main part of the high cross is usually between 3 meters and 4.5 meters, although in some cases it can be 6 meters high. The high cross is crowned with a cap-stone, which is often made in the form of a miniature church. The whole structure is usually carved, both with figurative art and with interlacing patterns. The resulting high cross is an imposing structure, weighing a few tons, and it would have required great talent to construct and raise. Those who have never seen these monuments and have only seen the contemporary folkloric adaptations in modern graveyards can find it difficult to appreciate the sheer size of the originals (for a sense of scale, see figure 9 showing the author next to the high cross of Moone, Co. Kildare).

While there is still no consensus as to the exact purpose of the high crosses, it would seem that they were usually not funerary monuments. Building a high cross would have been very expensive and would have involved the patronage of important individuals: some of the high crosses bear inscriptions of the names of their royal patrons. It may well be that they were carved after the death of these patrons, but it is just as likely that they were carved as memorials when they were still alive. In many instances, more than one high cross survives at the same site, and these may have marked out the boundaries of the monastic enclosure where one could look for sanctuary.[235] It is possible that their seventh-century origin could be connected with the introduction of the feast of the Exaltation of the Cross in seventh-century Rome.[236] It also seems to be the case that in some instances the high cross marked the site of a miracle performed by the saint who founded the monastery. Adomnán reports one such instance with Columba where two crosses were erected: "in the place where Ernán died, in front of the door of the corn-kiln, a cross was set up, and another on the spot where Columba was standing at the moment of Ernán's death. These are still standing today."[237] Muirchú likewise reports that at Slíab Miss, the site of Patrick's earlier slavery, "to the present day a cross stands there to mark (the spot of) his first view of the district."[238]

Many of the high crosses are completely covered in figurative carvings. Intricate iconographical programming has been worked out drawing mainly from scriptural sources. Some works point to these high crosses as an instrument used to catechize the illiterate lay folk, but this view is somewhat simplistic and does not do justice to the complexity of these monuments.[239] Given the specialist knowledge necessary, it is more probable that they were created with educated clerics and monastics in mind.[240]

The high crosses that are engraved with scriptural scenes usually have the Crucifixion at the center of the cross and ring on one side, and the Last Judgment on the other. Other biblical scenes from both the Old and the New Testaments abound.[241] There does not seem to be a canonical arrangement of scenes; other than having the Crucifixion of Christ in the center, each high cross is arranged in a different way, but the biblical scenes on the different panels, while in a different order, are usually of the same scenes.

One expert analysis of the whole body of high cross iconography suggests that "the arrangement of scenes from the Old Testament to parallel the New Testament are not randomly selected but often give importance to the two sacraments of baptism and the Eucharist." The biblical scenes that have particular eucharistic overtones in their iconography and are most prevalent on the high crosses is the Marriage Feast at Cana (seven instances), the Multiplication of the Loaves and the Fishes (nine instances), and the Sacrifice of Isaac (twenty-two instances).[242]

There is also a nonbiblical scene that is of great eucharistic significance and that often appears on the Irish high crosses—the Meeting of Paul and Anthony. Indeed, the many instances of this scene on the Irish high crosses constitute the vast majority of all first-millenium artistic portrayals worldwide of this scene.[243] This is one of the few nonbiblical scenes to appear on the high crosses, and the only nonbiblical scene to appear on a number of high crosses. This image is inspired by an incident in the *Life of Paul, the First Hermit* written by St Jerome. This story tells how it is revealed to St Anthony the Great that he was not, after all, the first monk; he is inspired to go on a journey even further into the desert where he meets St Paul. He stays with him a while and then attends St Paul as he dies. One particular incident in this story was seen to have eucharistic connotations, and it is precisely this scene that is portrayed on many Irish high crosses:

> Accordingly, having returned thanks to the Lord, they sat down together on the brink of the glassy spring. At this point a dispute arose as to who should break the bread, and nearly the whole day until eventide was spent in the discussion. Paul urged in support of his view the rites of hospitality, Anthony pleaded age. At length it was arranged that each should seize the loaf on the side nearest to himself, pull towards him, and keep for his own the part left in his hands. Then on hands and knees they drank a little water from the spring, and offering to God the sacrifice of praise passed the night in vigil.[244]

Fortunately, a comprehensive study has been published on the Paul and Anthony panels on the high crosses. On the basis of this corpus of iconography, we can see how this event was particularly important in Irish monastic tradition, remembering that Ireland had a non-Benedictine Western monastic tradition. Another indication of the importance of this story in Irish spirituality is the fact that chapter 26 of the *Navigatio* of St Brendan rewrites this story, making Paul into one of the original monks in St Patrick's monastery who has a mysterious meeting with St Brendan. Although there is no mention of bread in this version of the story (even though the *Navigatio* reworking does have clear eucharistic resonances), this use of the story underlines its importance and further helps the attribution of the iconography.[245]

The panels usually feature the bread between the two saints. This "between" is important because in medieval and Irish iconography Christ is often framed by two characters, inspired by the Vulgate text of Habakkuk 3:2 where God is *in medio duorum animalium* (between two animals). Although the original context of two animals is pejorative, and this was taken over into popular exegesis as signifying the two thieves who were crucified with Christ, in early Irish ecclesiastical art many manuscript illustrations and crucifixion scenes on the high crosses and in other places give greater importance to the fact that Christ is framed than to the negative quality of the framers.[246] This suggests an identification between the bread and the eucharistic presence of Christ.[247]

Another possible eucharistic motif in the Irish high crosses, and Irish iconography in general, is the presence of a high number of chalices on the crosses themselves and particularly in the Crucifixion scene. Obviously crosses and chalices are two universal and ancient Christian objects that are common throughout the world. However, if we compare the incidence of occurrence of chalices in Irish art as compared to Anglo-Saxon art, for example, there is a higher rate of occurrence in the Irish iconography. The association between the cross and a chalice could be part of a trend to give particular value to the blood of Christ shed on the cross and present in the eucharistic chalice. Perhaps it is no coincidence that the great Irish chalices contain many more crosses than comparable ornate chalices from other places.[248]

As with the round towers, the Irish high crosses represent an attempt to recreate the holy places in the local church. Perhaps this influence of the Holy Land was mediated through Rome, as there is some suggestion that the high crosses paralleled the tombs that Irish pilgrims would have seen in Rome and thus have been a way of forming a "local" Rome at home.[249] While typically Irish, this form is also a witness to a common element in all Christian spiritualities and local churches, and it would not be advisable to read too much into parallel occurrences of the same image in Christian art of other far-flung regions such as Armenia or Egypt.[250]

THE *BOOK OF KELLS*

The Ogham alphabet was introduced into Ireland shortly before the advent of Christianity, but it is unlikely that anything other than inscriptions was ever written in it. Therefore, literacy and the coming of Christianity were intrinsically connected in Ireland. Many of the lives of Irish saints and annalistic entries make reference to saints "wielding their own pens"; indeed, the association of sanctity with writing may be connected to the apocryphal work of *Carta dominica,* where it is Christ himself who writes.[251] This can help explain the importance given to books in pre-Norman Ireland. In contrast to the plain churches, books were lavishly illustrated, and Irish scribes (as well as scribes from Irish-influenced scriptoria in Britain and the Continent) made a significant impact on the art of illumination in the early Middle Ages.[252]

Of the different manuscripts belonging to early Ireland, the *Book of Kells* is undoubtedly the most famous and beautiful. Moreover, it possesses a unique corpus of eucharistic iconography.[253] The celebrated manuscript is from a Columban foundation, probably Iona itself, and can be dated to around the year 800.[254] Today it is known by the title of the *Book of Kells,* but it is probably to be identified with the book referred to in the annals as the "Great Gospel of Colum Cille" (or "Soiscelae Mor Coluim Cille"). Kells was built in the early ninth century as a new monastery under the auspices of the monastery of Iona. However, it did not originally serve as a new site for the Iona monastery, but rather as a place of safekeeping for its treasures, which were now at risk from Viking raids. Nonetheless it did eventually assume a preeminence in the federation of Columban monasteries in the early eleventh century.[255] The Viking destruction of Iona may also explain the fact that the *Book of Kells* was never finished. Even in its new home the book was not safe: in the year 1007 it was stolen, and by the time it was recovered the thief had torn off its precious metal cover and left the *Book* "with a sod over it."[256]

The *Book* is a lavishly illuminated copy of the Gospels. It is unlikely that it was used frequently as a regular manuscript for proclamation in the liturgy or for study, but rather it seems more likely that it was displayed during the liturgical celebration.[257] It may well have been used in processions and for display, perhaps on the altar, during the solemn feasts of the church year, or being involved in some other way with a stational liturgy.[258]

The complex iconography of the *Book of Kells* is, among other things, a statement of faith in the Eucharist.[259] The main source of its eucharistic symbolism is that within many larger illustrations eucharistic hosts seem to be present (for example, fol. 29r, figure 13). This is the only logical explanation for these small white disks marked with the cross. There are also illustrations of grapes in different places (for example, fol. 188r) and about forty chalices throughout the *Book* (for example, fol. 201v).[260]

Perhaps the most intriguing image of the Eucharist in the *Book of Kells* is that of cats chasing after mice (or rats) who have the host in their mouths (folios 48r and 34r, figures 11 and 12). In later scholastic treatments of eucharistic theology, the problem of a mouse eating the eucharistic host was a favorite "worst-case scenario."[261] The cat was an important animal in the ancient Irish monastery: cats were often kept as pets by the monks, and there are even a number of cats sculpted on the bases of the high crosses. It has been proposed that "in popular Irish lore cats were specially created by God to keep down the number of mice which swarmed Noah's ark and threatened to consume the food needed to sustain its passengers."[262]

Here we can see the playfulness of the early Irish monks. By invoking horror at mice eating the eucharistic host, they underline its importance. Rather than emphasizing a disdain for the Eucharist, it is a powerful reminder of its importance, and perhaps the fact that the eucharistic host is portrayed as being between two mice could be another iconographic use of the motif of God being *in medio duorum animalium.* Analysis of this and other features show that the *Book of*

Kells is very rich in its details, and many of these details are concerned with eucharistic themes.[263] This attention to the small details seems to be a hallmark of the Irish worldview. As chalices and manuscripts, high crosses and churches are made up of smaller, highly detailed parts, which fit together into a harmony, so the eucharistic imagery of the *Book of Kells* fits together with other elements as a vital part of Christian life.

CONCLUSION

Robert Taft, the great liturgist of the Christian East, stated at the end of one of his works that his "conclusions may seem banal in the extreme. But the history of liturgy is a mosaic of reconstruction, a work-in-progress, and it is not guesswork but only the recovery, cleaning and repositioning of each small tessera that renders this reconstruction possible."[1] The same statement could be made at the end of this work, but I hope that as a result of this work that it is possible to appreciate the Eucharist in pre-Norman Ireland in a fresh light based on modern scholarship. Indeed, the only sure way forward for liturgical studies of the early Irish church is to be anchored in what the remaining texts and material objects can really tell us, to consider these in their proper contexts, and to avoid theoretical and ideological concepts of how the church and liturgy of this period *should* have been. In this sense I am hesitant to overreach in drawing conclusions at the end of this study. I prefer to present the evidence with a preliminary reading mainly focusing on contextualization of the data, thus making available the necessary evidence to allow the incorporation of the study of the Eucharist in early Ireland into the liturgical history of the West in particular and into the general social history of pre-Norman Ireland.

In presenting my conclusions, I start by saying that I think that the evidence paints a picture of the pre-Norman Irish experience of the Eucharist as being much more mainstream than is often proposed. There is little hard evidence to imply the existence of a separate Celtic or Irish eucharistic rite, and it is much more probable that the Irish Christians of the time used a form of the Gallican rite that was common to most of the West. While it would be anachronistic to expect to find Gallican uses in Ireland identical to any given Continental center, nonetheless, the liturgical experience in Ireland would probably have closely paralleled those in contemporary France or Germany.

The texts we have examined show that, at least at the higher levels of society, the laity were concerned that the church provide pastoral care within easy reach and ideally in every *túath*. This pastoral care included, at a minimum, the weekly celebration of the Eucharist, along with provisions for the administration of baptisms, the viaticum, and prayers for the protection of the place and for the dead. Tithes and other subsidies of the church were paid in order to guarantee these celebrations. The concern for the celebration of the Eucharist, however, seems not always to have encompassed an equal concern that the laity actually be in attendance. It may have been the case that the laity placed more importance on having the Eucharist celebrated and having the priest pray for themselves and their dead than on being physically present themselves at that eucharistic celebration. In common with much of the rest of Christendom, the laity ideally received the Eucharist on a small number of important occasions each year, such as Easter and Christmas. The emphasis was placed more on the quality of the spiritual preparation for these infrequent Communions rather than on having a greater number of occasions to receive Communion. In addition, pastoral care in pre-Norman Ireland often seems to have focused on preparation for death, in which the Eucharist is received as viaticum at the end of the Christian's mortal life.

While the church in pre-Norman Ireland seems to have been fairly typical for Western Europe of its day, there were, undoubtedly, some regional characteristics in her eucharistic practice. Perhaps the clearest example was the use of the chrismal whereby the eucharistic species were carried on the person of an ecclesiastic almost like a talisman. While the use of the chrismal was not specifically connected with the strong emphasis placed on the reception of the Eucharist as a viaticum, the fact that many early Irish ecclesiastics did carry the Eucharist on their person facilitated this reception. Apart from the use of the chrismal, it would seem that the Irish were sometimes slightly ahead of the Continent regarding certain practices and at other times behind it. Judging on the basis of fragmentary evidence (both from Ireland and the Continent), the Irish were at the forefront regarding the adoption of the Roman Canon, as they were likewise at the forefront in attributing the exact moment of the eucharistic transformation to the institution narrative of the eucharistic prayer. The rehabilitation of Western hymnography, especially in the celebration of the Eucharist, was also encouraged by the Irish. Whether or not the practice of private Masses as well as the offering of Masses for various intentions were born in an Irish milieu, they did fit in well with the Irish mentality and were adopted by the Irish at an early stage. It would seem, however, that the practice of offering Masses in order to expiate penances was not an Irish innovation nor was it popular there during our period.

The Passion of Christ was central to the devotion of medieval Christians, and this devotion permeates both the written and physical sources that we have examined. In particular it would seem that this devotion was actualized in two distinct manners in the pre-Norman Irish church. The first of these, which has already been commented on in much of the secondary literature, is seen in the elaborate performance of the *fractio panis,* whereby this moment of the liturgy was understood to actualize the Passion. The breaking of the eucharistic bread represented the breaking of Christ's mortal body upon the wood of the Cross. The second manner, which is not as noted in the secondary literature, is a strong devotional emphasis on the blood of Christ. The blood of Christ, made present in the eucharistic chalice, is emphasized in devotional literature such as Blathmac's poetry, magnificent eucharistic chalices, the presence of chalices in other aspects of iconography, and in many other texts.

By the time of the coming of the Normans, the religious climate in Ireland was probably closer to the Continent than ever before. While the Norman arrival undoubtedly affected the history of the Irish church in many other areas, the results of my analysis of the evidence suggests that their arrival only led to superficial differences in the area of eucharistic practice. This is suggested particularly by the success of the Franciscans, the champions of liturgical unification in the thirteenth and fourteenth centuries, in the Gaelic areas, which happened almost independently of the Normans. The current confusion about the dates of the *Corpus, Rosslyn,* and *Drummond Missals,* including the fact that some authors claim that these might well be pre-Norman, shows just how mainstream the eucharistic practice of the pre-Norman Irish church was.[2] The main liturgical effect of the Norman arrival was more in emphasis that in actual change: undoubtedly certain processes were accelerated, the Normans did encourage the growth of the (already present) new religious orders, Norman bishops were appointed in Ireland, and Norman clergy were imported. Perhaps the only element of eucharistic practice that may have been noticeably different after the Norman arrival was the construction of larger churches, although, once again, this development may have already been taking place in the Hiberno-Viking towns and early Cistercian abbeys prior to the Norman arrival, and may have been the result of increased population density in some areas as well as the new emphasis on actual church attendance.

It is my hope that this study will contribute a renewed appreciation of the role of the Eucharist in pre-Norman Ireland. The Eucharist was central to church practice at the time, it was the motor of the cultural revolution that accompanied the Christianization of Ireland, the reason behind the construction of the churches that still dot the Irish landscape, and was held in the highest awe by the people of the day. Unfortunately, many studies of the period pay little attention to the Eucharist. It is possible to read recent comprehensive books that deal with church organization, saints' lives, or church construction and archaeology in pre-Norman Ireland in which the actual celebration of the Eucharist does not merit even a passing reference. The present book makes current liturgical scholarship available to students of this period.

It is likewise my hope that my introduction to the corpus of contemporary material on the Eucharist in pre-Norman Ireland will allow students of the liturgy to reintegrate Ireland into the history of the Eucharist in the West. The time period covered in this book is a fascinating period in the history of the Eucharist, but it is also a period about which scholars often lament the access to contemporary sources. If, as is my contention, Ireland is to be placed firmly within the Western liturgical tradition, then a whole array of source materials are opened to scholars. Finally, it is true that not everyone will agree with all of my positions, but if this book encourages other authors to study the early Irish material dealing with the Eucharist then I feel that it has fulfilled its mission.

APPENDIX

The Old Irish Mass Tract

The texts and translation are taken from MacCarthy, "On the *Stowe Missal*," 245–65. However, in McCarthy's edition the *Stowe Missal* version is given first and followed by the *Lebar Breac* version, here they have been placed in parallel columns. As the Latin is not translated in McCarthy, I have translated these passages into English.

Stowe Missal	Lebar Breac

Lebar Breac

On the figurative and spiritual senses of the order of the sacrificial oblation

The figure of the incarnation of Christ from [His] conception to His Passion and to His Ascension, that explains the Order of Mass.

1. The church that shelters the people and the altar, a figure of the shelter of the Godhead divine, of which was said: you guard me under the shelter of your wings.

Stowe Missal

2. The altar, a figure of the persecution that was inflicted.

2. The altar in the Temple, a figure of the persecution of the Christians, wherein they bear tribulation in union with the Body of Christ. As the Holy Spirit said from the person of Isaiah: I have trodden the winepress alone; that is, him with his members.

3. The chalice, it is a figure of the Church which was set and founded upon the persecution and upon the martyrdom of the prophets and others.

3. The chalice of the Mass, [a figure] of the Church which was placed and founded upon the persecution and martyrdom of the prophets and elect of God besides. As Christ says: Upon this rock I will build my Church; that is, upon the firmness of the faith of the first martyrs who were laid in the foundation of the building, and of the last martyrs up to Elias and Enoch.

4. Water first into the chalice, and what is chanted by them is: I ask you, O Father; I beseech you, O Son; I implore you, O Holy Spirit; that is, a figure of the people that was poured into the Church.

4. Water into the chalice at first by the minister, it is what is meet. And he says I ask you, O Father,—a drop with that; I beseech you, O Son, a drop with that; I implore you, O Holy Spirit,—the third drop with that; a figure of the people that was poured into knowledge of the new law through the unity of the will of the Trinity and through the presence of the Holy Spirit. As it is said: I will pour out my Spirit upon all flesh and they shall prophesy and it will remain. And, as it is said: They will come from the East and the West and from the North and recline with Abraham and Isaac and Jacob in the kingdom of God; that is, the first in the earthly Church will be last in the kingdom of heaven.

Stowe Missal

Lebar Breac

De figuris et spiritualibus sensibus obaltionis sacrificii ordinis
Figuir tra inchollaigthi Crist o chompert co a chesad, ocus co a fresgabail-inchoiscid sin ord innaifrind.
1. In tempul ditnes in popul ocus ind altoir-figuir inna nditem diadacda, dianebrad: sub umbra alarum tuarum protégé me.

2. Ind altoir, fugor ind ingrimme immabred.

2. Ind altoir isin tempul-figuir ingrema na Cristaide imofolgnat fochaide inellach cuirp Crist. Prout Spiritus sanctus ex persona Isaiae dixit: Torcular conculcavi solus; id est, ipse cum membris suis.

3. In cailech, is figor inna eclaise foruirmed ocus rofothaiged for ingrimmim ocus for martri inna fathe et aliorum.

3. In cailech aifrind—[figuir] inna heclaise rofuirmed ocus rofothaiged for ingreim ocus marta na fhatha ocus tuicse nDe archena. Sicut Christus dixit: Super hanc petram edificabo ecclesiam meam, i. for sonairti irsi na martirech toisech rolaitea I fotha in chumtaig ocus inna martirech ndedinach conice hElii ocus Enoc.

4. Huisce prius in calicem, ocus issed canar occo: Peto te, Pater; deprecor te, Filii; obsecro te, Spiritus Sancte; idon, figor in phopuil toresset in ecclesia.

4. Usci isin cailech artus icon timthirthid, ised istechta. Et dicis: quaeso te, Pater, banna lassin; deprecor te, fili, banna lassin; obsecro te, Spiritus Sanctae, in tres banna—figuir in populi doroiset in eolus in rechta nui tre oentaid thoile na Trinoti, ocus tria erlathar in Spirta Noib. ut dictum est: Effundam de Spiritu meo super omnem carnem et prophetabunt, et reliqua. Et, ut dictum est: Venient ab Oriente et ab Occidente et ab Aquilone, et recumbent cum Abraham et Isaac et Jacob in regno Dei; id est, in ecclesia terrena primo, ultimo in regno caelesti.

Stowe Missal	Lebar Breac

5. The oblation afterwards upon the altar, that is, it enters. What is chanted by them is: Jesus Christ, Alpha and Omega: that is, the beginning and the end. A figure of the body of Christ, which was placed in the linen cloth of the womb of Mary.

6. Wine afterwards upon water in the chalice, namely, the divinity of Christ upon his humanity, and upon the people, at the time of the Incarnation. It is what is chanted hereat: May the Father forgive; may the Son be indulgent; may the Holy Spirit have mercy.

6. Wine afterwards into the chalice upon the water, to wit, the Divinity of Christ upon the humanity [and] upon the people at the time of his begetting and of the begetting of the people. That is: The Angel spoke, Christ was conceived by the Virgin; namely, it was then the Divinity came to meet the humanity. It is of the people however he said: I did not conceive this people in my womb. And again: in sadness and pain you will conceive your children. The Church said that. As the Apostle said: My little children, whom I am again giving birth to, so that Christ may be formed in you.

What is chanted in putting wine into the Chalice of the Mass is: May the Father forgive, a drop with that; may the Son be indulgent, another drop with that; may the Holy Spirit have mercy, the third drop with that.

7. What is chanted of the Mass after that—both Introit and Prayers and Augment—up to the Lection of the Apostles and the bigradual Psalm, it is a figure of the law of Nature, wherein was renewed [the knowledge of] Christ through all his members and deeds.

7. Now what is chanted in the Mass after that, both Introit and Orations and Augment, as far as the Lection of the apostles and bigradual Psalm, that is a figure of the Law of nature, wherein was renewed the knowledge of Christ through mysteries and deeds and convulsions of nature. As it is said: Abraham saw my day and rejoiced. For it was through the law of nature Abraham saw.

Stowe Missal

5. Oblae iarum super altare, id est, intrat. Issed canar occo, idon, Jesus Christus, A et Ω: hoc est, principium et finis. Figor cuirp Crist, rosuidiged hi linannart brond Marie.

6. Fin iarum ar huisce hi caelech, idon, deacht Crist ar a doenacht, ocus ar in popul, in aimsir thuisten. Issed canar oc suidiu: Remittat Pater; indulgeat Filius; miseratur Spiritus Sanctus.

7. A canar dind offriund forsen, inter introit ocus Orthana ocus Tormach, corrigi Liacht nApstal ocus Salm ndigrad, is figor recto aicnith insin, in roaithnuiged [aithgne] Crist tria huili baullo ocus gnimo.

Lebar Breac

6. Fin iarum isin cailech ar in usce .i. deacht Crist ar doenacht [ocus] for in popul, in aimsir a thusten ocus tusten in popuil. Ut est: Angelus sermonem fecit, Christum virgo concepit .i. is annsin tanic in deacht ar cend na doenachta. Is don popul dino atbert: namquid ego in utero concepi omnem populem istum. Et iterum: In tristitia et in dolore concipies filios tuos. In eclais atbert sin. ut apostolus dicit: Filioli mei, quos iterum parturio, donec Christus formetur in vobis.

Ised chanair ic tabairt fina isin cailech nofrind: [Re]mittat Pater, banna annsin; indulgeat Filius, banna aile andsin; miseratur Spiritus Sanctus, in tres banna andsin.

7. Acanar dino icon ofrind iarsin, itir Intrait ocus Orthanaib ocus Imthormach, corice Liachtain nan Apstal ocus Psalm digraid .i. figuir rechta aicnid sin, in rohathnuiged aichne Crist tria runaib ocus gnimaib ocus tomoltod naicnid. Ut dictum est: Vidit Abraham diem meum et gravisus est. Uair is tria recht naicnid itconnairc Abraham.

Stowe Missal	Lebar Breac
8. The Lection of the Apostles, moreover, and bigradual Psalm and from that to the Uncovering, it is a memorial of the law of the Letter, wherein was figured Christ, who was not known as yet, though he was figured therein.	**8.** The Lection of the Apostles and the bigradual Psalm, and from that to the uncovering of the Chalice of Mass, that is a figure of the letter...? Wherein was figured Christ; and he was not known as yet [although] he was figured therein, and the thing [that is, the reality] came not, and perfection was not wrought through it. Nobody is brought to perfection by the Law.
9. The Uncovering as far as half, of the oblation and of the chalice, and what was chanted by them—both Gospel and benediction, as far as *Oblata*, it is a memorial of the law and the Prophets, wherein Christ was foretold clearly, but was not seen until he was born.	**9.** The uncovering, as far as half, of the chalice of the Mass and of the host, and what is chanted by them, both Gospel and Benediction, a figure of the Law of the letter [is] that, therein Christ was proclaimed manifestly, but he was not seen until he was born.
10. The raising of the Chalice after its full uncovering, when *Oblata* is chanted, that is a memorial of the birth of Christ and of His exaltation through signs and miracles.	**10.** The raising up of the chalice of Mass and of the paten after fully uncovering them, whereat is chanted this verse: Offer God a sacrifice of praise, [is] a figure of the birth of Christ and of His glory through deeds and marvels. The beginning of the New Testament [is] that.
11. When *Accepit Jesus panem* is chanted, the priest bows thrice for sorrow for their sins; he offers them [that is, the bread and wine] to God; and the people prostrates; and there comes not a sound then, that it not disturb the priest; for it is his duty that his mind separate not from God whilst he chants this Lection. It is from this that *Periculosa Oratio* is its name.	**11.** The time, now, *Accepit Jesus panem, stans in medio discipulorum suorum* is chanted, the priests bow thrice for sorrow for the sins they did, and they offer to God, and they chant all this psalm: Have mercy on me, O God; and no sound is sent forth by them (the people) then, that the priest be not disturbed, for what is meet is that his mind separate not from God, even in one vocable at this prayer: for it is guilty of the spiritual order and of bad reception from God, unless it is like that it is done; wherefore it is from this that the name of this prayer is *Periculosa Oratio.*

Stowe Missal

8. Liacht nApostol, immorro, ocus Salm digrad ocus ho shuidiu co Dinochtad, is foraithmet rechta litre in rofiugrad Crist, nadfess cadacht, cid rofiugrad and.

9. In dinochtad corrici leth inna oblae ocus in cailich ocus a canar occo, iter Soscel ocus Ailloir, corrici *Oblata*, is foraithmet rechta fathe, hi tarc(h)et Crist co follus, acht nathnaicess co rogenir.

10. Tocbal in cailich iarn a landiurug, quando canitur *Oblata*, is foraithmet gene Crist insin [ocus] a indocbale tre airde ocus firto.

11. Quando canitur: *accipet jesus pacem*, tanaurnat in sacart fet(h)ri du aithrigi dia pecthaib; atnopuir Deo; ocus slecthith in popul: ocus ni taet guth isson ar -na tar ⏐ masca in sacardd; ar issed a thechta ar na rascra a menme contra Deum, cene canas in liachtso. Is de is *Periculosa Oratio* a nomen.

Lebar Breac

8. Liacht nan Apstal ocus in Salm digraid [ocus] oshein co dinochtud choilig ofrind-is figuir sin rechta littri inbertar in rofiugrad Crist; ocus ni fes cadacht, [cid] rofiugrad ann, ocus ni roacht inni, ocus ni roforbthiged trit. Neminem ad perfectum duxit lex.

9. In dinochtad coleth in cholig oifrind ocus inna hablainne ocus icantar occu, itir Shoscel ocus Alleoirfiguir rechta litri sin, in roterchanad Crist cofollus, acht na facus ha cein congenir.

10. Comgabail in choilig oifrind ocus na mesi iarn a landirguid. icanair infersa .i. Immola Deo sacrificium laudism—figuir gene Crist ocus a inocbala tria fertaib ocus mirbulib. Novi Testamenti initium sin.

11. Intan tra chanar: *Accepit Jesus panem, stans in medio discipulorum suorum*, usque in finem, dotoirnet fotri na sacairt do aitrige do na pecthaib doronsat, ocus idprait do Dia, ocus canait in salmsa uli *Miserere mei, Deus;* ocus ni theit guth ison leo, co na tairmescthar in sacart, uair ised is techta co na roscara a menma fri Dia, cid in oen vocabulo, icon ernaigthisea: uair is bidbu in uird spiritalla ocus mihairtin fri Dia, menip amlaid sin is denta. Conid desin ise ainm na hernaigthisea .i. *Periculosa Oratio.*

Stowe Missal

12. The three steps that the ordained man steps backwards and that he steps in return, that is the triad wherein sinneth every person, to wit, in word, in thought, in deed; and that is the triad through which he is renewed again, and through which he is moved to the Body of Christ.

13. The examination wherewith the priest examines the chalice and the Host, and the assault that the fraction implies, a figure of the contumelies and of the stripes and of the capture (is) that.

14. The Host upon the paten, the Body of Christ upon the tree of the Cross.

15. The fraction upon the paten, the Body of Christ being broken with nails upon the Cross.

16. The meeting whereby the two halves come together after the fraction, a figure of the integrity of the Body of Christ after the Resurrection.

17. The submersion wherewith the other half is submerged, a figure of the submersion of the Body of Christ in His Blood, after the wounding on the Cross.

18. The part that is taken from the bottom of the half that is wont to be on the left-hand, a figure of the wounding with the spear in the armpit of the right side; for it is westward the face of Christ was on the Cross, namely, towards the city: and it is eastward the face of Longinus was; what was left for this person was right for Christ.

Lebar Breac

12. The three steps the man of order takes backwards and takes again forward—that is the triad wherein man falls, to wit, in thought, in word, in deed. And that is the triad through which man is renewed again to God.

13. The aim that the priest aims at the chalice of Mass and at the paten, and the attack which he makes upon the Host to break it, that is a figure of the contumelies and of the stripes and of the capture that Christ underwent. And that is its literal explanation.

14. And the Host upon the paten, the Body of Christ upon the Cross.

15. The confraction upon the paten, the Body of Christ being broken against the tree of the Cross.

16. The meeting wherein the two halves come together after the confraction, a figure of the integrity of the body of Christ after the resurrection.

17. The submersion whereby the other half is submerged afterwards, that [is] a figure of the submersion of the blood that the Jews drained from the Body of Christ.

18. The portion that is taken from the lower part of the half that is in the left hand of the priest, that is a figure of the wounding with the spear in the hand of Longinus, in the armpit of the right side of Jesus: for westward was the face of Christ on His Cross, to wit, towards the city, Jerusalem, and eastward was the face of Longinus; and the thing that was left for this person the same in deed was right for Christ.

Stowe Missal

12. Na tri chemmen cingeds in fer-
graith for a culu, ocus tocing afrit-
hisi, ised a trede in imruimdethar cach
duine, idon, himbrethir, hi cocell,
hingnim; ocus ised trede tressanaith-
nuigther iterum, ocus trisatoscigther
do Chorp Crist.

13. In mesad mesas in sacart in
cailech ocus in obli, ocus int ammus
adminidethar a combach, figor nan
aithisse ocus nan esorcon ocus inna
(aur) gabale insen.

14. Ind oblae forsin meis, coland
Crist hi crann cruche.

15. A combag forsin meis, Corp
Crist do chombug co cloaib forsin
c(h)roich.
16. in comrac conrectar in da (l)leth
iarsin chombug, figor oge chuirp Crist
iarn esergo.

17. In fobdod fombaiter indalled,
figor fobdotha cuirp crist inna fhuil,
iarn aithchumbu hi croich.

18. In pars benar a hichtur ind lithe
bis for laim cli, figor ind aithchummi
cosind lagin in oxil in tuib deiss; ar is
siar robui aiged Crist in cruce, id est,
contra civitatem: ocus i[s] sair robui
aigeth Longini; arrobo thuairse do
shuidiu, issed ropo desse do Crist.

Lebar Breac

12. na tri ceimend chindes in fer
graid for a chula, ocus chinnes iterum
for a gnuis-ise sin tredi ituitend in
duine .i. in imradud, imbrethir, ing-
nim. Ocus ise sin tredi tresanathnui-
digther in duine iterum co Dia.

13. Int aimsiugud aimsiges in sacart
in cailech oifrind ocus in meis ocus in
ablaind, ocus int amus dosbeir forsin
ablaind dia combach-figuir sin inna
haitise ocus inna hesoircne ocus inna
nergabal forfhulaing Crist. Ocus ise
sin a thaithmech sianside.
14. Ocus in abland forsin meis-col-
and Crist forsin croich.

15. A combach forsin meis-coland
Crist dochombach fri crand crochi.

16. In comrac chomracithir in da
leth iarsin combach-figuir oige Chuirp
Crist iarn esergi.

17. In fodbugud fhodbaigther ind-
alleth iarum-figuir sin fhodbaigiti inna
fuile dothebrensat Iudaide a Colaind
Crist.

18. In rand benair a hichtar in lethi
bis i laim cli in sacairt-figuir sin ind
athcumai cusin lagin i laim Longini,
isind achsaill toibe deiss Isu: uair is
siar boi aiged Crist in a chroich .i. frisin caraig, Ierusalem, ocus is siar roboi
aiged Longini; ocus inni ropu tuathbel
dosum, issed on robo dess do Crist.

Stowe Missal

There are seven kinds upon the Fraction: that is, five parts of the common Host, in figure of the five senses of the soul. Seven of the Host of Saints and Virgins, except the chief ones, in figure of the seven gifts of the Holy Spirit. Eight of the Host of Martyrs, in figure of the octonary New Testament. Nine of the Host of Sunday, in figure of the nine folks of heaven and of the nine grades of the Church. Eleven of the Host of Apostles, in figure of the imperfect number of Apostles after the scandal of Judas. Twelve of the Host of the calends [of January, that is Circumcision] and of [Last] Supper day, in remembrance of the perfect number of Apostles. Thirteen of the host of little Easter [Low Sunday] and of the feast of Ascension—at first, although they were distributed more minutely afterwards, in going to communion—in figure of Christ with his twelve Apostles.

Lebar Breac

For the face of Christ was towards us coming to us as it is said: in those days, for you who fear the name of the Lord, the sun of justice shall arise. And God comes from the East.

His back, however, toward us, in going from us, and He calling each and every one to Himself after him, saying: Come all of you to me and after me.

The simultaneous holding wherewith the hand of the priest holds the chalice of Mass—that [is,] a figure of the assembling of the people of heaven and of earth into one people: to wit, the people of heaven by the paten, the people of earth by the chalice.

Stowe Missal

Lebar Breac

Uair issed boi aiged Crist frinde, oc tidecht chucaind, ut dictum est: orietur in diebus illis vobis, timentibus nomen Domini, sol justitiae. Et: Deus ab Oriente veniet.

A chul, immorro, frind, ic tocht uaind, ocus se ic togairm chaich uli chuci in a diaid, dicens: Venite omnes ad me, post me.

In chongbail congbus lam int shacairt in mias ocus in coilech aifrind—figuir comthinoil sin muintire nime ocus talman in oen muintir: .i. muintir nime per mensam, muintir thalman per calicem.

Ataat secht ngne forsin chombug: idon, cuic parsa de obli choitchinn, hi figur cuic sense animae. A secht di obli noeb ocus huag, acht na huaisli, hi figuir ind nui fhiadnisi ochti. A noe di obli domnich, hi figuir noe montar nimae ocus noe ngraith aecalsa. A oen deac di obli Apstal, hi figuir inna airme anfuir[b]t(h)e Apostolorum iarn immamus Iudae. A di deac di obli calann ocus c(h)enlai, hi foraithmut airmae foirbte inna nAp-stal | A teora deac di obli minchasc ocus fregabale-prius, ce fodailter ni bes miniu iarum, oc techt do laim-, hi figuir Crist cona dib nApstalaib deac.

Inna cuic, ocus inn scht, ocus inna ocht, ocus deac, ocus inna teora deacithe a cuic sescot samlith; ocus is hae lin pars insin bis in obli Casc, ocus Notlaic, ocus Chenncigis; ar congaibther huils hi Crist insin.

Stowe Missal	Lebar Breac

The five, and the seven, and the eight, and the nine, and the eleven, and the twelve, and the thirteen—they are five [and] sixty together; and that is the number of parts which is wont to be in the Host of Easter, and of the Nativity, and of Pentecost; for all that is contained in Christ.

And it is all arranged in the form of a cross upon the paten; and on the incline is the upper part on the left hand, as hath been said: Inclining His head He handed over His Spirit.

The arrangement of the Fraction of Easter and of the Nativity—thirteen [fourteen] parts in the tree of the crosses; nine [fourteen] in their cross-piece; twenty parts in the circuit-wheel (five parts of each angle); sixteen between the circuit and the body of the crosses (that is, four of each portion).

The middle part, that is the one to which the celebrant goes [partakes of]: namely, a figure of the breast with the mysteries.

What is from there upwards of the tree to bishops.

The thwart-piece on the left-hand to the priests.

The portion [athwart] on the right hand, to all undergrades.

The portion from the thwart-piece downwards, to anchorites of . . . penance.

The portion that is in the upper left-hand angle, to true clerical students.

The upper right-hand (portion), to innocent youths.

The lower left-hand (portion), to folk of penance.

The lower right-hand (portion), to folk of lawful wedlock and to folk who have not gone to hand [that is, to Communion] before.

Stowe Missal	Lebar Breac

Ocus is hi torrund cruisse suidigthir huile forsin meis; ocus is for cloen in pars ochtarach for lam cli, ut dictum est: Inclinato capite, tradidit spiritum.

Suidigoth combuig Casc ocus Notlaic;—teora parsa deac in eo na cros; a noe inna tarsno; fiche pars inna cuairtroth (cuic parsae cache oxile); a se deac iter in cuairt ocus chorp na cros (idon, a cetheora [ca]cha rainne).

In pars medonach, is hi diatet in tii oifres; idon, figor in bruinni cosna runaib.

Ambis ho shen suas dind eo, do epscopbaib.

A tarsno for laim cli, do sacardaib.

ani for laim des, do huilib fogradaib.

ani ond tarsno sis, do anchordaib . . . aithirge

Ani bis isinid oxil ochtarthuaiscer-daig, do firmacclerchib.

Ind ochtardescerdach, do maccaib enngaib.

An ichtarthuaiscerdach, do aes aithirge.

An ichtardescerdach, do aes lanam-nassa dligthig, ocus do aes na tet do laim riam.

Stowe Missal	Lebar Breac

Now the effect of this is (to cause) a meaning to be in [these?] figures and that this be your meaning, as if the part that you receive of the Host were a member of Christ from off His Cross; and as if it were this Cross whence runs upon each one his own draught [lit. run], since it is united to the crucified Body.

It is not proper to swallow it, the part, without tasting it; as it is not proper to pause in tasting the mysteries of God.

It is not proper to have it go under back teeth; in figure that it is not proper to dwell overmuch upon the mysteries of God, that hearsay be not forwarded thereby.

The End. Amen. Thanks be to God.

Stowe Missal	**Lebar Breac**

Issed tra as brig lades[in], men-
mae dobuith hi figraib in . . ., ocus co
rop –he tomenme | ind rann arafoemi
din bli, amail bith ball di Crist assa
chroich, ocus arambe croch [a] sa [rit?]
hir for cach a rith fhein, hore noenige-
thir frisin chorp crochte.

Ni techte a shlocod in[na] parsa cen
a mlaissiuth; amal nan coer cen saigith
mlas hirruna De.

Ni coir a techt fo culfhiachli; hi
figuir nan coir rosaegeth forruna De,
na forberther heres nocco.

Finit. Amen. Deo gratias.

NOTES

CHAPTER ONE. Historical Background

1. Alfred J. Smyth, "The Golden Age of Early Irish Monasticism: Myth or Reality?" in *Christianity in Ireland: Revisiting the Story,* ed. Brendan Bradshaw and Dáire Keogh (Dublin: Columba Press, 2002), 21.

2. Wendy Davies, "The Myth of the Celtic Church," in *The Early Church in Wales and the West: Recent Work in Early Christian Archaeology, History and Place-Names,* ed. Nancy Edwards and A. Lane, Oxbow Monograph 16 (Oxford: Oxbow Books, 1992), 12.

3. Philip Freeman has collected all of the classical references to Ireland in his work *Ireland and the Classical World* (Austin: University of Texas Press, 2001). If this slim volume, with entries from 32 authors, of 168 pages of length, is compared to a similar book on the Jewish people, Menahem Stern, *Greek and Latin Authors on Jews and Judaism,* 2 vols. (Jerusalem: The Israel Academy of Sciences and Humanities, 1974–1980), where there are entries from 570 authors taking up 1,324 pages of text, it can be seen that there was little real interest in Ireland.

4. Freeman, *Ireland and the Classical World,* 28–33.

5. Ibid., 35.

6. Ibid., 45–46.

7. "Hibernia inhumana incolarum ritu aspero, alias ita pabulosa, ut pecua, nisi interdum a pastibus arceantur, ad periculum agat satias. Illic nullus anguis, avis rara, gens inhospita et bellicose. Sanguine interemptorum hausto prius victores vultus suos oblinunt. Fas ac nefas eodem loco ducunt. Apis nusquam, advectum inde pulverem seu lapillus si quis sparserit inter alvearia, examina favos deserent": *Collectanea Rerum Memorabilium* 22.2–6; Latin and English translation in Freeman, *Ireland and the Classical World,* 87.

8. "Quid loquar de caeteris nationibus, cum ipse adolescentulus in Gallia atticotos (al. Scotos), gentem Britannicam, humanis vesci carnibus: et cum per silvas porcorum greges et armentorum pecudumque reperiant, pastorum nates et feminarum, et papillas solere abscindere, et has solas ciborum delicias arbitrary? Scotorum natio uxores proprias non habet: et quasi Platonis politiam

legerit, et Catonis sectetur exemplum, nulla apud eos coniux propia est, sed ut cuique libitum fuerit, pecudum more lasciviunt": *Adversus Juovinianum* 2.7; Latin and English translation in Freeman, *Ireland and the Classical World*, 99. It could be added in Jerome's defense that (even if his claims are historically mistaken and he probably never saw members of this group who ravaged Britain and not Gaul) he thought that his arch-rival Pelagius was of Irish stock, and as part of this fight he felt the need to disparage the Irish. Also in this quotation Jerome was not particularly singling the Irish out for special treatment, as he was one of the best practitioners of satire among all writers of Latin both classical and Christian; see J. N. D. Kelly, *Jerome: His Life, Writings and Controversies* (Peaboy, MA: Hendrickson, 1975), 26 and 108.

9. Freeman, *Ireland and the Classical World*, 12. However, for a more favorable summary of the material evidence see Catherine Swift, *Ogham Stones and the Earliest Irish Christians* (Maynooth: Cardinal Press, 1997), 3–11. This work's primary focus is relevant to this discussion because the Ogham system is itself intrinsically linked to Roman culture.

10. Damian McManus, "The So-Called *Cothrige* and *Pátraic* Strata of Latin Loan-Words in Early Irish," in *Irland und Europa: Die Kirche im Frühmittelalter*, ed. Próinséas Ní Chatháin and Michael Richter (Stuttgart: Klett-Cotta, 1984), 195.

11. Peter Harbison, *Pre-Christian Ireland: From the First Settlers to the Early Celts*, 2nd ed. (London: Thames & Hudson, 1994), 15–26.

12. Ibid., 27.

13. Peter Harbison, *Treasures of the Boyne Valley* (Dublin: Gill and Macmillan, 2003), 100–123.

14. Harold Mytum, *The Origins of Early Christian Ireland* (New York: Routledge, 1992), 49.

15. Harbison, *Pre-Christian Ireland*, 168–72.

16. Stuart Piggott, *The Druids*, 2nd ed. (London: Thames & Hudson, 1985), 123–82.

17. "Quia ualde 'debitor sum' Deo, qui mihi tantam gratiam donauit ut populi multi per me in Deum renascerentur et postmodum consummarentur. Et ut clerici ubique illis ordinarentur ad plebem nuper uenientem ad credulitatem, quam sumpsit Dominus 'ab extremis terrae.' Sicut olim promiserat per prophetas suos: 'Ad te gentes uenient ab extremis terrae et dicent, "Sicut falsa comparauerunt patres nostri idola et non est in eis utilitas."' Et iterum 'Posui te lumen in gentibus ut sis in salutem usque ad extremum terrae'": St Patrick, *Confessio* 38, from David R. Howlett, trans. and ed., *The Book of Letters of Saint Patrick the Bishop* (Dublin: Four Courts Press, 1994), 76; English translation from Ludwig Bieler, trans. and ed., *The Works of St Patrick and St Secundinus' Hymn on St Patrick*, Ancient Christian Writers 17 (Mahwah, NJ: Paulist Press, 1953), 32–33.

18. "Ultimi habitatores mundi": *Epistula* 5.23, in G. S. M. Walker, trans. and ed., *Sancti Columbani Opera,* Scriptores Latini Hiberniae 2 (Dublin: School of Celtic Studies, Dublin Institute for Advanced Studies, 1957), 38–39.

19. Peter Brown, *The Rise of Western Christendom,* 2nd ed. (Malden, MA: Blackwell, 2003), 21.

20. Ibid., 46.

21. This theme is amply proven in Michael McCormick, *Origins of the European Economy: Communications and Commerce, AD 300–900* (Cambridge: Cambridge University Press, 2001).

22. P. Brown, *The Rise of Western Christendom,* 104–5.

23. Ibid., 103.

24. James Campbell, ed., *The Anglo-Saxons* (Ithaca: Cornell University Press, 1982), 8.

25. Kathleen Hughes, *The Church in Early Irish Society* (London: Methuen, 1966), 21.

26. Nicholas Higham, *Rome, Britain and the Anglo-Saxons* (London: Seaby, 1992), 70.

27. P. Brown, *The Rise of Western Christendom,* 126–27.

28. Climatic change seems to have accompanied both the Roman arrival in Britain and the Roman withdrawal, contributing to a population growth at the start of the period of colonization and shrinkage at the end of the period; Higham, *Rome, Britain and the Anglo-Saxons,* 79–82.

29. Garth Fowden, *Empire to Commonwealth: Consequences of Monotheism in Late Antiquity* (Princeton: Princeton University Press, 1993), 85–93.

30. Higham, *Rome, Britain and the Anglo-Saxons,* 214–16.

31. Thomas M. Charles-Edwards, *Early Christian Ireland* (Cambridge: Cambridge University Press, 2000), 202. Modern language scholars point to a linguistic relationship between the Old Welsh that these British missionaries would have spoken and Old Irish. By the seventh century, the earliest time for which significant knowledge of these languages exists, they were mutually unintelligible. In the fourth and fifth centuries, as Irish and British Ogham texts testify, these languages were closer, but it is impossible to say precisely to what degree they were mutually intelligible. However, it is also true that at this time there was no concept of Celtic languages, and the new "cultural zone" that was formed between the Irish and the British had to be founded on Latin as a common language of scholarship and liturgy and not on any common Celtic spirit; see ibid., 239.

32. Unless otherwise specified, in this work Augustine refers to St Augustine of Canterbury and not St Augustine of Hippo.

33. Marie-Therese Flanagan, "The Contribution of Irish Missionaries and Scholars to Medieval Christianity," in Bradshaw and Keogh, *Christianity in Ireland,* 31.

34. There is a much later precedent for the wholesale use of a local language in the introduction of Christianity, when in the ninth century Saints Cyril and Methodius translated the liturgy and the scriptures into the language of the Slavic tribes that they were evangelizing, inventing a new alphabet to aid them in their task. However, even if a new alphabet, Glagolitic, was invented that was quite good for expressing Slavic sounds, in reality that alphabet had a very short life, being replaced by the Cyrillic alphabet (a more mainstream, if misleadingly named alphabet); see Anthony-Emil Tachiaos, *Cyril and Methodius of Thessalonica: The Acculturation of the Slavs* (Crestwood, NY: St. Vladimir's Seminary Press, 2001), 77–91, 119–21. Furthermore, the evangelization of the Slavs entailed a significant introduction of Byzantine culture and literature into a Slavic context where, unlike the Irish experience, very little of the pre-Christian culture remained and the native literature was not nearly as significant; see Helen C. Evans, "Christian Neighbors," in *The Glory of Byzantium: Art and Culture of the Middle Byzantine Era, AD 843–1261*, ed. Helen C. Evans and William D. Wixom, 272–79 (New York: The Metropolitan Museum of Art, 1997).

35. For more on the process of evangelizing a nation see James C. Russell, *The Germanization of Early Medieval Christianity: A Sociohistorical Approach to Religious Transformation* (New York: Oxford University Press, 1994), 26–44.

36. John J. Contreni, "The Irish Contribution to the European Classroom," in *Proceedings of the Seventh International Congress of Celtic Studies,* ed. D. Ellis Evans, John G. Griffith, and E. M. Jope (Oxford: Ellis Evans, 1986), 81–82; also see J. N. Hillgarth, "Modes of Evangelization of Western Europe in the Seventh Century," in *Ireland and Christendom: The Bible and the Missions,* ed. Próinséas Ní Chatháin and Michael Richter, 311–31 (Stuttgart: Klett-Cotta 1987).

37. "Ad Scottos in Christum credentes ordinates a papa Caelestino Palladius primus episcopus mittitur": *PL* 51:595; English translation from James F. Kenney, *The Sources for the Early History of Ireland I: Ecclesiastical* (New York: Columbia, 1929; repr., Dublin: Four Courts Press, 1993), 165n40.

38. "Nec uero segniore cura ab hoc eodem morbo Britannias liberauit, quando, quosdam inimicos gratiae solum suae originis occupants etiam ab illo secreto exclusit Oceani, et ordinato Scotis episcopo, dum romanam insulam sttudet seruare catholicam, fecit etiam barbaram christianam": *Contra Collatorem* 21, in *PL* 51:271; English translation from Thomas M. Charles-Edwards, "Palladius, Prosper, and Leo the Great: Mission and Primatial Authority," in *St Patrick AD 493–1993,* ed. David N. Dumville (Suffolk: Boydell & Brewer, 1993), 1.

39. "In the eighth year of his reign Palladius was sent by Celestinus the pontiff of the Roman church to the Irish believers in Christ to be their first

bishop"; "Cuius anno impeii octauo Palladius ad Scottos in Christum creden-
tes a pontifice Romanae ecclesiae Celestino primus mittitur episcopus": Bede,
Ecclesiastical History 1.13, text and translation from Bertram Colgrave and
R. A. B. Mynors, trans. and eds., *Bede's Ecclesiastical History of the English
People* (Oxford: The Clarendon Press, 1969), 46–47.

40. Thomas O'Loughlin, *Celtic Theology: Humanity, Word and God in
Early Irish Writings* (New York: Continuum, 2000), 25–26.

41. One trace of Palladius's pre-Patrick mission is in an eighth-century
life of Ailbe of Emly. Ailbe is said to have arrived in Ireland before Patrick and
to have been endorsed by Palladius (and naturally later on also by Patrick); see
Vita S. Albei, cols 29–30, cited in Thomas M. Charles-Edwards, "Introduction" in *A New History of Ireland,* vol. 1, *Prehistoric and Early Ireland,* ed.
Dáibhí Ó Cróinín (Oxford: Oxford University Press, 2005), lxxvii.

42. Thomas M. Charles-Edwards has proposed that Pope St Leo the
Great (d. 461), a friend of Prosper of Aquitaine, takes credit for the evangelization of Ireland on behalf of the papacy, a mere decade after Celestine's dis-
patching of Palladius. This is a plausible theory, given the political and social
situation of a Rome reeling from sackings and facing the rising prestige of Constantinople, but it is not easy to prove its historical accuracy; see Charles-
Edwards "Palladius, Prosper, and Leo the Great."

43. Charles-Edwards, *Early Christian Ireland,* 213.

44. "Nos enim sanctorum Petri et Pauli et omnium discipulorum divinum
canonem spiritu sancto scribentium discupuli sumus, toti Iberi, ultimi habitatores mundi, nihil extra evangelicam et apostolicam doctrinam recipients; nullus hereticus, nullus Iudaeus, nullus schismaticus fuit; sed fides catholica, sicut
a vobis primum, sanctorum videlicet apostolorum successoribus, tradita est,
inconcussa tenetur": *Letter* 53, in Walker, *Sancti Columbani Opera,* 38–39.

45. Dáibhí Ó Cróinín, *Early Medieval Ireland, 400–1200* (London:
Longman, 1995), 23.

46. The *First Synod of Patrick,* which dates to sometime in the sixth century, portrays a world where Christians and pagans are living together and
where the church feels a certain need to legislate against Christians becoming
too involved with their pagan neighbors; see Fergus Kelly, *A Guide to Early
Irish Law,* Early Irish Law Series 3 (Dublin: Dublin Institute for Celtic Studies,
1998), 40.

47. Charles-Edwards, *Early Christian Ireland,* 183.

48. Mytum, *The Origins of Early Christian Ireland,* 21.

49. For more on the role of agriculture in early Ireland see Fergus Kelly,
Early Irish Farming, Early Irish Law Series 4 (Dublin: Dublin Institute for
Celtic Studies, 2000), and the helpful summary Nancy Edwards, "The Archaeology of Medieval Ireland, *c.* 400–1169: Settlement and Economy," in *Prehistoric and Early Ireland,* ed. Ó Cróinín, 261–75, esp. 275.

50. Mytum, *The Origins of Early Christian Ireland,* 23–36, 49.

51. P. Brown, *The Rise of Western Christendom,* 125–26, 81.

52. Ibid., 129–30, 239.

53. Ibid, 344. For a fuller treatment of the link between Rome and what was to become the English church and nation, see Nicholas Brooks, "Canterbury, Rome and English Identity," in *Early Medieval Rome and the Christian West: Essays in Honour of David A. Bullough,* ed. Julia M. H. Smith, 221–47 (Leiden: Brill, 2000).

54. Bede, *Ecclesiastical History* 5.23, text and translation from Colgrave and Mynors, *Ecclesiastical History,* 560–61.

55. Indeed, the argument can be made that Bede invented the very concept of "Englishness," and that, prior to his theological project, Britain contained a number of different peoples, and that it is only with Bede that we have the intellectual underpinnings for England as a nation; see Benedicta Ward, *The Venerable Bede* (Harrisburg, PA: Morehouse Publishing, 1990), 143.

56. "Digniores memoratae praecones ueritatis": Bede, *Ecclesiastical History* 1.22, text and translation from Colgrave and Mynors, *Ecclesiastical History,* 68–69. Conversely, however, one could also note that the litany of saints at the start of the Eucharist in the *Stowe Missal* contains the names of Augustine's three immediate successors at Canterbury, but he himself is absent from the list; see Archdale A. King, *Liturgies of the Past* (London: Longmans, 1959), 264–65.

57. Bede, *Ecclesiastical History* 3.5, in Colgrave and Mynors, *Ecclesiastical History,* 226–29.

58. Bede, *Ecclesiastical History* 3.19, in Colgrave and Mynors, *Ecclesiastical History,* 268–77.

59. Bede, *Ecclesiastical History* 3.4, in Colgrave and Mynors, *Ecclesiastical History,* 220–25.

60. "Siquidem ubi Scottorum in praefata ipsorum patria quomodo et Brettonum in ipsa Brittania, uitam ac professionem minus ecclesiasticam in multis esse cognouit": Bede, *Ecclesiastical History* 2.4, text and translation from Colgrave and Mynors, *Ecclesiastical History,* 145–47.

61. Michael W. Herren and Shirley Ann Brown, *Christ in Celtic Christianity: Britain and Ireland from the Fifth to the Tenth Century* (Woodbridge: Boydell Press, 2002). Herren and Brown postulate a Pelagian church in the Celtic areas. While it is beyond the scope of this book to consider these claims, our general conclusions do not agree with Herren and Brown, as there is simply not enough evidence of a full-blown Pelagian church in the British Isles.

62. "Augustine's second question. Even though the faith is one, are there varying customs in the churches? and is there one form of mass in the Holy Roman Church and another in the Gaulish churches? Pope Gregory answered: My brother, you know the customs of the Roman Church in which, of course,

you were brought up. But it is my wish that if you have found any customs in the Roman or the Gaulish church or any other church which may be more pleasing to God, you should make a careful selection of them and sedulously teach the Church of the English, which is still new in the faith, what you have been able to gather from other churches. For things are not to be loved for the sake of place, but places are to be loved for the sake of their good things. Therefore choose from every individual Church whatever things are devout religious, and right. And when you have collected these as it were into one bundle, see that the minds of the English grow accustomed to it"; "Interrogatio Augustini: Cum una sit fides, sunt ecclesiarum diuersae consuetudines, et altera consuetudo missarum in sancta Romana ecclesia atque altera in Galliarum tenetur? Respondid Gregorius papa: Nouit fraternitas tua Romanae ecclesiae consuetudinem, in ua se meminit nutritam. Sed mihi placet ut, siue in Romana siue in Galliarum seu in qualibet ecclesiae aliquid inuenisti, quod plus omnipotenti Deo possit placere. Sollicite eligias, et in Anglorum ecclesia, quae adhuc ad fidem noua est, institutione praececipua, quae de multis ecclesiis colligere potuisti, infundas. Non enim pro locis res, sed pro bonis rebus loca amanda sunt. Ex singulis ergo quibusque ecclesiis quae pia, quae religiosa, quae recta sunt elige, et haec quasi in fasciculum collecta apud Anglorum mentes in consuetudinem depone": Bede, *Ecclesiastical History* 1.27, text and translation from Colgrave and Mynors, *Ecclesiastical History,* 80–83. For an analysis of this important text (which a number of scholars have rejected as spurious) see Paul Meyvaert, "Diversity within Unity: A Gregorian Theme," in *Benedict, Gregory, Bede and Others,* ed. Paul Meyvaert, 141–62 (London: Variorum, 1977).

63. The topic of baptism is another controversy that was raised by Bede, but this problem was never really as grave as the others. According to Bede, Augustine objected to the British practice, but Bede does not tell us what the difference was between the manner of baptism of the British bishops and "the rites of the holy Roman and apostolic church" ("iuxta morem sanctae Romanae et apostolicae ecclesiae"), *Ecclesiastical History* 2.2, text and translation from Colgrave and Mynors, *Ecclesiastical History,* 138–39.

64. H. Leclercq, "Paques," in *DACL* 13, col. 1495. See also the analysis of the various means of calculation in Dáibhí Ó Cróinín, "New Heresy for Old: Pelagianism in Ireland and the Papal Letter of 640," *Speculum* 60, no. 3 (1985): 505–16. For an in-depth study of the whole controversy see Caitlin Corning, *The Celtic and Roman Traditions: Conflict and Consensus in the Early Medieval Church* (New York: Palgrave Macmillan, 2006).

65. Benedicta Ward, *High King of Heaven: Aspects of Early English Spirituality,* Cistercian Studies Series 181 (Kalamazoo, MI: Cistercian Publications, 1999), 17.

66. For a summary of the various arguments see Edward James, "Bede and the Tonsure Question," *Peritia* 3 (1984): 86–87, and for a treatment of the

particularly important role that hair played in early Ireland see William Sayers, "Attitudes Towards Hair and Beards, Baldness and Tonsure," *Zeitschrift für Celtische Philologie* 44 (1991): 154–89.

67. Ward, *High King of Heaven*, 98.

68. Bede, *Ecclesiastical History* 5.22, in Colgrave and Mynors, *Ecclesiastical History*, 552–55.

69. Ward, *High King of Heaven*, 22.

70. "Eos qui uni Deo seruirent unam uiuendi regulam tenere, nec discrepare in celebratione sacramentorum caelestium, qui unum omnes in caelis regnum expectarent": Bede, *Ecclesiastical History* 3.25, text and translation from Colgrave and Mynors, *Ecclesiastical History*, 298–99.

71. The accusation was even made that Columbanus and other Irish churchmen were Quartodecimans. But this is untrue as, unlike the Quartodecimans, their Easter was always celebrated on Sunday; see Herbert Thurston, "Easter Controversy," in *CE* 5:229, and Daniel P. Mc Carthy and Aidan Breen, *The Ante-Nicene Christian Pasch*, De Ratione Paschali: *The Paschal Tract of Anatolius, Bishop of Laodicea* (Dublin: Four Courts Press, 2003), 175–77. Columbanus himself never changed his position; indeed, he addressed letters to two successive popes trying to bring them to change back their calculation to his own, but sometime after his death Luxeuil and his other foundations conformed to the local usage. Perhaps the lack of a reply from Gregory the Great to Columbanus may even show a tacit papal support of Columbanus's person and mission, even if Gregory knew that he could not agree with him on that point; see Charles-Edwards, *Early Christian Ireland*, 370.

72. P. Brown, *The Rise of Western Christendom*, 362–63.

73. Charles-Edwards, *Early Christian Ireland*, 321.

74. Kathleen Hughes, "Evidence for Contacts between the Churches of the Irish and English from the Synod of Whitby to the Viking Age," in *England Before the Conquest: Studies in Primary Sources Presented to Dorothy Whitelock*, ed. P. Clemoes and K. Hughes (Cambridge: Cambridge University Press, 1971), 49, and Denis Bethell, "English Monks and Irish Reform in the Eleventh and Twelfth Centuries," *Historical Studies* 8 (1971): 117.

75. Colmán Etchingham, "The Ideal of Monastic Austerity in Early Ireland," in *Luxury and Austerity: Papers Read before the Twenty-Third Irish Conference of Historians Held at St Patrick's College, Maynooth, 16–18 May, 1997*, ed. Jacqueline Hill and Colm Lennon (Dublin: University College Dublin Press, 1997), 16. Many twentieth-century scholars understood the church in pre-Norman Ireland to have an atypical structure due to its location outside the Roman empire and lack of centers of population to act as diocesan sees, but this traditional model is no longer sustainable. Kathleen Hughes initially modified it and then questioned it in her posthumously published work, *The Church in Early Irish Society*, 44–110, and in "The Celtic Church: Is This a Valid Con-

cept?" *Cambridge Medieval Celtic Studies* 1 (1981): 1–20. Patrick Corish also called it into question by adding the important dimension of pastoral care to the study; see his *The Christian Mission*, vol. 1 of *A History of Irish Catholicism* (Dublin: Gill and Macmillan, 1972), 32–40.

76. One particular article has added a much needed counterbalance to the overemphasis on the monastic dimension of the church in the pre-Norman period: Richard Sharpe, "Some Problems Concerning the Organization of the Church in Early Medieval Ireland," *Peritia* 3 (1984): 230–70. His intuitions have been further developed and elaborated in Colmán Etchingham, *Church Organisation in Ireland AD 650 to 1000* (Maynooth: Laigin Publications, 1999).

77. T. M. Charles-Edwards, "Beyond Empire II: Christianities of the Celtic Peoples," in *Early Medieval Christianities, c. 600–c. 1100*, ed. Thomas F. X. Noble and Julia M. H. Smith, vol. 3 of *The Cambridge History of Christianity* (Cambridge: Cambridge University Press, 2008), 101.

78. For an accessible account of the beginnings of monasticism, see Derwas Chitty, *The Desert a City: An Introduction to the Study of Egyptian and Palestinian Monasticism under the Christian Empire* (Crestwood, NY: St. Vladimir's Seminary Press, 1966). For more modern scholarship also see William Harmless, *Desert Christians: An Introduction to the Literature of Early Monasticism* (Oxford: Oxford University Press, 2004), and Susanna Elm, *"Virgins of God": The Making of Asceticism in Late Antiquity* (Oxford: Oxford University Press, 1994).

79. "Filii Scottorum et filiae regulorum monachi et uirgines Xpisti esse uidentur": St Patrick, *Confessio* 41, in Howlett, *The Book of Letters*, 80; English translation from Bieler, *The Works of St Patrick*, 34.

80. Ó Cróinín, *Early Medieval Ireland*, 162.

81. The case could be made that Irish monasticism tended to be more ascetical than the Continental varieties, at least if one compares the various Irish rules with that of Benedict; see Charles-Edwards, *Early Christian Ireland*, 384, and Dáibhí Ó Cróinín, "A Tale of Two Rules: Benedict and Columbanus," in *The Irish Benedictines: A History*, ed. Martin Browne and Colmán Ó Clabaigh, 11–24 (Dublin: Columba, 2005). It is significant that there is no widespread use of the *Rule of St Benedict* in Ireland prior to the twelfth-century reforms and Malachy's introduction of the Cistercians. The only exception to this is the Scottenkloster movement of Benedictine monasteries, which recruited Irish vocations for service in Benedictine monasteries in the Germanic regions; see Tomás Ó Fiaich, "Irish Monks in Germany in the Late Middle Ages," in *The Churches, Ireland and the Irish: Papers Read at the 1987 Summer Meeting and the 1988 Winter Meeting of the Ecclesiastical History Society*, ed. W. J. Shiels and Dianna Wood, 89–104 (Oxford: Basil Blackwell, 1989).

82. Colmán Etchingham, "Bishoprics in Ireland and Wales in the Early Middle Ages: Some Comparisons" in *Contrasts and Comparisons: Studies in*

Irish and Welsh Church History, ed. John R. Guy and W. D. Neely (Powys: Welsh Religious History Society, 1999), 14–15. Also see Etchingham, *Church Organisation,* chaps. 4 and 5.

83. Sharpe, "The Church in Early Medieval Ireland," 263.

84. Patrick J. Corish, "The Pastoral Mission in the Early Irish Church," *Léachtaí Cholm Cille* 2 (1971): 8–9.

85. "Si quis aduena ingressus fuerit plebem non ante baptizat neque offerat nec consecret nec ecclesiam aedificet nec permissionem accipiat ab episcopo, nam qui a gentibus sperat permissionem alienus sit": *The First Synod of Patrick* 24, in Ludwig Bieler, trans. and ed., *The Irish Penitentials,* Scriptores Latini Hiberniae 4, 2nd ed. (Dublin: School of Celtic Studies, Dublin Institute for Advanced Studies, 1975), 58–59. Hughes, *The Church in Early Irish Society,* 50, places this text in the sixth century whereas Etchingham, *Church Organisation,* 59–60, places it in the seventh. Regardless of whether it is of sixth- or seventh-century origin, it does accentuate the important role of the bishop (and not the abbot) as the overseer of pastoral care, at least in the mind of those who drafted this document.

86. "Monochi autem non debent baptizare neque accipere elimosinam. Si autem accipiant elimosiam, cur non baptizabunt?": *Penitential of Finnian* 50, in Bieler, *The Irish Penitentials,* 92–93.

87. "Non est monachorum baptizare, communicare, aut aliquod ecclesiasticum laicis ministrare nisi forte cogente necessitate imperanti episcopo obedient": *De statu ecclesiae* 45–48, in John Fleming, trans. and ed., *Gille of Limerick (c. 1070–1145) Architect of a Medieval Church* (Dublin: Four Courts Press, 2001), 148–49.

88. Paul Bradshaw, *The Search for the Origins of Christian Worship: Sources and Methods for the Study of Early Liturgy,* 2nd ed. (Oxford: Oxford University Press, 2002), 18–19.

89. Charles-Edwards, *Early Christian Ireland,* 124.

90. This is not to say that Christianity did not foster, for example, any improvement in society's general attitude to the poor (the Irish saints' lives contain many examples of Christian charity and mercy to the poor). Nonetheless, further study needs to be carried out on this topic in Ireland. Even though many significant differences would have existed between Ireland and France, an idea of the church's role in the care of the poor in this period can be gleaned from Henry Beck, *The Pastoral Care of Souls in South-East France during the Sixth Century,* Analecta Gregoriana 51 (Rome: Pontifical Gregorian Press, 1950), 317–44.

91. "Diverso ordine et uno animo Dominum omnipotentem orat": Cogitosus, *Vita Brigitae* 32.3, *PL* 75:789; English translation from Sean Connolly and Jean-Michel Picard, trans. and eds., "Cogitosius's *Life of St Brigit:* Content and Value," *Journal of the Royal Society of Antiquaries of Ireland* 117 (1987): 26.

92. I use the neutral term of "ecclesiastic" to refer to church personnel (bishops, priests, monks, and nuns) in preference to the more commonly used term of "monastic." As I have discussed, modern studies of pre-Norman Ireland have shown that the early Irish church was far from being thoroughly monastic, and hence the neutral term is more accurate.

93. For an attempt to analyze the complicated and often contradictory evidence of Irish society, see Charles-Edwards, *Early Christian Ireland*, 124–44.

94. Dorothy Hoogland Verkerk, "Pilgrimage *Ad Limina Apostolorum* in Rome: Irish Crosses and Early Christian Sarcophagi," in *From Ireland Coming: Irish Art from the Early Christian to the Late Gothic Period and Its European Context*, ed. Colum Hourihane, 9–26 (Princeton: Princeton University Press, 2001).

95. Charles Doherty, "The Basilica in Early Ireland," *Peritia* 3 (1984): 310.

96. Kelly, *A Guide to Early Irish Law*, 43–51.

97. Compare this view with the exalted view of Patrick's linguistic and general academic formation in Howlett, *The Book of Letters*.

98. Christine Mohrmann, "The Earliest Continental Irish Latin," *Vigiliae Christianae* 16, nos. 3/4 (1962): 216–33.

99. This may have contributed to the *peregrinatio* of many Irish clerics outside Ireland, because if they had merely moved from one *túath* to another they would have kept the status that they were liable to lose abroad and thus their spiritual sacrifice would be less meritorious in God's eyes; see Charles-Edwards, *Early Christian Ireland*, 103.

100. "Erant ibiden eo tempore multi nobilium simul et mediocrium de gente Anglorum, qui tempore Finani et Colmani episcoporum, relicta insula patria, uel diuinae lectionis uel continentioris uitae gratia illo secesserant. Et quidam quidem mox se monasticae consuersationi fideliter mancipauerunt; alii magis circueundo per cellas magistrorum lectioni operam dare gaudebant. Quos omnes Scotti libentissime suscipientes, uictum eis cotidianum sine pretio, libros quoque ad legendum et magisterium gratuitum praebere curabant": Bede, *Ecclesiastical History* 3.27, text and translation from Colgrave and Mynors, *Ecclesiastical History*, 312–13.

101. Flanagan, "The Contribution of Irish Missionaries," 37. For an enthusiastic view of the extent of the Irish ecclesiastical diaspora throughout modern France, Germany, and the Low Countries, see Róisín Ní Mheara, *In Search of Irish Saints: The* Peregrinatio Pro Christo (Dublin: Four Courts Press, 1994).

102. For more information, see Mary Garrison "The English and the Irish at the Court of Charlemagne," in *Charlemagne and His Heritage: 1200 Years of Civilization and Science in Europe*, ed. P. Butzer, M. Kerner, and

W. Oberschelp, 1:97–123 (Turnhout: Brepols, 1997). For another view that gives more importance to the specific Irish contribution to the Carolingian empire, see Michael Richter, "Das Irische Erbe der Karolinger," in *Charlemagne and His Heritage,* ed. Butzer, Kerner, and Oberschelp, 1:79–96.

103. Charles-Edwards, *Early Christian Ireland,* 592; see also Contreni, "The Irish Contribution."

104. Colmán Etchingham, "The Early Irish Church: Some Observations on Pastoral Care and Dues," *Ériu* 42 (1993): 102.

105. Richard Sharpe, "Churches and Communities in Early Medieval Ireland: Towards a Pastoral Model," in *Pastoral Care Before the Parish,* ed. John Blair and Richard Sharpe (Leicester: Leicester University Press, 1992), 89.

106. Some of the more recent work that has been done on individual sites is analyzed below: see pp. 155–60.

107. For a response to Sharpe's over-enthusiastic theory of pastoral care see Colmán Etchingham, "Pastoral Provision in the First Millennium: A Two-Tier Service?" in *The Parish in Medieval and Early Modern Ireland: Community, Territory and Building,* ed. Raymond Gillespie and Elizabeth FitzPatrick, 79–90 (Dublin: Four Courts Press, 2006).

108. "A nubarit, a ndechmad, a primite 7 a primgeine 7 a nudacht, a nimna": D. A. Binchy, *Corpus Iuris Hibernici* (1978): 529.5–24, quoted in Etchingham, "The Early Irish Church," 102.

109. It is worth noting that "the archaeological evidence suggests that in the pre-Viking period wealth was concentrated mainly in the hands of the many royal families"; Edwards, "The Archaeology of Medieval Ireland," 292.

110. "Each tribe [is] to have a chief bishop for the ordination of their clergy, for the consecration of their churches, and for the spiritual guidance of princes and chieftains, for the sanctification and blessing of their offspring after baptism"; "Prímepscop cec*h*a túait*h*e accu fri huirdned a n-óessa grá*i*d, fri coisecrad a n-eclas, 7 fri hanmc*h*airdes do flaithib 7 do airc*h*indc[h]ib, fri nóemad 7 bencac*h*ad a clainde iar mbat*h*ius": *Ríagail Pátraic* 1, in J. G. O'Keeffe, "The Rule of Patrick," *Ériu* 1 (1905): 218–21.

111. "Is é [epsc*op*] timairg f*or* cec*h* ecl*ais* co raib a durrt*h*ech 7 a relec hi nglai*n*e 7 co raib in altóir cona haidmib ar c[h]i*n*id óessa grá*i*d dogrés": *Ríagail Pátraic* 6, in ibid., 219–22.

112. "Go raib idbairt c*h*uirp Críst f*or* cec*h* altóir": *Ríagail Pátraic* 7, in ibid.

113. "Ocus nac*h* eclas oc ná bé túara ma*n*ach do bait*h*is 7 comna 7 gabáil écnairce ní dlig dec*h*mad ná train n-i*m*nai": *Ríagail Pátraic* 8, in ibid.

114. The *manaig* were lay tenants working on church-owned lands. They cannot really be considered to be semi-monastics (as some earlier authors have done), but, as the church had a special responsibility to them, they do receive special mention in many texts with a reference to pastoral care; see Charles-Edwards, *Early Christian Ireland,* 118–19.

115. "Ai*t*ire dogó *f*ria lái*m* de manc*h*aib ce*ch* ecl*a*isi bes *f*ora c*h*ubu*s* fri túar*u*stul cóir e*ter* lóg mbai*th*is 7 téc*h*ta co*m*na 7 gabáil écnairce ne n-uile man-ach e*ter* bíu 7 marbu 7 oiffrend ce*ch*a do*m*naig 7 ce*ch*a prímsoll*amain 7* ce*ch*a prim-féile 7 ceileab*r*ad ce*ch*a trá*th*q do c*h*étal, m*a*ni *th*airmesca forcetul *nó* an*m*chairdes . i. ongad 7 bai*th*is. Má be*th* *t*rai do húaithe ind áessa grá*i*d lasna túa*th*a, cia beit trí hecailsi *nó* a cet*h*air *f*or cubu*s* ce*ch* *f*ir grá*i*d ac*h*t rosó com-mand 7 bai*th*ius do anma*i*n c*h*áic*h* 7 oiffrend hi soll*amnaib* 7 féilib for a n-altóir. It é a fri*th*folaidi-seom dond fir grá*i*d . i. lá air n-i*n*draic ceich blí*adna* co*n*a síl 7 a i*th*ir 7 a let*h*gabol étaig do brutt *nó* do inur. Pruind c*h*et*h*ruir ar notlaic 7 *ch*aisc 7 c*h*ingcís": *Ríagail Pátraic* 12–14, in J. O'Keeffe, "The Rule of Patrick," 219; English translation from Etchingham, "The Early Irish Church," 108.

116. The idea that the eucharistic celebration was more important than the actual reception of Communion will be examined more fully in chapter 2, as well as the possible connection between the "meal for four at Christmas and Easter and Pentecost" and communitarian reception of Communion at these times.

117. It could be that this group of churches constituted a *túath*, so that this petty-kingdom would fall within the pastoral ministration of a single priest or bishop; see Etchingham, "Pastoral Provision in the First Millennium," 84.

118. Sharpe, "Churches and Communities," 82 (citing *Hibernensis* 2.25).

119. "Coteat mífolad dóertho ecalso? Ní hansae: buit cen bathais, cen chmnai, cen oifrend, cen immon n-anmae, cen phrecept, cen áes n-aithrige, cen achtáil, cen teoir; uisce tree for altóir, esáin oíged úaidi; nac, díchmairc, sain-chron, fodord, frithairle chéile; athláech inna hairitiu, gillae inna ferthigsiud, caillech do fócru a tráth; a fodergad co fuil, a cor fo flaith, a tascnam íar fogail, a fothlae fo mnáib, mórad fíach fuiri, a fochnam co peccad, a fochraic do flaith nó fini": *Bretha Nemed Toísech* 1.6, in Liam Breatnach, "The First Third of *Bretha Nemed Toísech*," *Ériu* 40 (1989): 10–11.

120. Corish, "The Pastoral Mission," 20.

121. "Ar ní fuil aitreb ni*m*e do a*n*main dui*n*e nad baithister o baithus dligthech re ce*ch* rét, conid aire for*ta* anmanda fer ner*enn* cona flaithib 7 a nairechaib 7 a nairchi*n*dchib co raib baithius 7 comna 7 gabail écnairce o ce*ch* ecl*a*is do manchaib techtaib; ar as octrít 7 miscad patraic co noemaib er*enn* for cech flaith 7 for cech manach na ti*m*airg *f*ora eclais saindiles baithius 7 co*m*nai 7 gabail ecnoirce i*n*ti": Daniel A. Binchy, *Corpus Iuris Hibernici: Ad Fidem Codicum Manuscriptorum Recognovit* (Dublin: Dublin Institute for Advanced Studies, 1978), 6:2129, lines 32–37; English translation from Thomas Charles-Edwards, "The Pastoral Role of the Church in the Early Irish Laws," in Blair and Sharpe, *Pastoral Care Before the Parish*, 70.

122. Sharpe, "Churches and Communities," 109.

123. Etchingham, "The Early Irish Church," 118.

124. Etchingham, "The Ideal of Monastic Austerity," 17–18.

125. Etchingham, *Church Organisation*, 290–318. The penitential texts that are the basis for this interpretation will be examined in chapter 2; see below, pp. 90–102.

126. P. Brown, *The Rise of Western Christendom*, 467.

127. "Longas tre-fhichet long di Norddmannaibh *for* Boinn; longas . ii. tre-fhichet long *for* abaind Liphi. Ro slatsat iar*u*m in di longais-sin Magh Liphi & Magh m-Bregh et*er* cealla & dune & treba. Roiniudh re feraib Bregh *for* Gallaibh ec Deoninni i Mughdornaibh Bregh conid-torc*h*radar se fichit diibh": *AU* 837.3.

128. The annals are a very important, but unfortunately understudied, source of early Irish history. For more background see Daniel P. McCarthy, *The Irish Annals: Their Genesis, Evolution and History* (Dublin: Four Courts Press, 2008).

129. Conleth Manning, "References to Church Buildings in the Annals," in *Seanchas: Studies in Early and Medieval Irish Archaeology, History and Literature in Honour of Francis J. Byrne,* ed. Alfred Smyth (Dublin: Four Courts Press, 2000), 49.

130. Colmán Etchingham, *Viking Raids on Irish Church Settlements in the Ninth Century: A Reconsideration of the Annals,* Maynooth Monograph, Series Minor 1 (Maynooth: An Sagart, 1996), 32–33, 45–47.

131. James A. Graham-Campbell, "The Viking-Age Silver Hoards of Ireland," in *Proceedings of the Seventh Viking Congress,* ed. Bo Almqvist and David Greene, 39–74 (Dublin: Royal Irish Academy, 1976).

132. Etchingham, *Viking Raids on Irish Church Settlements,* 44.

133. It must be admitted that the two great eucharistic chalices that are now in the National Museum in Ireland seem to have been hidden for safekeeping precisely during the period of the Viking, or Viking-inspired, raids (and then not found until our own days), and so, paradoxically, we could owe some of our best evidence for early Irish eucharistic devotion to these raids.

134. Liam de Paor, "The Age of the Viking Wars: The Ninth and Tenth Centuries," in *The Course of Irish History,* 4th ed., ed. T. W. Moody and F. X. Martin (Lanham, MD: Roberts Rinehart Publishers, 2001), 76. The fact that the Vikings did not conquer bigger territories in Ireland can probably be attributed to the fact that they only needed trading bases from which they could conduct more efficient raiding and not that they were unable to conquer more territory; see Bart Jaski, "The Vikings and the Kingship of Tara," *Peritia* 9 (1995): 314.

135. Corish, *The Christian Mission,* 60. The role of the Vikings with particular reference to the succession of the kingship of Tara has been fully developed in Jaski, "The Vikings and the Kingship of Tara," 310–51.

136. Perhaps the best-known example of this Christianization of society is the *Cáin Adomnáin* promulgated in 697 to protect noncombatants from violence in time of war. For more on this important *Cáin* (or law) see Thomas

O'Loughlin, ed., *Adomnán at Birr,* AD *697: Essays in Commemoration of the Law of the Innocents* (Dublin: Four Courts, 2001). A modern study of the evangelization of Europe has found that it usually took about two hundred years for Christianity to penetrate a given culture after its initial official adoption of Christianity; see Richard Fletcher, *The Barbarian Conversion: From Paganism to Christianity* (New York: Henry Holt and Company, 1997), 307.

137. Corish, *The Christian Mission,* 61.

138. Alfred P. Smyth, "The Effect of Scandinavian Raiders on the English and Irish Churches: A Preliminary Reassessment," in *Britain and Ireland 900–1300: Insular Responses to Medieval European Change,* ed. Brendan Smith (Cambridge: Cambridge University Press, 1991), 4.

139. St Patrick, *Confessio* 38, in Howlett, *The Book of Letters,* 76.

140. "Non solum in aestiuo solstitio sed in diebus circa illud in uspertina hora occidens sol abscondit se quasi trans paruulum tumulum, ita ut nihil tenebrarum in minimo spatio ipso fiat, sed quicquid homo operari uoluerit uel peduculos de camisia abstrahere tamquam in presentia solis potest": *Liber de Mensura Orbis Terrae* 8.11, in J. J. Tierney, trans. and ed., *Dicuili Liber de Mensura Orbis Terrae* (Dublin: Dublin Institute for Advanced Studies, 1967), 74–75.

141. "Illae insulae sunt aliae paruulae, fere cunctae simul angustis distantes fretis; in quibus in centum ferme annis heremitae ex nostra Scottia nauigantes habitauerunt. Sed sicut a principio mundi desertae semper fuerunt ita nunc causa latronum Normannorum uacuae anchoritis": *Liber de Mensura Orbis Terrae* 8.15, in ibid. 76–77.

142. Kristján Ahronson, "Further Evidence for a Columban Iceland: Preliminary Results of Recent Work," *Norwegian Archaeological Review* 33, no. 2 (2000): 117–24.

143. Jaski, "The Vikings and the Kingship of Tara," 318.

144. Tadhg O'Keeffe, *Romanesque Ireland: Archaeology and Ideology in the Twelfth Century* (Dublin: Four Courts Press, 2003), 38. It is worth noting that native Irish artisans refrained from using Viking motifs and forms in their work until the eleventh and twelfth centuries, perhaps due to a hesitancy to assume artistic ideas from their enemies; see Hilary Richardson, "Visual Arts and Society," in *Prehistoric and Early Ireland,* ed. Ó Cróinín, 711.

145. De Paor, "The Age of the Viking Wars," 79.

146. Peter O'Dwyer, *Céli Dé: Spiritual Reform in Ireland, 750–900,* 2nd ed. (Dublin: Editions Tailliura, 1981), 29.

147. Patrick J. Corish, *The Irish Catholic Experience: A Historical Survey* (Wilmington, DE: Michael Glazi *r*, 1985), 36.

148. Campbell, *The Anglo Saxons,* 229–31.

149. Aubrey Gwynn, *The Irish Church in the Eleventh and Twelfth Centuries,* ed. Gerard O'Brien (Dublin: Four Courts Press, 1992), 68–69.

150. Bethell, "English Monks and Irish Reform," 125.

151. Throughout the earlier period, however, many Irish churchmen seemed to have recognized a certain preeminence in Canterbury for the church in Britain. Some famous archbishops, such as Theodore (d. 690), naturally received the respect of the Irish. But, at times, there seems to be more than devotion to individual prestigious archbishops, and the see of Canterbury in and of itself demanded a certain respect from the Irish; see Marie-Therese Flanagan, *Irish Society, Anglo-Norman Settlers, Angevin Kingship: Interactions in Ireland in the Late Twelfth Century* (Oxford: The Clarendon Press, 1989), 43–44.

152. Ibid., 50. While not all the details of this recourse to Canterbury are clear, it seems that the Hiberno-Vikings were not acting totally independently from the native Irish power structures. Toirdelbach Ua Briain (d. 1086), king of Munster and overlord of Dublin at this time, would probably have given his assent to their plan; ibid., 17.

153. A. Gwynn, *The Irish Church*, 69.

154. Ibid., 83. It is quite probable that this petition was made with the consent of both Toirdelbach Ua Briain and also Muirchertach Ua Briain, another claimant to the high-kingship of Ireland; see Flanagan, *Irish Society*, 21.

155. A. Gwynn, *The Irish Church*, 110–11.

156. Anselm, *Epistola* 31, in Fleming, *Gille of Limerick*, 166–69. For an examination of the relationship between Canterbury and the Irish Reform movement see Martin Brett, "Canterbury's Perspective on Church Reform and Ireland, 1070–1115," in *Ireland and Europe in the Twelfth Century: Reform and Renewal*, ed. Damian Bracken and Dagmar Ó Riain-Raedel, 13–35 (Dublin: Four Courts Press, 2006).

157. It is worth noting that, with the exception of the work of Bishop Gille of Limerick, there is very little reference to the Eucharist throughout this period until the end of the Norman domination. The abuses dealt with at these synods mainly have to do with marriage laws, the protection of the church's economic and political welfare, and the structuring of dioceses.

158. A. Gwynn, *The Irish Church*, 49, 84.

159. Bethell, "English Monks and Irish Reform," 111; see also Marie-Therese Flanagan, "Irish Church Reform in the Twelfth Century and Áed Ua Cáellaide, Bishop of Louth: An Italian Dimension," in *Ogma: Essays in Celtic Studies Presented to Próinséas Ní Chatháin*, ed. Michael Richter and Jean-Michel Picard (Dublin: Four Courts Press, 2001), 104.

160. A. Gwynn, *The Irish Church*, 193.

161. Ibid., 117.

162. Ibid., 117–54. However, Gwynn's identification of Mael Muire Ua Dúnáin as the first papal legate has been recently challenged as resulting from an overdependence on the late and, at times, unreliable *Annals of the Four Masters*. This would imply that Gille of Limerick may well have been the first

papal legate and that the Synod of Cashel, the first of the Irish reforming synods, took place without an official papal representative; see Donnchadha Ó Corráin, "Mael Muire Ua Dúnáin (1040–1117), Reformer," in *Folia Gadelica: Essays Presented by Former Students to R. A. Breatnach, M.A., M.R.I.A.,* ed. Pádraig de Brún, Seán Ó Coileáin, and Pádraig Ó Riain (Cork: Cork University Press, 1983), 48.

163. Peter Harbison, *Pilgrimage in Ireland: The Monuments and the People* (Syracuse, NY: Syracuse University Press, 1992), 30–31. For details of earlier Irish attitudes to Roman authority see Corning, *The Celtic and Roman Traditions,* 94.

164. "Eogan, cend manach na Gaedel h-i Roim": *AI* 1095.13.

165. Colmán Etchingham, "Episcopal Hierarchy in Connacht and Tairdelbach Ua Conchobair," *Journal of the Galway Archaeological and Historical Society* 52 (2000): 18.

166. Charles-Edwards, *Early Christian Ireland,* 272. This superabundance of bishops may also have been the case in the pre-Augustinian British church; see Charles-Edwards, "Beyond Empire II," 89–90.

167. Evidence for these synods is patchy. We do not have complete acts for them, and there is even some confusion over dates and places. It is certain that more synods and meetings of bishops took place than are normally covered in the history books, such as Martin Holland, "The Synod of Dublin in 1080," in *Medieval Dublin III: Proceedings of the Friends of Medieval Dublin Symposium 2001,* ed. Seán Duffy, 81–94 (Dublin: Four Courts Press, 2002).

168. A. Gwynn, *The Irish Church,* 155–79.

169. T. O'Keeffe, *Romanesque Ireland,* 45.

170. See below, pp. 135–37.

171. This arrangement may reflect the lines of organization of the English church based on a primacy for Canterbury and York; T. O'Keefe, *Romanesque Ireland,* 47. But it is also quite likely that this twofold division (and also the later fourfold one) was due to "a degree of political gerrymandering" to fashion the church structures on a parallel to political ones; see Katherine Simms, "The Origins of the Diocese of Clogher," *Clogher Record* 10, no. 1 (1979): 187.

172. No Irish source mentions Malachy's connections to this (or the actual introduction of this particular form of Augustinian observance), but a statement by Gaultier, abbot of Arrouaise, suggests that Malachy visited their abbey in 1179: "Malachy of holy memory, archbishop of the Irish, visited us while on a journey. He inspected our constitutions and approved them, he had our books and usages transcribed and had them brought to Ireland. There he made all the clerics in the episcopal sees and in many other places in Ireland accept and observe the precepts of our constitutions, order and habit and especially observe the praying of divine office in the church"; "Sanctae memoriae

Malachias, Hiberniensium archiepiscopus, per nos iter faciens, inspectis con-suetudinibus nostris et approbatis, libros nostros et usus ecclesiae transciptos suam in Hiberniam detulit, et fere omnes clericos in episcopalibus sedibus et in multis aliis locis per Hiberniam constitutos, ordinem nostrum et habitum et maxime divinum in ecclesia officium suscipere et observare praecepit": *PL* 217:68; the English translation is my own. It is worth noting that, in contrast to his contacts with the Cistercians, Malachy simply brought the rule and other written documents back to Ireland and no monks from this foundation came to introduce them; see Patrick J. Dunning, "The Arroasian Order in Medieval Ireland," *Irish Historical Studies* 4, no. 16 (1945): 299–300.

173. For more on this observance, see Sarah Preston, "The Canons Regu-lar of St Augustine: The Twelfth Century Reform in Action," in *Augustinians at Christ Church: The Canons Regular of the Cathedral Priory of the Holy Trinity Dublin,* ed. Stuart Kinsella, 23–40 (Dublin: Christ Church Cathedral Publications, 2000).

174. Fifty-seven of the ninety-six new Augustinian and thirteen of the thirty-four Cistercian monasteries of the twelfth century occupied sites for-merly occupied by Celtic monasteries; see Geraldine Carville, *The Occupation of Celtic Sites in Medieval Ireland by the Canons Regular of St Augustine and the Cistercians,* Cistercian Studies Series 56 (Kalamazoo, MI: Cistercian Publi-cations, 1982), 1–2. Carville also notes how the Augustinian monasteries were more likely to be located close to centers of population so as to be able to en-gage in ministerial duties, 92.

175. Tadhg O'Keeffe, *An Anglo-Norman Monastery: Bridgetown Priory and the Architecture of the Augustinian Canons Regular in Ireland* (Kinsale: Cork County Council/Grandon Editions, 1999), 107.

176. From a liturgical point of view, many Augustinian houses took part in pastoral care, but unlike the Benedictines and Cistercians they had no pecu-liar liturgical usages that distinguished them from secular churches; see John Harper, *The Forms and Orders of Western Liturgy from the Tenth to the Eigh-teenth Century* (Oxford: Oxford University Press, 1991), 30.

177. This is not to doubt that his role was important and maybe even pre-eminent, but he was by no means the only reform-minded bishop at this time. Other bishops may have been as involved; see Flanagan, "Irish Church Re-form."

178. "Cum autem coepisset pro officio suo agere, tunc intellexit homo Dei, non ad homines se, sed ad bestias destinatum. Nusquam adhuc tales exper-tus fuerat in quantacunque barbarie: nusquam repererat sic protervos ad mores, sic ferales ad ritus, sic ad fidem impios, ad leges barbaros, cervicosos ad disci-plinam, spurcos ad vitam: christiani nomine, re pagani. Non decimas, non pri-mitias dare, non legitima inire conjugia, non facere confessiones; poenitentias nec qui peteret, nec qui daret, penitus inveniri. Ministri altaris pauci admodum

erant. Sed enim quid opus plurium, ubi ipsa paucitas inter laicos propemodum otiosa vacaret? Non erat quod de suis fructificarent officiis in populo nequam. Nec enim in ecclesiis aut praedicantis vox, aut cantantis audiebatur": *Vita Sancti Malachiae* 8.16, in J. Leclercq and H. M. Rochais, eds., *Sancti Bernardi Opera*, vol. 3, *Tractatus et Opuscula* (Rome: Editiones Cisterciensis, 1963), 325; English translation from Robert T. Meyer, trans. and ed., *Bernard of Clairvaux: The Life and Death of Saint Malachy the Irishman*, Cistercian Fathers Series 10 (Kalamazoo, MI: Cistercian Publications, 1978), 33–34.

179. "Consuetudines sanctae Romanae Ecclesiae": *Vita Sancti Malachiae* 3.7, in Leclercq and Rochais, *Sancti Bernardi Opera*, 3:316; English translation from Meyer, *Bernard of Clairvaux*, 72.

180. Francis Xavier Martin, "Ireland in the Time of St Bernard, St Malachy and St Laurence O'Toole," *Seanchas Ard Mhacha: Journal of the Armagh Diocesan Historical Society* 15 (1992): 34.

181. A. Gwynn, *The Irish Church*, 301–2. For a study on Bernard's actual opinion of Ireland see Diarmuid Scully, "The Portrayal of Ireland and the Irish in Bernard's *Life of Malachy:* Representation and Context," in *Ireland and Europe*, ed. Bracken and Ó Riain-Raedel, 239–58.

182. T. O'Keeffe, *Romanesque Ireland*, 180; John Watt, *The Church in Medieval Ireland*, 2nd ed. (Dublin: University College Dublin Press, 1998), 14. Some of the most famous examples of Hiberno-Romanesque architecture and works of ecclesiastical art may have been commissioned as parts of these campaigns. A typical example is the famous Cross of Cong; see Etchingham, "Episcopal Hierarchy in Connacht," 22–23.

183. T. O'Keeffe, *Romanesque Ireland*, 49.

184. Watt, *The Church in Medieval Ireland*, 26.

185. Francis Xavier Martin, "The Normans: Arrival and Settlement, 1169–c. 1300," in *The Course of Irish History*, ed. Moody and Martin, 95.

186. Martin, "Ireland in the Time of St Bernard," 18. For more on the life of Mac Murchada see the recent biography, Nicholas Furlong, *Diarmait King of Leinster*, 2nd ed. (Cork: Mercier Press, 2006).

187. Perhaps this interest was partly motivated by a desire to control all commerce in the important trading area of the Irish Sea; see Benjamin T. Hudson, "The Changing Economy of the Irish Sea Province: AD 900–1300," in *Britain and Ireland*, ed. Smith, 64–66.

188. "Nos itaque . . . impendentes assensum, gratum et acceptum habemus ut pro dilatandis ecclesie terminis pro vitiorum restringendo decursu, pro corrigendis moribus et virtutibus ingrediaris, pro Christiane religionis augmento, insulam illam ingrediaris et que ad honorem Dei et salutem illius terre spectaverint exequaris, et illius terre populus honorifice te recipiat et sicut dominum veneretur": *Laudabiliter,* as in Maurice P. Sheehy, ed., *Pontifica Hibernica: Medieval Papal Chancery Documents Concerning Ireland 640–1261* (Dublin: Gill, 1962), 1:16, English translation my own.

189. Marie-Therese Flanagan, "Hiberno-Papal Relations in the Late Twelfth Century," *Archivium Hibernicum* 34 (1977): 56.

190. On the debate on the authenticity of *Laudabiliter* and for a detailed analysis of the document see Watt, *The Church in Medieval Ireland*, 28–40.

191. Corish, *The Irish Catholic Experience*, 37.

192. Martin, "The Normans," 98.

193. At the time of Mac Murchada's request, Strongbow's lands in Wales and England had been sequestered by the king; see Flanagan, *Irish Society*, 112–36, esp. 118.

194. Martin, "Ireland in the Time of St Bernard," 22–23.

195. Martin, "The Normans," 101–3. It has often been pointed out that Mac Murchada did not have the legal right to designate Strongbow to succeed him. However, in a detailed study, Flanagan has shown that this offer may not have been as untraditional as once thought; *Irish Society*, 79–111.

196. Flanagan, *Irish Society*, 168.

197. Martin, "The Normans," 103.

198. For a discussion of the issues involved, see Flanagan, *Irish Society*, 167–228.

199. Ibid., 229–72.

200. Ibid., 272.

201. Martin, "The Normans," 105–6.

202. Marie-Therese Flanagan, "Henry II, the Council of Cashel, and the Irish Bishops," *Peritia* 10 (1996): 186–87.

203. Flanagan traces the various problems and background of the 1172 Council of Cashel in ibid.

204. Watt, *The Church in Medieval Ireland*, 62, 70, 48.

205. Ibid., 50.

206. Stephen J. P. Van Dijk and Joan Hazelden Walker, *The Origins of the Modern Roman Liturgy: The Liturgy of the Papal Court and the Franciscan Order in the Thirteenth Century* (Westminister, MD: Neuman Press, 1960), 358–411.

207. Watt, *The Church in Medieval Ireland*, 87–89.

208. Ibid., 53–59; also see Barry W. O'Dwyer, trans. and ed., *Stephen of Lexington: Letters from Ireland 1228–1229*, Cistercian Fathers Series 28 (Kalamazoo, MI: Cistercian Press, 1982), 5–6.

209. Watt, *The Church in Medieval Ireland*, 78–84.

210. Ibid., 56.

211. The advent of the printing press had a huge effect on the uniformity of the liturgy, reducing local liturgical variants to a minimum. It would be anachronistic to expect to find in this period identical liturgical books in use in even two churches in the same town never mind two churches hundreds of miles apart; see Cyrille Vogel, *Medieval Liturgy: An Introduction to the Sources,*

rev. and trans. William Storey and Niels Rasmussen (Portland: The Pastoral Press, 1986), 4–5. Most modern works hesitate to give a definition of exactly what a rite is, but it could be generally defined as "the manner of performing all services for the worship of God and the sanctification of men": Adrian Fortescue, "Rite," in *CE* 13:64. A more specific definition is "a coherent, unified corpus of liturgical usages followed by all churches within a single ecclesiastical conscription"; Robert F. Taft, *The Byzantine Rite: A Short History* (Collegeville, MN: Liturgical Press, 1992), 24. Although, as will be seen below, when applied to the Gallican rite this definition needs to be qualified, as the geographical area of its use was quite large, and the lack of metropolitan sees made its "ecclesiastical conscription" somewhat fluid.

212. Henry Chadwick, "Preface" to Frederick E. Warren, *The Liturgy and Ritual of the Celtic Church,* 2nd ed. with a monograph and updated bibliography by Jane Stevenson (Oxford: The Clarendon Press, 1881; 2nd fac. ed., Suffolk: Boydell Press, 1987), vii.

213. Kevin Collins, *Catholic Churchmen and the Celtic Revival, 1848–1916* (Dublin: Four Courts Press, 2003), 29–31.

214. Paradoxically there is one early source that does maintain an independent Eastern origin for Irish liturgy, the so-called *Ratio de cursus qui fuerunt eius auctores,* a somewhat eclectic document, probably written by an anonymous Irishman on the Continent (possibly Echternach) before 767. Here the author gives his understanding of the origins of the different liturgical traditions with reference to the Liturgy of the Hours. He lists six liturgical traditions of the "cursus" of the Divine Office: the Roman, the Gallican, the Irish, the Eastern, that of St Ambrose, and that of St Benedict. He traces the Irish lineage from St Peter to St Mark and through St Basil of Caesarea, Gregory Nazianzen, then through the Egyptian monasteries to Western Europe with Cassian, Honoratus of Lérin, and Caesarius of Arles, to Germanus of Auxerre who passed it to Patrick and from there to Ireland. This tradition then made its way with Colombanus onto the Continent, where the author is familiar with its use in his day. However this document makes no mention of the Eucharist, and there is no historical basis for accepting its theories of Eastern origins, even if it would be very appealing to latter-day followers of Warren. The text can be found in Kassius Hallinger, ed., *Corpus Consuetudinum Monasticarum Cura Pontificii Athenaei Sancti Anselmi de Urbe Editum,* vol. 1: *Initia Consuetudinis Benedictinae* (Siegburg: Franz Schmitt, 1963), 83–91. For more information on the document see Kenney, *The Sources for the Early History of Ireland,* 687–88.

215. Joseph A. Jungmann, *The Mass of the Roman Rite: Its Origins and Development (Missarum Solemnia),* 2 vols. (New York: Benziger Brothers, 1951), 1:44–48.

216. For a modern treatment of the New Testament evidence on the Eucharist see Étienne Nodet and Justin Taylor, *The Origins of Christianity: An*

Exploration (Collegeville, MN: Liturgical Press, 1998), and Jerome Kodell, *The Eucharist in the New Testament* (Collegeville, MN: The Liturgical Press, 1988).

217. Many of the proposed reconstructions were based on *De Traditione Divinae Missae,* a spurious document purporting to be by Proclus, a mid-fifth-century bishop of Constantinople (this text is available in *PG* 65:849–52; for details of this forgery see F. J. Leroy, "Proclus *De Traditione Divinae Missae:* Un Faux de C. Palaeocappa," *Orientalia Christiana Periodica* 28 [1962]: 288–99). These theories claimed that "the earliest apostolic liturgies had been very long but were deliberately abridged in later centuries in order to retain the participation of less fervent generations of Christians"; see John R. K. Fenwick, *Fourth Century Anaphoral Construction Techniques,* Grove Liturgical Studies 45 (Bramcote: Grove, 1986), 4. For a modern summary of earlier scholarship see P. Bradshaw, *The Search for the Origins of Christian Worship,* 1–6.

218. Gregory Dix, *The Shape of the Liturgy,* 2nd ed. (London: Dacre Press, 1945; repr. with intro. by Simon Jones, London: Continuum, 2005), 5, 48.

219. Perhaps the most popular and influential example of this is the work of Louis Bouyer, *Eucharist Theology and Spirituality of the Eucharistic Prayer,* trans. Charles Quinn (Notre Dame, IN: University of Notre Dame Press, 1968).

220. For example, Jungmann, *The Mass of the Roman Rite,* 1:12.

221. Paul Bradshaw is the most influential voice of this school; see *The Search for the Origins of Christian Worship,* passim.

222. *First Apology* 67.3–6, in Anton Hänggi and Irmgard Pahl, eds., *Prex Eucharistica: Textus e Variis Liturgiis Antiquioribus Selecti* (Fribourg: Éditions Universitaires Fribourg Suisse, 1968), 70–73; English translation available in R. C. D. Jasper and G. J. Cuming, trans. and eds., *Prayers of the Eucharist: Early and Reformed,* 3rd ed. (Collegeville, MN: Liturgical Press, 1990), 29–30.

223. P. Bradshaw, *The Search for the Origins of Christian Worship,* 140.

224. Maxwell E. Johnson, "The Apostolic Tradition," in *The Oxford History of Christian Worship,* ed. Geoffrey Wainwright and Karen B. Westerfield Tucker (Oxford: Oxford University Press, 2006), 52. Even Bradshaw (one of the pioneers of the current view that there was no common shape of the Eucharist in the early church) will admit that this may have taken place, albeit in very general terms, "long before" the fourth century; Paul Bradshaw, *Eucharistic Origins,* Alcuin Club Collections 80 (London: SPCK, 2004), 146.

225. Robert F. Taft, "Mass Without the Consecration? The Historic Agreement on the Eucharist between the Catholic Church and the Assyrian Church of the East Promulgated 26 October 2001," *Worship* 77, no. 6 (2003): 482–509.

226. Allan Bouley, *From Freedom to Formula: The Evolution of the Eucharistic Prayer from Oral Improvisation to Written Texts* (Washington DC: Catholic University of America Press, 1981), 89–90.

227. The need to guarantee a legitimate celebration of the Eucharist so that Christians might bring blessings to the empire by their sanctification of Sunday was an important consideration in the reasoning of the emperor Constantine leading to his legalization of Christianity with the edict of Milan; Arnold H. M. Jones, *Constantine and the Conversion of Europe* (Toronto: University of Toronto Press, 1948), 87.

228. John F. Baldovin, "The Empire Baptized," in *The Oxford History of Christian Worship*, ed. Wainwright and Westerfield Tucker, 84.

229. Paul Bradshaw, "The Homogenization of Christian Liturgy— Ancient and Modern," *Studia Liturgica* 26 (1996): 6–9.

230. P. Bradshaw, *The Search for the Origins of Christian Worship*, 220.

231. Robert Taft has made an important contribution in the analysis of this phenomenon with his theory of "soft points" of the eucharistic liturgy, whereby some between parts and silent actions of the "shape" of the Eucharistic celebration were gradually overlaid with rituals and prayers; see his *Beyond East and West: Problems in Liturgical Understanding*, 2nd ed. (Rome: Edizioni Orientalia Christiana, 1997), 201–2.

232. Edward J. Kilmartin, *The Eucharist in the West: History and Theology*, ed. Robert J. Daly (Collegeville, MN: Liturgical Press, 1998), 110.

233. Tom Elich, "Using Liturgical Texts in the Middle Ages," in *Fountain of Life in Memory of Niels K. Rasmussen, O.P.*, ed. Gerard Austin (Washington DC: The Pastoral Press, 1991), 71.

234. Ibid., 76; see 74–77.

235. King rightly points out that the term "Gallican" can refer to as many as five different types of liturgy: "(1) The rite existing in Gaul before the reforms of Pepin and Charlemagne; (2) the Roman rite as altered and enriched in Gaul and Germany by the Carolingian school of liturgists; (3) a French use introduced by the Normans into Apulin and Sicily; (4) the Franco-Roman rite, which, at the instigation of Pope St Gregory VII (1073–85), supplanted the Mozarabic rite in Spain at the end of the 11th century . . .; (5) the liturgical books in many of the dioceses of France in the 18th century, which, in defiance of the Tridentine regulations, had been altered by the bishops"; *Liturgies of the Past*, 77. Today I would add a sixth possible usage: the liturgical uses of some of the "Western Rite Orthodox" groupings; see Gregory Woolfenden, "Western Rite Orthodoxy: Some Reflections on a Liturgical Question," *St Vladimir's Theological Quarterly* 45, no. 2 (2001): 163–92. The multiplicity of meanings can be confusing and, in this section, "Gallican" can be taken to signify King's first meaning, "the rite existing in Gaul before the reforms of Pepin and Charlemagne." However, as will be explained in this section, I believe that this was a rather broad liturgical category that was in use in much of the non-Roman West, including the British Isles.

236. Jordi Pinell i Pons, "History of the Liturgies in the Non-Roman West," in *The Pontifical Liturgical Institute Handbook for Liturgical Studies,*

vol. 1, *Introduction to the Liturgy,* ed. Anscar J. Chupungco (Collegeville, MN: Liturgical Press, 1997), 184.

237. Ibid., 186.

238. Jordi Pinell i Pons, "Gallicana (Liturgia)," in *DPI* 1:911; cf. Johannes Quasten, "Oriental Influence in the Gallican Liturgy," *Traditio* 1 (1943): 55–78. Here Quasten argues, unsuccessfully in my opinion, for an Eastern and, in particular, Syriac origin for the Gallican rite. Duchense argues for Milan being the "principal center" of the genesis of the Gallican rite. He assumes that the Ambrosian and Gallican liturgies are one and the same thing in the early period and that both came into contact with the Roman liturgy at different times and in different ways explaining the later differences between them; see Louis Duchense, *Christian Worship: Its Origin and Evolution; A Study of the Latin Liturgy up to the Time of Charlemagne,* 5th ed., trans. M. L. McClure (London: SPCK: 1919), 86–105.

239. Pinell i Pons, "History of the Liturgies in the Non-Roman West," 187.

240. W. S. Porter, *The Gallican Rite* (London: Mowbray, 1958), 10.

241. One theory that is often advanced in popular works is that of early Irish Christianity having some sort of direct contact with non-Chalcedonian forms of Eastern Christianity (e.g., the Coptic church). Yet there is very little evidence of any such direct contacts. There may be some scholarly basis for proposing such contacts because of the presence of apocryphal scriptural material in Ireland that originated in the East. However, the most modern treatment of this material has been unable to find any direct links to the East that would explain its presence in Ireland; see Martin McNamara, "Apocalyptic and Eschatological Texts in Irish Literature: Oriental Connections?" in *Apocalyptic and Eschatological Heritage: The Middle East and Celtic Realms,* ed. Martin McNamara, 75–97 (Dublin: Four Courts Press, 2003).

242. Edmund Bishop, *Liturgica Historica: Papers on the Liturgy and Religious Life of the Western Church* (Oxford: The Clarendon Press, 1918), 165.

243. Jungmann, *The Mass of the Roman Rite,* 1:469.

244. Marc Schneiders, "The Origins of the Early Irish Liturgy," in *Ireland and Europe in the Early Middle Ages: Learning and Literature,* ed. Próinséas Ní Chatháin and Michael Richter (Stuttgart: Klett-Cotta 1996), 80. However, cf. Michael Curran, *The Antiphonary of Bangor and the Early Irish Monastic Liturgy* (Dublin: Irish Academic Press, 1984), 151. Here Curran traces four definite and fifteen possible Spanish prayers in the *Antiphonary of Bangor,* perhaps suggesting stronger Irish-Spanish links. Although considering that this book comes from an Irish center in the north of Italy (and if the fifteen possible identifications are, in fact, accurate), this could suggest a Spanish-Ambrosian link.

Another area that will require future study is the links between Irish liturgy and various north Italian liturgies. North Italy was particularly rich in liturgical creativity in the period of late antiquity due to its political importance as a contact between the West and the Byzantine Empire. The metropolitan sees of this region were also fortunate in having liturgically prolific and important bishops, the most famous of these being Ambrose of Milan (d. 397). However (apart from some remnants of the Ambrosian Rite in Milan), all of these churches adopted the Roman rite and only today are critical editions being prepared of the various liturgical material from this region. We also know that various Irish churchmen, including St Columbanus, were active in this region. For more information see Achille Triacca, "Liturgia Ambrosiana," in *NDL*, 55–56 and "La Liturgia Ambrosiana," in *Anàmnesis: Introduzione Storico-Teologica della Liturgia*, vol. 2, *La Liturgia: Panorma Storico Generale*, ed. Salvatore Marsilli (Casale Monoferrato: Marietti, 1978), 95–96. For the most recent work on the connection between Ireland and Northern Italy, even though it does not specifically treat liturgical matters, see Michael Richter, *Bobbio in the Early Middle Ages: The Abiding Legacy of Columbanus* (Dublin: Four Courts Press, 2008).

245. King, *Liturgies of the Past*, 183.

246. Jordi Pinell i Pons, "La Liturgia Gallicana," in *Anàmnesis*, ed. Marsilli, 66.

247. Jordi Pinell i Pons, "Hispanica (Liturgia)," in *DPA* 1:912.

248. Bouley, *From Freedom to Formula*, 192.

249. Taft, *Beyond East and West*, 51.

250. Beck, *The Pastoral Care of Souls*, 128.

251. Matthieu Smyth, *La Liturgie Oubliée: La Prière Eucharistique en Gaule Antique et dans l'Occident non Romain* (Paris: Éditions du Cerf, 2003), 24. For a detailed reconstruction of a typical celebration of Sunday Mass in southeast France in the sixth century (based mainly on the homilies of the bishops of the period, local councils, and the *Expositio Antiquae Liturgiae Gallicane*), see Beck, *The Pastoral Care of Souls*, 136–50. This very thorough reconstruction is of particular note as it uses exclusively southeastern French material. However, the approach, while interesting, is dated precisely because it does not use any Irish material. Another very detailed reconstruction can be found in M. Smyth, *La Liturgie Oubliée*, 183–225. Here Smyth makes use of all available sources including much Irish material.

252. Charles Thomas, *Christianity in Roman Britain to AD 500* (Berkeley: University of California Press, 1981), 83–84, and Richard W. Pfaff, *The Liturgy in Medieval England: A History* (Cambridge: Cambridge University Press, 2009), 32–36.

253. Stevenson, "Introduction," xxx. Although some recent scholarship had rehabilitated the figure of Palladius in the evangelization of Ireland and his mission as sponsored by Rome, see Charles-Edwards, "Palladius, Prosper and Leo the Great," 7. This might lead to the question of whether early Irish liturgy owed something to Roman liturgy given that Roman liturgy was to be one of

the hallmarks of the later Roman mission to Canterbury. But Palladius was sent to Ireland from France and not directly from Rome like Augustine, so it is far more likely that he would have introduced some form of the Gallican rite as was practiced in fifth-century Gaul.

254. Speaking of Western Europe as a whole in the sixth to the eleventh centuries, Vogel reminds us that "a variety of ritual descriptions could coexist in regard to the same *acio liturgica* at the same period and in the same locality, even if they were of different ritual and cultic backgrounds"; *Medieval Liturgy*, 137.

255. For example, "One time when Coemgen was reciting his hours, he dropped his psalter into the lake; and a great grief and vexation seized him. And the angel said to him: 'Do not grieve.' Afterwards an otter came to Coemgen bringing the psalter with him from the bottom of the lake, and not a line or letter was blotted (*lit.* drowned)"; "Fecht náon dia raibhe Cáoimhgin ag gabail a trath ro thuit a psaltair uadh isin loch. Ro gabh sniomh 7 toirrsi mor-adbal é. Ocus do raidh an taingel fris: "nár bhad brónach" ar sé. Tainc an dobhrán iaramh go Caoimhgin, 7 tucc an tsaltair leis as iochtar an locha gan báthiad line no litre": *Life of Coemgen* (I) 9.14, in Charles Plummer, trans. and ed., *Bethada Náem nÉrenn: Lives of the Irish Saints Edited from Original Manuscripts* (Oxford: Oxford University Press, 1922; repr. 1968), 1:127; English translation from ibid., 2:123.

256. For these legendary accounts on the reasons for Columba's exile for Christ in Scotland see Martin McNamara, *Psalter Text and Psalter Study in the Early Irish Church, AD 600–1200* (Dublin: Royal Irish Academy, 1973), 210–13.

257. Bishop, *Liturgica Historica*, 166.

258. Stevenson, "Introduction," lxx.

259. Indeed, prior to the official promotion of Roman practices by Charlemagne, Vogel sees a great deal of evidence of "private initiatives" whereby various private individuals such as pilgrims or clerics and monastics who journeyed to Rome brought Roman books and traditions back to France particularly in the period after the mid-seventh century; see Cyrille Vogel, "Les Échanges Liturgiques entre Rome et les Pays Francs jusqu'á l'Époque de Charlemagne," in *Le Chiese nei Regni dell'Europa Occidentale e i loro Rapporti con Roma fino all'800*, Settimana di Spoleto 7 (Spoleto: Centro Italiano di Studi sull'Alto Medioevo, 1960) 1:293–95.

260. Vogel, *Medieval Liturgy*, 323. For a detailed history and analysis of the opinions of various scholars on the *Bobbio Missal*, see Yitzhak Hen, "Introduction: The *Bobbio Missal*—from Mabillon Onwards," in *The Bobbio Missal: Liturgy and Religious Culture in Merovingian Gaul*, ed. Yitzhak Hen and Rob Meens, 1–7 (Cambridge: Cambridge University Press, 2004).

261. While Columbanus was Irish, it seems that either his foundations adopted the local liturgy of the place or, perhaps, that the liturgy that Colum-

banus would have been familiar with in Ireland would not have been radically different from the Gallican rite as he found on the Continent. A study of the remaining manuscripts from the Columban foundation of Luxeuil indicates that the liturgical works are Gallican: "studies of the Luxeuil Lectionary, the *Missale Gothicum* and the *Missale Gallicanum Vetus,* all written at Luxeuil or in an affiliated center, demonstrate how predominantly Gallican liturgical usage was. Any Insular features occurring at Luxeuil are incidental"; Rosamond McKitterick, "The Scriptoria of Merovingian Gaul: A Survey of the Evidence," in *Columbanus and Merovingian Monasticism,* ed. H. B. Clarke and Mary Brennan (Oxford: British Archaeological Reports International Series, 1981), 185.

262. Hen and Meens, "Conclusion," in *The Bobbio Missal,* ed. Hen and Meens, 219.

263. For example, Jungmann, *The Mass of the Roman Rite,* 1:45; Henry Jenner, "The Celtic Rite," in *CE* 3:496; and Louis Gougaud "Celtiques (Liturgies)," in *DACL* 2/2, col. 2971.

264. Vogel, *Medieval Liturgy,* 323–24; Bernard Botte, *Le Canon de la Messe Romaine: Édition Critique, Introduction et Notes* (Louvain: Abbaye de Mont César, 1935), 11; Gregory Woolfenden, "The Medieval Western Rites," in *The Study of Liturgy,* ed. Cheslyn Jones et al., 2nd ed. (New York: Oxford University Press, 1992), 266; Bouyer, *Eucharist,* 319. Interestingly M. Smyth, *La Liturgie Oubliée,* 108–13, does not seem to come down on either side of the line, as he finds the eclectic composition of the book to be too haphazard to attribute it to the Gallican sphere of influence, and he suspects that it was written in the north of Italy under Irish influence. He does, however, use the evidence from it in the rest of his book when trying to reconstruct the Gallican rite.

265. Yitzak Hen, "The Liturgy of the *Bobbio Missal,*" in *The Bobbio Missal,* ed. Hen and Meens, 150.

266. Alban Dold and Leo Eizenhöfer, eds., *Das Irische Palimpsestsakramentar im CLM 14429: Der Staatsbibliothek München* (Beuron: Beuroner Kunstverlag, 1964).

267. George F. Warner, ed., *The Stowe Missal: MS. D. II.3 in the Library of the Royal Irish Academy, Dublin* (Suffolk: Henry Bradshaw Society/Boydell Press, orig. pub. 2 vols., 1906 and 1915; repr. 1 vol., 1989).

268. The tiny vestiges of the Hispanic liturgy celebrated in a handful of Spanish churches were the only other Western example of a eucharistic prayer for about one thousand years; see José Bohajar, "Liturgia Hispana," in *NDL,* 958–60.

269. Enrico Mazza, "The Eucharist in the First Four Centuries," in *The Eucharist,* vol. 3 of *The Pontifical Liturgical Institute Handbook for Liturgical Studies,* ed. Anscar J. Chupungco (Collegeville, MN: Liturgical Press, 1999), 52.

270. Owen Chadwick, *A History of Christianity* (London: Weidenfeld and Nicolson, 1995), 106–15.

271. Theodore Klauser, *A Short History of the Western Liturgy: An Account and Some Reflections*, trans. J. Halliburton, 2nd ed. (New York: Oxford University Press, 1979), 32–37.

272. John F. Baldovin, *The Urban Character of Early Christian Worship: The Origins, Development and Meaning of Stational Liturgy* (Rome: Pontifical Oriental Institute Press, 1987), 37.

273. A good introduction to the *Ordines Romani* can be found in Vogel, *Medieval Liturgy*, 135–224. More recent reflections on this type of literature can be found in Éric Palazzo, *A History of Liturgical Books: From the Beginning to the Thirteenth Century*, trans. Madeleine Beaumont (Collegeville, MN: Liturgical Press, 1998), 175–85. Michel Andrieu, *Les Ordines Romani du Haut Moyen Age*, 5 vols. (Louvaine: Spicilegium Sacrum Lovaniense, 1931–61) provides the best modern critical edition of the *Ordines Romani*. For an examination of how a papal Roman Eucharist would have appeared at around the year 700, see Klauser, *A Short History of the Western Liturgy*, 59–72.

274. Vogel, *Medieval Liturgy*, 138.

275. Ibid., 137.

276. Marcel Metzger, "The History of the Eucharistic Liturgy in Rome," in *The Eucharist*, ed. Chupungco, 125–28.

277. A number of different names are given to this new liturgy, including "Gallican Roman," "Frankish Roman," and "Romano Frankish." I follow Porter in the use of "Gallicanized Roman"; see Porter, *The Gallican Rite*, 54.

278. For an examination of the importation of Roman practices in the north of England in the seventh and eighth centuries see Éamonn Ó Carragáin, *Ritual and the Rood: Liturgical Images and the Old English Poem of the* Dream of the Rood *Tradition* (London: The British Library, 2005), 223–79. It is unlikely that contemporary Irish ecclesiastics would have been as zealous in their adoption of Roman traditions.

279. Yitzhak Hen, *The Royal Patronage of the Liturgy in Frankish Gaul: To the Death of Charles the Bald (877)* (Woodbridge: Henry Bradshaw Society/ Boydell Press, 2001), 68.

280. Ibid., 67.

281. For information on this sacramentary, see Vogel, *Medieval Liturgy*, 80–85, and Palazzo, *A History of Liturgical Books*, 50–54.

282. See Vogel, *Medieval Liturgy*, 85–92, and Palazzo, *A History of Liturgical Books*, 52–54. For more general background on Benedict, who is often overlooked in histories of the liturgy, see Allen Cabaniss, trans., *Benedict of Aniane, the Emperor's Monk: Aldo's Life*, Cistercian Studies 220 (Kalamazoo, MI: Cistercian Publications, 2008).

283. Hen, *The Royal Patronage of the Liturgy*, 78.

284. For example, Michael S. Driscoll, "The Conversion of the Nations," in *The Oxford History of Christian Worship*, ed. Wainwright and Westerfield Tucker, 189.

285. Hen, *The Royal Patronage of the Liturgy*, 65–95, esp. 78–81.

286. Vogel, *Medieval Liturgy*, 102–6, and Palazzo, *A History of Liturgical Books*, 54–56.

287. Edmond Bishop's paper on "The Genius of the Roman Rite," (in his *Liturgica Historica*, 1–19) is still the classic examination of this process of the melding together of the two rites with particular attention given to the differences between the two styles of euchology or prayer composition.

288. Baldovin, *The Urban Character*, 116.

289. Klauser, *A Short History of the Western Liturgy*, 72–77; Vogel, *Medieval Liturgy*, 104–5.

290. Driscoll, "The Conversion of the Nations," 197–202.

291. It is interesting to note that the earlier shift from Greek to Latin in Western liturgy "does not seem to have been a burning problem, there is scarcely a hint of a discussion on the matter"; see A. A. R. Bastiaensen, "The Beginnings of Latin Liturgy," *Studia Patristica* 30 (1993): 278.

292. Nathan Mitchell, *Cult and Controversy: The Worship of the Eucharist outside Mass* (New York: Pueblo, 1982), 68–70.

293. Donald Bullough, "The Carolingian Liturgical Experience," in *Continuity and Change in Christian Worship: Papers Read at the 1997 Summer Meeting and the 1998 Winter Meeting of the Ecclesiastical History Society*, ed. R. N. Swanson (Woodbridge: Boydell Press, 1999), 52. For the development of Latin as a liturgical language see Christine Mohrmann, *Liturgical Latin: Its Origins and Character, Three Lectures* (London: Burns and Oates, 1957).

294. Robert F. Taft, "Was the Eucharistic Anaphora Recited Secretly or Aloud? The Ancient Tradition and What Became of It," in *Worship Traditions in Armenia and the Neighboring Christian East: An International Symposium in Honor of the Fortieth Anniversary of St Nersess Armenian Seminary*, ed. Roberta R. Ervine, 15–57 (Crestwood, NY: St. Vladimir's Seminary Press, 2006).

295. Mitchell, *Cult and Controversy*, 51.

296. This new form of allegory was more than a development of early Christian interpretation, but, as will be seen below, was also a reorientation of the genre; see Enrico Mazza, *The Celebration of the Eucharist: The Origins of the Rite and the Development of Its Interpretation*, trans. Matthew J. O'Connell (Collegeville, MN: Liturgical Press, 1999), 163–64.

297. "Moyen de remettre en memoir les événements de l'histoire du salut à travers les rites": A. Häussling, "Messe (Expositiones Missae)," in *DSAM* 10, col. 1084; my translation.

298. "Un drame qui rejoue la vie du Christ, et meme l'histoire entière du salut, depuis le paradis terrestre jusqu'à la mort sur la croix et l'ensevelissement": ibid., col. 1085; my translation.

299. Kilmartin, *The Eucharist in the West*, 93.

300. Ibid., 92. While there was a drastic shift in the understanding of the Eucharist, Snoek's criticism of this type of allegorical interpretation as being

based on "pious and pseudo-historical meanderings of the ecclesiastical mind" is probably overly harsh, see G. J. C. Snoek, *Medieval Piety from Relics to the Eucharist: A Process of Mutual Interaction*, Studies in the History of Christian Thought 63 (Leiden: E. J. Brill, 1995), 35.

301. Mazza, *The Celebration of the Eucharist*, 164.

302. This theory is outlined in full in Russell, *The Germanization of Early Medieval Christianity*.

303. Joseph A. Jungmann, *Pastoral Liturgy* (New York: Herder and Herder, 1962), 38–47.

304. This new spirituality can be seen in *The Heliand*, an early Saxon adaptation of the gospel; G. Roland Murphy, *The Heliand: The Saxon Gospel* (New York: Oxford University Press, 1992). Murphy's introduction to this text was published as a separate volume, *The Saxon Savior: The Transformation of the Gospel in the Ninth-Century Heliand* (New York: Oxford University Press, 1989).

305. Mary Collins, "Evangelization, Catechesis, and the Beginning of Western Eucharistic Theology," *Louvain Studies* 23 (1988): 127.

306. Driscoll, "The Conversion of the Nations," 192–93.

307. Joseph A. Jungmann, *The Place of Christ in Liturgical Prayer* (New York: Alba House, 1965), 259.

308. Metzger, "The History of the Eucharistic Liturgy in Rome," 129.

309. Kilmartin, *The Eucharist in the West*, 113, and see 112–15.

310. Angelus Häussling and Karl Rahner, *The Celebration of the Eucharist* (New York: Herder and Herder, 1967), 1. For a detailed analysis of the theological issues involved with the multiplication of Masses, see 1–9. There is still some debate regarding the actual genesis of the *missa privata* or "Private Mass" (a term that does not occur much in the period but is often taken to be synonymous with *missa lecta* or *missa solitaria*). The ritual books really cannot provide explicit evidence that these liturgies took place without the presence of the faithful, but the fact that the priest now says every single word of the liturgy by himself (as opposed to the earlier practice of having a choir, lector, deacon, and congregational responses) is taken as evidence that nobody else was present. Vogel is of the opinion that it developed as a consequence of taking the Roman papal stational liturgy and introducing it into the new setting north of the Alps with the necessary replacing of the various stational churches with side altars; see Vogel, *Medieval Liturgy*, 156–59, and "La Multiplication des Messes Solitaires au Moyen Âge," *Revue des Sciences Religieuses* 55 (1981): 206–13. Häussling takes a different view that "private" must refer to a Mass for a group as opposed to the "public" Mass of Sundays. He says that these "private" Masses evolved from the ancient practice of Eucharists celebrated on the tomb of the martyrs, of funeral and anniversary Eucharists, and of Eucharists celebrated for devotional purposes such as those said for pilgrims at shrines; see

Angelus Häussling, *Moenchskonvent und Eucharistiefeier: Eine Studie ueber die Messe in der Abendländischen Klosterliturgie des Fruehen Mittelalters und zur Geschichte der Messhäufigkeit,* Liturgiewissenschaftliche Quellen und Forschungen 58 (Muenster: Westfalen, 1973), 249, 252, 319. But regardless of the reasons why this practice started, the fact is that the practice of the priest celebrating the liturgy by himself on a side altar became very common from this point onwards.

311. Cyrille Vogel, "La Vie Quotidienne du Moine en Occident a l'Époque de la Floraison des Messes Privées," in *Liturgie, Spiritualité, Cultures: Conferences Saint-Serge XXIXe* (Rome: Centro Liturgico Vincenziano: Edizioni Liturgiche, 1983), 345. The work of Daniel Callam is also relevant. He has studied the relationship between the daily celebration of the Eucharist and clerical celibacy. Callam concluded that in the West daily celebration of the Eucharist started in the fourth century. This developed from the earlier practice of Home Communion, as it had become impracticable for Christians to bring the Eucharist home due to the larger numbers of Christians and the fact that people in general were tending not to receive Communion even at Sunday Eucharist. At the same time there was a movement within asceticism and the nascent monasticism for monks to receive presbyteral ordination. This made it possible to change the practice of Home Communion to that of a daily celebration of the Eucharist in monastic circles. Gradually monastic and reform-minded bishops also encouraged the enforcement of the discipline of celibacy among the secular clergy. As the priest had to be celibate on the night previous to the celebration of the Eucharist, these new disciplinary measures also made it practical for the extension of a daily celebration of the Eucharist to nonmonastic circles. Thus monastic spirituality's emphasis on a daily eucharistic celebration passed to the secular clergy and the laity; see Daniel Callam, "The Frequency of Mass in the Latin Church ca. 400," *Theological Studies* 45 (1984): 613–50, esp. 648–50, and "Clerical Continence in the Fourth Century: Three Papal Decretals," *Theological Studies* 41 (1980): 3–50. Also see Eoin de Baldraithe, "Daily Eucharist: The Need for an Early Church Paradigm," *American Benedictine Review* 41 (1990): 378–440, and Taft, *Beyond East and West,* 87–110.

312. There is even good grounds to make the bold statement that the earliest monks were anti-liturgical; see Eligius Dekkers, "Were the Early Monks Liturgical?" *Collectanea Cisterciensia* 22 (1960): 120–37.

313. Susan A. Rabe, *Faith, Art and Politics at Saint-Riquier: The Symbolic Vision of Angilbert* (Philadelphia: University of Pennsylvania Press, 1995), 6–8. Eastern monasticism, however, held a certain indifference towards the liturgy. In some cases the monk is thought to be on a higher level than those in the world, and as he can see Christ directly he has no need for the Eucharist; see Robert E. Taft, "Home-Communion in the Late Antique East," in *Ars Liturgiae: Worship, Aesthetics and Praxis: Essays in Honor of Nathan D. Mitchell,* ed. Clare V. Johnson (Chicago: Liturgy Training Publications, 2003), 4–7.

314. Vogel, *Medieval Liturgy,* 156.

315. Vogel, "La Vie Quotidienne du Moine," 357.

316. Ibid., 347.

317. "Qui omnes tam festive, tam solemniter, tam diversi, tam propinqui, tam hilariter ipsam altarium consecratione missarum solemnem vcelebratione missarum solemnem celebrationem superius inferiusque peragebant, ut ex ipsa sui consonantia et cohaerente harmoniae grata melodia potius angelicus quam humanus concentue aestimaretur": *De Consecratione Ecclesiae Sancti Dionysii* 7, in Erwin Panofsky, trans. and ed., *Abbot Suger on the Abbey-Church of Saint-Denis and Its Art Treasures* (Princeton: Princeton University Press, 1946), 118–21.

318. Timothy Thibodeau, "Western Christendom," in *The Oxford History of Christian Worship,* ed. Wainwright and Westerfield Tucker, 213. This would also be the case in Ireland, where the Cistercian monasteries quickly adopted both decorative elements and fortification works; see Roger Stalley, *The Cistercian Monasteries of Ireland: An Account of the History, Art, and Architecture of the White Monks in Ireland from 1142 to 1540* (New Haven: Yale University Press, 1987), 141–45, 179–80.

319. The theme of stational liturgy will be dealt with more fully in chapter 3.

320. Bullough, "The Carolingian Liturgical Experience," 41. However, note that there are some examples of true stational liturgy in the Carolingian domain. In a recent study of the monastery of Saint Riquier, an important monastery reformed under Charlemagne's patronage in the late eighth century, it is clear that the laity did indeed participate in the monastic liturgy particularly on important feast days where they processed with the monks in the various elements of the stational liturgy; see Rabe, *Faith, Art and Politics,* 122–32.

321. Vogel, *Medieval Liturgy,* 157.

322. Mitchell, *Cult and Controversy,* 186.

323. "Missarum namque et sacrificiorum solemnia non solum pro eo, verum etiam pro omnibus fidelibus defunctis frequenter facias offerri. Nulla enim oratio in hac parte melior, quam sacrificiorum libamina. Dicitur de viro fortissimo Juda: *Sancta et salubris est cogitatio orare pro mortuis, et pro eis sacrificium offerre, ut a peccatis solvantur*": *PL* 106:116; English translation from Mitchell, *Cult and Controversy,* 102.

324. Louis de Bazelaire, "Communion Fréquente," in *DSAM* 2/1: col. 1237–38. Perhaps this practice developed from the age of persecutions. As the viaticum was an important obligation for Christians, so in the time of the persecutions, Christians, even the laity, were accustomed to bringing the eucharistic bread home so that they could receive Communion if they were about to be captured and martyred; see W. H. Freestone, *The Sacrament Reserved: A Sur-*

vey of the Practice of Reserving the Eucharist, with Special Reference to Communion of the Sick, during the first Twelve Centuries, Alcuin Club Collections 21 (London: Mowbray, 1917), 34. Freestone sees Home Communion as having developed from this practice, 37–38. It soon became apparent that this practice was open to abuses. The author of *De spectaculis* complains of Christians who go straight to pagan spectacles from the liturgy, and as they are carrying the Eucharist with them they expose it to contact with all kinds of obscenity (*De spectaculis* 5, in *PL* 4:784, cited in Freestone, *The Sacrament Reserved,* 39). There was also a tendency for some Christians to get carried away in their devotional practices involving the Eucharist species. St Gregory Nazianzen (d. 389) tells "how his seriously ill sister St Gorgonia smeared her whole body with the eucharistic species and was cured"; Robert F. Taft, "Is There Devotion to the Holy Eucharist in the Christian East? A Footnote to the October 2005 Synod of the Eucharist," *Worship* 80, no. 3 (2006): 215.

325. Taft, "Home-Communion," 3, also see 13–14. In the next two chapters, the practice of the reservation of the Eucharist on the person of Irish ecclesiastics in vessels called chrismals, which were hung around their necks, will be examined as perhaps an example of the development and perseverance of a custom based on the practice of domestic reservation by monks for later daily reception of Communion.

326. Robert F. Taft, "The Order and Place of Lay Communion in the Late Antique and Byzantine East," in *Studia Liturgica Diversa: Studies in Church Music and Liturgy; Essays in Honor of Paul F. Bradshaw,* ed. Maxwell E. Johnson and L. Edward Phillips (Portland: Pastoral Press, 2004), 130–31.

327. Mitchell, *Cult and Controversy,* 45.

328. "Et cum quaedam arcam suam, in qua Domini sanctum fuit, manibus indignis temptasset aperire, igne inde surgente deterrita est ne auderet attingere": *De lapsis* 26, in M. Bévenot, ed., *Sancti Cypriani Episcopi Opera: Pars I,* Corpus Christianorum Series Latina 3 (Turnhout: Brepols, 1972), 235; English translation from Roy J. Deferrari, trans. and ed., *Saint Cyprian Treatises,* Fathers of the Church 36 (Washington DC: Catholic University of America Press, 1958), 79.

329. De Bazelaire, "Communion Fréquente," col. 1243. Taft notes that it was often these very same pastors who so frightened their congregations and filled them with an appreciation of their unworthiness that there is little surprise that they did not approach the altar; see his *A History of the Liturgy of St John Chrysostom,* vol. 5, *The Precommunion Rites,* Orientalia Christiana Analecta 261 (Rome: Edizioni Orientalia Christiana, 2000), 130, and Bradshaw, *Eucharistic Origins,* 143.

330. Pierre M. Gy, "Penance and Reconciliation," in *The Sacraments,* vol. 3 of *The Church at Prayer,* vol. 3: *The Sacraments,* ed. A. G. Martimort, trans. Matthew J. O'Connell (Collegeville, MN: Liturgical Press, 1988), 103.

331. As well as general conversion and change of life, the notion sometimes entered that "physical purity was procured through abstinence from marital relations in the period before the feast"; see Beck, *The Pastoral Care of Souls,* 152–53.

332. Adrien Nocent, "Questions About Specific Points," in *The Eucharist,* ed. Chupungco, 311.

333. De Bazelaire, "Communion Fréquente," col. 1255.

334. There are even cases of injunctions to priests obliging them to receive, which probably implies that at some times a Eucharist may have been celebrated in which absolutely no one received. "To *sacordotes.* It is understood that some priests celebrate mass and do not themselves partake in the sacrament, something which one reads in the apostolic canons to be utterly forbidden"; "Ad sacerdotes. Auditum est aliquos presbyteros missam celebrare et non communicare: quod omnio in canonibus apostolorum interdictum esse legitur": *Admonitio Generalis* 6, in Alfredus Boretius, ed., *Monumenta Germaniae Historica, Legum Sectio II: Capitularia Regum Francorum* (Hanover: Impensis Bibliopolii Haniani, 1883), 1:54; English translation from P. D. King, trans. and ed. *Charlemagne: Translated Sources* (Kendal: self-published, 1987), 210.

335. After the end of our period, these culminated with the still-obligatory twenty-first canon of the Fourth Lateran Council (1215), which mandates that all adult Catholics have to make an annual Confession of mortal sins and receive Communion in the Easter season; see Norman P. Tanner, trans. and ed., *Decrees of the Ecumenical Councils* (Washington DC: Georgetown University Press, 1990), 1:245. Early medieval examples are given in Beck, *The Pastoral Care of Souls,* 150–51.

336. Henri Leclercq, "Communion," in *DACL* 3/2, col. 2463.

337. Ibid., col. 2464.

338. Mitchell, *Cult and Controversy,* 90. Mitchell traces the changes in the practices of giving Communion on 86–104. From an art history point of view, a recent survey of icons and other paintings of the Last Supper has no unambiguous pre-eleventh-century evidence, but all of the post-eleventh-century medieval iconography has Jesus administering the Eucharist to the apostles on either a spoon or in the form of a host directly into the mouth; see Julia Hasting, ed., *Last Supper* (London: Phaidon, 2000). However, some medieval liturgical manuscripts, dating from the tenth to the twelfth centuries and originating in Italy and France, provide liturgies for Communion services where an abbess could distribute Communion to her nuns when no priest was available to celebrate Mass for them; see Jean Leclercq, "Eucharistic Celebration without Priests in the Middle Ages," in *Living Bread, Saving Cup: Readings on the Eucharist,* ed. R. Kevin Seasoltz, 222–30 (Collegeville, MN: Liturgical Press, 1987). However, while female monastics were important in Ireland and some female saints (Brigit in particular) are presented as handling chrismals, for ex-

ample, there is no Irish evidence for nuns distributing Communion; see Christina Harrington, *Women in a Celtic Church: Ireland 450–1150* (Oxford: Oxford University Press, 2002), 93.

339. Robert Cabié, *The Eucharist*, vol. 2 of *The Church at Prayer*, ed. A. G. Martimort, trans. Matthew J. O'Connell (Collegeville, MN: Liturgical Press, 1986), 135–36.

340. Ibid., 132–33.

341. Mitchell, *Cult and Controversy*, 96.

342. Taft, "Is There Devotion," 217.

343. A good introduction to the devotion to relics is provided by Peter Brown, *The Cult of the Saints: Its Rise and Function in Latin Christianity* (Chicago: University of Chicago Press, 1981). Snoek, *Medieval Piety*, gives an up-to-date study on the whole phenomenon of the place of relics in early Christianity.

344. José Antonio Iñiguez Herrero, *El Altar Cristiano*, vol. 1, *De los Origines a Carlomagno* (Pamplona: Eunsa, 1978), 64–65.

345. Snoek, *Medieval Piety*, 9–14.

346. Angelus Häussling, "Motives for the Frequency of the Eucharist," *Concilium* 152 (1982): 27.

347. Snoek, *Medieval Piety*, 18.

348. But where enough relics were found, the desire to honor these relics with the celebration of the Eucharist may have been another contributing factor to the multiplication of Masses; see ibid., 42.

349. Dating from the first half of the eighth century, *Ordo Romanus* 42 mentions that as part of the consecration of a church that "three particles of the body of the Lord are placed in the *confessio* (saint's tomb)" of the altar. "Tres protiones corporis domini intus in confessione": *Ordo Romanus* 42.11, in Andrieu, *Les Ordines Romani*, 4:400; English translation my own.

350. Archadale A. King, *Eucharistic Reservation in the Western Church* (New York: Sheed and Ward, 1965), 42–45. The texts cited by King contain references to metallic "doves" associated with altars, perhaps even as early as the third century. It is only in the eighth century that there is positive evidence of "doves" containing the eucharistic species.

351. For example, the ninth-century local Synod of Verona requires that "the altar should be covered with clean linen; nothing should be placed on the altar except reliquaries and relics and the four gospel-books, and a pyx with the body of the Lord for the viaticum of the sick; other things should be kept in some seemly place": "Altare coopertum de mundis linteis; super altare nihil ponatur nisi capsae et reliquiae, aut forte quatuor Evangelia et buxida cum corpore Domini ad viaticum infirmis; caetera in nitido loco recondantur": *PL* 136:559; English translation from Benedict Groeschel and James Monti, *In the Presence of the Lord: The History, Theology and Psychology of Eucharistic Devotion* (Huntington, IN: Our Sunday Visitor Books, 1997), 191.

352. Mazza, *The Celebration of the Eucharist,* 195. This desire for ocular Communion was much more prevalent in the West than in the Christian East; see Dix, *The Shape of the Liturgy,* 15.

353. In this treatment I have followed Mitchell and other liturgical scholars in a somewhat minimalist reading of the evidence for popular eucharistic devotion. However, for a (very) maximalist view, see James Monti's treatment of the subject in Groeschel and Monti, *In the Presence of the Lord,* 187–208. However it is advisable to check the original sources that Monti refers to, as his work is overly dependent on secondary materials. For a view of how the eucharistic celebration developed after this period (with some references to earlier history) see John Bossy, "The Mass as a Social Institution: 1200–1700," *Past and Present* 100 (1983): 29–61.

354. Mitchell, *Cult and Controversy,* 163.

355. Jaroslav Pelikan, *The Christian Tradition: A History of the Development of Doctrine,* vol. 2, *The Growth of Medieval Theology (600–1300)* (Chicago: University of Chicago Press), 185. Internal quotations from Odo of Cluny *Collationum Libri Tres* 2.28. ("Hoc enim beneficium majus est inter omnia bona, quae hominibus concessa sunt, et hoc est quod Deus majori charitate mortalibus indulsit, quia in hoc mysterio salus mundi tota consistit": *PL* 133:572.)

CHAPTER TWO.   Written Sources

1. Robert F. Taft, *Through Their Own Eyes Liturgy as the Byzantines Saw It* (Berkeley, CA: InterOrthodox Press, 2006), 68.

2. There are two main published editions of the *Stowe Missal.* Most scholars use the more widely available edition edited by Warner, which remains very valuable and up until now has been much more accessible (it also includes a facsimile of the manuscript itself). However, a slightly earlier edition by Bartholomew MacCarthy has by no means been superceded. In terms of textual reconstruction MacCarthy is sometimes more accurate than Warner, and in addition to providing a critical edition of the text of the *Stowe Missal* he also supplies material on the *Old Irish Mass Tract of the Stowe Missal* that Warner does not. As MacCarthy's edition can be hard to locate today, those interested are recommended to consult Fredrick Edward Warren, *The Liturgy and Ritual of the Celtic Church,* with a new introduction by Neil Xavier O'Donoghue, Gorgias Liturgical Studies 64 (Oxford: The Clarendon Press, 1881; 3rd fac. ed., Piscataway, NJ: Gorgias Press, 2010). This publication contains the full text of MacCarthy's edition of the *Stowe Missal* as an appendix.

3. Warner, *The Stowe Missal,* xxxii. Warner discusses earlier opinions on the possible dates on xxii–xxiv and xxxii–xxxvii.

4. Many of the surviving sources for the Eucharist in pre-Norman Ireland have at one time or another been associated with the Céli Dé, but today

many of these associations are no longer trustworthy. For more on the Céli Dé, see Westley Nicholson Follett, "Monastic Devotion in Ireland: The Celi De Movement in the Eighth and Ninth Centuries" (PhD diss., University of Toronto, 2002).

5. Folio 33 in Warner, *The Stowe Missal*, 89. Botte also notes that in the *Te igitur* mention is made of "et abate nostro N. episcopo" (fol. 24r, in ibid., 10) and not the more normal "et Antístite nostro N."; see Botte, *Le Canon de la Messe Romaine*, 32–33. However, this is only an indication of a possible monastic provenance and does not really have any bearing on whether or not the *Stowe Missal* is associated with the Céli Dé movement.

6. Pádraig Ó Riain, "The Shrine of the *Stowe Missal* Redated," *Proceedings of the Royal Irish Academy* 91C (1991): 294–95. In which case the Missal was used in the church of Lorrha (figure 18).

7. These will be dealt with below, pp. 71–77, 79–83, and 143.

8. Marion J. Hatchett, "The Eucharistic Rite of the *Stowe Missal*," in *Time and Community: In Honor of Thomas Julian Talley*, ed. J. Neil Alexander, NPN Studies in Church Music and Liturgy (Washington DC: Pastoral Press, 1990), 154.

9. Botte, *Le Canon de la Messe Romaine*, 11–13. The early-ninth-century *Book of Armagh*, whose material on St Patrick will be examined below, also contains a fragment of the Roman Canon in the New Testament section of the manuscript; see Warren, *Liturgy and Ritual*, 174–75.

10. "Le *Kyrie* de la Messe et le Pape Gélase," "Alcuin et l'Histoire du Symbole de le Messe," and "Le Rite de la Fraction dans la Messe Romaine," collected in Bernard Capelle, *Travaux Liturgiques de Doctrine et d'Histoire*, vol. 2, *Histoire La Messe* (Louvain: Centre Liturgique, Abbaye du Mont César, 1962).

11. Sven Meeder, "The Early Irish *Stowe Missal*'s Destination and Function," *Early Medieval Europe* 13:2 (2005): 182–83. In this sense it seems to have been akin to the *Bobbio Missal*; Hen, "The Liturgy of the *Bobbio Missal*," 152–53.

12. Hatchett, "The Eucharistic Rite of the *Stowe Missal*," 154.

13. I borrow the phrase from J. W. Hunwicke, "Kerry and Stowe Revisited," *Proceedings of the Royal Irish Academy* 102C (2002): 2.

14. Hatchett, "The Eucharistic Rite of the *Stowe Missal*," 162. Breen is of the opinion that these revisions were carried out soon after the missal was written, as they are in line with the Councils of Friuli (796/97) and Aachen (798), where a new version of the Creed was promulgated and on which these changes are based; see Aidan Breen, "The Text of the Constantinopolitan Creed in the *Stowe Missal*," *Proceedings of the Royal Irish Academy* 90 (1990): 121.

15. Meeder, "The Early Irish *Stowe Missal*'s Destination and Function," 185.

16. Hatchett, "The Eucharistic Rite of the *Stowe Missal*," 159.

17. Schneiders, "The Origins of the Early Irish Liturgy," 84.

18. I do not deny that certain liturgical characteristics and practices may have marked out various subgroups in pre-Norman Ireland (churches influenced by the *Romani* or the *Hiberni,* or those serviced by monastics connected with the Céli Dé or Columban charisms). But with the possible exception of the calculation of the date of Easter, there is not enough evidence to say anything more concrete about these possible differences, and Móel Cáich cannot be assigned to any particular movement.

19. Preliminary attempts at such an analysis can be found in King, *Liturgies of the Past,* 248–74, and Hatchett, "The Eucharistic Rite of the *Stowe Missal.*" A more developed analysis can be found in Hugh P. Kennedy, "Tinkering Embellishment or Liturgical Fidelity? An Investigation into Liturgical Practice in Ireland before the Twelfth Century Reform Movement as Illustrated in the *Stowe Missal*" (DD thesis, St Patrick's College, Maynooth, 1994). On a contemporary proposal to use the preface from the *Stowe Missal* see Thomas O'Loughlin, "A Celtic Preface," *Furrow* 51 (2000): 34–38.

20. O'Loughlin, *Celtic Theology,* 136–37.

21. "Peccavimus, Domine, Peccavimus parce peccatis nostris et salva nos. Qui gubernasti Noe super undas diluvii, exaudi nos; et Jonam de abysso verbo revocasti libera nos. Qui Petro mergenti manum porrexisti auxiliare nobis, Christe, Fili Dei. Fecisti mirabilia, Domine, cum patribus nostris, et nostris propitiare temporibus. Emitte manum tuam de alto, libera nos. Christe, audi nos; Christe, audi nos; Christe audi nos. Kyrie, eleison.

Sancta Maria,	[ora pro nobis]
Sancte Petre,	[ora pro nobis]
Sancte Paule,	[ora pro nobis]
Sancte Andrea,	[ora pro nobis]
Sancte Jacobe,	[ora pro nobis]
Sancte Bartholomaee,	[ora pro nobis]
Sancte Thoma,	[ora pro nobis]
Sancte Matthaee,	[ora pro nobis]
Sancte Jacobe,	[ora pro nobis]
Sancte Thaddaee,	[ora pro nobis]
Sancte Matthia,	[ora pro nobis]
Sancte Marce,	[ora pro nobis]
Sance Luca,	[ora pro nobis]
Omnes sancti,	orate pro nobis.
Propitius esto,	parce nobis, Domine
Ab omni malo,	libera nos Domine
Per crucem tuam,	libera nos Domine
[*] Sancte Stephane,	ora pro nobis.
Sancte Martine,	ora pro nobis.
Sancte Hieronyme,	ora pro nobis.

Sancte Augustine,	ora pro nobis.
Sancte Gregori,	ora pro nobis.
Sancte Hilari,	ora pro nobis.
Sancte Patrici,	ora pro nobis.
Sancte Ailbei,	ora pro nobis.
Sancte Finnio,	ora pro nobis.
Sancte Finnio,	ora pro nobis.
Sancte Ciarani,	ora pro nobis.
Sancte Ciarani,	ora pro nobis.
Sancte Brendini,	ora pro nobis.
Sancte Brendini,	ora pro nobis.
Sancte Columba,	ora pro nobis.
Sancte Columba,	ora pro nobis.
Sancte Comgilli,	ora pro nobis.
Sancte Cainnichi,	ora pro nobis.
Sancte Findbarri,	ora pro nobis.
Sancte Nessani,	ora pro nobis.
Sancte Factni,	ora pro nobis.
Sancte Lugidi,	ora pro nobis.
Sancte Lacteni,	ora pro nobis.
Sancte Ruadani,	ora pro nobis.
Sancte Carthegi,	ora pro nobis.
Sancte Coemgeni,	ora pro nobis.
Sancte Mochonne,	ora pro nobis.
Sancta Brigita,	ora pro nobis.
Sancta Ita,	ora pro nobis.
Sancta Scetha,	ora pro nobis.
Sancta Sinecha,	ora pro nobis.
Sancta Samdine,	ora pro nobis.
Omnes sancti,	orate pro nobis.
Propitius esto,	parce nobis, Domine.
Propitius esto,	libera nos, Domine.
Ab omni malo,	libera nos, Domine.
Per Crucem tuam,	libera nos, Domine.
Peccatores,	te rogamus audi nos.
Filii Dei,	te rogamus audi nos.
Ut pacem dones,	te rogamus audi nos.

Agne Dei qui tollis peccata mundi, miserere nobis.
Christe, audi nos; Christe, audi nos; Christe, audi nos": *Stowe Missal* fols.
12a, 28a–29a, in Bartholomew MacCarthy, "On the *Stowe Missal*," *Transactions of the Royal Irish Academy* 27 (1886): 192–94; English translation from O'Loughlin, *Celtic Theology*, 137–39.

22. Jungmann, *The Mass of the Roman Rite*, 1:333–46.

23. This is marked in the text by [*]. At some stage the page containing these additions was bound in the wrong place at some later date; King, *Liturgies of the Past*, 249.

24. Willibrord Godel, "Irish Prayer in the Early Middle Ages II," *Milltown Studies* 5 (1980): 85–96.

25. This assumes the modern Western distinction between liturgy and popular devotion (see Mark R. Francis, "Liturgy and Popular Piety in a Historical Perspective," in *Directory on Popular Piety and the Liturgy: A Commentary*, ed. Peter Phan [Collegeville, MN: Liturgical Press, 2005], 26–27). While this distinction may be somewhat forced at this time, it is likely that Christians in pre-Norman Ireland would have acknowledged a difference between the Eucharist and other contexts where litanies were used.

26. I am indebted to Dr Colmán Etchingham for these insights.

27. *Stowe Missal* fols. 30a–31b, in MacCarthy, "On the *Stowe Missal*," 216–18. This is also the place where the famous mention is made of St Maelruin, the founder of the Céli Dé movement, along with the one hundred other saints. For a table of dates and other information of the Irish saints mentioned in the *Stowe Missal*, see Warner, *The Stowe Missal*, xxiv–xxxii.

28. King, *Liturgies of the Past*, 264–65. King also notes that, while Laurence, Melitus, and Justus—the three successors of Augustine of Canterbury—are commemorated in this list, Augustine himself is not commemorated, which might hint at some antipathy towards the founder of Anglo-Saxon Christianity.

29. "Cognoverunt Dominum, *alleluia*, in fractione panis, alleluia. Panis quem frangimus Corpus est Domini nostri, Jesu Christi, alleluia. Calix quem benedicimus, alleluia, Sanguis est Domini nostri, Jesu Christi, *alleluia,* in remisionem peccatorum nostrorum, *alleluia.* Fiat Domine, *misericordia tua super nos, alleluia quemadmodum speravimus in te, alleluia.* Cognoverunt Dominum, alleluia. Credimus, Domine, credimus in hac confractione Corporis et effussione Sanguinis nos esse redemptos; et confidimus, sacramenti hujus assumptione muniti, ut quod spe interim hic tenemus, mansuri in celestibus veris fructibus perfruamur. Per Dominum"*: Stowe Missal* fols. 32a—33a, in MacCarthy, "On the *Stowe Missal*," 219–20; English translation from O'Loughlin, *Celtic Theology*, 142. I have slightly modified O'Loughlin's translation.

30. O'Loughlin, *Celtic Theology*, 142.

31. "Pacem mandasti, pacem dedisti, pacem dereliquisti. Pacem tuam, Domine, da nobis de caelo, et pacificum hunc diem et caeteros dies vitae nostrae in tua pace disponas. Per Dominum.
Conmixto Corporis et sanguinis Domini nostri, Jesu Crsto, sit nobis salus in vitam perpetuam. Amen.
Ecce agnus Dei; ecce quo tollit peccata mundi.
Pacem meam do vobis, alleluia; pacem relinquo vobis, alleluia.

Pax multa diligentibus legem tuam, Domine, alleluia; et non est in illis scanda-
lum, alleluia.
Regem caeli cum pace, alleluia,
Plenum odorem vitae, alleluia,
Novum carmen cantate, alleluia,
Omnes sancti, venite, alleluia.
Venite comedite panem meum, alleluia, et bibite vinum quod miscui vobis,
alleluia.
Dominus regit me.
Qui manducat Corpus meum, et bibit meum Sanguinem, alleluia, ipse in me
manet, [et] ego in illo, alleluia.
Domini est terra.
Hic est panis vivus, qui de caelo discendit, alleluia; qui manducat ex eo, vivet in
aeternum, alleluia.
Ad te, Domine, levavi animam meam.
Panem caeli dedit eis Dominus, alleluia; panem angelorum manducavit homo,
alleluia
Judica me, Domine.
Comedite, amici mei, alleluia; et inebriamini, charissimi, alleluia
Hoc sacrum Corpus Domini,
Salvatoris Sanguinem, alleluia,
Sumite vobis
In vitam aeternam, alleluia.
In labis meis meditabor hymnum, alleluia; cum docueris me, et ego justitias
respondebo, alleluia.
Benedicam Dominum in omni tempore, alleluia; semper laus eius in ore meo,
alleluia.
Gustate et videte, alleluia, quam suavis est Dominus, alleluia.
Ubi ego fuero, alleluia, ibi erit et minister meus, alleluia.
Sinite parvulos venire ad me, alleluia, et nolite eos prohibere, alleluia; talium est
enim regnum caelorum, alleluia.
Penitentiam agite, alleluia; appropinquavit enim regnum caelorum, alleluia.
Regnum celorum vim patitur; alleluia et violenti rapiunt illud, alleluia.
Venite, benedicti patris mei, possidete regnum, alleluia, quoe vobis paratum est
ab origine mundi, alleluia.
  Gloria. Venite. Sicut erat. Venite": *Stowe Missal* fols. 33b–35a, in MacCarthy,
"On the *Stowe Missal*," 221–23; English translation from O'Loughlin, *Celtic
Theology,* 143–44.
    32. Although the *Mass Tract* is not a liturgical manuscript per se and per-
haps ought to have been treated in the second half of this chapter, it is treated
here as it is so closely related to the *Stowe Missal*.
    33. Warner, *The Stowe Missal*, ix.

34. The translation in Warner, *The Stowe Missal*, 40–42, is taken from Whitley Stokes and John Strachan, eds., *Thesaurus Palaeohibernicus*, 2 vols. (Cambridge: Cambridge University Press, 1901–3) 2:252. This same translation seems to have been taken and modernized in Oliver Davies, *Celtic Spirituality*, The Classics of Western Spirituality (Mahwah, NJ: Paulist Press, 1999), 311–13. Both versions of the *Tract* are available in the 1886 edition of MacCarthy, "On the *Stowe Missal*," 245–65. Pádraig Ó Néill also mentions that there are two versions and introduces the reader to linguistic differences in the Irish originals; see his "The *Old-Irish Tract on the Mass* in the *Stowe Missal*: Some Observances on Its Origin and Textual History," in Smyth, *Seanchas*, 199–204.

35. Regarding a date for the actual composition of the original *Tract*, MacCarthy calls attention to the fact that the *Gloria* and Creed are not mentioned (although they are present within the *Stowe Missal* itself), which might indicate an early date of composition; "On the *Stowe Missal*," 248. The fact that they are not mentioned, however, does not necessarily mean that they were not part of the liturgy at that time. In addition, given the differences that existed from one church to another, perhaps the author came from a church that retained older usages; his work may have been incorporated into the Stowe Missal shortly after he composed it. The actual manuscripts date to the early ninth (*Stowe*) and early fifteenth (*Leabhar Breac*) centuries; see Ó Néill, "The *Old-Irish Tract on the Mass* in the *Stowe Missal*," 199.

36. MacCarthy is of the opinion that the scribe who transcribed the version in the *Leabhar Breac* "displays complete illiteracy with respect to the Latin." Because a cleric would be expected to have some knowledge of Latin, this suggests at least some use of this text in lay (albeit literate) circles; see MacCarthy, "On the *Stowe Missal*," 262.

37. Willibrord Godel, "Irish Prayer in the Early Middle Ages IV," *Milltown Studies* 7 (1981): 28.

38. *Stowe Missal Tract* 2, in MacCarthy, "On the *Stowe Missal*," 245. As the complete text is given in parallel columns in appendix 1 of this volume, the Irish text will not be quoted here.

39. *Leabhar Breac Tract* 1, in ibid., 259.

40. "Oblae iarum super altare," in ibid., 246.

41. See Warner, *The Stowe Missal*, 40. For more information on the fifth-century origins of the eucharistic dove, see Iñiguez, *El Altar Cristiano*, 1:105–10. If this really is a reference to the practice of a eucharistic dove, it would be quite significant as there is virtually no evidence for the use of the eucharistic dove between the seventh and eleventh centuries; ibid., 1:197. This text might then either constitute evidence of a practice being preserved in Ireland at a time when it was lost on the Continent, or point to an early date for the original *Tract*. For an alternative view of eucharistic doves in this period, cf. King, *Eucharistic Reservation in the Western Church*, 42–45. Dr Michael Ryan, the Director of the Chester Beatty Library in Dublin and an expert on early

Irish metalwork and eucharistic vessels, is of the opinion that this could refer to a chrismal being hung above the altar (personal communication, October 15, 2002).

42. "Peto te, Pater; deprecor te, Filii; obsecro te, Spiritus Sancte": *Stowe Missal Tract* 4, in MacCarthy, "On the *Stowe Missal*," 245. The fact that *Stowe* says that this prayer is sung ("canar") is taken by MacCarthy to mean that "the service was choral"—this is paralleled by *Leabhar Breac Tract* 4, in ibid., 260. However, this version does not mention the prayer being sung, but uses the generic "dicis."

43. "Remittat Pater; indulgeat Filius; miseratur Spiritus Sanctus": *Stowe Missal Tract* 6, in ibid., 246–47. This is paralleled by *Leabhar Breac Tract* 6, in ibid., 261.

44. *Leabhar Breac Tract* 11, in ibid., 262–63. The parallel section in *Stowe* reads, "When *Accepit Jesus panem* is chanted, the priest bows thrice for sorrow for their sins; he offers them [i.e., the bread and wine] to God; and the people prostrates; and there comes not a sound then, that it not disturb the priest; for it is his duty that his mind separate not from God whilst he chants this Lection. It is from this that *Periculosa Oratio* gets its name": in ibid., 249.

45. Jungmann, *The Mass of the Roman Rite*, 2:205.

46. *Stowe Missal Tract* 18, in MacCarthy, "On the *Stowe Missal*," 251–54.

47. "Innumerabiles populos": Cogitosus, *Vita Brigitae* 32.9, in *PL* 75:790; English translation from Connolly and Picard, "Cogitosius's *Life of St Brigit*," 26. This text will be treated in more detail in chapter 3.

48. *Stowe Missal Tract* 18, in MacCarthy "On the *Stowe Missal*," 254–57.

49. For possible reconstructions of the pieces of eucharistic bread on the paten, see ibid., 256, and Thomas O'Loughlin, "The Praxis and Explanation of Eucharistic Fraction in the Ninth Century: The Insular Evidence," *Archiv für Liturgiewissenschaft* 45 (2003): 13.

50. MacCarthy, "On the *Stowe Missal*," 255.

51. It is possible to find allusions to similar practices in Gallican and Hispanic areas, but these texts are not nearly as detailed as the *Tract*; see José Antonio Iñiguez Herrero, *El Altar Cristiano*, vol. 2, *De Carlomagno al Siglo XIII* (Pamplona: Eunsa, 1991), 109–14, and O'Loughlin, "Praxis and Explanation," 13.

52. *Stowe Missal Tract* 18, in MacCarthy, "On the *Stowe Missal*," 257–58.

53. Dold and Eizenhöfer, *Das Irische Palimpsestakramentar*, 125, 34.

54. Ibid., 125–26.

55. Schneiders, "The Origins of the Early Irish Liturgy," 79–80. For a very interesting alternative reading of this evidence, see Yitzhak Hen, "Rome, Anglo-Saxon England and the Formation of Frankish Liturgy," *Revue Bénédictine* 112, nos. 3–4 (2002): 301–22. Hen presupposes that the *Palimpsest Sacramentary* is not Irish but comes from an Irish-influenced scriptorium in Northumbria. He then proposes that this type of sacramentary was later revised

under Archbishop Theodore of Canterbury (or someone close to him) and then passed to the Continent in the company of some English ecclesiastic, "most probably . . . from the circle of Boniface. A copy of this modified version, I believe, was one of the main sources used by the compiler of the Gothic Missal"; ibid., 315–16. While this is a fascinating theory worthy of further study, I believe that until that study is carried out, it is better to maintain Irish provenance for this work, in line with the exhaustive scholarship of Dold and Eizenhöfer.

56. Dold and Eizenhöfer, *Das Irische Palimpsestakramentar,* 127.

57. For an outline of the contents, including a comparison of the *Palimpsest Sacramentary*'s sanctoral to that of other Gallican manuscripts, see ibid., 90–99.

58. Ibid., 127.

59. Ibid., 127. The significance of the presence of Roman material should be balanced by the traces of Gnostic texts. The *Palimpsest Sacramentary* contains traces of the Gnostic hymn *Veni Epiclesis* from the *Acts of Thomas.* These take the form of quotations within a prayer, however, and the eucharistic liturgy of the *Palimpsest Sacramentary* does not resemble that of Gnostic texts; for more on these Gnostic eucharistic texts see G. Rouwhorst, "La Célébracion de l'Eucharistie selon les Actes de Thomas," in *Omnes Circumadstantes: Contributions Towards a History of the Role of the People in the Liturgy,* ed. Charles Caspers and Marc Schneiders, 51–77 (Kampen: J. H. Kok, 1990).

60. Michael Richter, *Ireland and Her Neighbours in the Seventh Century* (Dublin: Four Courts Press, 1999), 173.

61. John Hennig, "Old Ireland and Her Liturgy," in *Old Ireland,* ed. Robert E. McNally (New York: Fordham University Press, 1965), 68. Although the goal of the whole article, in fact, seems to be to try to prove "the absence of a *Sanctorale*" in old Ireland than to actually introduce us to her liturgy.

62. Klaus Gambler rejected the *Palimpsest Sacramentary* as being an imposition of the Gallican rite in Ireland; quoted in Leo Eizenhöffer, "Zu dem Irischen Palimpesakramentar im Clm 14429," *Sacris Erudiri Jaarboek voor Godsdienstwetenschappen* 17, no. 1 (1966): 358–59. Stevenson also rejected it as being "completely un-Irish in its contents"; see Stevenson, "Introduction," lxvii. But we do not have enough other primary sources to be able to eliminate this source. Moreover, it has to be considered that this is only one piece of evidence among many that Ireland was using a basically Gallican liturgy.

63. Dold and Eizenhöfer, *Das Irische Palimpsestakramentar,* 126.

64. Frederick S. Paxton, *Christianizing Death* (Ithaca: Cornell University Press, 1990), 85.

65. Ibid., 79.

66. Technically speaking this rite could be called a viaticum as it always contains the reception of Communion in addition to the anointing with oil

(Gougaud, in "Celtiques [Liturgies]," *DACL* 2/2, col. 3021, refers to the rite as "saint viatique"). But here I follow other authors in referring to the rite as the "rites of the sick." Additionally the term viaticum presupposes that there is no chance that the individual will return to health, seeing it as a liturgical preparation for death. However, while it is very possible (and judging from the other evidence dealing with the viaticum it is even probable) that these were rites used to administer the viaticum when somebody was clearly dying, the prayers of the rite itself do speak of healing. It is likewise possible that the rite may have been repeated if the sick person recovered and later became sick again, even if later on in the High Middle Ages the repetition of the sacrament of the sick was to be strictly forbidden.

67. Though the *Book of Deer* contains a short liturgical section, the manuscript is principally an evangelarium and is the only remaining Scottish liturgical manuscript from this period. As the Scottish church was so linked to the Irish at this time, and this remaining fragment is so related to Irish material, it can appropriately be treated in this section. Warren's analysis and edition of the text is still valuable; see *Liturgy and Ritual,* 163–66. For a detailed modern treatment of the rite as found in the *Book of Deer,* see Gilbert Márkus, "The Sick and the Dying in the *Book of Deer,*" in *Studies on the Book of Deer,* ed. Katherine Forsyth, 67–97 (Dublin: Four Courts Press, 2008). The side-by-side comparison of the various rites dealt with in this section provided by Márkus is useful, but I believe that he is overly eager to draw conclusions from this sole-surviving fragment of liturgical material of Scottish provenance which amounts to a single page inserted into the manuscript.

68. Jenner, "The Celtic Rite," *CE* 3:503.

69. Two of the scripture passages deal with the Resurrection and the third with the Last Judgment.

70. Ibid., 503–4.

71. *"Oratio communis pro infirmo incipit*
Oremus, frateres carissimi, pro spiritu cari nostri .n. qui secundum carnem egritudinem patitur, ut dominus ei reuelationem dolorum presentet, uitam concedat, tutellam salutis remunerationem boborum operum impertiat, per dominum.
Prefatio communis incipit.
Oremus, fratres carissimi, pro fratre nostro .n. qui incommodo carnis et egretudine uexatur, domini pietas per angelum medicine celestisuisitare et corroborare dignetur, per dominum [*words missing from manuscript*]
[pate]r omnipotens, et consuera famulum tuum hanc .n. quem [sancti]ficasti et redemisti pre[tio] magno sanguinis tui, in saecula saeculorum.
Benedictio Super Aquam
Oremus et postulemus de domini misericordia, ut celesti spiritu hunc fontem benedicere et sanctificare dignetur, per dominum.

Benedictio Hominis
Benidicat tibi dominus et custodiat te; illuminet dominus faciem suam super te et misseriatur tui, conuertatque dominus uultum suum adte, et det tibi pacem et sanitatem. Misere n. d. a.
Tum ungens eum oleo.
Ungo te deoleo sanctificationis in nominee dei patris, et filí, et spiritus sancti, ut salus eris in nomine sancta trinitatis.
simul canit.
credo in deum patrem.
Tum dicitur et ut dimittat omnia
Collectio Orationis Dominicae
Creator naturarum omnium, deus, et pariens uniuersarum in cele et interra originum has trinitas populi tui relegiosas preces ex illo inaccesse lucis throno tuo suscipe, et inter hiruphin et seraph[in i]n-deffessas circu[m] st[an]tium laudes exudi spei non ambi[gue] precationes.
P[ater] noster.
Collectio nunc sequitur.
Libera nos a malo, domine christe ihesu, et custodies nos in omni opere bobo, auctor omnium bonorum, mamens et regnans in saecula saeculo-rum, amen.
Tum reficitur corpore et sanguine.
Corpus cum sanguine domini nostri ihesu Christi sanitas sit tibi in uitam eternam.
Oratio post sumptam euchari[s]tiam.
Custodi intra nos, domine, glorie tue munus, ut aduersus omnia presen-tis saeculi mala euchari[s]tiae quam percipimus uiribus muniamur, per dominum.
Alleluia.
Et sacrificent sacrificium laudis *usque* annuntiant opera eius in exultatione, alleluia.
Calicem salutaris accipiam et nomen domini inuocabo.
Reffecti Christi corpore et sanguine, tibi semper, domine, dicamus, alleluia.
Laudate dominum omnes.
Glo[ria patri].
sacrificate sacrificium iustitie et sperate in domino.
Deus, tibi gratias agimus, per quem misteria sancta celebrauimus, et ate sanctitatis dona deposcimus, per dominum nostrum ihesum christum fil-ium tuum, cui gloria in saecula saeculorum": my own translation of the Communion of the Sick in the *Book of Mulling* in Warren, *Liturgy and Ritual*, 171–73.

72. Cabié, *The Eucharist*, 2:131–32, and Eamon Duffy, *Saints and Sin-ners: A History of the Popes* (New Haven: Yale University Press, 1997), 84–86.

73. Jungmann, *The Mass of the Roman Rite*, 2:371.

74. Warren, *Liturgy and Ritual*, 224, 170, 173, 164; English translations are my own.

75. For more on the general background of the viaticum, see Damien Sicard, *La Liturgie de la Mort dans l'Eglise Latine des Origines à la Réforme Carolingienne*, Liturgiewissenschaftliche Quellen und Forschungen 63 (Muenster: Westfalen, 1978), 34–39.

76. Jan Michael Joncas, "Liturgy and Music," in *The Pontifical Liturgical Institute Handbook for Liturgical Studies*, vol. 2, *Fundamental Liturgy*, ed. Anscar J. Chupungco (Collegeville, MN: Liturgical Press, 1998), 283.

77. True to form Warren claims that the only thing that can possibly be said about music in the early Irish church is that it was not Roman; see *Liturgy and Ritual*, 126–27.

78. Judaism probably influenced early Christianity's musical practice. Jewish forms of cultic music would be quite unfamiliar to modern Western listeners and are somewhat like a lyrical type of speech; see Edward Foley, *Foundations of Christian Music: The Music of Pre-Constantinian Christianity*, 2 vols. bound as 1, Grove Liturgical Studies 22–23 (Bramcote: Grove, 1992), 38–40. This simple type of music was in stark contrast to the extravagant musical styles of the Roman and Greek religious traditions; see Johannes Quasten, *Music and Worship in Pagan and Christian Antiquity*, trans. Boniface Ramsey (Washington DC: National Association of Pastoral Musicians, 1983), 1–6, at 1. The associations with pagan cultic practices that the contemporary Greco-Roman musical styles had was probably the deciding factor in their rejection by the first Christians.

79. David Hiley, *Western Plainchant: A Handbook* (Oxford: The Clarendon Press, 1993), 479.

80. The two main problems to be dealt with are the interplay between Christians and the pagan cult of the dead, which, among other things, contained many musical elements, and the feasts of the martyrs, which again made use of music as a part of a feast that the church fathers could not reconcile with Christian decorum; see Quasten, *Music and Worship*, 149–77.

81. The other result of the emergence of a specialist class of singers was a split between music and text. This led to the possibilities of musicless Low Masses, which, in turn, contributed to the possibility of reciting the Canon in silence; see Edward Foley, "Music, Liturgical," in *NDSW*, 859.

82. Ibid., 858.

83. Joncas, "Liturgy and Music," 289.

84. Hiley, *Western Plainchant*, 485.

85. Ibid., 485–86.

86. Quasten, *Music and Worship*, 78–79.

87. The texts of these hymns in the *Antiphonary of Bangor* represent the earliest manuscript tradition; see Ann Buckley, "Music in Ireland to *c.* 1500," in *Prehistoric and Early Ireland*, ed. Ó Cróinín, 781.

88. Foley, "Music, Liturgical," *NDSW*, 858.

89. Jane Stevenson, "Hiberno-Latin Hymns: Learning and Literature," in *Ireland and Europe in the Middle Ages: Learning and Literature*, ed. Próinséas Ní Chatháin and Michael Richter (Stuttgart: Klett-Cotta, 1996), 103.

90. J. H. Bernard and R. Atkinson, eds., *The Irish Liber Hymnorum*, 2 vols., Henry Bradshaw Society 13–14 (London: Harrison & Sons, 1898).

91. The main aim of the editorial material in Curran's *Antiphonary of Bangor* is to prove this point.

92. Stevenson, "Introduction," lxxxvii.

93. Ann Buckley, "Music and Musicians in Medieval Irish Society," *Early Music* 28, no. 2 (2000): 167–72.

94. Ann Buckley, "Celtic Chant," in *NGDM* 5:344.

95. Buckley, "Music and Musicians," 185.

96. "Item precipitur, ut forma ordinis tam in cantu quam psalmodia teneatur secundum scriptum beati Bernardi. Nec aliquis contra ordinis simplicitatem uocibus duplicatis cantare presumat. Alioquin transgressor, quicumque fuerit, quotienscumque fecerit, et custodes cantus, nisi dictos presumptores cohibuerint in continenti, in crastino sint in pane et aqua et in capitulo uapulent absque dispensatione": Stephen of Lexington, *Letter* 80.76, in Bruno Griesser, ed., "Registrum Epistolarum Stephani de Lexinton Abbatis de Stanlegia et de Savigniaco," *Analecta Sacri Ordinis Cisterciensis* 2 (1946): 105; English translation from B. O'Dwyer, *Stephen of Lexington*, 167.

97. Patrick Brannon, "Medieval Ireland: Music in Cathedral, Church and Cloister," *Early Music* 28, no. 2 (2000): 195. Gerald of Wales, writing nearly half a century before Stephen of Lexington, also mentions the use of harmony in Ireland. However he was dealing with harp music in a passage that is more probably secular than liturgical; see *Topographia Hibernie* 3.94, in John O'Meara, trans. and ed., *Gerald of Wales: The History and Topography of Ireland* (London: Penguin, 1982), 103–4.

98. Buckley, "Music in Ireland," 783–98.

99. Curran, *The Antiphonary of Bangor,* is the most recent edition of the *Antiphonary*. Before consulting this work, however, the reader would be well advised to read the review by Jane Stevenson, "The Antiphonary of Bangor," *Peritia* 5 (1986): 430–37. An older version (the first volume of which is a facsimile of the manuscript) is that of Fredrick Edward Warren, ed., *The Antiphonary of Bangor*, 2 vols. (London: Harrison & Sons, 1893–95). To situate this work within the Western tradition as a whole and to see how it relates to other Irish evidence, see Robert F. Taft, *The Liturgy of the Hours in East and West: The Origins of the Divine Office and Its Meaning for Today*, 2nd ed. (Collegeville, MN: Liturgical Press, 1993), 113–15.

100. Stevenson, "Hiberno-Latin Hymns," 102.

101. Stevenson, "Introduction," lxxxvi.

102. "Ymnum quando communicarent sacerdotes. Sancti uenite, Christi corpus sumite, sanctum bibentes, quo redempti sanguine. Saluati Christi corpore et sanguine, a quo refecti laudes dicamus Deo. Hoc sacramento corporis et sanguinis omnes exuti ab inferni faucibus. Dator salutis, Christus filius Dei, mundum saluauit per crucem et sanguinem. Pro uniuersis inmolari hostias, qua adumbrantur diuina mysteria. Lucis indultor et saluator omnium praeclaram sanctis largitus est gratiam. Accedant omnes pura mente creduli, sumant aeternam salutis custodiam. Sanctorum custos, rector quoque, Dominus, uitae perennis largitor credentibus. Caelestem panem dat esurientibus, de fonte uiuo praebet sitientibus. Alpha et Ω ipse Christus Dominus uenit, uenturus iudicare homines": Latin from A. S. Warpole, *Early Latin Hymns with Introductions and Notes* (Cambridge: Cambridge University Press, 1922), 345; English translation adapted from Davies, *Celtic Spirituality,* 316–17.

103. Curran, *The Antiphonary of Bangor,* 47.

104. For a verse-by-verse analysis and comparison to other sources, see ibid., 47–49, 210–11.

105. "Doronsat *tra* síth and-sin, Patr*aic ocus* Sech*nall; ocus* cen batar [oc] tiachtain timchell na relgi, ro chualutar clais aingel oc cantain immo'n ídper*t* isin ec*lais; ocus* iss*ed* ro chansat in n-immon di-a n-ad tossach, 'sancti uenite Corpus, etc.,' *con*id o-sein ille chantar i n-Eir*inn* in immune-sa in tan tiagar do churp Crist": *Praefatio in Hymnum S. Secundini* 75–79, in Bernard and Atkinson, *The Irish Liber Hymnorum,* 1:5; English translation from John Carey, trans. and ed., *King of Mysteries: Early Irish Religious Writings* (Dublin: Four Courts Press, 2000), 150.

106. Here I am working under the presumption that it is the same hymn even though there is a slight variation in the title.

107. For a general introduction to these works see Kenney, *The Sources for the Early History of Ireland,* 705–6. A more modern treatment can be found in Buckley, "Music in Ireland," 782–94, 809–10.

108. Critical editions of these missals were published in the nineteenth century: Fredrick E. Warren, ed., *The Manuscript Irish Missal Belonging to the President and Fellows of Corpus Christi College, Oxford* (London: Henry Bradshaw Society, 1879); George Hay Forbes, ed., *Missale Drummondiense: The Ancient Irish Missal in the Possession of the Baroness Willoughby de Eresby* (Edinburgh: Pitsligo Press, 1882); and Hugh Jackson Lawlor, ed., *The Rosslyn Missal: An Irish Missal in the Advocate's Library, Edinburgh* (London: Henry Bradshaw Society, 1899). However, while Lawlor's edition of the *Rosslyn Missal* is still quite serviceable, the other two missals need to have new critical editions prepared. Some modern work has been done on the *Drummond Missal* in Sarah Casey, "The *Drummond Missal:* A Preliminary Investigation into Its Historical Liturgical and Musicological Significance in Pre-Norman Ireland" (MA thesis, University of Pittsburgh, 1995). Images of the full contents of the *Corpus Missal,*

from Corpus Christi College MS. 282, are available on-line from Oxford University at http://image.ox.ac.uk/show?collection=corpus&manuscript=ms282.

109. William O'Sullivan, "Manuscripts and Palaeography," in *Prehistoric and Early Ireland*, ed. Ó Cróinín, 543–54.

110. Martin Holland, "On the Dating of the Corpus Irish Missal," *Peritia* 15 (2001): 280.

111. A. Gwynn, *The Irish Church in the Eleventh and Twelfth Centuries*, 20.

112. Ibid., 23, 29–30, 105, 31.

113. Holland, "On the Dating of the Corpus Irish Missal," 282, see also 301.

114. The doubt as to whether these missals are post-Norman parallels the earlier confusion about whether the *Bobbio Missal* was from an Irish center.

115. Another problem that faces the student of these missals is the convoluted origins of the Sarum use, which in recent years has also been shown to be an overly simplistic category that cannot fully explain the nuances of early English liturgical history. For a general introduction to medieval English liturgical practice, see King, *Liturgies of the Past*, 276–374.

116. For example, Gy, "Penance and Reconciliation," 104–8.

117. O'Loughlin, *Celtic Theology*, 49.

118. Bieler, *The Irish Penitentials*, 3–4. Earlier authors have tended to see the penitentials, popularized by Irish ecclesiastics on the Continent, replacing public penance with private. But this distinction was probably not as fine-cut as once portrayed, with many churches retaining both types of penance and applying them as they saw fit; see Corning, *The Celtic and Roman Traditions*, 16–17. For more on the general Western European background, see Rob Meens, "The Frequency and Nature of Early European Penance," in *Handling Sin: Confession in the Middle Ages*, ed. Peter Biller and A. J. Minnis, 35–61 (Woodbridge: York Medieval Press, 1998); for a helpful summary of current scholarship, see Kate Dooley, "From Penance to Confession: The Celtic Contribution," *Bijdragen, Tijdschrift voor Filosofie en Theologie* 43 (1982): 390–411.

119. Bieler, *The Irish Penitentials*, 108–35.

120. Hugh Connolly, *The Irish Penitentials and Their Significance for the Sacrament of Penance Today* (Dublin: Four Courts Press, 1995), 21; also see Thomas O'Loughlin, "Penitentials and Pastoral Care," in *A History of Pastoral Care*, ed. G. R. Evans, 93–111 (London: Cassell, 2000).

121. Jungmann, *The Mass of the Roman Rite*, 1:170.

122. Many of the penitential texts deal with monks, so it is hard to know just how many of the laity participated in the penitential discipline.

123. "Puer qui sacrificium communicat pecans cum pecode .c. dies penitea cum pane et aqua": the *Penitential of Finnian* 1, in Bieler, *The Irish Penitentials*, 74–75. Also for Columbanus even the daily "mental disturbances" had

to be confessed before attending the Eucharist: *Penitential of Columbanus* B. 30, in Walker, *Sancti Columbani Opera,* 181.

124. For example, the *Penitential of Finnian* 47 says, "There is no crime which cannot be expiated through penance so long as we are in this body"; "Nullam crime quod non potest ridimi per penitentiam quamdiu sumus in hoc corpore": Bieler, *The Irish Penitentials,* 92–93. Stancliffe would propose a more stringent style of penitence that would basically turn the penitent into a quasi-monastic for the rest of his life, and might only finish with the viaticum on his death-bed; see Claire Stancliffe, "Red, White and Blue Martyrdom," in *Ireland in Early Medieval Europe: Studies in Memory of Kathleen Hughes,* ed. Dorothy Whitelock, Rosamond McKitterick, and David Dumville (Cambridge: Cambridge University Press, 1982), 45.

125. *The Rule of St Carthage* even goes so far as to imply that the priest must force Communion on a penitent in danger of death who still does not wish to receive: "If you go to give Holy Communion at the very moment of death, you shall accept their confession without shame and without reserve. It is your sacrifice that he receives, even if he does so unwillingly. That repentance is unworthy which does not abandon evil"; "Ar ité do sacarbuicc siu diacoi a coirp: nirb dillachtbin aitrige cen tintód on olc. Dia cuirter lám ar in grád ar is mór in bríg: co tairce toil da cech oen i mbriathan i ngním": *The Rule of St Carthage, The Duties of a Priest* 4–5, in Mac Eclaise (pseudonym), trans. and ed., "The Rule of St Carthage," *Irish Ecclesiastical Record* 27 (1910): 502; English translation from Uinseann Ó Maidín, *The Celtic Monk: Rules and Writings of Early Irish Monks,* Cistercian Studies Series 162 (Kalamazoo, MI: Cistercian Publications, 1996), 65. Unfortunately the text is slightly corrupt at this point of this ninth-century Céli Dé rule. This could also explain the passage in the *Communal Rule* of St Columbanus that states, "Let none be compelled by force to receive the sacrifice, except in case of necessity": "Nullus cogatur coactus accipere sacrificium praeer necessitates": *Communal Rule* 2.10, in Walker, *Sancti Columbani Opera,* 158–59.

126. "Si qui(s) in ultimo spiritu constitutus fuerit uel si qua sonstituta sit licet peccatrix uel peccator fuerit ex exposcerit communionem Christi, non negandum ei dicimus si promiserit uotum suum Deo et bene agat et accipiatur ab eo. Si conuersus fuerit in hunc mundum, impleat quod uouerit Deo; si autem non impleat uotum quod uoerit Deo in caput suum erit et nos quod debemus non negabimus ei. Non cessandum est eripere perdam ex ore leonis uel draconis, id est de ore diabuli, qui predam nostre anime deripere non desinit, licet in extremo line uite hominis adfectandum (et) nitendum sit. Si qui(s) autem laicus ex malis actibus suis consuersus fuerit ad Dominum et omne[m] malum egerit, id est fornicando et sanguinem effundeno, tribus annis peniteat et inermis existat nisi uirga tantum in manu eius et non maneat cum uxore sua, sed in primo anno cum pane et aqua et sale ieiunet per mensura et non maneat cum uxorem;

post penitentiam trium annorum det pecunia(m) pro redemptionem anime sue et fructum penitentie in manu[s] sacerdotis et cenam faciat seruis Dei et in cena consummabitur et recipietur ad communionem; intret ad uxorem suam post integram et perfectam penitentiam suam et si ita libuerit iungatur altario": the *Penitential of Finnian* 34–35, in Bieler, *The Irish Penitentials*, 86–87.

127. "Post annum et dimendium eucharistiam summat, ad pacem ueniat, psalmos cum fratribus canat, ne pernitus anima tanto etempore caelestis medicinae (ieiuna) intereat": the *Preface of Gildas on Penance* 1, in ibid., 60–61.

128. "DE SUMMENDA EUCHARISTIA POST LAPSUM. Post examinationem carceris sumenda est, maxime autem in nocte Pasche, in qua qui non communicat fidelis non est. Ideo breuia sunt et stricta apud eos spatial, ne anima fidelis interiat tanto tempore ieiuna medicinae, Domino dicente: *nisi manducaueritis carnem filí hominis non habebitis uitam in uobis*": the *Second Synod of St Patrick* 22, in ibid., 192–93. However the penitentials are not a fully consistent corpus, and at times they contradict each other. So, for example, the *Bigotian Penitential* contradicts the saying that one should only receive after the completion of penance when one is "perfect, whole and not infirm": "perfecta, sana et non infirma": *Bigotian Penitential* 4.7, in ibid., 230–33. In another parallel, it even seems that sometimes a penance could be carried out by a dead person's relatives. A Céli Dé document tells of the death of a virtuous layman who is married with ten sons. His *anamchara* advises one of the sons to do the seven years' penance that his father should have done. That day seven years later the son and wife come to Communion, where the dead father appears and thanks them because he has now left hell for heaven. It is important to note that the son's penitence ended with a reception of Communion: *The Monastery of Tallaght* 86, in Edward John Gwynn and Walter John Purton, "The Monastery of Tallaght," *Proceedings of the Royal Irish Academy* 39C (1911–12): 115–79, at 163–64.

129. "Qui sacrificium euomit causa uoracitatis, .xl. diebus. Si uero obtentu insoliti cybi pinguioris et non uitio saturitatis sed stomachi, .xxx. Si infirmitatis gratia, xx peniteat. Aliter alius dicit: Si infirmitatis causa, .vii. diebus; si in ignem proiecerit, .c. psalmos canet; si canis lambuerit talem uomitum, .c. diebus qui euomit poeniteat. Qui accipit post cibum sacrificium, .vii. dies peniteat": *Bigotian Penitential* 31–33, in Bieler, *The Irish Penitentials*, 214–15. This text has parallels in the *Preface of Gildas on Penance* 7, in ibid., 60; the *Penitential of Columbanus* B.12, in ibid., 100–103; the *Penitential of Cummean* 1.8, 11.7, in Bieler, *The Irish Penitentials*, 112, 130; and in the *Bigotian Penitential, De Remediis* 3, in ibid., 213.

130. "Qui bene non custodierit sacrificium et mus comedit illud, .xl. diebus peniteat. Qui autem perdiderit in ecclesia, id est, ut part ceciderit et non inuenta fuerit, .xx. diebus. Qui autem perdiderit suum crismal aut solum sacrificium in regione qualibet et non inueniatur, tres xlmas uel annum. Perfundens aliquid de calice super altare quando auferatur linteamen, .vii. diebus peniteat.

Si cadentis de manu effuderit, superpositionibus .vii. diebus peniteat a quo ceciderit. Qui effufit calicem in fine sollemnitatis misse, .xl. diebus peniteat. Sacrificium euomens grauatus saturitate uentris, si in ignem proiecerit, .xx. diebus,
sin autem, .xl. Si uero canes comederint talem uomitum, .c. Si autem dolore, et
in ignem proicierit, .c. psalmos canat. Si uero neglexerit quis sacrificium accipere et nec non interrogat nec aliquid nec aliquid causae excusabilis exsteterit,
superponat; et qui acciperit sacrificium pollutus nocturno somno, sic peniteat.
Diaconus obliuiscens oblationem adferre donec auferatur linteamen quando
recitantur pausantium nomina similiter peniteat. . . . Qui neglegentiam erga
sacrificium fecerit, ut siccans uermibusque consumptum ad nihilum deuenerit,
tres xlm cum pane et aqua peniteat. Si autem integrum, sed inuentum fuerit in
eo uermis, comburatur et cinis eius sub altari abscondatur, et qui neglexerit
quater denis diebus suam neglegentiam saluat. Si cum consummatione saporis
decoloratur sacrificium, .xx. diebus expleatur ieiunium; conglutinatum uero,
.vii. diebus. Qui merserit sacrificium, continuo bibat aquam quae in crismali
fuerit sumatque sacrificium et per .x. soles emendat culpam. Si sacfiricium ceciderit de manibus offerantis terratenus et non inueniatur, omne quodcumque inuentum fuerit sacrificium, locus scopa mundetur et stramen ut supra diximus
igne comburetur et sacerdos .xx. diebus peniteat. Si usque ad altare tantum fuerit lapsum, superponat. Si uero de calice aliquid per neglegentiam stillauerit in
terra, lingua lambetur, tabula radatur, igni sumatur, ut supra diximus celatur, .l,
diebus peniteat. Si super altare stillauerit calyx, sorbeat minister stillam et ternis
peniteat diebus et linteamina quae tangerit stilla per tres abluat uices calice sub-
ter posito et aquam ablutionis sumat. Si quando intra luitur calix stillauerit,
prima uice .xii. a minister canantur psalmi, si secunda uice, {. . .}, si tertia, .iii. Si
titubauerit sacerdotes super oratione dominica quae dicitur periculosa, si una
uice, .l. plagis emundatur, si secunda, .c., si tertia superponat": *Penitential of
Cummean* 11.1–11, 19–29, in ibid., 130–33. The section missing from the quotation contains duplicate material or material not related to the Eucharist.

131. Bieler, *The Irish Penitentials,* 6.

132. "Si casu neglegens quis sacrificium aliquod perdat, per .iii. xlmas,
reliquens illud feris et alitibus deuorandum": *Preface of Gildas on Penance* 9, in
ibid., 62–63. The *Communal Rule* of St Columbanus also mentions the possibility of losing the sacrifice, probably in the context of a journey, saying that
it may have "fallen from a boat or a bridge or a horse"; "De cimba uel de ponte
seu de equo": *Communal Rule* 15, in Walker, *Sancti Columbani Opera,* 162–63.
The passage has parallels in the *Penitential of Columbanus* 12, in Bieler, *The
Irish Penitentials,* 100; and the *Penitential of Cummean* 9.1, in ibid., 126.

133. John Ryan, *Irish Monasticism: Origins and Early Development,* 2nd
ed. (Dublin: Four Courts Press, 1972), 345–46, and Taft, "Home-Communion," 3.

134. There is a parallel to this passage in the same penitential (the *Penitential of Cummean* 9.9, in Bieler, *The Irish Penitentials,* 126), and the earlier
Preface of Gildas on Penance 20 likewise refers to it being sinful to "change any

of the words where danger is noted"; "Commotauerit aliquid de uerbis ubi periculum adnotatur": in ibid., 62–63. Crehan, commenting on Gildas, points out that "this document, from the Welsh Church of the sixth century, has the support of the Welsh language, for the word there used for a Mass priest was *periglawr* (from the late Latin *periculator*), and this says much for the popular understanding of the priest as 'danger man,' who takes upon himself to pronounce without stumbling the words of consecration"; Joseph H. Crehan, "The Theology of Eucharistic Consecration: The Role of the Priest in Celtic Liturgy," *Theological Studies* 40, no. 2 (1979): 335. MacCarthy lists a number of other parallels from penitential material not included in Bieler's collection; "On the *Stowe Missal*," 186. However the Irish are not unique in treating the Eucharist with fear. For a good presentation of the evidence for this sentiment in both East and West throughout the Patristic age, see Taft, *History of the Liturgy*, 130, esp. n. 7.

135. "*Quando recitantur pausantium nomina*": *Penitential of Cummean* 11.11 in Bieler, *The Irish Penitentials*, 247, esp. n. 29.

136. "Pro bonis regibus sacra debemus offerre, pro malis nequaquam. Presbiteri uero pro suis episcopis non prohibentur offerre": the *Preface of Gildas on Penance* 23–24, in ibid., 62–63. This passage has an almost exact parallel in the *Penitential of Cummean* 9.11–12, in ibid., 126. The early-ninth-century *Book of Armagh* tells us that Patrick is entitled to have a Mass offered for him on his feast day in all the monasteries he founded; *Tírechán* 3.57, in Ludwig Bieler, trans and ed., *The Patrician Texts in the Book of Armagh*, Scriptores Latini Hiberniae 10 (Dublin: School of Celtic Studies, Dublin Institute for Advanced Studies, 1979), 167.

137. "Nech nothoirc fadesin tria dasacht ernaigti aire 7 almsana hara hanmain mad craibdech riam. Mad ar derchainiuth ronoirnecht fadesin nó ar nach tucait ali is lecti immessair ndé ar ni lamther ernaigti airi .i. oifred *acht* mad nach n-ernaigti aile 7 almsan do thruadaib 7 do bochtaib": the *Old-Irish Penitential* 5.5, in Edward John Gwynn, "An Irish Penitential," *Ériu* 7 (1914): 166; English translation from Bieler, *The Irish Penitentials*, 272.

138. Charles-Edwards, *Early Christian Ireland*, 105–6.

139. Paxton, *Christianizing Death*, 99.

140. Ibid., 67–68.

141. Charles-Edwards, *Early Christian Ireland*, 221, and P. Brown, *The Rise of Western Christendom*, 31–33.

142. For example, Mitchell, *Cult and Controversy*, 109–10.

143. "Arra .uii. mbliadna durpende di ernaigtib glanaib du thesarcain anma duini a pianaib hifirnn .i. cet n-oiffrend cét coica(i)t salm cét mbieti cét slechtan *cacha* beit cét pr cét credo cét imna n-anma": the *Old-Irish Table of Commutations* 36, in Daniel Anthony Binchy, "The Old-Irish Table of Penitential Commutations," *Ériu* 19 (1962): 6; English translation from Bieler, *The*

Irish Penitentials, 279. This work seems to date from the second half of the eighth century and originated in the Céli Dé monastery of Tallaght. While not a penitential per se, it belongs to the general penitential literature.

144. Vogel, "La Vie Quotidienne du Moine," 347–51.

145. Ó Maidín, *The Celtic Monk,* 81.

146. This Early Irish technical term for receiving Communion, *teit do láim* (stretching out one's hands), would imply that the recipient received on the hand and not directly in the mouth. The Early Irish rubrics of the *Stowe Missal* also have a similar phrase, *oc teacht do láim,* for receiving Communion.

147. "Inti teti pruis do midnocht do sacarbhaicc nama theit, acas ni theit iterum usqque de finem anni. Teit iaram do midnocht dibliadna acas do churp na casc ara barach. Tertia uice di midnocht acas di churp na casc acas notlac. Tertia uice ar notlaic acas di chairc acas cingcedir. Quinto anno ar sollamnu acas cind .xl. oidche beos. Sexto anno cind cech mis. Septimo anno cind cec coecthigir. Post .uii. anno is and teit cech domnaig. Pater siar prius acas Deus in adiutorium usque festina acas da dhí láim suas fria nem acas airrdhe na croiche cot laim ndeiss iaram similiter in cech aird sic + ris acas suass. Is hi tra comrair chrábuid leosaide, acht is crosfigell prius, luirech léire din a ammhide. In tan na tiagar do láim dia domnaig tiagar dia dhardain ina dhegair, ar is ro fhata anad cu domnaig; uair is aurdhalta leosom do grér in dí lá sin fri hoifrend": the *Rule of the Céli Dé,* in William Reeves, "On the Céli Dé, Commonly Called the Culdees," *Transactions of the Royal Irish Academy* 24:3 (1873): 204–5; English translation from Ó Maidín, *The Celtic Monk,* 85–86.

148. One might ask how often lay people received Communion. If the novice starts off at once a year, as a layperson prior to monastic life had he been accustomed to receive at all? On top of this it cannot simply be assumed that the laity were always prepared to receive Communion. Aside from questions of morality, we see that St Columbanus had to legislate against monks biting the chalice, striking the altar, and spitting at the altar by mistake. If these were normal behavior for monks we can only imagine what the laity were like. See Walker, *Sancti Columbani Opera,* 149, 143, 163. However the Irish were not the only people to spit in church: John Cassian chides the Western monks in his *Institutes* by telling them that, unlike Gaul, in Egypt during the offices "no one spits, nor hawks, nor cough is heard": "Non sputum emittitur, non exscreatio obstrepit, non tussis intersonat": *Institutes* 2.10, in *PL* 49:98; English translation from Jerome Bertram, trans., *St John Cassian, The Monastic Institutes: On the Training of a Monk and the Eight Deadly Sins* (London: Saint Austin Press, 1999), 21.

149. A very close parallel of this scheme of a "novitiate" type initiation into the Eucharist that culminates in weekly Communion appears in the ninth-century *Rule of Tallaght,* where it takes nine years to reach weekly Communion. Regarding the monk not receiving from the chalice the *Rule of Tallaght* gives

the impression that the monk could not receive from it for the full nine years. In the next section it adds an interesting detail that "those guilty of shedding blood and those who sinned seriously were allowed to receive the Body of Christ, but denied the chalice, even though they had made expiation through penance": *The Rule of Tallaght* 4–5, in Ó Maidín, *The Celtic Monk*, 101.

150. "Menibe cech én lathi iar digi cech cláin": *The Rule of St Carthage, The Duties of the Anam-Cara* 12, in Mac Eclaise, "The Rule of St Carthage," 504; English translation from Ó Maidín, *The Celtic Monk*, 66.

151. "An toes graid don ernaigthi don oifrind co cert": *The Rule of St Carthage, The Duties of the Céli Dé* 8, in Mac Eclaise, "The Rule of St Carthage," 510; English translation from Ó Maidín, *The Celtic Monk*, 70.

152. "Intan tiastan don aifrind is uasal in dán: congain cride telcud dén turcabál na lám. Cen fáilte cen folabrad co cendsa co coi: con dilgud cech aincride fil bias rotoboi. Co sid dria cech coimnesaim co imecla máir: co fóistin dualche tan tiagar do láim . . . óir is glan an coirp dia téis rob glan no téir dá": *The Rule of Carthage, Anam-Cara* 16–18, 21, in Mac Eclaise, "The Rule of St Carthage," 504–6; English translation from Ó Maidín, *The Celtic Monk*, 67.

153. This document was probably written between 831 and 840; Gwynn and Purton, "The Monastery of Tallaght," 122. For a detailed examination of this text, which is perhaps the most important of the Céli Dé works, see Follett, "The Celi De Movement," 132–48.

154. "IS cumme dano forich in biat nó an offrend in oen ocus in sochaidhe ar ni luga cumung naernaighthi dosom cit lir quam si sibi soli assignetus amail nach moa soillsi na grene don oenfer for leith indas don sochaidhe. IS mor leisim in mile cemenn nó eo amplius do aithidhigh in deissi I domnuch is foracbadh in mile cemind fri torrome fir galair fri tabairt comne do 7 do ocaib 7 tuathibh biti fo anmchairtes dotiagat do airsemh offrind 7 do etsecht procepti 7 do rætaibh trieibh cene 7cetera": *The Monastery of Tallaght* 70–71, in Gwynn and Purton, "The Monastery of Tallaght," 156–57.

155. Follett, "Monastic Devotion in Ireland," 145–48.

156. "Ni dligid dechmhadu, nab o chendaith, na train annoti, na dire seoit do mhainib mina bet a frithfholaid thechta na heclaisi innte do bathis acas chomnai, acas gabail necnairce a manach etir biu acas marbu, acas corroib oifrend for altoir i ndhomnaighib acas sollamnaib, acas corrabut aidme oga cech altoir dib. Nach eclair Dé, acht is uaim thagut acas latrand a hainm la Crist. Cech eclais tra i mbi fer graid domhieclaisib tuaithe ni dligh tuarastul auird .i. tech acas airlisse acas dergub, acas decellt cecha bliadna amuil bias hi cumang na heclaisi. Miach cona indud, bo blicht in cech raithe acas airier imm cech coir an chena. Bathis din uadesium accas comna .i. sacarbaic, acas gabail necnairce beo acas cech primshollaman acas cech domnaig acas cech primshollaman acas cech primfheli. Celebrad cach tratha; na .lll. do checul cech die acht mina toirmesci forcetul no anmchairduis. Nach fer graid din lar na bi tualaing

celebrad acas oifriund for belaib rig acas epscop, nis dlig saire fir ghraidh hi thuaith no i n-eclais . . . Nach oen tra las a legait na meic audparthar and do Dia acas Patric dlegairside fochraic acas dulchinde i n-aimseraib corib .i. loilgech i fochraice na .lll. co na nimnaib acas cantacaib acas liachtanaib acas combathir acas comna, acas gabail n-ecnarci acas co neolar a n-ordaigthe olchena com ba tualaing airiten grad: ag acas mucc acas tri meich bracha, acas miach arba bid ina duilchinde cecha bliadna cenmotha gaire acas ailgine do étiud acas biathad illog mbendactain. Acht iar tiasfenad na salm acas na nimond fo chetóir dorenar in loilghech, iar taisfenad din in ordusa dlegar in duilchinde acas in decelt. Dlighid imorro in thsui ni in tesroc dia tairfentar na sailm proind cuicir de chormaimm acas buid in oidche sin": *The Rule of the Céli Dé*, in Reeves, "On the Céli Dé," 211–14; English translation from Ó Maidín, *The Celtic Monk*, 92–94.

157. Richard Sharpe, *Medieval Irish Saints' Lives: An Introduction to Viatae Sanctorum Hiberniae* (Oxford: The Clarendon Press, 1991), 5–6.

158. For an introduction to the cares and concerns of the medieval authors of Irish hagiography see Ludwig Bieler, "The Celtic Hagiographer," *Studia Patristica* 5 (1962): 243–65.

159. Kenney, *The Sources for the Early History of Ireland*, 297.

160. I take this definition from Professor Pádraig Ó Riain's public lecture on "Recent Work on Saints' Lives and Martyrologies," given at St Patrick's College, Maynooth, on April 25, 2006.

161. Ibid.

162. A. Gwynn, *The Irish Church*, 193.

163. Richard Sharpe, trans. and ed., *Adomnán of Iona: Life of St Columba* (London: Penguin, 1995), 43–44.

164. See *Life of St Columba* 3.11–12.

165. "Hi uno eodemque consensus elegerunt ut sanctus Colum coram ipsis in eclesia sacra eucharistiae consecraret misteria. Qui eorum obsecundans iusioni simul cum eis die dominica ex more post euangelii lectionem eclesiam ingreditur. Ibidemque dum misarum sollemnia celebrarentur sanctus Brendenus mocu Alti, sicut post Comgello et Cainnecho intimauit, quendam criniosum igneum globum et ualde luminosum de uertice sancti Columbae ante altare stantis et sacram oblationem consecrantis tamdiu ardentem et instar alicuius columnae sursum ascendentem uidit donec eadem perficerentur sacrosancta ministeria": *Life of St Columba* 3.17, in Alan Orr Anderson and Marjorie Ogilive Anderson, trans. and eds., *Adomnán of Iona: Life of Columba*, 2nd ed. (Oxford: Oxford University Press, 1991), 206; English translation from Sharpe, *Adomnán of Iona*, 219.

166. Sharpe, *Adomnán of Iona*, 368–69.

167. "Alio in tempore quidam de Muminensium prouincia proselytus ad sanctum uenit qui se in quantum potuit occultabat humiliter, ut nullus sciret quod esset episcopus. Sed tamen snctum hoc non poterat latere. Nam alia die

dominica a sancto iusus Christi corpus ex more conficere sanctum aduocat, ut simul quasi duo prespiteri dominicum panem frangerent. Sanctus proinde ad altarium accendens repente intuitis faciem eius sic eum conpellat: 'Benedicat te Christus, frater. Hunc solus episcopali ritu frange panem. Nunc scimus quod sis episcopus: quare hucusque te occultare conatus es, ut tibi a nobis debeta non redderetur ueneratio?' Quo audito sancti uerbo humilis perigrinus ualde stupefactus Christum in sancto ueneratus est. Et qui inerant praesentes nimis ammirati glorificarunt deum": *Life of St Columba* 1.44, in Anderson and Anderson, *Adomnán of Iona,* 80; English translation from Sharpe, *Adomnán of Iona,* 147; also see 3.12.

168. Warren, *Liturgy and Ritual,* 128–30.

169. Saving time by an expedient performance of the liturgy was not as big a concern for Christians in the early Middle Ages as it is for today's Roman Catholics.

170. "Post septenorum sicut tibi dictum est expletionem annorum, diebus ad me huc quadragensimalibus uenies, ut in pascali sollemnitate ad altarium accedas, et eucharistiam sumas": *Life of St Columba* 3.39, in Anderson and Anderson, *Adomnán of Iona,* 156; English translation from Sharpe, *Adomnán of Iona,* 189.

171. Etchingham, *Church Organisation,* 317.

172. "Tu ergo Silnane nunc mecum discendens de monte nauigationem praepara crastina die, uita comite et deo uolente, a me pane accepto dei inuocato nomine benedicto; quo in aqua intincto homines ea consparsi et pecora celerem recuperabunt salutem": *Life of St Columba* 2.4, in Anderson and Anderson, *Adomnán of Iona,* 98; English translation from Sharpe, *Adomnán of Iona,* 157.

173. A similar miracle can be found in Bede's *Life of Cuthbert* 31. Here a layman is visiting a sick friend and remembers that in his pocket he has some bread blessed by St Cuthbert. He breaks off a small piece of the bread, places it in a cup of water and gives it to the sick man, who, on drinking it, is cured; J. F. Webb, trans., *The Age of Bede,* ed. D. H. Farmer (London: Penguin, 1988), 82–83. The *Communal Rule* of St Columbanus 4, also mentions monks receiving the Eulogia with dirty hands ("Eulogias inmundus accipiens"), in Walker, *Sancti Columbani Opera,* 148.

174. Taft, "Home-Communion," 1–3.

175. Henri Leclercq, "Eulogie," in *DACL* 5, cols. 733–34.

176. "Et cum forte post nonam coepisset horam in refectorio eulogiam frangere, ocius deserit mensulam, unoque in pede inherente calceo et altero pro nimia festinatione relicto festinanter pergit hac cum uoce ad eclesiam: 'Non est nobis nunc temporis prandere quando in mari periclitatur nauis sancti Columbae'": *Life of St Columba* 2.13, in Anderson and Anderson, *Adomnán of Iona,* 112; English translation from Sharpe, *Adomnán of Iona,* 164.

177. "Quid plura? Lugaido obsecundanti et consequenter emigranti sanctus pineam tradit cum benedictione capsellam, dicens: 'Benedictio quae in hac capsellula contenetur quando ad Mauginam peruenies uisitandam in aquae uasculum intinguatur; eademque benedictionis aqua super eius infundatur coxam. Et statim inuocato dei nominee coxale coniungetur os et densebitur; et sancta uirgo plenam recuperabit salutem'": *Life of St Columba* 2.5, in Anderson and Anderson, *Adomnán of Iona,* 102; English translation from Sharpe, *Adomnán of Iona,* 158.

178. Connolly and Picard, "Cogitosius's *Life of St Brigit,*" 5.

179. "Caput pene omnium Hiberniensium Ecclesiarum, et culmen praecellens omnia monasteria Scotorum, cujus parochia per totam Hibernensem terram diffusa, a mari usque ad mare extensa est": Cogitosus, *Vita Brigitae* Preface 4, in *PL* 75:775–77; English translation from Connolly and Picard, "Cogitosius's *Life of St Brigit,*" 11.

180. Harrington, *Women in a Celtic Church,* 92–93.

181. "Prudenti dispensatione de animabus eorum regulariter in omnibus procurans, et de Ecclesiis multarum provinciarum sibi adhaerentibus sollicitans, et secum revolvens, quod sine summo sacerdote, qui ecclesias consecraret, et ecclesiasticos in eis gradus subrogaret, esse non posset; illustrem virum et solitarium, omnibus moribus ornatum, per quem Deus virtutes operatus est plurimas, convocans eum de eremo et de sua vita solitaria, et ibi sibi obviam pergens, ut Ecclesiam in episcopali dignitate cum ea gubernaret, atque ut nihil de ordine sacerdotali in suis deesset Ecclesiis, accersivit": Cogitosus, *Vita Brigitae* Preface 4, in *PL* 75:777; English translation from Connolly and Picard, "Cogitosius's *Life of St Brigit,*" 11.

182. "Nam vestimenta transmarina et peregrina episcopi Conleath decorati luminis, quibus in solemnitatibus Domini et vigiliis apostolorum sacra in altaribus offerens mysteria utebatur, pauperibus largita est": Cogitosus, *Vita Brigitae* 28.2, in *PL* 75:786; English translation from Connolly and Picard, "Cogitosius's *Life of St Brigit,*" 23. Mention is also made of a silver chalice, which Brigit breaks into three pieces as alms for three lepers. It was probably not for liturgical use: Cogitosus, *Vita Brigitae* 27.2.

183. Sean Connolly, trans. and ed., "*Vita Prima Sanctae Brigitae,*" *Journal of the Royal Society of Antiquaries of Ireland* 119 (1989): 8. When Sean Connolly published his 1989 English edition of the *Vita Prima* he intended to follow this by publishing a new critical edition of the Latin text (on which he had based his translation). Unfortunately this critical edition has yet to be published and, therefore, when quoting from the Latin I use a seventeenth-century Latin edition of the *Vita Prima,* which is the most modern published edition. In some cases the variants in the English translation are to be preferred to this precritical Latin edition.

184. "Sequenti autem die dixit Patricius ad Brigida; ex hac die non licet uoi ambulare sine sacerdote; Auriga tuus semper tuus sacerdos fiat. Ordinavit

autem sacerdotem nomine *Nathfrioch:* & ipse in tota vita sua auriga S. Brigidae fuit": *Vita Prima Sanctae Brigitae* 40.6 in John Colgan, ed., *Trias Thaumaturga* (Louvain: Cornelius Coenesteius, 1647; repr., Dublin: Edmund Burke, 1997), 531; English translation from Connolly, *"Vita Prima Sanctae Brigitae,"* 24.

185. "Et ita fecerunt, & versi sunt isti duo serpents in duos Eucheas in pascha & in nataliis Domini": *Vita Prima* 52.4, in Colgan, *Trias Thaumaturga,* 532; English translation from Connolly, *"Vita Prima Sanctae Brigitae,"* 27.

186. "Iussit autem S. Patritius aquam illam asseruari, & in Ecclesiis omnibus illius regionis diuidi, vt ad Eucharistiam sanguinis Christi mitteretur, & vt aspergerentur agri de illa aqua in fanitatem": *Vita Prima* 60.3, in Colgan, *Trias Thaumaturga,* 534; English translation from Connolly, *"Vita Prima Sanctae Brigitae,"* 30.

187. "Quoque missas, quae domino procul in terra celebrantur, quasi prope ipsas essem": *Vita Prima* 88.8, in Colgan, *Trias Thaumaturga,* 538; English translation from Connolly, *"Vita Prima Sanctae Brigitae,"* 40.

188. "In vrbe Romana iuxta Petri & Pauli corpora audiui missas: & nimis desidero, vt ad me istius ordo & vniuersa regula feratur a Roma. Tunc misit Brigida viros sapientes & detulerunt inde missas, & regulam. Item dixit post aliquantu tempus Brigida ad illos viros; ego sentio quod quidam commutautauerunt in Roma missas postquam venistis ad ea. Exite iterum. Et illi exierunt & detulerunt vt inuenerunt": *Vita Prima* 90.4–5, in Colgan, *Trias Thaumaturga,* 539; English translation from Connolly, *"Vita Prima Sanctae Brigitae,"* 41.

189. Corning, *The Celtic and Roman Traditions,* 176.

190. "Post haec exiuit S. Brigida vt peregrinaretur in regione quadam cum simul secum comitantibus, & habitauerunt in campo Air. Quadam ergo die accessit ad altare vt eucharistiam sumeret de manu Episcopi, & calicem desuper intuens, vidit in eo deforme prodigium, id est vmbram hirci vidit in calice: vnus quippe de pueris Episcopi tenebat calicem. Tunc Brigida noluit ex hoc calice bibere. Dixitque Episcopus; cur non bibis ex hoc calice. Brigida autem ei manifestauit quod in calice vidit. Tunc Episcopus puero dixit; quid fecisti? da gloriam Deo. Puer autem confessus est se fecisse furtu in capario, & vnum occidisse hircorum suorum, & ex parte comedisse. Dixit ei Episcopus; paenientiam age, & funce lachrymas cum fletu. Et iussis obediuit & paenitentiam egit. Iterum vocata Brigida, venit ad calicem & nihil in calicem & nihil in calice vidit hirci Lachrymae enim illius culpam foluerunt": *Vita Prima* 92.1–6, in Colgan, *Trias Thaumaturga,* 539; English translation from Connolly, *"Vita Prima Sanctae Brigitae,"* 42.

191. "Alio tempore S. Brigida missalia Conlaidi episcopi pauperibus dedit; quia aliud quod daret non habebat, & statim in hora sacrificij Conlaidus suum vestimentum quaesuit dicent; corpus & sanguinem Christi non immolabo sine meis vestimentis. Tunc Brigida orante similia vestimenta Deus praeparuit. 7 omnes videntes glorificabunt Deum. Alio tempore Sancta Brigida

vestimenta in scrinio super mare misit, vt deuenirent per longissimum maris spatium ad Senanum Episcopum in alia insula in mari habitantem. Et ille revelante spiritu subito fratribus dixit; Ite quantocyus ad mare, & quidquid illic inveneritis, huc voniscum ducite. Illi autem exeuntes, invenerunt scrinium cum vestimento, vt diximus. Senanus ergo videns gratias egit deo & Brigidae. Quo enim homines ire non possunt sine maximo labore, ibi serinium solo, deo gubernante perrexit": *Vita Prima* 111.1–112.2, in Colgan, *Trias Thaumaturga*, 540–41; English translation from Connolly, "*Vita Prima Sanctae Brigitae*," 46.

192. In a slightly later work we are told that "the chasuble [cassula] of holy Patrick" was miraculously preserved from fire. But this reference is somewhat ambiguous, and it is not altogether clear if this refers to a liturgical vestment or simply Patrick's clothes; *Muirchú* 1.20, in Bieler, *The Patrician Texts*, 97. The *Leabhar Breac* provides us with a definite reference to liturgical vestments when it discusses the significance of the priest's white vestments, stating that "what the white is intended for, when the priest looks upon it, is, that he should blush at it with sensitiveness and shame, if he should not be chaste and pure in heart and mind, like the froth of the wave, or like the *cailei* on the *bendchobar* of a *duirtheach*, or like the colour of the swan before the sun; without any kind of sin, small or great, remaining in his heart": "Ir ead do forne in gel in tan fhegur in racart fain, cura immdergthar imme an fhele 7 naire, menip genmnaid taitne mach a cridè 7 a menma, amail uan tuinde, no amail chailc for benachobar daurhige, no amail bath géiri frigréin, cenach n-epnail pecad, do bic no mor, do airririum in a cride": *Leabhar Breac* fol. 54 (now 44), as quoted and translated in George Petrie, *The Ecclesiastical Architecture of Ireland: An Essay on the Origin and Uses of the Round Towers of Ireland*, 2nd ed. (Dublin: Hodges & Smith, 1845), 349–50.

193. *Bethu Brigte*, available through the online Corpus of Electronic Texts at http://www.ucc.ie/celt/published/G201002/index.html.

194. "7 nibo thesbaid fleth": *Bethu Brigte* 21, in Donncha Ó hAodha, trans. and ed., *Bethu Brigte* (Dublin: Dublin Institute for Advanced Studies, 1978), 7, 25.

195. "Do-luid Mél dia Luain arabarach doc[h]*um* Brigite do precept 7 do ofriund di eter di C[h]aisc. Tuc*ad* bó di-si d*ano* a laa n-í-ssin. Do-breth d*ano* d'epsc*up* Mél iar mbreith na bó aili. Do-fobair crith-galar ingin de mun*tir* Brigite co tabrath com*an* di. 'In fil nib eth mian duit?' ar Brig*it*. 'Fil,' olsi, 'manamthi lemlacht at-bel nunc': Con-gair Brigit cuci ingin, 7 dixit: 'Tuc dam mochuad feisin lán, isi n-ibim linn, de uisce, Du-n-uc for choim': Do-breth di-di iarum, 7 sensi combo lemnacht inbrothach, 7 ba ógslan statim filia ubi gustavit. Condat da firt sin simul, id est lactis de aqua factis, sanitas filia[e]': *Bethu Brigte* 24, in Ó hAodha, *Bethu Brigte*, 8, 25–26.

196. "Dia Mairt arabarach baí fer maith i fochraib cobdelach do Brig*ti*. Blia*dain*lan dó I siurc. 'Berid da*m*,' ol suidi, 'Boin bes dech bes ima indesi

indiu do Brigiti, 7 gudeth Dia n-erum dus im slan.' Bret[h]a[e] in bó, 7 is-bert B*rigit* fri cach noda-bert.' 'Berid fo chetuair do Mel.' N*us*-mbertata iterum dia tig 7 *con*oimcloisi boin I n-ecmais a fir galair. At-fes do Bri*git*, 'isait coin altai in deg-boin do-ratad formu seilb 7 nat rucad duit-siu,' ol sisi fri Mel, '7 isait .vii. n-os impi.' At-fes iarum dond fiur galair a n-i-sin. 'Arcib tra.' ol suide, 'berid di .vii. n-os de forclu na indesi.' Do-gnith samlaith. 'Deo gratias,' ar Brigit. 'Bertar tra do Mél dia recle*us*. Ata .vii. laa eter di Cháisc oc precept 7 oc oifriund dún; bó cech la*œ* dau da*no* ara opair, ní mó a dán; 7 berid bennacht leu .viiii. hule bennacht for cach o tuctha,' ar B*rigit*. Deth as-bert-se(*n*) a focul n-í-sin ba slan-side fo c[h]etuair. [. . .] Ta(i)nic doib iarum co Minchaisc. 'Ni beoda[e] lem nunc,' ar B*rigit* fria ingena, 'cen chorim aran Minchaisc dond epscup pridcha-bus 7 of-.' Dan as-bert-sí a n-í-sin, lo*tar* di ingin dond *us*ciu do t[h]abairt usque isi tech 7 mundi mór leu do ergnam, 7 ni fitir B*rigit*. In tan do-lotar a frithisi, ata-condairc B*rigit* i(*n*) suidiu. 'Deo gratias,' ar B*rigit*. 'Celiam dedit nobis Deus episcopo nostro.' Gabit[h] fait*ches* na caillecha la sodain. 'Don-fair Dia, ammo ingen.' 'Cia bet as-rubart ni erbart na olc, a c[h]aillecha.' 'Uisci tuc*ad* issa tech, acht huairi ro-mbennachais-[s]is do dighni Dia erat, statim ro-soad ho 7 bolad fina *fair*, 7 ni rolad for descdu isin domun choirm ba *ferd*.' Ro-fe*r* iarum cona n-oegeduib 7 ind eps*cup* int oenmudi": *Bethu Brigte* 25, 28, in Ó hAodha, *Bethu Brigt,* 8–9, 26–27.

197. As, e.g., in *The Rule of the Céli Dé;* see above, p. 304, n. 156.

198. Kenney, *The Sources for the Early History of Ireland,* 337.

199. Bieler, *The Patrician Texts,* 3.

200. "Egressus ad sedem apostolicam uisitandam et honorandam, ad caput utique omnium ecclesiarum totius mundi, ut sapientiam diuina(m) sanc-taque misteria ad quae uocauit illum Deus ut disceret atque intellegeret et im-pleret, et ut praedicaret et donaret diuinam gr(aci)am in nationibus exter[n]is conuertens ad fidem Christi": *Muirchú* 2.15, in Bieler, *The Patrician Texts,* 70–71.

201. This concern with fidelity to the Pope's way of celebrating the Mass can be seen later in the mid-twelfth-century *Life of St Flannan of Killaloe.* Here, among the other achievements of this saint we are told that he brings an up-to-date version of the Mass back with him from Rome: "Then he told of the additions by the holy Church throughout the four corners of the world and the rites and the solemn Masses of the supreme pontiff John"; "Deinde incrementa sancte ecclesie per iiii fines orbis, ritus etiam ac missarum sollempnia summi pontificis Iohannis, iuculenta oratione enucliatim enarravit": *Vita S. Flannani* 13, in William W. Heist, ed., *Vitae Sanctorum Hiberniae e Codice olim Salman-ticensi nunc Bruxellensi,* Subsidia Hagiographica 25 (Brussels: Société des Bol-landistes, 1965), 297; the English translation is my own.

202. "Portauit Particius per Sininn secum quinquaginta clocos, quinqua-ginta patinos, quinquaginta calices, altaria, libros legis, aeuanguelii libros et rel-iquit illos in locis nouis": *Tírechán* 2.1, in Bieler, *The Patrician Texts,* 123–24.

203. "Missam Patricii acceperunt": *Tírechán* 3.37 in ibid., 152–53.

204. Kenney, *The Sources for the Early History of Ireland*, 334.

205. "Aeclessia Scottorum immo Romanorum ut Christiani ita ut Romani sitis ut decantetur uobiscum oportet omni hora orationis uox illa laudabilis Curie lession Christe lession. Omnis aecl[esia] quae seqitur me canet Cyrie lession Chriest lession Deo gratias": Bieler, *The Patrician Texts,* 124; English translation from *The "Sayings" of Patrick* 3, in Thomas O'Loughlin, trans. and ed., *Discovering St. Patrick* (Mahwah, NJ: Paulist Press, 2005), 184–85.

206. Jungmann, *The Mass of the Roman Rite,* 1:336.

207. O'Loughlin, *Discovering St. Patrick,* 108.

208. Webb, *The Age of Bede,* 11.

209. Ibid.

210. "Iterum conuersus uir Dei ad predicum fratrem ait: 'Sume corpus et sanguinem Domini, quia anima tua modo egredietur de corpore. Hic etenim habes locum sepulture tue' . . . itaque accepta eucharistia, anima fratris egressa est de corpore, suscepta ab angelis lucis uidentibus fratribus. Corpus autem eius conditum est in eodem loco a predicto sancto patre": *Navigatio* 8, in Carl Selmer, ed., *Navigatio Sancti Brendani Abbatis* (Notre Dame, IN: University of Notre Dame Press, 1959), 16; English translation from Webb, *The Age of Bede,* 217.

211. "Mane autem facto precepit sacerdotibus ut singuli missas cantarent, et ita fecerunt. Cum sanctus Brendanus et ipse cantasset [missam] in naui, ceperunt fratres carnes crudas portare foras de naui ut condirent sale [illas], et etiam pisces quos secum tulerunt de alia insula": *Navigatio* 10, in Selmer, *Navigatio Sancti Brendani Abbatis,* 20–21; English translation from Webb, *The Age of Bede,* 219.

212. "Quodam uero tempore, cum sanctic Brendanus celebrasset Sancti Petri Apostoli festiuitatem in sua naui, inuenerunt mare clarum ita ut possent uidere quicquid subtus erat. Cum autem aspexissent intus in profundum, uiderunt diuersa genera bestiarum iacentes super arenam. Videbatur quoque illis quod potuissent manu tangere illas pre nima claritate illius maris. Erant enim sicut greges iacentes in pascuis. Pre multitudine tali uidebantur sicut ciuitas in girum, applicantes capita ad posteriora iacendo. Rogabant fratres uenerabilem patrem ut celebraret cum silencio [suam] missam, ne bestie audissent ac leuassent se eos ad persequendos. Sanctus pater subrisit atque dicebat illis: 'Miror ualde uestram stulticam. Cur timetis istas bestias et non timuistis omnium bestiarum maris deuoratorem et magistrum, sedentes uos atque psallentes multis uicibus in dorso eius? Immo et siluam scidistis et ignem succendistis carnemque coxistis. Ergo cur timstis istas? Nonne Deus omnium bestiarum est Dominus noster Jhesus Christus, qui potest humiliare omnia animancia?' Cum hec dixisset, cepit cantare in quantum potuit alcius. Ceteri namque ex fratribus aspiciebant semper bestias. Cum autem audissent bestie [uocem cantantis], leuauerunt se a terra et natabant in ciricitu nauis, ita ut non potuissent fratres ultra in omni

parte pre multidudine diuersarum natancium. Tamen non appropinquabant nauicule, sed longe lateque natabant, et ita huc atque illus, dones uir Dei finisset missam, se retinebant": *Navigatio* 21, in Selmer, *Navigatio Sancti Brendani Abbatis*, 56–58; English translation from Webb, *The Age of Bede*, 235–36.

213. "Sanctus uir cum suis fratribus missam cantasset": *Navigatio* 11, in Selmer, *Navigatio Sancti Brendani Abbatis*, 27. Webb's translation of "community Mass" (*The Age of Bede*, 222), while not strictly literal, nonetheless conveys the meaning.

214. See *Navigatio* 15, in Selmer, *Navigatio Sancti Brendani Abbatis*, 41.

215. It would be a mistake, however, to write off this early medieval text as total fiction. A modern attempt to recreate St Brendan's voyage discovered that many minor details of the *Navigatio* are probably true; see Tim Severin, *The Brendan Voyage: Across the Atlantic in a Leather Boat* (New York: Modern Library, 2000).

216. *Navigatio* 12.

217. Warren, *Liturgy and Ritual*, 143.

218. *Navigatio* 26. This image of Paul and Antony will be fully treated below; see pp. 194–95.

219. *Muirchú* 2.9, in Bieler, *The Patrician Texts*, 119.

220. "Praind da*no* do tomailt la marb hi tig ceth naob is a hurcul *acht* sailmchetal 7 aurnaigti occo. Cid i*n*d fe*r* geai*d* dobeir sac*ra*fic dond fir galir dlegai*r* dó dual astig statim iar*um* ne p*re*senti illo morit*ur*. Ar diambe hi fiadnaisi ind bais istig nic*o*taldad dó oifre*n*n do denam c*o*n*i*dcisrecad epscob. Tocaomnacair do diarmaid 7 do blathm*a*c m*a*c flaind fecht robói c*o*n*i*d eite*r* a lamaib rothathamir cú rui q*uando* mortuus *est* tarmartsom oifrend do denam iar*um* cen a coisc*ra*d c*o*nditoirmesc colcu díob uctaras ind leuitic 7 diarmait da*no* abb ía lais occo": *The Monastery of Tallaght* 65, in Gwynn and Purton, "The Monastery of Tallaght," 153. In another section of the same document it allows for those still undergoing penance to receive the viaticum: "This is what Colchu approves, to give the sacrament [*sacrafic*] to those that are lying sick at the hour of death, provided they have made a renunciation of every vanity. Leave it, however, to God to judge the mind of such, whether it be true conversion; and if it be so [be sure that] the sacrament can bring salvation to them in that moment. It is not proper, however, to repeat the sacrament thereafter *in extremis*"; "Is *sed* da*no* is choir la colchin sac*ra*fic do tab*ir*t dond aos bís illobrae f*ri* huar mhbáis acht doratat fretech c*e*ch espi. Lecsiu immu*rg*o ildeth nde mess fo*r* a menmai*n*som dús ind fircomtúd ac*us* mad ed ón rombeir ind sac*ra*fic sláne doib den chursin. Ni dóig immu*r*gu sac*ri*fic doatarrachtar ite*r*um f*ri* degenca iars*in*": *The Monastery of Tallaght* 56, in Gwynn and Purton, "The Monastery of Tallaght," 148.

221. "Eirigh 7 caith corp C*ri*st 7 a fhuil, 7 eircc docum na bethad suthaine, uair achluinim si claiscettal aingel 'gud gair*m* ara nam*mus*": *Betha Brenainn Clúana Ferta*, in Plummer, *Bethada Náem nÉrenn*, 1:52; English translation

from ibid., 2:53. Also see *Betha Ciarán Saigre II,* in ibid, 1:120. The texts edited by Plummer in two works—one containing a collection of Irish saints' lives in Latin, the other in Early Irish—are, strictly speaking, outside of our period. The manuscripts were compiled mainly by Irish Franciscan scholars in the Irish seminaries on the Continent in the period of the Counter-Reformation. However, many of these were copied from earlier manuscripts that are no longer extant and oftentimes, other than linguistic modernization, reflect texts and situations from pre-Norman Ireland. For more on Plummer's methods of editing these collections see Sharpe, *Medieval Irish Saints' Lives,* 78–88.

222. "Dochuaidh dochum nimhe focéttoir": *Betha Máedóc Ferna* 2.52.143, in Plummer, *Bethada Náem nÉrenn,* 1:231; English translation from ibid., 2:225.

223. "Murchad h. Flaithbertaich do dhul *for* creich I Cinel Conaill co tuc gabail mór coni[d] tarraidh oenghai 7 con erbailt de oc Dun Cloitighe do cummain 7 aithrighe": *AU* 974.1.

224. "Céle mc. Donnacáin, cenn crabuid Herend, quieuit in Christo hi Glind da Locha": *AI* 1076.4.

225. "Sadb ingen U Concubuir Ciarraigi quieuit i l-Lis Mór fo buaid ailitre acus aterge": *AI* 1126.6.

226. Stancliffe, "Red, White and Blue Martyrdom." The eighth-century *Bretha Nemed Toísech* speaks of an ex-layman (*athláech*) who, under the direction of a confessor initially cannot receive Communion, gradually reaches the degree of being able to receive; see Etchingham, "The Ideal of Monastic Austerity," 21–22.

227. Jacques Dubois, "Monachisme (Relations des moines avec les prétres et les laics [11e–13e S.])," in *DSAM* 10, col. 1578.

228. "Bliadan co leith isin ngalar a n-eibelad 7 corp *Cristi do caithem do gacha domnaig frisin re sin*": *Irish Life of Colum Cille: Appendix* 5, in Máire Herbert, *Iona, Kells and Derry: The History and Hagiography of the Familia of Columba* (Oxford: The Clarendon Press, 1988), 245, 267.

229. Perhaps this was the persistence and transformation of the earlier practice of Home Communion in Ireland; see Freestone, *The Sacrament Reserved,* 55.

230. Ibid., 206. It is true that there are some Continental occurrences of the word as "the vessel in which the Eucharist was kept in churches," but these are rare and none appear exclusively in non-Irish sources; ibid., 207. See also Anthony Harvey and Jane Power, eds., *Non-Classical Lexicon of Celtic Latinity* (Dublin: Brepols 2005), s.v. "c(h)rismal/c(h)rismale."

231. Otto Nußbaum, *Die Aufbewahrung der Eucharistie* (Bonn: Hanstein, 1979), 111. The *Three Irish Canons* mentions the case of someone "breaking into the place of the keeping of the chrismal of any saint" ("refugium crismalis alicuis sancti") to steal it: *Three Irish Canons* 1, in Bieler, *The Irish Penitentials,* 182–83. While it is unclear from the text whether this was the case,

if this was simply the storage place where a living monk stored his chrismal or a reliquary for a deceased saint, nonetheless it does seem that the chrismal was worth stealing.

232. William Greenwell, ed., *The Pontifical of Egbert: Archbishop of York, AD 732–766*, Publications of the Surtees Society 27 (London: The Surtees Society, 1854), xvii–xviii.

233. "Prefatio chrismalis. oremus, dilectissimi et fraters karissimi, ut Deus Omnipotens hoc ministerium corporum Filii sui Domini nostri Jesu Christi gerulum benedictione sanctificationis, tutamine defensionis, donationis implere dignetur orantibus nobis. per eudem. Alia. Omnipotens Deus, trinitas inseparabilis, minibus nostris opem tue benedictionis infunde, ut, per nostram benedictionem, hoc vasculum sanctificetur, et corporis Christi novum sepulchrum Spiritus Sancti gratia perficiatur. Per": *The Pontifical of Egbert* 48; the English translation is my own.

234. "Habentes stigmata diabolica": *Vita Prima Sanctae Brigitae* 65.1, in Colgan, *Trias Thaumaturga*, 534; English translation from Connolly, *"Vita Prima Sanctae Brigitae,"* 32. Also see *Vita Prima Sanctae Brigitae* 67.1, in Connolly, *"Vita Prima Sanctae Brigitae,"* 33.

235. Neither Ambrose nor Augustine saw anything wrong with using the eucharistic bread as a talisman; see Ambrose, *De excessu fratris* 1.43, and Augustine, *Opus imperfectum contra Julianum* 3.162, cited in Freestone, *The Sacrament Reserved*, 39.

236. "Sanctus Episcopus Broon feuersus est ad suam regionem, & portauit secum chrisma a S. Brigida; ille autem habitabat iuxta mare. Quadam autem die Episcopus Broon laborabat in litore maris, & vnus puer secum, & venit mare ad plenitudinem suam. tunc puer recordatus est Chrismatis, & fleuit. Dixitque Episcopus; noli flere: credo enim quod chrisma S. Brigidae non peribit, & fic completum est. chrisma enim siccum super saxum fuit & non mutatum est fluctibus maris: & decrescente mari inuenerunt illud sicut positum est": *Vita Prima Sanctae Brigitae* 86.1–4, in Colgan, *Trias Thaumaturga*, 538; English translation from Connolly, *"Vita Prima Sanctae Brigitae,"* 39.

237. Snoek, *Medieval Piety*, 94.

238. *Vita S. Comgalli* 57, in Charles Plummer, trans. and ed., *Vitae Sanctorum Hiberniae Partim Hactenus Ineditae: Ad Fidem Codicum Manuscriptorum Recognovit Prolegomenis Notis Indicibus Instruxit*, 2 vols. (Oxford: Oxford University Press, 1910), 2:20.

239. *Vita S. Moluae* 52, in ibid., 2:223.

240. Snoek, *Medieval Piety*, 95.

241. Nußbaum is of the opinion that in certain cases the chrismal only had the function of talisman because the host was held in the container *together* with the holy oil, which rendered both of them unusable for sacramental purposes. Therefore the chrismal had the single function of talisman; *Die Aufbe-*

wahrung der Eucharistie, 88. However, while there are a good number of examples of the viaticum being administered from the chrismal, I have found no Irish evidence of the practice of such a mixture as proposed by Nußbaum.

242. A. King, *Eucharistic Reservation in the Western Church,* 24–25.

243. "Quodam die, cum sanctus Comgallus esset solus in agro foris operans, posuit crismale suum super uestem suam. In illa die gentiles latrunculi multi de Pictonibus irruerunt in illam uillam, ut raperent omnia que ibi errant, siue hominess, siue peccora. Cum ergo uenis[s]ent gentiles ad sanctam Comgallum foris operantem, et crismale eius super capam suam vidissent, putauerunt crismal illud deum sancti Comgalli esse; et non ausi sunt tangere eum latrunculi causa timoris dei sui": *Vita S. Comgalli* 22, in Plummer, *Vitae Sanctorum Hiberniae,* 2:11; English translation my own.

244. *Vita Sancti Mochiemog* 18, in ibid., 2:172–73.

245. Freestone, *The Sacrament Reserved,* 56.

246. In the introduction to Alan J. Fletcher and Raymond Gillespie, eds., *Irish Preaching 700–1700* (Dublin: Four Courts Press, 2001), 12.

247. Ibid.

248. Thomas O'Loughlin, "Irish Preaching before the End of the Ninth Century: Assessing the Extent of Our Evidence," in Fletcher and Gillespie, *Irish Preaching,* 39.

249. O. Davies, *Celtic Spirituality,* 53.

250. Although these sermons have circulated as a collection attributed to Columbanus from an early date in modern times, their attribution to Columbanus has been questioned. The doubts arise principally from a reference that is made to Faustus as the teacher of the author. This was often understood to refer to Faustus of Riez, who died over a hundred years before Columbanus. But Stancliffe's in-depth analysis has successfully defended the traditional authorship; see Claire Stancliffe, "The Thirteen Sermons Attributed to Columbanus and the Question of Their Authorship," in *Columbanus: Studies on the Latin Writings,* ed. Michael Lapidge, Studies in Celtic History 17 (Woodbridge: Boydell Press, 1997), 199.

251. Walker, *Sancti Columbani Opera,* xliii.

252. Charles-Edwards, *Early Christian Ireland,* 357–58.

253. Perhaps this is due to the influence of St Jerome's *Life of St Paul, The First Hermit,* which was extremely influential in Irish monastic circles. The meeting of Anthony and Paul was one of the most important images of the Eucharist for the Irish monks and, as we shall see in the next chapter, this scene was very important for early Irish depictions of the Eucharist. However, in the account of Jerome, the saints shared bread and water and not bread and wine. While there are no overt parallels in St Columbanus, there may well be an underlying appeal to this account. The influence of this story will be examined in chapter 3; see below, pp. 194–95.

254. "Videte unde iste fons manat; inde enim unde et panis descendit; quia idem est qui Panis et Fons, Filius unicus, Deus noster Christus Dominus, quem semper esurire debemus. Licet eum edamus amando, devoremus licet desiderando, adhuc eum quasi esurientes desideremus. simili modo ut fontem, eum semper dilectionis nimietate bibamus, eum semper desiderii plenitudine bibamus, et suavitate quadam eius dulcedinis delectemur. Dulcis enim est et suavis Dominus; licet eum edamus et bibamus, tamen semper esuriamus et sitiamus, quia cibus noster et potus non totus umquam sumi potest est bibi; qui licet sumitur non consumitur, licet bibitur non admitur, quia panis noster aeternus est, et fons noster, perennis est, fons noster dulcis est": St Columbanus, *Sermon* 13.2 as found in Walker, *Sancti Columbani Opera*, 116–19.

255. Kenney, *The Sources for the Early History of Ireland*, 739. A general introduction to Irish homiletic material in the medieval period, where the homilies from the *Leabhar Breac* are the most important source, can be found in Brian Murdoch, "Preaching in Medieval Ireland: The Irish Tradition," in Fletcher and Gillespie, *Irish Preaching*, 40–55.

256. "Isu Crist Mace Rig nime 7 talman, in Tres Persu na Trinóti is comoesa 7 is cutruma frisin athair 7 frisin Spirut Nóeb, in Fír-Dia 7 in Fírduine, int Uasalsacurt 7 int Ard-epscop roédpá(i)r he fén for altoir na crochi do cendach 7 do fuaslucud in chinedu doenna-is é roedpair isin oídche ria n-a c(h)ésad a fuil 7 a feoil, 7 dorat dia apstalaib dia caithium. Ocus forácaib oc na hapstalaib sin 7 icon eclais uile cu forba in tsaegail gnáthugud dénma na hedparta cetna do cuimniugud na cét-edparta dia rothairbir he fén fri croich 7 bás ar umalóit don Athair némda do comallud a tholi. Is hé in édpairt a raibe lánbuidecus Dé 7 féthnugud a fergi fri síl n-Ádaim escainte. Ar is ínnte robui forbair umalóti 7 inísle, forbair deirci 7 cridircisechta, 7 lán-chomaiditiu fri trógi in chineda doenna cu coiteend": *Homilies from the Leabhar Breac* 27–28, in Edmund Hogan, trans. and ed., *The Irish Nennius from L. Na hUidre and Homilies and Legends from L. Breac: Alphabetical Index of Irish Neuter Substances,* Todd Lecture Series 6 (Dublin: Academy House, 1895), 17–81. Also see *Homilies from the Leabhar Breac* 30, in ibid., 19.

257. "Cech duine tra risnad ail in bethu suthain cuitiged in edpa(i)rt-si 7 caithed in sásad némda co hirisech 7 co trathaigtech 7 co haithrigech. Ar cech oen chaithes hé con a airmitin in in a chride, bid aittreb 7 bid tempul coisecartha do Dia hé; bid malairt bithbluan imorro hí dá cech oen noseaithfe co heceomadais .i. cen aithIriIgi dia pecdaib 7 cen colma aice conid fírfuil in tSlainíccedu caithes, 7 cen anoir ndlestenaig dó in a cride acht a gabail amal cech mbiad archéna": *Homilies from the Leabhar Breac* 37, in ibid., 23–24.

258. "Cech oen caithes a chorp 7 a fuil, no ren-a duthracht a caithem dia fagbad": *Homilies from the Leabhar Breac* 32, in ibid., 20. The Eucharist as nourishment is mentioned in another section dealing with the sacraments in general. Using the image of nourishment it says that as "the child after birth

needs food to support its life, so after regeneration the food of the body and blood of Christ is needed to keep (him) up as regards the spiritual life which was got in baptism": *"Ocus amal ric a less imorro in náidiu iarna túsmiud biad do fulang a bethad, is amlaid sin recar a less iarsin athgene(m)ain sásad chuirp Crist 7 a fola dia congbail immon mbiethiaid spiritalda frith isin bathis"*: *Homilies from the Leabhar Breac* 42, in ibid., 27. This might lend support to the reception of Communion with baptism, but the text does not explicitly say this.

259. "Co fétfad comsód a chuirp 7 a fola im mbairgin 7 hi fín": *Homilies from the Leabhar Breac* 39, in ibid., 24–25. For more on this see Martin McNamara, "The Inverted Eucharistic Formula *Conversio Corporis Christi in Panem et Sanguinis in Vinum:* The Exegetical and Liturgical Background in Irish Usage," *Proceedings of the Royal Irish Academy* 87C (1987): 573–93. This builds on insights in Jean Rittmueller, "The Gospel Commentary of Máel Brigte Ua Maelruanaig and Its Hiberno-Latin Background," *Peritia* 2 (1983): 185–214. This idea is also found in the *Liber Questionum in Evangeliis,* an anonymous early-eighth-century commentary written in Ireland but popular in many British and Continental sources. When commenting on the Last Supper (Mt 26:27) it mentions that "the body was transfigured within the bread" ("transfigurato corpore 'in' panem"); see Jean Rittmueller, ed., *Liber Questionum in Evangeliis,* Corpus Christianorum Series Latina 108F, Scriptores Celtigenae (Turnhout: Brepols, 2003), 411. There is little else of interest for eucharistic practice or spirituality in this commentary. But the fact the Irish commentary was accepted without question in a number of foreign centers and was even attributed to Alcuin in some later studies shows, yet again, how close some Irish material was to the general Western synthesis of the time.

260. "Ar amal roedpair in Rígscart coitchend, .i. Isu Crist fodessin, in edpairt sin artus darcend in chinedu doenna, is amlaid édprais cech sacart dia síl apersain 7 a nerit briathar, in edpairt sin. Ni hinand doré amal dorinde-sium rompu, 7 amal rothescaisc doib conadernatís; acht iar fír cena didiu is esium fén .i. Isu Crist in Sacart cínnte oc bendachad 7oc noemad na nemaicside na hedparta cech lathi cia beth in sacart ele co haicside oc timthirecht fria laim": *Homilies from the Leabhar Breac* 31, in Hogan, *The Irish Nennius,* 19–20.

261. "Ni messu didiu a bec inas a mor in chuirp-si Crist, 7 ní mó is airberu a rand oltás a thoitt, at ata ulídetaid 7 toitt chómlan chuirp Crist in cech errandus dé; ocus ata lánnert legis 7 slánaigthe cech duine inntiblegis 7 slánaigthe cech duine inntib. Ni ferr didiu, nó ní messa, o duine, sech araile in glanrúin sin chuirp Crist 7 a fhola; ar ní thic do pecad duine no ar a nóime fásus a maith-si 7 a noemad; ar is íse maithiges 7 noemas cách iter thuaith 7 eclais": *Homilies from the Leabhar Breac* 41, in ibid., 26.

262. "Is annsin rolínad in úaim do boltnugud amal bid o u(n)gain 7 o fín 7 o fírchumra in betha uli rolínta in uama cor sássta iad uli desin frí re fota co nfacus in rétlu dermáir derscaigthech os cind na huamad o matain co fescor, 7 ni

factus a macsamla riam na iarom na bud chutruma fria. Rochóraig tra Muiri a mac in a lige iarsin co mbrétib lín gil imbe .i. hi crú ind assain 7 ind ócdaim, ar ni frith inad ele do istin tig óiged. Ocus tucsat na dúile indligtecha annsin aichne for a nDuilemain, uair batar oca lige 7 oc(a) adrad .i. int assan 7 int ócdam, 7 se amedon etorru. Is annsin rocomallad and-epert in fáid noem ochéin .i. Ezecias mac Amois": *Homilies from the Leabhar Breac* 70, in ibid., 48.

263. Driscoll, "The Conversion of the Nations," 197–202, and A. Gwynn, *The Irish Church,* 84–98.

264. "Fuit quidam clericus in Lesmor, probabilis (ut fertur) vitae, sed fidei non ita. Is sciolus in oculis suis, praesumpsit dicere, in Eucharistia esse tantummodo sacramentum, et non rem sacramenti, id est solam sanctificationem, et non corporis veritatem. Super quo a Malachia secreto, et saepe conventus, sed incassum, vocatus ad medium est, seorsum tamen a laicis, ut, si fieri posset, sanaretur, et non confunderetur. Itaque in conventu clericorum data facultas homini est pro sua sententia respondendi. Cumque totis ingenii viribus, quo non mediocriter callebat, asserere et defendere conaretur errorem, Malachia contra disputante et convincente, judicio omnium superatus, de conventu confusus quidem exiit, sed non correctus": *Vita Sancti Malachiae* 26.57, in Leclercq and Rochais, *Sancti Bernardi Opera,* 3:360; English translation from Meyer, *Bernard of Clairvaux,* 71.

265. "Eadem hora accitur Episcopus, agnoscitur veritas, abjicitur error. Confessus reatum absolvitur, petit Viaticum, datur reconciliatio: et uno pene momento perfidia ore abdicatur, et morte diluitur": *Vita Sancti Malachiae* 26.57, in Leclercq and Rochais, *Sancti Bernardi Opera,* 3:361; English translation from Meyer, *Bernard of Clairvaux,* 72.

266. Gerard Murphy, "Eleventh or Twelfth Century Irish Doctrine Concerning the Real Presence," in *Medieval Studies Presented to Aubrey Gwynn,* ed. J. A. Watt, J. B. Morrall, and F. X. Martin (Dublin: Colm O'Lochlainn, 1961), 19.

267. Ó Maidín, *The Celtic Monk,* 143.

268. Ibid., 143–44.

269. "A dhuine nach creit íar cóir in fleidh caithe 'con altóir, fogébha brieth ngairbh co ngail, maircc do ghein do gheineamain": *Treatise on the Eucharist* 1, in A. G. van Hamel, "Poems from Brussels Ms. 5100–4," *Revue Celtique* 37 (1919): 345; English translation from Ó Maidín, *The Celtic Monk,* 147.

270. "Ma dorigne cen adbar dúile nimhe acus talman, doghéna d'abhlainn is d'fín corp acus fuil cen anfír. Amal dorighne Día dil do fleiscc Moysi derbhnat[h]raigh, amal dorighne in fleiscc fóill don nathraigh sin fochédóir": *Treatise on the Eucharist* 17–18, in van Hamel, "Poems from Brussels," 346; English translation from Ó Maidín, *The Celtic Monk,* 147.

271. In Irish texts, the title "King" is one of the favorite titles for Christ.

272. "Iúdas, gerb olc in fer gráidh, da tucadh corp Críst, d'fir cháidh íar creidimh íar cói cinad ropad edbairt ógh-idhan": *Treatise on the Eucharist* 25,

in van Hamel, "Poems from Brussels," 346; English translation from Ó Maidín, *The Celtic Monk,* 149.

273. *Treatise on the Eucharist* 56–66.

274. *Treatise on the Eucharist* 67–73.

275. "Mbláith": *Treatise on the Eucharist* 32, in van Hamel, "Poems from Brussels," 346; English translation from Ó Maidín, *The Celtic Monk,* 150.

276. "Pars forsin teisc": *Treatise on the Eucharist* 72, in van Hamel, "Poems from Brussels," 348; English translation from Ó Maidín, *The Celtic Monk,* 153.

277. "Is áirithe a mbí de sin do áiritin in c[h]*uir*p sin, fogébha nemh, búan in breath, no if*ren* úar ainbhtenach": *Treatise on the Eucharist* 78, in van Hamel, "Poems from Brussels," 349; English translation from Ó Maidín, *The Celtic Monk,* 154. The idea that damnation entails "cold stormy hell" is very typical of Irish spirituality, and upon visiting the windswept island monasteries it is easy to realize how the monks came to that conclusion.

278. Taft, *Beyond East and West,* 53.

279. Michael Maher, "Sunday in the Irish Church," *Irish Theological Quarterly* 60 (1994): 161.

280. For the Irish role in the spreading of this document in the greater European context and its sabbatarian view of Sunday, see Robert E. McNally, ed., *Scriptores Hiberniae Minores Pars I,* Corpus Christianorum Series Latina 108B, Scriptores Celtigenae (Turnhout: Brepols, 1973), 175–79.

281. *Muirchú* 1.24, in Bieler, *The Patrician Texts,* 107.

282. "Ut a uespera dominicae noctis usque ad mane secundiae feriae": *Muirchú* 2.3, in Bieler, *The Patrician Texts,* 114–15.

283. Thomas O'Loughlin, "The Significance of Sunday: Three Ninth-Century Catecheses," *Worship* 64 (1990): 535.

284. Ibid.

285. "Eipistil do thiachtain lasin ailithir docum n-E*renn* co Cain Domnaigh & co forcetlaibh maithibh ailibh," *AU* 887.3.

286. "Ité féich thairmthechta in domnaig .i. unga arcait for fer imthéit co n-eri and 7 a thimthach do loscad 7 dílsi a eri. Leth n-unga for fer n-dilmain imt[h]éit and 7 a thimthach do loscud. Nech imrét ech I n-domnach dílsi a eich 7 a thimthaig. Mleth I muilind I n-domnach iar luga chána, mad muilend túathi, unga arcait ind 7 cóic suidiu anund. Mad muilend ecalsa tra, is cumal díra I mbleith ann I n-domnach. Nach bró melar I n-domnach, a brisiud 7 leth n-unga argait for fer nó mnái nodamela. Mad fer-amus nó ban-amus nodamela, loscad a thimthaig 7 a indarba asin mendut": *Cáin Domnaig* 23, in J. G. O'Keeffe, "Cáin Domnaig I: The Epistle of Jesus," *Ériu* 2 (1905): 204–5.

287. Maher, "Sunday in the Irish Church," 163.

288. Donnchadh Ó Corráin, "Ireland *c.* 800: Aspects of Society," in *Prehistoric and Early Ireland,* ed. Ó Cróinín, 606–7.

289. "Luss bongar ind domnuch *nó* brais*ech* nó arán fonit*her* nó mérai nó cnoi bongar dia domnaich ní fogní leisim a cathim na ráod sin na*ch* Lasna fir-clerchiu . . . Teclaim ubald da*no* dia domnaich no gluasacht cen ubuild díob de lar ní fogni leusom": *The Monastery of Tallaght* 13.49, in Gwynn and Purton, "The Monastery of Tallaght," 132, 145.

290. "Ante praedicationem uero die dominica toti exceptis certis necessi-tatibus simul sint conglobati, ut nullus desit numero praeceptum audientium excepto coco ac portario; qui et ipsi si possint sati agant, ut adsint quando toni-truum euangelii auditur": the *Penitential of St Columbanus* B.29, in Bieler, *The Irish Penitentials,* 106–7.

291. "In tí na bui oc tairisim offroind dia domnaig .l. do chetul do ina shessam hi tig dúnta, acas a shuile senta: ir e a luag in oifroind issed delece .i. cét slechtaim acas crosfhigill fri bliait": *The Rule of the Céli Dé,* in Reeves, "On the Céli Dé," 208; English translation from Ó Maidín, *The Celtic Monk,* 88.

292. James Carney, trans and ed., *The Poems of Blathmac Son of Cú Bret-tan Together with the Irish Gospel of Thomas and a Poem on the Virgin Mary,* Irish Texts Society 47 (Dublin: Irish Texts Society, 1964), ix.

293. Ibid., xi. However, cf. Pádraig Ó Riain, "The *Book of Glendalough* or Rawlinson B502," *Éigse* 18 (1981): 171–74, and "Rawlinson B502 alias *Lebar Glinne Dá Locha:* A Restatement of the Case," *Zeitschrift fur Celtische Philo-logie* 51 (2000): 141–42. Here Ó Riain disagrees with Carney and posits that the *Book of Glendalough* actually survives in part as Rawlinson B502.

294. Carney, *The Poems of Blathmac,* xiv–xv, although account must be made for mid-twentieth-century tendencies to ascribe any religious text that came from certain centuries to the Céli Dé. For more on the possible Céli Dé connection, see Brian Lambkin, "Blathmac and the *Céli Dé:* A Reappraisal," *Celtica* 23 (1999): 132–54.

295. Diarmuid MacIomhair, "The History of Fir Rois," *County Louth Ar-chaeological Journal* 15 (1964): 338–42, and "The Poems of Blathmac," *County Louth Archaeological Journal* 15 (1964): 358.

296. "Ó fu-rócbath a chride, mac ríg na secht noebnime, do-rórtad fín fu roenu, fuil Críst triä geltoebu. Toesca toebraith coimdeth dil ro-bathais mul-lach nÁdaim, dég ad-rumedair int eú cruchae Críst ina béulu. Dond fuil chét-nai – ba cain n-am! – is trait ron-ícc in n-ógdall, ossé díb dornnaib co glé oc imbeirt inna láigne": *Poems of Blathmac* 56–58, in Carney, *The Poems of Blath-mac,* 20–21. The canonical Gospels do not mention any details about the Roman soldier who pierced the side of the dead Christ so that blood and water flowed out. However some apocryphal texts mention that this solider was blind and was healed of his blindness by the blood and water that fell on his face. This particular story seems to have been popular in pre-Norman Ireland: see Séan Ó Duinn, *Where Three Streams Meet: Celtic Spirituality* (Dublin: Co-lumba Press, 2002), 91.

297. *Poems of Blathmac* 178, in Carney, *The Poems of Blathmac,* 60–61.

298. Perhaps one can find parallels in the other texts in which the body and blood of Christ become bread and wine in the Eucharist, such as the homiletic material of the *Leabhar Breac* examined above; see McNamara, "The Inverted Eucharistic Formula," 573–74.

299. "Is corp do maisc imman-ric dia tiagar do sacarfaic, is I fuil maic ind ríg do-roäd dúnn a fífín. Is corp do maic—mad-tulaid!—dia mbí bithflaith bithsubaid; is inna fuil cen acht do-nnig cach noeb a geltlacht. Fuil in maic ríg corp do chrí roindid hi crú rogili; fuil do maic-siu, maic Dé bí, do-gní dí a étrachtai": *Poems of Blathmac* 203–5, in Carney, *The Poems of Blathmac,* 68–71.

300. Fleming, *Gille of Limerick.*

301. Anselm, *Epistola* 31, in Fleming, *Gille of Limerick,* 166–69.

302. Fleming, *Gille of Limerick,* 43, 47, 115–16.

303. Bradshaw, *The Search for the Origins of Christian Worship,* 18–19.

304. "Ut nulus Judaeus vel Gentilis sive catechumenus hora sacrificii intersit nec omnio canis aut aliquis immundud sive sanguinolentus in eam intret": *De Statu Ecclesiae* 101–4, in Fleming, *Gille of Limerick,* 152–53.

305. "Luminaria certis horis accendere et extinguere": *De Statu Ecclesiae* 110, in ibid., 152–53.

306. "Cimbarium id est, altaris umbraculum, crucem, tintinnabulum": *De Statu Ecclesiae* 259–60, 266, in ibid., 160–61.

307. "Offere autem ejus est; panem et vinum cum aqua singulis diebus immolare . . . et ante sacrificium thus super et circa altare et sacrificium": *De Statu Ecclesiae* 139–44, in ibid., 154–55.

308. "Sicut ergo septem gradus sunt quibus sacerdos elevatur ita septem sunt vestes quibus ordinatur: indumentum quotidianum, amicta, alba, cingulum, fanon, stola et casual. Et caetera quidem omnia official sine casual, et cum stola sola aliquando potest. Quotiniana ad Missam ut paucissima sunt quatuor: camisia, tunica, femoralia, calceamenta, addunt tamen Romani caligas. Dicitquoque Amelarius sacerdotem debere indui sandaliis et dalmatica: sed pontifices apud nos his utuntur. . . . Haec autem sunt utensilia sacerdoti oportuna quae sine benedictione episcopi sufficient: aqua benedicta aspergit, textus sancti Evangelii, psalterium, missale, horarius, manuale et synodalis liber, vela, candelabra cum candelis, arca vestimentorum, pixis cum oblates et ferrum eorum, ampulla cum vino et altera cum aqua, pelvis ad manus lavandas cum manutergio, truncus aut lapis cavus ubi aqua unde sacra lavantur effunditur, absconsa etiam sub candela et lecturiale sub libro": *De Statu Ecclesiae* 215–21, 229–36, in ibid., 158–61.

309. "Aquam et vinum calici infundere": *De Statu Ecclesiae* 116–17, in ibid., 152–53.

310. "Diaconorum est dicere *Exeant qui non communicant* et *Humiliate vos ad benedictionem* et *Humiliate capita vestra Deo* et *Ite missa est* et *Benedicamus Domino* et evangelium legere et pronunciare, sacrificii super corporalia statuere, sacerdoti ministrare": *De Statu Ecclesiae* 123–26, in ibid., 154–55.

311. "Communicare statim debet baptizatos et fideles omnes ter in anno in Pascha, in Pentecoste et natali Domini et prope mortem positos si quaesierint verbo vel signo vel teste fideli qui prius quaesissent. Commendare debet orando animas fideles de corporibus egredientes et earum memoriam in Missa et orationibus frequentare": *De Statu Ecclesiae* 192–97, in ibid., 156–57.

312. *De Statu Ecclesiae* 192; this text will be quoted later on in this chapter, see below, p. 143.

313. Gerald is familiar with Bede's *Ecclesiastical History*, and he takes it to task in its geographic description of Ireland. This passage that deals with the possibility of the cultivation of grape-vines in Ireland will be examined in chapter 3; see below, p. 183.

314. "In australia Momonia circa partes Corchagie est insula quedam, ecclesiam continens sancti Michaelis, antique nimis et autentice religionis. Vbi lapis quidem est extra hostium ecclesiae a dextris, ipsi fere coherens hostio; in cuius superioris partis concauitate, cotidie mane, per merita sanctorum loci illius, tantum uini reperitur quantum ad missarum sollempnia, iuxta numerum sacerdotum qui ibidem eodem die celebraturi fuerit, conuenienter sufficere posit": *Topographia Hibernie* 2.63, in John J. O'Meara, "Giraldus Cambrensis *In Topographia Hibernie:* Text of the First Recension," *Proceedings of the Royal Irish Academy* 50C (1949): 149; English translation from O'Meara, *Gerald of Wales,* 80.

315. Ann O'Sullivan and John Sheehan, *The Iveragh Peninsula: An Archaeological Survey of South Kerry* (Cork: Cork University Press, 1996), 278–90.

316. "Et sic usque ad extremam communionem a sacerdote cuncta rite peracta suscepit: quam et ipsa constanter efflagitans, attencius supplicauit ut uiatici largitione benefitium consummaret. Quo sacerdos cum se carere firmiter asseruisset, lupus qui parumper abscesserat iterum accessit, ostendens ei perulam, librum manualem et aliquot hostias consecratas continentem; que more patrie presbiter itinerns a collo suspensa deferebat": *Topographia Hibernie* 2.52, in O'Meara, "Giraldus Cambrensis," 144; English translation from O'Meara, *Gerald of Wales,* 71.

317. "Est fons in Momonia, qui si tactus ab homine, uel etiam uisus fuerit, statim tota prouincia pluuiis inundabit. Que non cessabunt, donec sacerdos ad hoc deputatus, qui et uirgo fuerit tam ente quem corpore, misse celebratione, in capella que non procul a fonte ad hoc dinoscitur esse fundata, et aque benedicite, lactisque uacce unius coloris aspersione, barbaro satis ritu et ratione carente, fontem reconciliauerit. Inter alia multa artis inique figmenta, hoc unum habent tanquam precipuum argumentum. Sub religionis et pacis obtentu ad sacrum locum aliquem conueniunt, cum eo quem oppetere cupiunt. Primo compaternitatis federa iungunt: deinde ter circa ecclesiam se inuicem portant: postmodum ecclesiam intrantes, coram altari reliquiis sanctorum appositis, sac-

ramentis multifarie prestitis, demum misse celebratione, et orationibus sacerdotum, tanquam desponsatione quadam indissolubiliter federantur. Ad ultimum uero, ad maiorem amicitie confirmationem, et quasi negotii consummatione, sanguinem sponte ad hoc fusum uterque alterius bibit": *Topographia Hibernie* 2.40, 3.101, in O'Meara, "Giraldus Cambrensis," 138, 167; English translation from O'Meara, *Gerald of Wales,* 63, 108.

318. "Nos nihil fecimus, nec derelictio cibo et poculo Domini ad profana contagia sponte properauimus: perdidit nos aliena perfidia, parentes sensimus parricidas": *De lapsis* 9, in Bévenot, *Sancti Cypriani Episcopi Opera,* 225; English translation from Deferrari, *Saint Cyprian Treatises,* 65.

319. Mark Dalby, *Infant Communion: The New Testament to the Reformation* (Cambridge: Grove Joint Liturgical Studies, 2003), 10.

320. Ibid., 11.

321. "Vbi uero sollemnibus adimpletis calicem diaconus offerre praesentibus coepit, et accipientibus ceteris locus eius aduenit, faciem suam paruula instinctu diuinae maiesatis auerters, os labiis obdurantibus premere, calicem recusare. Perstitit tamen diaconus et reluctanti licet de sacramento calicis infudit. Tunc sequitur singultus et uomitus: in corpore adque ore uiolato eucharistia permanere non potuit, sanctificatus in Domini sanguine potus de pollutis uisceribus erupit": *De lapsis* 25, in Bévenot, *Sancti Cypriani Episcopi Opera,* 235; English translation from Deferrari, *Saint Cyprian Treatises,* 79.

322. Dalby, *Infant Communion,* 13.

323. Ibid., 14.

324. Kilmartin, *The Eucharist in the West,* 31–34.

325. *Ordo* 11 may well have appeared around 650–700 and is therefore one of the oldest *ordines* to have survived; see Vogel, *Medieval Liturgy,* 164–65.

326. "Post hoc ingrediuntur ad missas et communicant omnes ipsi infants nam hoc praevidendum est ne, postquam baptizanti fuerint, ullum cibum accipiant neque ablactentur antequam communicent": *Ordo Romanus* 11.103, in Andrieu, *Les Ordines Romani,* 2:446; English translation from E. C. Whitaker, *Documents of the Baptismal Liturgy,* 3rd ed., rev. Maxwell E. Johnson (Collegeville, MN: Liturgical Press, 2003), 251.

327. "Et dixit Patricius: 'Si creditis per baptismum patris et matris iecere paccatum?' Responderunt: 'Credimus.' 'Si poenitentiam creditis post peccatum?' 'Credimus.' 'Si creditis uitam post mortem? Si creditis resurrectionem in die iudicii?' 'Credimus.' 'Si creditis unitatem aeclessiae?' 'Credimus.' Et baptitzatae sunt et cadida ueste in capitibus earum. Et postulauerunt uidere faciem Christi, et dixit eis sanctus: 'Nissi mortem gustaueritis, non potestis uidere faciem Christi, et nissi sacrificium accipietis.' Et responderunt: 'Da nobis sacrificium, ut possimus Filium, nostrum sponsum, uidere,' et acciperunt eucharitziam Dei et dormierunt in morte, et posuerunt illas in lectulo uno uestimentis coopertas, et fecerunt ulututum et planctum magnum amici earum": *Tírechán* 3.26, in Bieler, *The Patrician Texts,* 144–45.

328. The *pedilavium* was a ritual washing of the feet that was practiced in various ancient baptismal liturgies in many places including Milan, North Africa, Spain, Gaul, and Syria; Maxwell E. Johnson, *The Rites of Christian Initiation: Their Evolution and Interpretation*, 2nd ed. (Collegeville, MN: Liturgical Press, 2007), 21. The fact that, in the West, Rome was the only place that did not practice this rite shows that the *Stowe Missal* is in keeping with the Ambrosian, Hispanic, and Gallican sources on this point.

329. "Corp*us* et sanguinis d*o*m*i*ni *n*ost*ri* iesu chr*is*ti sit t*i*b*i* i*n* uita*m* aeter-na*m* amen. Redecti sp*i*ritalib*us* esc*í*s cibo caelesti corpore et sanguine d*o*m*i*ni recreati d*e*o d*o*m*i*no *n*ost*ro* iesu chr*is*to debitas laudes et gratias referamus oran-tes indefessa*m* *eius* misericordia*m* ut diuini muneris sacramentu*m* ad *i*ncremen-tu*m* fidei et profectu*m* aet*er*nae salutis habeam*us*: p*er*": *Stowe Missal* fols. 58v–59r, in Warner, *The Stowe Missal*, 32; English translation from Whitaker, *Documents of the Baptismal Liturgy*, 283.

330. Maxwell Johnson is of the opinion that the *Stowe Missal's* order of baptism dates from the ninth century, that the infants did in fact receive Communion, and that this is not an unused anachronistic rite, whereas if the manu-script gave the full texts of a Mass at this stage it would have been (personal communication, January 12, 2005).

331. *Stowe Missal Tract* 18, in MacCarthy, "On the *Stowe Missal*," 257.

332. "Communicare statim debet baptizatos": *De Statu Ecclesiae* 192, in Fleming, *Gille of Limerick*, 156–57.

333. This was probably due to a fear that the child could vomit the Com-munion and thus "sin" and also it has to be seen in the context of the end of the first millennium when Christians received Communion less frequently; see above, pp. 56–59.

334. At the time, this posed a particularly complex theological problem and it should be noted that "if Augustine himself could not sustain his position consistently, it was hardly to be expected that lesser minds could do so"; Dalby, *Infant Communion*, 16.

335. Holland, "On the Dating of the Corpus Irish Missal," 294.

336. "Reura et procul pulsa omni ambiguitate sciatis neque transmarinas aecclesias neque nos Anglos hanc de infantibus tenere sententiam quam putatis. Credimus enim generaliter omnes omnibus aetatibus plurimum expedire tam uiuentes quam morientes Dominici corporis et sanguinis perceptione sese mu-nire. Nec tamen, si prius quam corpus Christi et sanguinem sumant contingat baptizatos statim de hoc in aeternum petite. Alioquin Veritas non esset uerax quae dicit: 'Qui crediderit et baptizatus fuerit, saluus erit.' et per prophetam: 'Effundam super uos aquam / mundam, et mundabimini ab omnibus inquina-mentis uestris.' Quod de baptismo esse dictum omnes huius sententiae expositors concorditer asseuerant. Et Petrus apostolus: 'Et uos nunc similis formae saluos facit baptisma.' Et Paulus apostolus: 'Quotquot in Christo baptizati estis, Christum induistis.' Christum est enim induere, habitatorem Deum per

remissionem peccatorum in se habere. Nam sentential illa quam Dominus in euangelio dicit: 'Nisi manducaueritis carnem Filii hominis et biberitis eius sanguinem, non habebitis uitam in uobis,' quantum ad comestionem oris non potest generaliter dicta esse de omnibus. Plerique etenim sanctorum martirum ante baptismum quoque diuersis excruciati poenis de corpore migrauerunt. Eos tamen in numero martirum computat et saluos credit aecclesia, per illud testimonium Domini quo dicitur: 'Qui me confessus fuerit coram hominibus, confitebor et ego eum coram Patre meo qui est in caelo.' Infantem quoque non baptizatum, si morte imminente urgeatur, a fideli laico si praesbiter desit baptizari posse canones precipiunt; nec eum tamen si statim moriatur a consortio fidelium seiungunt. Necesse est ergo predictam Domini sententiam sic intelligi, quatinus fidelis quisque diuini misterii per intelligentiam capax carnem Christi et sanguinem non solum ore corporis sed etiam amore et suauitate cordis comedat et bibat: uidelicet amando et in conscientia pura dulce habendo quod pro salute nostra Christus carnem assumpsit, pependit resurrexit ascendit, et imitando uestigia eius, et communicando passionibus ipsius in imitando uestigia eius, et communicando passionibus ipsius in quantum humana infirmitas patitur et diuina ei gratia largiri dignatur": Letter 49.13–49, in Helen Clover and Margaret Gibson, trans. and eds., *The Letters of Lanfranc, Bishop of Canterbury* (Oxford: Oxford University Press, 1979), 156–59.

337. "Corpus et sanguinem Domini Romana ecclesia ex antiquo tempore capacibus tribuit. Non capaces solius sanguinis infusione reficere consueuit. Denique quod Dominus dicit in evangelio, 'Nisi manducaveritis carnem meam et biberitis sanguinem meum non habebitis vitam in vobis,' de capacibus dicit": Robert Somerville, *Scotia Pontificia: Papal Letters to Scotland before the Pontificate of Innocent III* (Oxford: Clarendon Press, 1982), 21; English translation my own. For a good introduction to the historical background of this problem see David Bethell, "Two Letters of Pope Paschal II to Scotland," *Scottish Historical Review* 49 (1970): 33–45, esp. 39–40. Bethell notes that in the Scottish manuscript tradition this letter of Pope Paschal II is sometimes joined to that of Lanfranc examined above. He also points out that Lanfranc gives a clearer answer. However, Bethell's treatment of the liturgical context is confused, as he seems to indiscriminately take elements from different centuries and areas and apply them to the Scottish situation.

338. Holland, "On the Dating of the Corpus Irish Missal," 295.

CHAPTER THREE.   Archaeological and Iconographic Sources

1. James White, *Roman Catholic Worship: Trent to Today,* 2nd ed. (Collegeville, MN: Liturgical Press, 2003), xiii.

2. Louis Bouyer, *Liturgy and Architecture* (Notre Dame, IN: University of Notre Dame Press, 1967), 39–60.

3. St Patrick does mention pious women throwing their gifts onto the altar in his *Confessio*, but this text adds little to our overall knowledge. "For although I be rude in all things, nevertheless I have tried somehow to keep myself safe, and that, too, for my Christian brethren, and the virgins of Christ, and the pious women who of their own accord made me gifts and laid on the altar some of their ornaments; and I gave them back to them, and they were offended that I did so"; "Nam 'esti imperitus sum in omnibus' tamen conatus sum quippiam seruare me etiam et fratribus Xpistianis et uirginibus Xpisti et mulieribus religiosis, quae mihi ultronea munuscula donabant et super altare iactabant ex ornamentis suis et iterum reddebam illis et aduersus me scandalizabantur cur hoc faciebam": *Confessio* 49, in Howlett, *The Book of Letters*, 84; English translation from Bieler, *The Works of St Patrick*, 36–37. I disagree with Hanson who takes this as evidence that Patrick himself constructed purpose-built wooden church buildings; see R. C. Hanson, "The Mission of St Patrick," in *An Introduction to Celtic Christianity*, ed. James Mackey (Edinburgh: T&T Clark, 1995), 39.

4. Ann Hamlin, "The Study of Early Irish Churches," in *Irland und Europa*, ed. Ní Chatháin and Richter, 117.

5. Harold G. Leask, *Irish Churches and Monastic Buildings*, vol. 1, *The First Phases and the Romanesque* (Dundalk: Dundalgan Press, 1955), 1.

6. Ibid., 17. One early text that supports the traditional theory is found in the *Book of Armagh*. It tells how in Foirrgea, Patrick "made there a square earthen church of clay because no timber was near"; "Et fecit ibi aeclessiam terrenam de humo quadratam, quia non prope erat silua": *Tírechán* 3.44, in Bieler, *The Patrician Texts*, 158–59. In this text, when there is no wood, clay is used, and it seems that the possibility of using stone was not contemplated. But it is hard to draw firm conclusions from this because whereas wood is clearly preferred, there is no explicit rejection of stone.

7. Manning, "References to Church Buildings in the Annals," 38. The first reference to a stone church is the entry for 789, which mentions an *oratorii lapidei* (stone church), *AU* 789.8.

8. For a distribution map of mortared churches, see Tomás Ó Carragáin, "Habitual Masonry Styles and the Local Organisation of Church Building in Early Medieval Ireland," *Proceedings of the Royal Irish Academy* 105C (2005): 141.

9. Timber and wattle construction was used even for important secular structures. For example, when Henry II visited Ireland in 1171, a wooden palace was built for him; see Flanagan, *Irish Society*, 172.

10. Ireland was not the only place where wood was used in the construction of churches. There still survives an early wooden church in Essex, there are many wooden churches in Scandinavia, and excavations after the destruction of World War II have also unearthed a number of examples of wooden churches

under later stone churches in the Netherlands and Germany; see Christie Håkon, Olaf Olsen, and H. M. Taylor, "The Wooden Church of St Andrew at Greensted, Essex," *Antiquaries Journal* 59 (1979): 105.

11. Nancy Edwards, "The Archaeology of Early Medieval Ireland," 245–46.

12. This rejection of the traditional round shape of domestic construction could show the idea of sacred space; Jenny White Marshall and Grellan D. Rourke, *High Island: An Irish Monastery in the Atlantic* (Dublin: Townhouse, 2000), 51–55. Even in ecclesiastical sites where round buildings were the norm, this form was rejected for churches. In Skellig Michael, the round *clochaun* (cell or hut) is the preferred form for construction, and the site contains six of these round buildings, but there are three rectangular churches; see O'Sullivan and Sheehan, *The Iveragh Peninsula*, 278–90. Indeed, it would seem that from the ninth century, rectangular houses began to replace round ones, perhaps as an influence of church architecture; see Edwards, "The Archaeology of Early Medieval Ireland," 248.

13. "Qui in insula Lindisfarnensi fecit ecclesiam episcopali sedi congruam, quam tamen more Scottorum non de lapide sed de robore secto totam composuit atque harundine texit; quam tempore sequente reuerentissimus archepiscopus Theodorus in honore beati apostoli Petri dedicauit. Sed et episcopus loci ipsius eadberet ablata harundine plumbi lamminis eam totam, hoc est et tectum et ipsos quoque parietes eius, cooperire curauit": Bede, *Ecclesiastical History* 3.25, text and translation from Colgrave and Mynors, *Ecclesiastical History*, 294–95.

14. "Porro oratorium intra paucos dies consummatum est de lignis quidem laevigatis, sed apte firmiterque contextum, opus Scoticum, pulchrum satis": *Vita Sancti Malachiae* 6.14, in Leclercq and Rochais, *Sancti Bernardi Opera*, 3:323; English translation from Meyer, *The Life and Death of St Malachy*, 32.

15. "Scoti sumus, non Galli": *Vita Sancti Malachiae* 28.61, in Leclercq and Rochais, *Sancti Bernardi Opera*, 3:365. English translation from Meyer, *Bernard of Clairvaux*, 77.

16. Tadhg O'Keeffe, *Medieval Ireland: An Archaeology* (Stroud: Tempus, 2000), 128.

17. Tomás Ó Carragáin, "Skeuomorphs and Spolia: The Presence of the Past in Irish Pre-Romanesque Architecture," in *Making and Meaning in Insular Art*, ed. Rachel Moss (Dublin: Four Courts Press, 2007), 98–101.

18. Peter Harbison, "Early Irish Churches," in *Die Iren und Europa im Früheren Mittelalter*, ed. Heinz Löwe, 2 vols. (Stuttgart: Klett-Cotta, 1982), 2:627.

19. Although we are reminded that "contrary to the prevailing impression, the stone church (or *daimhliag*) was not fireproof, since such buildings

were generally covered by timber-framed roofs"; Richard Stalley, "Ecclesiastical Architecture before 1169," in *Prehistoric and Early Ireland*, ed. Ó Cróinín, 725.

20. Edwards, "The Archaeology of Early Medieval Ireland," 300.

21. "Nec et de miraculo in reparatione ecclesiae tacendum est, in qua gloriosa amborum, hoc est episcopi Conleath et hujus virginis sanctae Brigidae corpora a dextris et a sinistris altaris decorati, in monumentis posita ornatis, vario cultu auri et argenti et gemmarum, et pretiosi lapidis, atque coronis aureis et argenteis desuper pendentibus requiescunt. Ecclesia namque crescente numero fidelium et utroque sexu, solo spatiosa, et in altum minaci proceritate porrecta, ac decorata pictis tabulatis, tria intrinsecus habens oratoria, ampla et divisa parietibus tabulatis, sub uno culmine majoris domus, in quo unus paries decoratus, et imaginibus depictus, ac linteaminibus tectus, per latitudinem in orientali ecclesiae parte, a pariete ad alterum parietem ecclesiae se tetendit; qui in suis extremitatibus duo habet in sua ostia; et per unum ostium in extera parte positum intratur ad sanctuarium ad altare summus pontifex cum sua regulari scola et his sacris sunt deputati ministeriis, sacra ad dominica et immolare sacrificia. Et per alterum ostium in sinistra parte parietis supra dicti et transversi positum, abbatissa cum suis puellis et viduis fidelibus tantum iverat [*Leg.* intrat], ut convivio corporis et sanguinis fruantur Jesu Christi. Atque alius paries pavimentum domus in duas aequales dividens partes, a parte orientali usque ad transversum in latitudine parietem extensus est. Et haec tenet Ecclesia in se multas fenestras, et unam in latere dextro ornatam portam, per quam sacerdotes et populus fidelis masculini generis sexus intrat Ecclesiam; et alteram portam in sinistro latere, per quam virgines et fidelium feminarum congregatio intrare solet. Et sic in una basilica maxima, populus grandis in ordine, et gradibus, et sexu, et locis diversis interjectis et inter se partibus, diverso ordine et uno animo Dominum omnipotentem orat": Cogitosus, *Vita Brigitae* 32.1–3, in *PL* 75:788–89; English translation from Connolly and Picard, "Cogitosius's *Life of St Brigit*," 25–26.

22. Various modern reconstructions of the cathedral can be seen in Carol Neuman De Vegvar, "Romanitas and Realpolitik in Cogitosus' Description of the Church of St Brigit, Kildare," in *The Cross Goes North: Process of Conversion in Northern Europe, AD 300–750*, ed. Martin Carver, 153–70 (Suffolk: York Medieval Press, 2003). She sees a strong Roman influence, particularly with the style of liturgy as described by *Ordo Romanus* 1, in the design of this church. However, as no manuscripts of the *Ordines* remain from pre-Norman Ireland, there is no evidence of direct influence of the *Ordines Romani* in Ireland. Nonetheless, the style of liturgy promoted by these documents was to become very common in France between 700 and 750; see Vogel, "Les Échanges Liturgiques," 217–29.

23. Michael W. Herren, trans. and ed., *The Hisperica Famina*, vol. 1, *The A-Text: A New Critical Edition with English Translation and Philological Commentary* (Toronto: Pontifical Institute of Mediaeval Studies, 1974), 38–39.

24. "Hoc arboreum candelatis plasmatum est oratorium tabulis, gemellis conserta biiug[u]is artat latera; quadrigona edicti stabilitant fundamenta templi, quis densum globoso munimine creuit tabulatum, supernam compaginat camaram, quadrigona comptis plextra sunt sita tectis. Ageam copulat in gremio aram, cui collecti cerimonicant uates missam. Unicum ab occiduo limite amplectitur ostium, quod arborea strictis fotis cluditur regia. Extensum tabulosa stipat porticum collectura, quaternas summo nectit pinnas. Innumera congellat plasmamina, quae non loqueloso explicare famulor turno": *Hisperica Famina* 547–60, in ibid., 108–9.

25. Niall Brady, "*De Oratorio: Hisperica Famina* and Church Building," *Peritia* 11 (1997): 329–30.

26. Ibid., 333.

27. Manning, "References to Church Buildings in the Annals," 37. For more on another less used term, *reiclés,* see Aidan Mac Donald, "Reiclés in the Irish Annals to AD 1200," *Peritia* 12 (1999): 259–75.

28. Manning, "References to Church Buildings in the Annals," 41.

29. "Cinaedh m. Conaing, rex Ciannachtae, du frithtuidecht Mael Sechnaill a nneurt Call *cor* indridh Ou Neill o Sinaind co *m*m[uir] etir cella 7 tuatha, 7 *cor*[o] ort innsi Locha Gabur dolose corbo comardd fria lar, 7 *cor*o loscad leis derthach Treoit 7 tri .xx. dec di doinibh ann": *AU* 850.3. Note that I have emended the translation of Mac Niocaill and Mac Airt as the number of people in the church was actually 260 and not 70. The original text reads "tri .xx.it dec," which Mac Niocaill and Mac Airt have expanded as "tri fichit dec," which translates as "three twenties and ten," or 70. However, this is an incorrect reading of the syntax of the Irish phrase, which actually means "thirteen times twenty," that is, 260. I am indebted to Dr Colmán Etchingham for his help in reconciling the various translations of this passage.

30. Stalley, "Ecclesiastical Architecture before 1169," 721.

31. Neumann De Vegvar, "Romanitas and Realpolitik," 161.

32. An interesting theory has been proposed by Patrick Wallace on the basis of his study of tenth- and eleventh-century buildings of Viking Dublin. In Viking construction the posts were not placed at the corners of the building but in the center, and a roof frame was placed on these so that walls were not weight bearing and might have left no trace. If this were the case it would dramatically increase the size of the early churches so that the area enclosed by a roof could be up to three times greater than others have projected. This theory rests on shaky grounds, however, as it is unlikely that early Irish church-builders would have used later Scandinavian construction techniques. The iconographic portrayals of early Irish churches show steep pitched roofs (a style that was carried over in many later stone churches), which would have been difficult to reconcile with this construction technique and the general lack of hard archaeological evidence regarding earlier wooden constructions. See Patrick Wallace, "Irish Early Christian 'Wooden' Oratories—A Suggestion," *North Munster Antiquities Journal* 24 (1982): 19–23.

33. Stalley, "Ecclesiastical Architecture before 1169," 729. However, Ó Carragáin has attempted to find regional styles of pre-Romanesque architecture, although his stylistic division has little bearing on our analysis of eucharistic practice; see Tomás Ó Carragáin, "Regional Variation in Irish Pre-Romanesque Architecture," *Antiquaries Journal* 85 (2005): 23–56.

34. Stalley, "Ecclesiastical Architecture before 1169," 728, and Ó Carragáin, "Habitual Masonry Styles," 138.

35. There may have been some wooden sculpture, but none has been preserved. And while there is evidence of stained glass in England in the seventh and eighth centuries, there is none for Ireland; see Michael Hare and Ann Hamlin, "The Study of Early Church Architecture in Ireland: An Anglo-Saxon Viewpoint," in *The Anglo-Saxon Church: Papers on History, Architecture and Archaeology in Honour of Dr H. M. Taylor,* ed. L. A. S. Butler and R. K. Morris, Council for British Archaeology Research Report 60 (London: Bond Hall, 1986), 135. The earliest archaeological evidence surviving for stained or painted glass in Ireland is dated to between the thirteenth and fifteenth centuries, well within the Norman period; see Josephine Moran, "The Shattered Image: Archaeological Evidence for Painted and Stained Glass in Medieval Ireland," in *Art and Devotion in Late Medieval Ireland,* ed. Rachel Moss, Colmán Ó Clabaigh, and Salvador Ryan (Dublin: Four Courts, 2006), 125. Regarding the use of flowers as decorative elements in churches in pre-Norman Ireland, Kelly informs us that, while floral decoration may have been present in the ancient Middle East and Mediterranean, there is no evidence of any cultivation or use of flowers in pre-Norman Ireland; see Kelly, *Early Irish Farming,* 270–71.

36. Conleth Manning, "Clonmacnoise Cathedral," in *Clonmacnoise Studies,* vol. 1, *Seminar Papers 1994,* ed. Heather A. King (Dublin: Dúchas—The Heritage Service, 1998), 57.

37. Ibid., 60. By way of comparison the famous small stone church of Gallarus Oratory (figure 1) has the dimensions of 6.86 m by 5.74 m; Judith Cuppage, *Archaeological Survey of the Dingle Peninsula: A Description of the Filed Antiquities of the Barony of Corca Dhuibhne from the Mesolithic Period to the Seventeenth Century AD* (Ballyferriter: Oidhreacht Chorca Dhuibhne, 1986), 286.

38. Manning accepts the *Chronicum Scotorum* date of 909; see Manning, "Clonmacnoise Cathedral," 71.

39. Tomás Ó Carragáin, "The Architectural Setting of the Mass in Early-Medieval Ireland," *Medieval Archaeology* 53 (2009):123–24.

40. Edward James, "Archaeology and the Merovingian Monastery," in *Columbanus and Merovingian Monasticism,* ed. Clarke and Brennan, 34.

41. T. Ó Carragáin, "Skeomorphs and Spolia," 98–100.

42. T. Ó Carragáin, "Church Buildings and Pastoral Care in Early Medieval Ireland," in *The Parish in Medieval and Early Modern Ireland,* ed. Gillespie and FitzPatrick, 108–9.

43. Ibid., 108.

44. Sharpe, "Churches and Communities," 109.

45. Tadhg O'Keefe, "The Built Environment of Local Community Worship between the Late Eleventh and Early Thirteenth Centuries," in *The Parish in Medieval and Early Modern Ireland,* ed. Gillespie and FitzPatrick, 127–28.

46. Leask, *Irish Churches and Monastic Buildings,* 76, but cf. Tomás Ó Carragáin, "Church Buildings and Pastoral Care," 104–8.

47. Stalley, "Ecclesiastical Architecture before 1169," 730.

48. T. O'Keeffe, *Romanesque Ireland,* 25.

49. Tadhg O'Keeffe, "Romanesque as Metaphor: Architecture and Reform in Early Twelfth Century Ireland," in *Seanchas,* ed. A. Smyth, 313.

50. Ibid., 315.

51. T. O'Keeffe, *Romanesque Ireland,* 39.

52. T. O'Keeffe, "Romanesque as Metaphor," 316.

53. T. Ó Carragáin, "Skeomorphs and Spolia," 108–9.

54. The best among many examples is Clonfert cathedral; T. O'Keeffe, *Romanesque Ireland,* 92–93. The idea of the doorway being somehow special may not have been unique to this time period, as archaeologists have identified a spectacular eighth-century door handle and fittings for a church door from Donore, Co. Meath; see Hillary Richardson, "Visual Arts and Society," 692–93.

55. Stalley, *The Cistercian Monasteries of Ireland,* 7–9.

56. T. O'Keeffe, *An Anglo-Norman Monastery,* 107.

57. Stalley, "Ecclesiastical Architecture before 1169," 735.

58. "Ro rad ben Tighearnain Uí Ruairc inghean Ui Mhaoileachlainn an ccomatt cedna 7 caileach óin ar altoir Mhairi, 7 edach ar gach naltóir do na naoi naltoraibh oile bátan isin tempall isin": *AFM* 1157.9. As the *Annals of the Four Masters* was only completed in the seventeenth century, its historical accuracy for earlier periods is debated by historians (now-lost earlier sources were used, but it is also sure that editorial changes were introduced to favor a Roman Catholic Counter-Reformation view). So this cannot be regarded as conclusive proof for the presence of ten altars in the great church of Mellifont. The parallel entry in the *Annals of Ulster* mentions the same bequest, but does not specify that there were ten altars. It is possible that this is a genuine historical detail, and it has been accepted in Flannagan, *Irish Society,* 92–93.

59. Stalley, *The Cistercian Monasteries of Ireland,* 235–38.

60. "Pauci sunt habitantes in communi, sed per ternarium aut quaternarium in paruis casellis extra claustrum cateruatim constitut": Stephen of Lexington *Letter* 21, in Griesser, "Registrum Epistolarum," 35; English translation from B. O'Dwyer, *Stephen of Lexington,* 44.

61. *Letter* 10, in B. O'Dwyer, *Stephen of Lexington,* 29.

62. T. O'Keeffe, *An Anglo-Norman Monastery,* 108.

63. T. O'Keeffe, *Romanesque Ireland,* 104.

64. T. O'Keeffe, "The Built Environment of Local Community Worship between the Late Eleventh and Early Thirteenth Centuries," unpublished paper. This is an earlier version of a paper that was later revised for publication in Gillespie and FitzPatrick, *The Parish in Medieval and Early Modern Ireland;* I have taken the statistic from the unpublished version (for which I am grateful to Dr O'Keeffe).

65. T. O'Keeffe, "The Built Environment," in *The Parish*, 128–32.

66. Tadhg O'Keeffe, *Ireland's Round Towers* (Stroud: Tempus, 2004), 17.

67. Roger Stalley, *Irish Round Towers* (Dublin: Country House, 2000), 35.

68. Stalley, "Ecclesiastical Architecture before 1169," 733.

69. Ibid., 734.

70. Stalley, *Irish Round Towers*, 10.

71. Petrie, *The Ecclesiastical Architecture of Ireland*.

72. T. O'Keeffe, *Ireland's Round Towers*, 15–28.

73. "Cloichtech Sláne do loscadh do Ghallaibh Ath Cliath. Bachall ind erlama 7 cloc ba dech di clocaibh Caenechair fer leigind, soschaide mór imbi do loscadh": *AU* 950.7. This is the first entry in the annals that mentions a round tower and hence the period shortly before 950, the date of this entry, is taken as the date of the building of the first round tower. This may well be the case, but there is no reason to take this date as an absolute starting point. It is during this same period that the annals become more detailed, and this first mention may simply be a case of the annalist providing more detail, or this could be the first event of note to happen in connection with a round tower.

74. A typical example of this theory is de Paor, "The Age of the Viking Wars," 75.

75. Stalley, *Irish Round Towers*, 33.

76. T. O'Keeffe, *Ireland's Round Towers*, 97, and *Romanesque Ireland*, 74.

77. Harbison, *Pilgrimage in Ireland*, 238.

78. For example, see the reconstruction of early-twelfth-century Cashel in T. O'Keeffe, *Romanesque Ireland*, 137 (figure 15 in this volume).

79. It cannot be denied, however, that the principal identification of these buildings as *cloigtheach* or bell-houses in the annals must allude to at least one of their functions; see Stalley, *Irish Round Towers*, 11.

80. Edwards, "The Archaeology of Medieval Ireland," 297. However, from the ninth century onwards the use of rectangular houses gradually became more popular, 299.

81. Paradoxically, there are indications that the square north tower in Cormac's Chapel at Cashel did contain a chapel; see Stalley, "Ecclesiastical Architecture before 1169," 738.

82. T. O'Keeffe, *Ireland's Round Towers*, 106. While intriguing, O'Keeffe's theories have not been accepted by many scholars; cf. Roger Stalley, "Sex, Symbol, and Myth: Some Observations on the Irish Round Towers," in *From*

Ireland Coming, ed. Hourihane, 40–42, and for a more balanced summary of the current scholarly consensus see Stalley, "Ecclesiastical Architecture before 1169," 731–34.

83. Walter Horn and E. Born, *The Plan of St Gall,* 3 vols. (Berkeley: University of California Press, 1979), 1:129, 1:166.

84. One text that bears relevance to the idea of round churches is Adomnán of Iona's *De Locis Sanctis.* Adomnán wrote this text in the late seventh century based on the accounts of Arculf, a Gaulish bishop returning from a pilgrimage to the Holy Land who was shipwrecked in Iona. Adomnán used his notes from his conversations with Arculf and the books available to him to produce this work, which was popular in the early Middle Ages and accurately portrayed the topography of the Holy Land. See Kenney, *The Sources for the Early History of Ireland,* 285–86; also see John Wilkinson, *Jerusalem Pilgrims Before the Crusades,* 2nd ed. (Warminster: Aris and Phillips, 2002), 18–19. While there may be no link between the round towers and those round churches described by Adomnán's work, which was about two hundred years old when the first round tower was built, nonetheless, this work may well have influenced the programming of the ecclesiastical sites in Ireland. Those who designed these worship complexes would naturally have desired to re-create some elements of the Holy Land. Of special significance in any attempted reconstruction of the sacred geography of Jerusalem is Adomnán's description of the *Anastasis* or the church of the Resurrection: "This extremely large church, all of stone, and shaped to wondrous roundness on every side, rises up from its foundations in three walls. Between each two walls there is a broad passage, and three altars too are in three skilfully constructed places of the center wall. Twelve stone columns of wondrous magnitude support this round and lofty church, where are the altars mentioned, one looking south, the second north, the third towards the west"; "Quae utique ualde grandis eclesia tota lapidea mira rotunditate ex omni parte conlocata, a fundamentis in tribus consurgens parietibus, inter unum quemque parietem et alterum latum habens spatium uiae, tria quoque altaria in tribus locis parietis medii artifice fabricates. Hanc rotundam et summam eclesiam supra memorata habentem altaria, unum ad meridiem respiciens, alterum ad aquilonem, tertium ad occasum uersus, duodecim mirae magnitudinis sustentant columnae": *De Locis Sanctis* 1.2.3–4, in Denis Meehan, trans. and ed., *Adamnán: De Locis Sanctis,* Scriptores Latini Hiberniae 3 (Dublin: The Dublin Institute for Advanced Studies, 1983), 42–45. Later on in the work Adomnán mentions another three round churches (*De Locis Sanctis* 1.23.11–13, 2.12, and 3.3).

85. Iñiguez, *El Altar Cristiano,* 1:33–35, 1:38–46, 1:64–65, 1:131–38.

86. H. Leclercq, "Autel," in *DACL* 1/2, cols. 3171–72.

87. The Manx stone example (figure 17) may have mirrored similar examples on the Irish mainland.

88. Iñiguez, *El Altar Cristiano,* 1:211–14.

89. Elizabeth Coatsworth, "The Pectoral Cross and Portable Altar from the Tomb of St Cuthbert," in *St Cuthbert, His Cult and His Community to* AD *1200,* ed. Gerald Bonner, David Rollason, and Clare Stancliffe (Woodbridge: Boydell Press, 1989), 300, 295–96.

90. While it is quite probable that Irish altars would have resembled the English examples such as St Cuthbert's altar, it is likely that there were some differences in the fixed altars in churches. Some recent scholarship has advanced the interesting theory that in some Anglo-Saxon English churches the altar may have stood between the sanctuary and nave with a bench for the clergy in the center of the apse. This would imply that the priest would have celebrated the Eucharist facing the people; see David Parsons, *Liturgy and Architecture in the Middle Ages* (Deerhurst: Friends of Deerhurst Church, 1989), 18–21. This theory is quite intriguing and is based mainly on archaeology study of some of the oldest English churches noting the position of the ablution drains, the foundation of ancient altars at the center of the church (at the edge of the sanctuary facing the nave), and the clergy bench being positioned behind the altar. Much work still needs to be done to clarify these matters, and the archaeological evidence of these English churches is not repeated in Ireland. For a summary of the evidence as the state of study now stands, see David Parsons, "*Sacrarium:* Ablution Drains in Early Medieval Churches," in *The Anglo-Saxon Church,* ed. Butler and Morris, 105–20. This theory has been more recently supported by Carol F. Davidson, "Change and Change Back: The Development of English Parish Church Chancels," in *Continuity and Change,* ed. Swanson, 75–76. For a general study on the practice of the celebrant of the Eucharist facing east, see Cyrille Vogel, "L'Orientation vers l'Est du Célébrant et des Fidèles pendant la Célébration Eucharistique," *L'Orient Syrien* 9:1 (1964): 3–38. In any event, regardless of whatever may have happened in Britain, in pre-Norman Ireland it is almost certain that the Eucharist was celebrated with the priest facing east; see T. Ó Carragáin, "The Architectural Setting of the Mass," 128–32.

91. For more on this synod see Watt, *The Church in Medieval Ireland,* 152–57.

92. James Ware, *The Whole Works of Sir James Ware Concerning Ireland,* ed. and rev. Walter Harris (Dublin: Printed for R. Bell in Stephen-Street, opposite Aungier Street; and John Fleming, in Sycamore-Alley, 1764), 1:316. I have modernized the eighteenth-century English spelling.

93. "Quae coram Deo et episcopo ac altari genua humiliter flectens, et suam virginalem [*F.* virginitatem] coram Domino Omnipotente offerens, fundamentum ligneum, quo altare fulciebatur, tetigit": Cogitosus, *Vita Brigitae* 2.2, in *PL* 75:779; English translation from Connolly and Picard, "Cogitosius's *Life of St Brigit,*" 14.

94. "Item cum ego parua puella esse in feci altare lapidem ludo puellari, venitque angelus domini, & perforauit lapidem in quator angulis: & supporuit quatuor pedes ligneos": *Vita Prima Sanctae Brigitae* 88.11, in Colgan, *Trias Thaumaturga*, 538; English translation from S. Connolly, *"Vita Prima Sanctae Brigitae,"* 40.

95. Kenney, *The Sources for the Early History of Ireland*, 688. However, this is not the earliest reference to the practice of consecrating churches: the *Book of Armagh* tells how Patrick in the course of his ministry consecrated a church at the well of Stringell; *Tírechán* 3.37, in Bieler, *The Patrician Texts*, 153.

96. "§17. IS hi in cèlna fodal coisecartha na haltora -i- ablu 7 usce 7 fín comes[c]tar a n-oenlestar immalle 7 coisecarthar amal rogab tincetul a coise-cartha isin libur escuip, 7 is aire coisecarthar in[n]a tri sin I tosach, fobith it e adopretar fuirri dogres ic oiffrind. §18. IS hi in fodal tànaisi àsas asin altoir -i-coisecrad clair na haltora budessin -i- doforni in [t]epscop fessin cetheora crossa cona scín I cethri hardaib in[n]a altora, 7 doforni tri) crossa tar a medon ina altora -i- crosstar a medon tai roc a hor, 7 cross tar a medon tiar oc a hor, 7 cross tar a firmedon fessin, 7 doing clar na altora anuas cusin usce 7 cusin fín 7 cusin abluind, 7 inni a mbi don usci dofórti im fortha, 7 doderna in altoir dia anart becco mbi trim, 7 adanna inchís il-lestar bec forsin altoir, 7 canaid 'Dirigat[ur] oratio mea sicut incensum' usque 'uespertinum,' amal doríme isin libur escuip, 7 ongaid con-ole choisecartha na -uii- crossa tóraind isin altoir, et dicit: ungore altare de oleo sanctificato, cosin tinchetul dot-coisc) isin libur es-cuip": Whitley Stokes, "The *Lebar Brecc* Tractate on the Consecration of a Church," in *Miscellanea Linguistica in Onore di Graziadio Ascoli* (Turin: Casa Editrice Ermanno Loescher, 1901), 370–73. As Stokes's edition can be hard to locate today, I recommend my third edition of Warren, *The Liturgy and Ritual of the Celtic Church*, which will also contain Stokes's edition of the *Lebar Brecc* tractate as an appendix, pp. 471–97.

97. Stokes himself follows this interpretation in his notes for this section.

98. *Tírechán* mentions incense (or literally "blessed smoke," *fumum benedictum*) in the *Book of Armagh*, when Patrick is fighting with King Loí-guire and his druids. However, while Bieler tends to see this as incense, he also leaves open the possibility that it could have been the smoke of the paschal fire; *Tírechán* 3.8, in Bieler, *The Patrician Texts*, 131.

99. A. M. Cubbon, "The Early Church in the Isle of Man," in *The Early Church in Western Britain and Ireland: Studies Presented to C. A. Ralegh Radford*, ed. Susan M. Pearce, BAR British Series 102 (Oxford: BAR, 1982), 262.

100. Tomás Ó Carragáin, "A Landscape Converted: Archaeology and Early Church Organisation on Iveragh and Dingle, Ireland," in *The Cross Goes North*, ed. Carver, 133. Ó Carragáin's illustration of the surface of this "Mass Rock" has been reproduced as figure 16.

101. Ibid.

102. "Cui indicauit altare mirabile lapideum in monte neoptum Ailelo, quia inter nepotes Ailello erat": *Tírechán* 3.19, in Bieler, *The Patrician Texts,* 138–39.

103. Harbison, *Pilgrimage in Ireland,* 73.

104. "Semper ita apti et ita rationabiles, ut ita ipsam rem pertineant": *Egeria's Travels* 25.5, in Pétré Hélène, trans. and ed., *Éthérie: Journal de Voyage,* Sources Chrétiennes 21 (Paris: Éditons du Cerf, 1948), 200; English translation from John Wilkinson, trans. and ed., *Egeria's Travels,* 3rd ed. (Warminster: Aris and Phillips, 1999), 120. This travel log kept by Egeria from her late-fourth- or early-fifth-century visit to Jerusalem is the most important witness to this form of hagiopolite stational liturgy. Older works tend to criticize this form of liturgy as a degeneration of a primitive norm, but for a more modern interpretation see Taft, *Beyond East and West,* 31–49.

105. Victor Saxer, "L'Utilisation par la Liturgie d'Espace Urbain et Suburbain: L'Exemple de Rome das l'Antiquité en le Haut Moyen Âge," in *Collection de l'École Française de Rome,* vol. 123, printed in 2 vols., *Actes du XIe Congrès International d'Archéologie Chrètienne* (Rome: Ecole Francaise de Rome, 1989), 2:983–86.

106. Baldovin, *The Urban Character,* 35–37.

107. The importation of the stational liturgy north of the Alps in the *Ordines Romani* and the possible influence of stational liturgy on the development of the private Mass were examined in chapter 1.

108. Charles Doherty, "The Monastic Town in Early Medieval Ireland," in *The Comparative History of Urban Origins in Non-Roman Europe: Ireland, Wales, Denmark, Germany, Poland and Russia from the Ninth to the Thirteenth Centuries,* ed. H. D. Clarke and Anngret Simms, BAR International Series 225, printed in 2 vols. (Oxford: BAR, 1985), 1:68.

109. Baldovin, *The Urban Character,* 249, 413, 250.

110. While little has been written on this theme, for a consideration on the introduction of elements of Roman stational elements into Northumbria see Éamonn Ó Carragáin, *The City of Rome and the World of Bede: The 1994 Jarrow Lecture* (n.p., 1994).

111. *Vita Prima Sanctae Brigitae* 90.4–5, quoted in chapter 2 above, p. 110.

112. Baldovin, *The Urban Character,* 407–8.

113. Stalley, "Ecclesiastical Architecture before 1169," 719–20.

114. Nancy Edwards, "Celtic Saints and Early Medieval Archaeology," in *Local Saints and Local Churches in the Early Medieval West,* ed. Alan Thacker and Richard Sharpe (Oxford: Oxford University Press, 2002), 226, 230, 265.

115. P. Brown, *The Cult of the Saints,* 38.

116. It is possible that these initiatives were inspired by the example of Rome; see Harbison, *Pilgrimage in Ireland,* 236–37.

117. Edwards, "Celtic Saints and Early Medieval Archaeology," 226.

118. "At-be*rt Colum Cille* ind sin rá m*u*ntir: 'Is maith dún ar fréma do dul fó thalm*ain* súnd,' 7at be*rt* fr*iu*: 'Is cet díb nech écin uaib do dul fo úir na hinnsi-se dia coisecr*ad*.' At*r*acht suas Ódran erlattad 7 *is ed at*-be*rt*, 'Dianam-gabtha,' olse. 'is erlo, le, sin.' 'A Odrain,' ol *Colm Cille*, 'rot-bia a lóg sin .i. ni tibe*r*th*ar* a itghe do nech icom ligesi mina fo*r*tsa shirfes ar thus.' Luid iar*u*m Odran docum nime": *Irish Life of Colum Cille* 52, in Herbert, *Iona, Kells and Derry,* 237, 261.

119. While there are a number of important examples of these shrine chapels, they were by no means an essential element in the development of an Irish saint's cult; see Tomás Ó Carragáin, "The Architectural Setting of the Cult of Relics in Early Medieval Ireland," *Journal of the Royal Society of Antiquaries of Ireland* 133 (2003): 136-37.

120. Kathleen Hughes and Ann Hamlin, *The Modern Traveller to the Early Irish Church,* 2nd ed. (Dublin: Four Courts Press, 1997), 68.

121. After a detailed study of the architectural descriptions in Adomnán's *Life of Columba* Aidan MacDonald was unable to say anything specific about how Iona or any other typical Irish monastery might have looked in the period; see "Aspects of the Monastery and Monastic Life in Adomnán's *Life of Columba,*" *Peritia* 3 (1984): 299–300.

122. Stalley, "Ecclesiastical Architecture before 1169," 717.

123. Cuppage, *Archaeological Survey of the Dingle Peninsula,* 257.

124. Nicholas B. Aitchison, *Armagh and the Royal Centres in Early Medieval Ireland: Monuments, Cosmology and the Past* (Suffolk: Cruithne Press/Boydell & Brewer, 1994), 224–25.

125. Leo Swan, "Monastic Proto-towns in Early Medieval Ireland: The Evidence of Aerial Photography, Plan Analysis and Survey," in *The Comparative History of Urban Origins,* ed. Clarke and Simms, 1:100–101.

126. This theory is expressed in Leask, *Irish Churches and Monastic Buildings,* 60, and Sharpe, *Adomnán of Iona,* 368–69. For a possible example, consult fol. 202v of the *Book of Kells* (figure 2) which shows the Temptation of Christ. Jesus is on top of the temple being put to the test by Satan, but the temple is in fact in the form of an early Irish church. The figure coming out could just as easily be a Christian priest as a Jewish Old Testament one (or perhaps may represent both). As an aside, it could also be pointed out that in the period of Late Antiquity and the early Middle Ages Ireland experienced a much warmer climate than today, and it would not have been as uncomfortable to attend the Eucharist outside as it would be today; see H. H. Lamb, *Climate, History and the Modern World* (London: Methuen, 1982), 170–71.

127. A recent article has tried to build on an older proposal by Françoise Henry that the "church" would have only been used as a sacristy and a tabernacle while the whole eucharistic celebration would have taken place outside:

Hunwicke, "Kerry and Stowe Revisited." However, the article tries to construct too much from very little evidence, and moreover freely calls on present-day Byzantine practice as much as early Irish evidence. On the basis of our current knowledge (and excepting pilgrimage and particular feast days) I do not believe that it is possible to propose a habitual celebration of the liturgy with the people participating outside. For a very thorough treatment of this topic that lays to rest the theory of the people usually staying outside the church, which is only entered by the clergy, see T. Ó Carragáin, "The Architectural Setting of the Mass."

128. *Life of St Columba* 3.17. This text is quoted above, p. 104.

129. The *Second Synod of St Patrick* makes reference to bringing the Eucharist outside to the faithful, which it forbids at the paschal vigil. This could imply that in some other instances (apart from the paschal vigil) the Eucharist was brought outside the church to the laity waiting outside. But the text is somewhat ambiguous and it would be best not to read too much into it. "OF THE SACRIFICE. On the even of Easter, whether it is possible to carry it outside. *It is not to be carried outside*, but to be brought down to the faithful. What else signifies it that the Lamb is taken *in one house*, but that Christ is believed and communicated under one roof of faith?"; "DE SACRIFICIO. In nocte Paschae, si fas est ferre foras. *Non foras feretur*, sed fidelibus deferatur. Quid aliud significant quod *in una domo* sumitur agnus quam: sub uno fidei culmine creditur est communicatur Christus?": *Second Synod of St Patrick* 13, in Bieler, *The Irish Penitentials*, 188–89.

130. Aitchison, *Armagh and the Royal Centres*, 198–295 passim.

131. Taft, *Beyond East and West*, 96.

132. Marilyn Dunn, *The Emergence of Monasticism: From the Desert Fathers to the Early Middle Ages* (Oxford: Oxford University Press, 2000), 189–90.

133. T. Ó Carragáin, "Church Buildings and Pastoral Care," 111.

134. See Gerald of Wales, *Topographia Hibernie* 2.63 (quoted above at p. 138) and T. Ó Carragáin, "Church Buildings and Pastoral Care," 109–12.

135. "Et quis sermone explicare potest, maximum decorem hujus ecclesiae, et innumera illius civitatis qui dicemus miracula? si fas est dici civitas, de qua vita in se multorum nomen accepit. Maxima haec civitas et metropolitana est, in cujus suburbanis, quae sancta certo limite designavit Brigida, nullus carnalis adversarius, nec cursus timetur hostium. Sed civitas est refugii tutissima de foris suburbanis in tota Scotorum terra, cum suis omnibus fugitivis in qua servantur thesauri regum, et decorati culminis excellentissima esse videntur. Et quis enumerare potest diversas turbas et innumerabiles populos de omnibus provinciis confluentes: alii ob epularum abundantiam, alii languidi propter sanitates, alii ad spectaculum turbarum; alii cum magnis donis venientes ad solemnitatem nativitatis sanctae Brigidae, quae in die Kalendarum Februarii mensis

dormiens secure sarcinam dejecit carnis, et Agnum Dei in coelestibus mansionibus secuta est?": Cogitosus, *Vita Brigitae* 32.8–10, in *PL* 75:790; English translation from Connolly and Picard, "Cogitosius's *Life of St Brigit*," 26–27.

136. Kelly, *A Guide to Early Irish Law*, 4.

137. A. Smyth, "The Effect of Scandinavian Raiders," 21.

138. Harbison, *Pilgrimage in Ireland*, 182.

139. Tomás Ó Carragáin, "The Saint and the Sacred Centre: Characterising the Early Medieval Pilgrimage Landscape of Inishmurray, Co. Sligo," in *The Archaeology of the Early Medieval Celtic Churches*, ed. Nancy Edwards (London: Maney Publishing, 2009), 214–15.

140. Michael Ryan, *Early Irish Communion Vessels* (Dublin: Country House, Dublin, in association with The National Museum of Ireland, 2000), 12. This volume contains many useful photographs and illustrations that can help the understanding of these impressive vessels.

141. Ibid., 34.

142. F. J. Byrne, "Derrynaflan: The Historical Context," *Journal of the Royal Society of Antiquaries of Ireland* 110 (1980): 116.

143. M. Ryan, *Early Irish Communion Vessels*, 12.

144. "Argentus calix sextarii Gallici mensuram habens duasque in se ansulas ex utraque parte altrinsecus contenens compositas": *De Locis Sanctis* 2.7.1, in D. Meehan, *Adamnán: De Locis Sanctis*, 50–51.

145. Michael Ryan, *Studies in Early Irish Metalwork* (London: Pindar Press, 2002), 178.

146. Ibid., 284–86.

147. The Ardagh and Derrynaflan Chalices are slightly larger than the norm for early Byzantine chalices, although later Byzantine chalices were even larger than these. The Derrynaflan Paten was within the normal dimensions for early Byzantine patens. See Taft, "The Order and Place of Lay Communion," 147–49.

148. M. Ryan, *Studies in Early Irish Metalwork*, 338–40.

149. Egon Wamers, "Some Ecclesiastical and Secular Insular Metalwork Found in Norwegian Viking Graves," *Peritia* 2 (1983): 277–306.

150. Egon Wamers, "Insular Finds in Viking Age Scandinavia and the State Formation of Norway," in *Ireland and Scandinavia in the Early Viking Age*, ed. Howard Clarke, Máire Ní Mhaonaigh, and Raghnall Ó Floinn (Dublin: Four Courts Press, 1998), 42.

151. Cormac Bourke, *Patrick: The Archaeology of a Saint* (Belfast: H.M.S.O. Ulster Museum, 1993), 32.

152. Warren lists a number of examples of chalices that were found and then lost in earlier centuries but he is unable to provide a detailed description for any of them; see his *Liturgy and Ritual*, 143–44. For an accessible account of the use of glass in general in Ireland in the first millennium, see Edward

Bourke, "Glass Vessels of the First Nine Centuries AD in Ireland," *Journal of the Royal Society of Antiquaries of Ireland* 124 (1994): 163–209. He deals with the possibility of glass eucharistic chalices on 174–75; however, I am unable to agree with his analysis as I judge the texts he uses to have too symbolic a tone to be read literally.

153. A famous account of such a vision can be found in *Navigatio* 12 where St Brendan visits the mysterious island of the community of St Ailbe where the whole church and everything in it, including the chalices and other cruets, are made of crystal (*cristallo*).

154. Mytum, *The Origins of Early Christian Ireland,* 221, and M. Ryan, *Studies in Early Irish Metalwork,* 344–46.

155. Cormac Bourke, "The Bells of Saints Caillín and Cuana: Two Twelfth-Century Cups," in *Seanchas,* ed. A. Smyth, 331–40.

156. M. Ryan, *Studies in Early Irish Metalwork,* 313. Ryan himself provides a useful summary of the state of scholarship on the study of the non-Irish Western European chalices on 288–334.

157. Ibid., 279–81.

158. Ibid., 328.

159. Ibid., 550–52.

160. See Ó Duinn, *Where Three Streams Meet,* 91–92, and Salvador Ryan, "'Reign of Blood': Aspects of Devotion to the Wounds of Christ in Late Medieval Ireland," in *Irish History: A Yearbook,* ed. Joost Augusteijn and Mary Ann Lyons (Dublin: Four Courts Press, 2002), 138.

161. Richardson, "Visual Arts and Society," 705.

162. Edward Foley, *From Age to Age: How Christians Have Celebrated the Eucharist,* 2nd ed. (Collegeville, MN: Liturgical Press, 2008), 220. In most of the East the laity were given the eucharistic bread on a spoon that had been dipped in a chalice; Stefano Parenti, "The Eucharistic Celebration in the East: The Various Orders of Celebration," in *The Eucharist,* ed. Chupungco, 66.

163. One pre-ninth-century Irish text does mention a particular type of square paten made on the order of Patrick. "Assicus the holy bishop was a coppersmith (in the service) of Patrick, and he made altar-plates and square casks for the patens of our holy saint in honour of bishop Patrick, and three of these square patens I have seen, that is, a paten in Patrick's church at Armagh and another in the church of Ail Find and a third in the great church of Seól on the altar of the holy bishop Felartus"; "Asicus sanctus episcopus faber aereus erat Patricio et faciebat altaria (et) bibliothicas qua(drata)s faciebat in patinos sancti nostri pro honore Patricii episcopi, et de illis tres patinos quadratos uidi, id est platinum in aeclessia Patricii in Ardd Machae et alterum in aeclessia Alo Find et tertium in aeclessia magna Saeoli super altare Felarti sancti episcopi": *Tírechán* 3.22, in Bieler, *The Patrician Texts,* 140–41. Here the paten is seen as an important relic of Patrick and is treated in isolation from any accompanying chalice. While tantalizing, it is hard to deduce much information from this story.

164. M. Ryan, *Early Irish Communion Vessels,* 39.

165. Close scientific examination of the Derrynaflan Paten has revealed that it contains a minuscule engraving of an anagram whose letters are less than 1 millimeter high. Unfortunately, it has not been possible to deduce what words these letters stand for; see Michelle P. Brown, "Paten and Purpose: The Derrynaflan Paten Inscriptions," in *The Age of Migrating Ideas: Early Medieval Art in Northern Britain and Ireland,* ed. R. Michael Spearman and John Higgitt (Gloucester: Sutton, and Edinburgh: National Museum of Scotland, 1993).

166. Ibid.

167. M. Ryan, *Early Irish Communion Vessels,* 311. For further textual references, see O'Loughlin, "Praxis and Explanations," 7.

168. M. Ryan, *Studies in Early Irish Metalwork,* 569.

169. M. Brown, "Paten and Purpose," 165.

170. M. Ryan, *Early Irish Communion Vessels,* 43.

171. C. Bourke, *Patrick,* 32.

172. Purely utilitarian actions have sometimes been preserved in later liturgies with a spiritual meaning attached to them; see P. Bradshaw, *The Search for the Origins of Christian Worship,* 19–20.

173. Raghnall Ó Floinn, "The Bronze Strainer-Ladle," in *The Derrynaflan Hoard,* vol. 1, *A Preliminary Account,* ed. Michael Ryan (Dublin: National Museum of Ireland, 1983), 33.

174. M. Ryan, *Studies in Early Irish Metalwork,* 550.

175. "Ornato vere altare, tunc archidiaonus summit amulam pontificis de subdiacono oblationario et refundit super colum in calicem, deinde diaconorum": *Ordo Romanus* 1.79, in Andrieu, *Les Ordines Romani,* 2:93; English translation from Jasper and Cuming, *Prayers of the Eucharist,* 169.

176. For a list of other archaeological parallels, see Ó Floinn, "The Bronze Strainer-Ladle," 33.

177. Ibid., 33–34.

178. Stevenson, "Introduction," liii–lvii.

179. For example in the vernacular life of St Columba we are told: "On one occasion, Finnén lacked wine for the Mass. Colum Cille blessed the water, and it was changed into wine and placed in the Mass-chalice"; "Fechtus an testa fin (bairgen) ar Finden on aiffriund. Bennachais Colum Cille in usce cor soad hi fhìn co tartad isin coilech n-aiffrind": *Irish Life of Colum Cille* 24, in Herbert, *Iona, Kells and Derry,* 227, 254.

180. "Diues lactis et mellis insula nec uinearum expers, piscium uolucrumque sed et ceruorum caprearumque uenatu insiginis": Bede, *Ecclesiastical History* 1.1, text and translation from Colgrave and Mynors, *Ecclesiastical History,* 20–21. It is very unlikely that Bede was speaking from firsthand experience (particularly given that in the sentence just before this he has informed how scrapings from Irish manuscripts cure people suffering from poisonous snake bite).

181. "Pascuis et pratis, melle et lacte, unius, non uineis, diues est insula. Beda tamen inter alias insule laudes dicit eam uinearum expertem non esse. Solinus uero apibus eam career asserit. Sed salua utriusque venia, circumspectius e diuerso scripsissent: vineis ipsam carere, et apium expertem non esse. Vineis enim et earum cultoribus semper caruit et caret insula. Vina tamen transmarine ratione commertii tam habunde terram replent, ut uixpropaginis prouentusque naturalis in aliquo defectum percipias": *Topographia Hibernie* 1.2, in O'Meara, "Giraldus Cambrensis," 144; English translation from O'Meara, *Gerald of Wales*, 35.

182. See Lamb, *Climate, History and the Modern World*, 151.

183. Kelly, *Early Irish Farming*, 262–63.

184. Ibid., 358.

185. Charles Thomas, "Imported Pottery in Dark-Age Western Britain," *Medieval Archaeology* 3 (1959): 89–111. Furthermore, it has been proposed that the majority of wine would have been imported in wooden casks, which would have left little evidence in the archaeological record; see Edwards, "The Archaeology of Medieval Ireland," 290.

186. Kelly, *Early Irish Farming*, 319, but cf. Mytum, *The Origins of Early Christian Ireland*, 51, where Mytum proposes that wine was not imported directly from Gaul to Ireland but that British merchants brought the wine to Ireland acting as middle men.

187. "Him who has bitten the chalice of salvation with his teeth, it is ordained to correct with six blows"; "Similiter qui pertunderit dentibus calicem salutaris, vi percussionibus": *Communal Rule* 2.4, in Walker, *Sancti Columbani Opera*, 148–49; also see the parallel section in 1.3 in ibid., 142–43.

188. *The Rule of the Céli Dé*, in Reeves "On the Céli Dé," 204–5, quoted above on p. 99.

189. *The Rule of Tallaght* 5, in Ó Maidín, *The Celtic Monk*, 101. Perhaps this text refers to individuals who have entered a semimonastic state in repentance for some serious sin, but these individuals were neither fully lay nor fully monastic; see Stancliffe, "Red, White and Blue Martyrdom," 45.

190. *Vita Prima Sanctae Brigitae* 92.1–6, quoted above on p. 111.

191. MacCarthy, "On the *Stowe Missal*," 261.

192. Ware, *The Whole Works of Sir James Ware Concerning Ireland*, 1:316.

193. Mary Regina Sexton, "Cereals and Cereal Foodstuffs in Early Historic Ireland" (MA thesis, University College Cork, 1993), 91, 93–95.

194. Kelly, *Early Irish Farming*, 220–21.

195. Sexton, "Cereals and Cereal Foodstuffs," 92. Gerald of Wales also recounts a miracle performed by the bishop of Cork, who changes a field of *suillech* (spelt wheat or rye) into *triticum* (wheat); see *Topographia Hibernie* 2.78, in O'Meara, *Gerald of Wales*, 89.

196. Reginald Maxwell Wooley, *The Bread of the Eucharist*, Alcuin Club Tracts 10 (London: Mowbray, 1913), 1–23. Wooley imagines that Ireland was

probably typical in this respect, using first leavened and then unleavened as anywhere else in Western Europe, but cf. Warren, *Liturgy and Ritual,* 131–22 (which Wooley, in turn, dismisses on 17–18).

197. Sexton, "Cereals and Cereal Foodstuffs," 106–7. In this sense another canon of the 1186 Dublin Synod is significant. It mandates that "the Host, which represents the Lamb without spot, the Alpha and the Omega, should be made so pure and white that the partakers thereof may thereby understand the purifying and feeding of their souls, rather than their bodies": Ware, *The Whole Works of Sir James Ware Concerning Ireland,* 1:316. Perhaps this is evidence of a new, whiter, unleavened type of bread being used in the wake of the Norman arrival.

198. "Si cum consummatione saporis decoloratur sacrificium, .xx. diebus expleatur ieiunium; conglutinatum uero, .vii. diebus": *Penitential of Cummean* 9.21, in Bieler, *The Irish Penitentials,* 132–33.

199. Sexton, "Cereals and Cereal Foodstuffs," 106–7.

200. Helen Geake, "Medieval Britain and Ireland," *Medieval Archaeology* 48 (2004): 244–46.

201. Personal communication, January 7, 2005, from Cormac Bourke, Curator of Medieval Antiquities, Department of Archaeology and Ethnography, Ulster Museum.

202. For more information on this object, see George Petrie, *Christian Inscriptions in the Irish Language* (Dublin: Royal Historical and Archaeological Association of Ireland, 1878), 2:111.

203. "Adherentem lateri suo capsulam cum sanctorum reliquiis collo auulsam": Bede, *Ecclesiastical History* 1.18, text and translation from Colgrave and Mynors, *Ecclesiastical History,* 58–59.

204. *The Glory of Martyrs* 83, in *PL* 71:779–80.

205. H. Leclercq, "Pyxide," in *DACL* 14.2, cols. 1983–95.

206. *Encolopia* were "small round containers suspended on a chain about the neck and worn upon the breast"; J. M. Franik, "Reliquaries," in *NCE* 12, 335.

207. C. Bourke, *Patrick,* 11.

208. King, *Eucharistic Reservation in the Western Church,* 39. While probably of no direct bearing on this artifact, a modern reconstruction of the life of St Columbanus has placed Columbanus in Chur on two occasions during his life; see Donald Bullough, "The Career of Columbanus," in *Columbanus,* ed. Lapidge, 20, 22.

209. Nußbaum, *Die Aufbewahrung der Eucharistie,* 88. For more information, see Patrick Périn and Laurie-Charlotte Feffer, *La Neustrie: Les Pays au Nord de La Loire de Dagobert à Charles Le Chauve (VIIe–IXe Siècles)* (Créteil: Museés et Monuments Départmentaux de Seine-Maritime, 1985), 141–42, with color photographs on page 90.

210. King, *Eucharistic Reservation in the Western Church,* 39.

211. Leslie Webster, "England and the Continent," in *The Making of England: Anglo-Saxon Art and Culture AD 600–900*, ed. Leslie Webster and Janet Backhouse (London: British Museum Press, 1991), 175–76.

212. It is also noteworthy that the Irish textual sources that deal with chrismals imply that they had economic value as they were worth stealing; see Nußbaum, *Die Aufbewahrung der Eucharistie*, 111.

213. Edwards, "Celtic Saints and Early Medieval Archaeology," 246–47, and Richardson, "Visual Arts and Society," 697.

214. Ken Parry and Archimandrite Ephrem, "Rhipidion," in Ken Parry et al., *The Blackwell Dictionary of Eastern Christianity* (Malden, MA: Blackwell Publishing, 1999), 404–5.

215. H. Leclercq, "Flabellum," in *DACL* 5, col. 1610.

216. Ibid., 1611–12.

217. Klauser, *A Short History of the Western Liturgy*, 35.

218. P. Bradshaw, *The Search for the Origins of Christian Worship*, 84–86.

219. "Ὡν γενομενων οι διαχονοι προσαγετωσαν τα δωρα τω επισχοπω προς το θυσιαστηριον, και δωρα τω επισκοπω προς το θσιαστητιον, και οι πρεσδθτεροι εκ δεξιων αθτου και εξ ευωνυμων στηκετωσαν, ως αν μαθηςται παρεστωτες διδασκαλω δυο δε διακονοι εξ εκατερων των μερων του θυσιαστηριου κατεχετςσαν εξ υμρνων λεπτων ριπιδιον η πτερον ταωνος, και ηπεμα αποσοδειτωσαν τα μικρα των ιπταμενων ξωων, οπως αν μη εγχριμπτωνται εις τα κυπελλλα": *Apostolic Constitutions* 8.2.123, in Marcel Metzger, trans. and ed., *Les Constitutions Apostoliques III: Livres VII et VIII*, Sources Chrétiennes 336 (Paris: Les Éditons du Cerf, 1987), 178; English translation from W. Jardine Grisbrooke, trans. and ed., *The Liturgical Portions of the Apostolic Constitutions: A Text for Students*, Alcuin/GROW Liturgical Study 13–14 (Bramcote: Grove Books, 1990), 31.

220. Leclercq, "Flabellum," col. 1615; cf. Raghnall Ó Floinn, "*Insignia Columbae I*," in *Studies in the Cult of Saint Columba*, ed. Cormac Bourke (Dublin: Four Courts Press, 1997), 157.

221. Leclercq, "Flabellum," cols. 1615–16.

222. Ó Floinn, "*Insignia Columbae I*," 158.

223. Ibid., 157.

224. Hilary Richardson, "Remarks on the Liturgical Fan, Flabellum or Rhipidion," in Spearman and Higgitt, *The Age of Migrating Ideas*, 30.

225. It has been proposed that "three cones and silver pommel," from the Scottish St Ninian's Isle treasure, may be the remains of an Insular *flabellum*, but there is no way to substantiate this claim; Stevenson, "Introduction," xc–xci.

226. Ó Floinn, "*Insignia Columbae I*," 155–56.

227. "M*ai*cnia H. Uchtan fer leiginn Cenannsa, do bath*ad* ic tiachtain a hAlb*ain*, 7 culb*ead* Colu*im* Cille 7 tri minna do m*inn*aib Pat*raicc* 7 tricha fer impu": *AU* 1034.9.

228. "Gnim granna anaithnigh ainiarmartach ro thoill escoine fer nErenn *eter* loech 7 cleirech do nach frit macsamhla i nErinn riam do dhenamh do Thigernan H. Ruairc 7 do hUi[b] Bruin .i. comarba Patraic do nocht-sharughadh ina fhiadhnuise .i. a chuidechta do shlat 7 dream dibh do marbadh ann. Ise imorro an iarmuirt do fhass don mbignimsa conach fuil in Erinn comuirce is tairisi do dhuine fodhesta ho curo dhighailter o Dhia 7 o dhoeinibh in t-olc-sa. In dinsemh-a tra tucadh for comarba Patraic iss amal 7 dinsim in Comdhegh uair adrubart in Coimdheo fein isin tshoiscéla: Qui uos spernit me spernit, qui mé spernit spernit eum qui mé misit": *AU* 1128.5. I have emended McÁirt and Mac Niocaill's translation of the central line, which gives the translation "a young cleric of his own household that was *in* a *cuilebadh* was killed." The original Early Irish reads: "& mac-cleirech dia mhuinntir fein do bi fo chuilebadh do marbadh ann." While somewhat unclear, this carries the meaning that the individual was "under," "holding," or "carrying" the *cuilebadh* and not "in" it. I am indebted to Dr Colmán Etchingham for alerting me to this occurrence.

229. Bernard Meehan, *The Book of Kells: An Illustrated Introduction to the Manuscript in Trinity College, Dublin* (New York: Thames and Hudson, 1994), 48.

230. The identifications of *flabella* in stone carvings are modern identifications, and it is impossible in every case to be certain that these are not simply stylized crosses; cf. Ó Floinn, "*Insignia Columbae I*," 157–58, and cf. J. G. Higgins, *The Early Christian Cross Slabs, Pillar Stones and Related Monuments of County Galway*, BAR International Series 375, printed in 2 vols. (Oxford: BAR, 1987), 1:109–13. For an example of these carvings see figure 19 from a standing stone at Caherlehillian on the Iveragh Peninsula, Co. Kerry.

231. Hilary Richardson and John Scarry, *An Introduction to Irish High Crosses* (Cork: Mercier Press, 1990), plates 33, 66; also see Peter Harbison, *Ireland's Treasures: 5,000 Years of Artistic Expression* (Westport, CT: Hugh Lanter Levin Associates, 2004), 87–88.

232. Richardson, "Remarks on the Liturgical Fan," 27–34.

233. Indeed, perhaps the clearest sculpture of a *flabellum* is to be found on a standing stone at Caherlehillian on the Iveragh Peninsula, Co. Kerry, on a site that has no Columban connections; see Peter Harbison, *The Golden Age of Irish Art: The Medieval Achievement 600–1200* (London: Thames & Hudson, 1999), plate 1, page 9.

234. Roger Stalley, *Irish High Crosses* (Dublin: Country House, 1996), 5.

235. Ibid., 39.

236. For more on the introduction of this feast into Rome from the East and its importation into England, see E. Ó Carragáin, *Ritual and the Rood*, 189–95.

237. "Vnde in eodem loco ante ianuam canabae crux infixa est; et altera ubi sanctus restitit illo exspirante similiter crux hodieque infixa stat": *Vita Columba* 1.45, in Anderson and Anderson, *Adomnán of Iona*, 82; English transla-

tion from Sharpe, *Adomnán of Iona,* 148. Also see note in Sharpe, *Adomnán of Iona,* 309–10.

238. "Ubi nunc usque crux habetur in signum ad uissum primun illius regionis": *Muirchú* 1.12, in Bieler, *The Patrician Texts,* 80–81.

239. Stalley, *Irish High Crosses,* 42.

240. Hilary Richardson, "Celtic Art," in Mackey, *An Introduction to Celtic Christianity,* 373–74; for example, the cross of Moone is "a monument which has been conceived in mathematical terms, with the proportions and measurements of each shape carefully worked out," 376.

241. However, these scenes generally are chosen from a biblical-artistic corpus that "continues a programme found in the earliest Christian art in the catacombs and on sculptured sarcophagi"; Richardson, "Visual Arts and Society," 709.

242. Peter Harbison, *The High Crosses of Ireland,* 3 vols. (Bonn: Habelt, 1992), 1:334–35, 1:252, 1:256, 1:299.

243. Ibid., 1:332. There is also an incidence of a Paul and Anthony scene from a high cross in the Isle of Man dating from around the ninth century. But this was also within a context that was markedly Irish; see Cubbon, "The Early Church in the Isle of Man," 262.

244. "Igitur Domino gratiarum actione celebrata super vitrei marginem fontis uterque consedit. Hic vero quis frangeret panem oborta contentio, pene iem duxit in vesperum. Paulus more cogebat hospitii, Antonius jure refellebat aetatis. Tandem consilium fuit, ut apprehenso e regione pane, dum ad se quisque nititur, pars sua remaneret in manibus. Dehinc paululum aquae in fonte prono ore libaverunt: et immolantes Deo sacrificium laudis, noctem transegere vigiliis": St Jerome, *The Life of Paul, the First Hermit* 11, in *PL* 23:25; English translation from W. H. Fremantle, trans., *Jerome: Letters and Select Works,* Nicene and Post-Nicene Fathers Second Series 6 (New York: Christian Literature Publishing Company, 1893; repr., Peabody, MA: Hendrickson, 2004), 301. Note that this St Paul the Hermit is not to be confused with the apostle, St Paul of Tarsus.

245. Éamonn Ó Carragáin, "The Meeting of Saint Paul and Saint Anthony: Visual and Literary Uses of a Eucharistic Motif," in *Keimelia: Studies in Medieval Archaeology and History in Memory of Tom Delaney,* ed. G. Mac Niocaill and P. F. Wallace (Galway: Galway University Press, 1988), 44, 35–38.

246. Ibid., 20–22.

247. We can also see this principle at work in the cross of Moone, Miracle of the Loaves and Fishes, which has the loaves and fishes *between* stylized monsters (figure 10). A magnificent example of both Sts Paul and Anthony and two animals on either side of the chalice and host can be seen in the Nigg stone, Roshire, Scotland; see E. Ó Carragáin, *Ritual and the Rood,* fig. 33, 159, and see 158–60.

248. Catherine Karkov, "The Chalice and the Cross in Insular Art," in *The Age of Migrating Ideas,* ed. Spearman and Higgitt, 238–39.

249. Dorothy Hoogland Verkerk, "Pilgrimage *Ad Limina Apostolorum.*"

250. Hilary Richardson, "The Jewelled Cross and Its Canopy," in *From the Isles of the North: Early Medieval Art in Ireland and Britain,* ed. Cormac Bourke (Belfast: H.M.S.O., 1995), 185.

251. Lawrence Nees, *Early Medieval Art,* Oxford History of Art (Oxford: Oxford University Press, 2002), 166–67.

252. For details of this contribution see ibid., 153–71.

253. The uniqueness of this eucharistic iconography in Insular sources was confirmed by Dr Bernard Meehan, the Keeper of Manuscripts, Trinity College Library, Dublin (personal communication, December 9, 2002).

254. Carol Farr, *The Book of Kells: Its Function and Audience* (London: The British Library Press, 1997), 14.

255. Herbert, *Iona, Kells and Derry,* 68, 88.

256. "Fot tairis": *AU* 1007.11.

257. Éamonn Ó Carragáin, "'*Traditio Evangeliorum*' and '*Sustenatio*': The Relevance of Liturgical Ceremonies to the Book of Kells," in *The Book of Kells: Proceedings of a Conference at Trinity College Dublin, 6–9 September 1992,* ed. Felicity O'Mahony (Aldershot: Scolar Press, 1994), 398. Later on the records of some land grants were inscribed on blank spaces. Perhaps this was because the manuscript was seen as being a particularly sacred place to record these.

258. Farr, *The Book of Kells,* 141.

259. Suzanne Lewis, "Sacred Calligraphy: The Chi Rho Page in the *Book of Kells,*" *Traditio* 36 (1980): 159.

260. Meehan, *The Book of Kells,* 44, 46.

261. Gary Macy, *The Banquet's Wisdom: A Short History of the Theologies of the Lord's Supper,* 2nd ed. (Akron, OH: OSL Publications, 2005), 98.

262. Lewis, "Sacred Calligraphy," 147.

263. Ibid., 158. In her analysis of folio 114r (the Taking of Christ), a page that at first glance seems to have little eucharistic significance, Jennifer O'Reilly concludes that this icon is ultimately centered on the eucharistic body of Christ; see her "*The Book of Kells:* Folio 114r, a Mystery Revealed Yet Concealed," in *The Age of Migrating Ideas,* ed. Spearman and Higgitt, 113–14.

Conclusion

1. Taft, "The Order and Place of Lay Communion," 130.

2. It is also interesting that a generation ago there was a similar confusion about the origins of the *Bobbio Missal,* when many authors proposed an Irish origin for this missal.

BIBLIOGRAPHY

Ahronson, Kristján. "Further Evidence for a Columban Iceland: Preliminary Results of Recent Work." *Norwegian Archaeological Review* 33, no. 2 (2000): 117–24.

Aitchison, Nicholas B. *Armagh and the Royal Centres in Early Medieval Ireland: Monuments, Cosmology and the Past.* Suffolk: Cruithne Press/ Boydell and Brewer, 1994.

Anderson, Alan Orr, and Marjorie Ogilive Anderson, trans. and eds. *Adomnán of Iona: Life of Columba.* 2nd ed. Oxford: Oxford University Press, 1991.

Andrieu, Michel, ed. *Les Ordines Romani du Haut Moyen Age.* 5 vols. Louvain: Spicilegium Sacrum Lovaniense, 1931–61.

Baldovin, John F. "The Empire Baptized." In *The Oxford History of Christian Worship,* edited by Wainwright and Westerfield Tucker, 77–130.

———. *The Urban Character of Early Christian Worship: The Origins, Development and Meaning of Stational Liturgy.* Rome: Pontifical Oriental Institute Press, 1987.

Bastiaensen, A. A. R. "The Beginnings of Latin Liturgy." *Studia Patristica* 30 (1993): 271–90.

Beck, Henry. *The Pastoral Care of Souls in South-East France during the Sixth Century.* Analecta Gregoriana 51. Rome: Pontifical Gregorian Press, 1950.

Bernard, J. H., and R. Atkinson, eds. *The Irish Liber Hymnorum.* 2 vols. Henry Bradshaw Society 13–14. London: Harrison & Sons, 1898.

Bertram, Jerome, trans. *St John Cassian, The Monastic Institutes: On the Training of a Monk and the Eight Deadly Sins.* London: Saint Austin Press, 1999.

Bethell, David. "English Monks and Irish Reform in the Eleventh and Twelfth Centuries." *Historical Studies* 8 (1971): 111–35.

———. "Two Letters of Pope Paschal II to Scotland." *Scottish Historical Review* 49 (1970): 33–45.

Bévenot, M., ed. *Sancti Cypriani Episcopi Opera Pars I.* Corpus Christianorum Series Latina 3. Turnhout: Brepols, 1972.

Bieler, Ludwig, trans. and ed. "The Celtic Hagiographer." *Studia Patristica* 5 (1962): 243–65.

————, trans. and ed. *The Irish Penitentials.* Scriptores Latini Hiberniae 4, 2nd ed. Dublin: School of Celtic Studies, Dublin Institute for Advanced Studies, 1975.

————, trans. and ed. *The Patrician Texts in the Book of Armagh.* Scriptores Latini Hiberniae 10. Dublin: School of Celtic Studies, Dublin Institute for Advanced Studies, 1979.

————. *The Works of St Patrick and St Secundinus' Hymn on St Patrick.* Ancient Christian Writers 17. Mahwah, NJ: Paulist Press, 1953.

Binchy, Daniel A. *Corpus Iuris Hibernici: Ad Fidem Codicum Manuscriptorum Recognovit.* Dublin: Dublin Institute for Advanced Studies, 1978.

————. "The Old-Irish Table of Penitential Commutations." *Ériu* 19 (1962): 47–72.

Bishop, Edmund. *Liturgica Historica: Papers on the Liturgy and Religious Life of the Western Church.* Oxford: The Clarendon Press, 1918.

Blair, John, and Richard Sharpe, eds. *Pastoral Care Before the Parish.* Leicester: Leicester University Press, 1992.

Boretius, Alfredus, ed. *Monumenta Germaniae Historica, Legum Sectio II: Capitularia Regum Francorum.* Hanover: Impensis Bibliopolii Haniani, 1883.

Bossy, John. "The Mass as a Social Institution: 1200–1700." *Past and Present* 100 (1983): 29–61.

Botte, Bernard. *Le Canon de la Messe Romain: Édition Critique, Introduction et Notes.* Louvain: Abbaye de Mont César, 1935.

Bouley, Allan. *From Freedom to Formula: The Evolution of the Eucharistic Prayer from Oral Improvisation to Written Texts.* Washington DC: Catholic University of America Press, 1981.

Bourke, Cormac. "The Bells of Saints Caillín and Cuana: Two Twelfth-Century Cups." In *Seanchas,* edited by A. Smyth, 331–40.

————. *Patrick: The Archaeology of a Saint.* Belfast: H.M.S.O. Ulster Museum, 1993.

Bourke, Edward. "Glass Vessels of the First Nine Centuries AD in Ireland." *Journal of the Royal Society of Antiquaries of Ireland* 124 (1994): 163–209.

Bouyer, Louis. *Eucharist: Theology and Spirituality of the Eucharistic Prayer.* Translated by Charles Quinn. Notre Dame, IN: University of Notre Dame Press, 1968.

————. *Liturgy and Architecture.* Notre Dame, IN: University of Notre Dame Press, 1967.

Bracken, Damian, and Dagmar Ó Riain-Raedel, eds. *Ireland and Europe in the Twelfth Century: Reform and Renewal.* Dublin: Four Courts Press, 2006.

Bradshaw, Berndan, and Dáire Keogh, eds. *Christianity in Ireland: Revisiting the Story.* Dublin: Columba Press, 2002.

Bradshaw, Paul. *Eucharistic Origins.* Alcuin Club Collections 80. London: SPCK, 2004.

———. "The Homogenization of Christian Liturgy—Ancient and Modern." *Studia Liturgica* 26 (1996): 1–15.

———. *The Search for the Origins of Christian Worship: Sources and Methods for the Study of Early Liturgy.* 2nd ed. Oxford: Oxford University Press, 2002.

Brady, Niall. "*De Oratorio: Hisperica Famina* and Church Building." *Peritia* 11 (1997): 327–35.

Brannon, Patrick V. "Medieval Ireland: Music in Cathedral, Church and Cloister." *Early Music* 28:2 (2000): 193–202.

Breatnach, Liam. "The First Third of *Bretha Nemed Toísech.*" *Ériu* 40 (1989): 1–40.

Breen, Aidan. "The Text of the Constantinopolitan Creed in the *Stowe Missal.*" *Proceedings of the Royal Irish Academy* 90 (1990): 107–21.

Brett, Martin. "Canterbury's Perspective on Church Reform and Ireland, 1070–1115." In *Ireland and Europe,* edited by Bracken and Ó Riain-Raedel, 13–35.

Brooks, Nicholas. "Canterbury, Rome and English Identity." In *Early Medieval Rome and the Christian West: Essays in Honour of David A. Bullough,* edited by Julia Smith, 221–47. Leiden: Brill, 2000.

Brown, Michelle P. "Paten and Purpose: The Derrynaflan Paten Inscriptions." In *The Age of Migrating Ideas,* edited by Spearman and Higgitt, 162–67.

———. "The Saint as Exemplar in Late Antiquity." In *Saints and Virtues,* edited by J. S. Hawley, 3–14. Berkeley, CA: The University of California Press, 1987.

Brown, Peter. *The Cult of the Saints: Its Rise and Function in Latin Christianity.* Chicago: University of Chicago Press, 1981.

———. *The Rise of Western Christendom.* 2nd ed. Malden, MA: Blackwell Publishing, 2003.

Browne, Martin, and Colmán Ó Clabaigh, eds. *The Irish Benedictines: A History.* Dublin: Columba, 2005.

Buckley, Ann. "In Search of the Music of the Medieval Irish Church: Irish, Sarum and Gregorian." *New Liturgy* 125 (2005): 9–15.

———. "Music and Musicians in Medieval Irish Society." *Early Music* 28, no. 2 (2000): 165–90.

———. "Music in Ireland to *c.* 1500." In *Prehistoric and Early Ireland,* edited by Ó Cróinín, 744–808.

Bullough, Donald. "The Career of Columbanus." In *Columbanus: Studies on the Latin Writings,* edited by Lapidge, 1–28.

———. "The Carolingian Liturgical Experience." In *Continuity and Change,* edited by Swanson, 29–64.

Butler, L. A. S., and R. K. Morris, eds. *The Anglo-Saxon Church: Papers on History, Architecture and Archaeology in Honour of Dr H. M. Taylor.*

Council for British Archaeology Research Report 60. London: Bond Hall, 1986.

Butzer, P., M. Kerner, and W. Oberschelp, eds. *Charlemagne and His Heritage: 1200 Years of Civilization and Science in Europe.* 2 vols. Turnhout: Brepols, 1997.

Byrne, Francis John. "Derrynaflan: The Historical Context." *Journal of the Royal Society of Antiquaries of Ireland* 110 (1980): 116–26.

———. "The *Stowe Missal.*" In *The Great Books of Ireland*, edited by Liam de Paor, 38–50. Dublin: Four Courts Press, 1967.

Cabaniss, Allen, trans. *Benedict of Aniane, the Emperor's Monk: Aldo's Life.* Cistercian Studies Series 220. Kalamazoo, MI: Cistercian Publications, 2008.

Cabié, Robert. *The Eucharist,* vol. 2 of *The Church at Prayer,* edited by A. G. Martimort and translated by Matthew J. O'Connell. Collegeville, MN: Liturgical Press, 1986.

Cabrol, F. "Les Origines de la Liturgie Gallicane." *Revue d'Histoire Ecclésiastique* 26 (1930): 951–62.

Callam, Daniel. "Clerical Continence in the Fourth Century: Three Papal Decretals." *Theological Studies* 41 (1980): 3–50.

———. "The Frequency of Mass in the Latin Church ca. 400." *Theological Studies* 45 (1984): 613–50.

Campbell, James, ed. *The Anglo-Saxons.* Ithaca: Cornell University Press, 1982.

Capelle, Bernard. *Travaux Liturgiques de Doctrine et d'Histoire.* Vol. 2: *Histoire: La Messe.* Louvain Centre Liturgique, Abbaye du Mont César, 1962.

Carey, John, trans. and ed. *King of Mysteries: Early Irish Religious Writings.* Dublin: Four Courts Press, 2000.

Carney, James, trans. and ed. *The Poems of Blathmac Son of Cú Brettan together with the Irish Gospel of Thomas and a Poem on the Virgin Mary.* Irish Texts Society 47. Dublin: Irish Texts Society, 1964.

Carver, Martin, ed. *The Cross Goes North: Process of Conversion in Northern Europe, AD 300–750.* Suffolk: York Medieval Press, 2003.

Carville, Geraldine. *The Occupation of Celtic Sites in Medieval Ireland by the Canons Regular of St Augustine and the Cistercians.* Cistercian Studies Series 56. Kalamazoo, MI: Cistercian Publications, 1982.

Casey, Sarah G. "The *Drummond Missal:* A Preliminary Investigation into Its Historical Liturgical and Musicological Significance in Pre-Norman Ireland." MA thesis, University of Pittsburgh, 1995.

———. "'Through a Glass, Darkly': Steps Towards Reconstructing Irish Chant from the Neumes of the *Drummond Missal.*" *Early Music* 28, no. 2 (2000): 205–15.

Chadwick, Owen. *A History of Christianity.* London: Weidenfeld and Nicolson, 1995.

Charles-Edwards, Thomas M. "Beyond Empire II: Christianities of the Celtic Peoples." In *Early Medieval Christianities, c. 600–c. 1100,* edited by Thomas F. X. Noble and Julia M. H. Smith, 86–106. Vol. 3 of *The Cambridge History of Christianity.* Cambridge: Cambridge University Press, 2008.

———. *Early Christian Ireland.* Cambridge: Cambridge University Press, 2000.

———. "Introduction." In *A New History of Ireland,* ed. Ó Cróinín, lvii–lxxxii.

———. "Palladius, Prosper, and Leo the Great: Mission and Primatial Authority." In *St Patrick AD 493–1993,* edited by David N. Dumville, 1–12. Suffolk: Boydell & Brewer, 1993.

———. "The Pastoral Role of the Church in the Early Irish Laws." In *Pastoral Care Before the Parish,* edited by Blair and Sharpe, 62–80.

Chitty, Derwas. *The Desert a City: An Introduction to the Study of Egyptian and Palestinian Monasticism under the Christian Empire.* Crestwood, NY: St. Valdimir's Seminary Press, 1966.

Chupungco, Anscar J., ed. *The Eucharist.* Vol. 3 of *The Pontifical Liturgical Institute Handbook for Liturgical Studies.* Collegeville, MN: Liturgical Press, 1999.

Clarke, Howard B., and Mary Brennan, eds. *Columbanus and Merovingian Monasticism.* Oxford: British Archaeological Reports International Series, 1981.

Clarke, Howard B., and Anngret Simms, eds. *The Comparative History of Urban Origins in Non-Roman Europe: Ireland, Wales, Denmark, Germany, Poland and Russia from the Ninth to the Thirteenth Centuries.* BAR International Series 225, printed in 2 vols. Oxford: BAR, 1985.

Clemoes, P., and Kathleen Hughes, eds. *England Before the Conquest: Studies in Primary Sources Presented to Dorothy Whitelock.* Cambridge: Cambridge University Press, 1971.

Clover, Helen, and Margaret Gibson, trans. and eds. *The Letters of Lanfranc, Bishop of Canterbury.* Oxford: Oxford University Press, 1979.

Coatsworth, Elizabeth. "The Pectoral Cross and Portable Altar from the Tomb of St Cuthbert." In *St Cuthbert, His Cult and His Community to AD 1200,* edited by Gerald Bonner, David Rollason, and Clare Stancliffe, 287–301. Woodbridge: Boydell Press, 1989.

Colgan, John. *Trias Thaumaturga.* Louvain: Cornelius Coenesteius, 1647; repr. Dublin: Edmund Burke, 1997.

Colgrave, Bertram, and R. A. B. Mynors, trans. and eds. *Bede's Ecclesiastical History of the English People.* Oxford: The Clarendon Press, 1969.

Collins, Kevin. *Catholic Churchmen and the Celtic Revival, 1848–1916.* Dublin: Four Courts Press, 2003.

Collins, Mary. "Evangelization, Catechesis, and the Beginning of Western Eucharistic Theology." *Louvain Studies* 23 (1988): 124–42.

Connolly, Hugh. *The Irish Penitentials and Their Significance for the Sacrament of Penance Today.* Dublin: Four Courts Press, 1995.

Connolly, Sean, trans. and ed. *"Vita Prima Sanctae Brigitae."* Journal of the Royal Society of Antiquaries of Ireland 119 (1989): 5–49.

Connolly, Sean, and Jean-Michel Picard, trans. and eds. "Cogitosius's *Life of St Brigit:* Content and Value." *Journal of the Royal Society of Antiquaries of Ireland* 117 (1987): 5–27.

Contreni, John J. "The Irish Contribution to the European Classroom." In *Proceedings of the Seventh International Congress of Celtic Studies,* edited by D. Ellis Evans, John G. Griffith, and E. M. Jope, 79–90. Oxford: Ellis Evans, 1986.

Corish, Patrick J. *The Christian Mission.* Vol. 1 of *A History of Irish Catholicism.* Dublin: Gill and Macmillan, 1972.

———. *The Irish Catholic Experience: A Historical Survey.* Wilmington, DE: Michael Glazier, 1985.

———. "The Pastoral Mission in the Early Irish Church." *Léachtaí Cholm Cille* 2 (1971): 14–25.

Corning, Caitlin, *The Celtic and Roman Traditions: Conflict and Consensus in the Early Medieval Church.* New York: Palgrave Macmillan, 2006.

Crehan, Joseph H. "The Liturgical Trade Route: East to West." *Studies* 65 (1976): 87–100.

———. "The Theology of Eucharistic Consecration: The Role of the Priest in Celtic Liturgy." *Theological Studies* 40, no. 2 (1979): 334–43.

Cubbon, A. M. "The Early Church in the Isle of Man." In *The Early Church in Western Britain and Ireland: Studies Presented to C. A. Ralegh Radford,* edited by Susan M. Pearce, 257–82. BAR British Series 102. Oxford: BAR, 1982.

Cuppage, Judith. *Archaeological Survey of the Dingle Peninsula: A Description of the Field Antiquities of the Barony of Corca Dhuibhne from the Mesolithic Period to the Seventeeth Century* AD. Ballyferriter: Oidhreacht Chorca Dhuibhne, 1986.

Curran, Michael. *The Antiphonary of Bangor and the Early Irish Monastic Liturgy.* Dublin: Irish Academic Press, 1984.

Dalby, Mark. *Infant Communion: The New Testament to the Reformation.* Cambridge: Grove Joint Liturgical Studies, 2003.

Davidson, Carol F. "Change and Change Back: The Development of English Parish Church Chancels." In *Continuity and Change,* edited by Swanson, 65–77.

Davies, Oliver, trans. and ed. *Celtic Spirituality.* The Classics of Western Spirituality. Mahwah, NJ: Paulist Press, 1999.

Davies, Wendy. "The Myth of the Celtic Church." In *The Early Church in Wales and the West: Recent Work in Early Christian Archaeology, History and Place-Names,* edited by Nancy Edwards and A. Lane, 12–21. Oxbow Monograph 16. Oxford: Oxbow Books, 1992.

De Baldraithe, Eoin. "Daily Eucharist: The Need for an Early Church Paradigm." *American Benedictine Review* 41 (1990): 378–440.

Deferrari, Roy J., trans. and ed. *Saint Cyprian Treatises.* Fathers of the Church 36. Washington DC: Catholic University of America Press, 1958.

Dekkers, Eligius. "Were the Early Monks Liturgical?" *Collectanea Cisterciensia* 22 (1960): 120–37.

De Lubac, Henri. *Corpus Mysticum—L'Eucharistie et l'Église au Moyen Age: Étude Historique.* 2nd ed. Paris: Aubier, 1949.

De Paor, Liam. "The Age of the Viking Wars: The Ninth and Tenth Centuries." In *The Course of Irish History,* edited by Moody and Martin, 67–80.

Dix, Gregory. *The Shape of the Liturgy.* 2nd ed. London: Dacre Press, 1945; repr. with an introduction by Simon Jones, London: Continuum, 2005.

Doherty, Charles. "The Basilica in Early Ireland." *Peritia* 3 (1984): 305–15.

———. "The Monastic Town in Early Medieval Ireland." In *The Comparative History of Urban Origins,* edited by Clarke and Simms, 1:45–75.

———. "The Use of Relics in Ireland." In *Die Kirche im Frühmittelalter,* edited by Ní Chatháin and Richter, 89–101.

Dold, Alban, and Leo Eizenhöfer, eds. *Das Irische Palimpsestsakramentar im CLM 14429: Der Staatsbibliothek München.* Beuron: Beuroner Kunstverlag, 1964.

Dooley, Kate. "From Penance to Confession: The Celtic Contribution." *Bijdragen, Tijdschrift voor Filosofie en Theologie* 43 (1982): 390–411.

Driscoll, Michael S. "The Conversion of the Nations." In *The Oxford History of Christian Worship,* edited by Wainwright and Westerfield Tucker, 175–215.

Duchense, Louis. *Christian Worship: Its Origin and Evolution; A Study of the Latin Liturgy up to the Time of Charlemagne.* 5th ed., translated by M. L. McClure. London: SPCK, 1919.

Duffy, Eamon. *Saints and Sinners: A History of the Popes.* New Haven: Yale University Press, 1997.

Dunn, Marilyn. *The Emergence of Monasticism: From the Desert Fathers to the Early Middle Ages.* Oxford: Oxford University Press, 2000.

Dunning, Patrick J. "The Arroasian Order in Medieval Ireland." *Irish Historical Studies* 4, no. 16 (1945): 297–315.

Edwards, Nancy. "The Archaeology of Medieval Ireland, *c.* 400–1169: Settlement and Economy." In *Prehistoric and Early Ireland,* edited by Ó Cróinín, 235–300.

———. "Celtic Saints and Early Medieval Archaeology." In *Local Saints and Local Churches in the Early Medieval West,* edited by Alan Thacker and Richard Sharpe, 225–65. Oxford: Oxford University Press, 2002.

Eizenhöffer, Leo. "Zu dem Irischen Palimpesakramentar im Clm 14429." *Sacris Erudiri Jaarboek voor Godsdienstwetenschappen* 17, no. 1 (1966): 355–64.

Elich, Tom. "Using Liturgical Texts in the Middle Ages." In *Fountain of Life in Memory of Niels K. Rasmussen, O.P.,* edited by Gerard Austin, 69–83. Washington DC: Pastoral Press, 1991.

Elm, Susanna. *"Virgins of God": The Making of Asceticism in Late Antiquity.* Oxford: Oxford University Press, 1994.

Empey, Adrian. "The Layperson in the Parish: The Medieval Inheritance, 1169–1536." In *The Laity and the Church of Ireland, 1000–2000: All Sorts and Conditions,* edited by Raymond Gillespie and W. G. Neely, 7–48. Dublin: Four Courts Press, 2002.

Etchingham, Colmán. "Bishoprics in Ireland and Wales in the Early Middle Ages: Some Comparisons." In *Contrasts and Comparisons: Studies in Irish and Welsh Church History,* edited by John R. Guy and W. D. Neely, 7–25. Powys: Welsh Religious History Society, 1999.

———. *Church Organisation in Ireland AD 650 to 1000.* Maynooth: Laigin Publications, 1999.

———. "The Early Irish Church: Some Observations on Pastoral Care and Dues." *Ériu* 42 (1993): 99–118.

———. "Episcopal Hierarchy in Connacht and Tairdelbach Ua Conchobair." *Journal of the Galway Archaeological and Historical Society* 52 (2000): 13–29.

———. "The Ideal of Monastic Austerity in Early Ireland." In *Luxury and Austerity: Papers Read before the Twenty-Third Irish Conference of Historians Held at St Patrick's College, Maynooth, 16–18 May, 1997,* edited by Jacqueline Hill and Colm Lennon, 14–29. Dublin: University College Dublin Press, 1997.

———. "Pastoral Provision in the First Millennium: A Two-Tier Service?" In *The Parish in Medieval and Early Modern Ireland,* edited by Gillespie and FitzPatrick, 79–90.

———. *Viking Raids on Irish Church Settlements in the Ninth Century: A Reconsideration of the Annals.* Maynooth Monograph, Series Minor 1. Maynooth: An Sagart, 1996.

Evans, Helen C. "Christian Neighbors." In *The Glory of Byzantium: Art and Culture of the Middle Byzantine Era, AD 843–1261,* edited by Helen C. Evans and William D. Wixom, 272–79. New York: The Metropolitan Museum of Art, 1997.

Farr, Carol. *The Book of Kells: Its Function and Audience.* London: The British Library Press, 1997.

Fenwick, John R. K. *Fourth Century Anaphoral Construction Techniques.* Grove Liturgical Studies 45. Bramcote: Grove, 1986.

Flanagan, Marie-Therese. "The Contribution of Irish Missionaries and Scholars to Medieval Christianity." In *Christianity in Ireland,* edited by Bradshaw and Keogh, 30–43.

———. "Henry II, the Council of Cashel and the Irish Bishops." *Peritia* 10 (1996): 184–211.

———. "Hiberno-Papal Relations in the Late Twelfth Century." *Archivium Hibernicum* 34 (1977): 55–70.

———. "Irish Church Reform in the Twelfth Century and Áed Ua Cáellaide, Bishop of Louth: An Italian Dimension." In *Ogma: Essays in Celtic Studies Presented to Próinséas Ní Chatháin,* edited by Michael Richter and Jean-Michel Picard, 94–104. Dublin: Four Courts Press, 2001.

———. *Irish Society, Anglo-Norman Settlers, Angevin Kingship: Interactions in Ireland in the Late Twelfth Century.* Oxford: The Clarendon Press, 1989.

Fleming, John, trans. and ed. *Gille of Limerick (c. 1070–1145): Architect of a Medieval Church.* Dublin: Four Courts Press, 2001.

Fletcher, Alan J., and Raymond Gillespie, eds. *Irish Preaching 700–1700.* Dublin: Four Courts Press, 2001.

Fletcher, Richard. *The Barbarian Conversion: From Paganism to Christianity.* New York: Henry Holt and Company, 1997.

Foley, Edward. *Foundations of Christian Music: The Music of Pre-Constantinian Christianity.* 2 vols. bound as 1. Grove Liturgical Studies 22–23. Bramcote, Nottingham: Grove, 1992.

———. *From Age to Age: How Christians Have Celebrated the Eucharist.* 2nd ed. Collegeville, MN: Liturgical Press, 2008.

Follett, Westley Nicholson. "Monastic Devotion in Ireland: The Celi De Movement in the Eighth and Ninth Centuries." PhD diss., University of Toronto, 2002.

Forbes, George Hay, ed. *Missale Drummondiense: The Ancient Irish Missal in the Possession of the Baroness Willoughby de Eresby.* Edinburgh: Pitsligo Press, 1882.

Fowden, Garth. *Empire to Commonwealth: Consequences of Monotheism in Late Antiquity.* Princeton: Princeton University Press, 1993.

Francis, Mark R. "Liturgy and Popular Piety in a Historical Perspective." In *Directory on Popular Piety and the Liturgy: A Commentary,* edited by Peter Phan, 19–43. Collegeville, MN: Liturgical Press, 2005.

Freeman, Philip. *Ireland and the Classical World.* Austin: University of Texas Press, 2001.

Freestone, W. H. *The Sacrament Reserved: A Survey of the Practice of Reserving the Eucharist, with Special Reference to Communion of the Sick, during the First Twelve Centuries.* Alcuin Club Collections 21. London: Mowbray, 1917.

Fremantle, W. H., trans. and ed. *Jerome: Letters and Select Works*. Nicene and Post-Nicene Fathers Second Series 6. New York: Christian Literature Publishing Company, 1893; repr. Peabody, MA: Hendrickson, 2004.

Furlong, Nicholas. *Diarmait King of Leinster*. 2nd ed. Cork: Mercier Press, 2006.

Gamber, Klaus. "Irische Liturgiebücher und ihre Verbreitung auf dem Kontinent." In *Die Iren und Europa im Früheren Mittelalter*, edited by Löwe, 1:536–48.

Garrison, Mary. "The English and the Irish at the Court of Charlemagne." In *Charlemagne and His Heritage*, edited by Butzer, Kerner and Oberschelp, 1:97–123.

Geake, Helen. "Medieval Britain and Ireland." *Medieval Archaeology* 48 (2004): 229–350.

Gillespie, Raymond, and Elizabeth FitzPatrick, eds. *The Parish in Medieval and Early Modern Ireland: Community, Territory and Building*. Dublin: Four Courts Press, 2006.

Godel, Willibrord. "Irish Prayer in the Early Middle Ages II." *Milltown Studies* 5 (1980): 72–114.

———. "Irish Prayer in the Early Middle Ages IV." *Milltown Studies* 7 (1981): 21–51.

Graham-Campbell, James A. "The Viking-Age Silver Hoards of Ireland." In *Proceedings of the Seventh Viking Congress*, edited by Bo Almqvist and David Greene, 39–74. Dublin: Royal Irish Academy, 1976.

Greenwell, William, ed. *The Pontifical of Egbert: Archbishop of York*, AD *732–766*. Publications of the Surtees Society 27. London: The Surtees Society, 1854.

Griesser, Bruno, ed. "Registrum Epistolarum Stephani de Lexinton Abbatis de Stanlegia et de Savigniaco." *Analecta Sacri Ordinis Cisterciensis* 2 (1946): 1–118.

Grisbrooke, W. Jardine, trans. and ed. *The Liturgical Portions of the Apostolic Constitutions: A Text for Students*. Alcuin/GROW Liturgical Study 13–14. Bramcote: Grove, 1990.

Groeschel, Benedict, and James Monti. *In the Presence of the Lord: The History, Theology and Psychology of Eucharistic Devotion*. Huntington, IN: Our Sunday Visitor Books, 1997.

Gwynn, Aubrey. *The Irish Church in the Eleventh and Twelfth Centuries*, edited by Gerard O'Brien. Dublin: Four Courts Press, 1992.

Gwynn, Edward John. "An Irish Penitential." *Ériu* 7 (1914): 121–95.

Gwynn, Edward John, and Walter John Purton. "The Monastery of Tallaght." *Proceedings of the Royal Irish Academy* 39C (1911–12): 115–179.

Gy, Pierre M. "Penance and Reconciliation." In *The Sacraments*, vol. 3 of *The Church at Prayer*, edited by A. G. Martimort and translated by Matthew J. O'Connell, 101–16. Collegeville, MN: Liturgical Press, 1988.

Håkon, Christie, Olaf Olsen, and H. M. Taylor. "The Wooden Church of St Andrew at Greensted, Essex." *Antiquaries Journal* 59 (1979): 92–112.

Hall, Dianne. *Women and the Church in Medieval Ireland, c. 1140–1540.* Dublin: Four Courts Press, 2003.

Hallinger, Kassius, ed. *Corpus Consuetudinum Monasticarum Cura Pontificii Athenaei Sancti Anselmi de Urbe Editum.* Vol. 1: *Initia Consuetudinis Benedictinae.* Siegburg: Franz Schmitt, 1963.

Hamlin, Ann. "The Study of Early Irish Churches." In *Die Kirche im Frühmittelalter,* edited by Ní Chatháin and Richter, 117–26.

Hänggi, Anton, and Irmgard Pahl, eds. *Prex Eucharistica: Textus e Variis Liturgiis Antiquioribus Selecti.* Fribourg: Éditions Universitaires Fribourg Suisse, 1968.

Hanson, R. P. C. "The Mission of St Patrick." In *An Introduction to Celtic Christianity,* edited by Mackey, 22–44.

Harbison, Peter. "Early Irish Churches." In *Die Iren und Europa im Früheren Mittelalter,* edited by Löwe, 2:618–29.

———. *The Golden Age of Irish Art: The Medieval Achievement 600–1200.* London: Thames & Hudson, 1999.

———. *The High Crosses of Ireland.* 3 vols. Bonn: Habelt, 1992.

———. *Ireland's Treasures: 5,000 Years of Artistic Expression.* Westport, CT: Hugh Lanter Levin Associates, 2004.

———. *Pilgrimage in Ireland: The Monuments and the People.* Syracuse, NY: Syracuse University Press, 1992.

———. *Pre-Christian Ireland: From the First Settlers to the Early Celts.* 2nd ed. London: Thames & Hudson, 1994.

———. *Treasures of the Boyne Valley.* Dublin: Gill and Macmillan, 2003.

Hare, Michael, and Ann Hamlin. "The Study of Early Church Architecture in Ireland: An Anglo-Saxon Viewpoint." In *The Anglo-Saxon Church,* edited by Butler and Morris, 131–45.

Harmless, William. *Desert Christians: An Introduction to the Literature of Early Monasticism.* Oxford: Oxford University Press, 2004.

Harper, John. *The Forms and Orders of Western Liturgy from the Tenth to the Eighteenth Century.* Oxford: Oxford University Press, 1991.

Harrington, Christina. *Women in a Celtic Church: Ireland 450–1150.* Oxford: Oxford University Press, 2002.

Harvey, Anthony, and Jane Power, eds. *Non-Classical Lexicon of Celtic Latinity.* Dublin: Brepols, 2005.

Hasting, Julia, ed. *Last Supper.* London: Phaidon, 2000.

Hatchett, Marion J. "The Eucharistic Rite of the *Stowe Missal.*" In *Time and Community in Honor of Thomas Julian Talley,* edited by J. Neil Alexander, NPN Studies in Church Music and Liturgy, 153–70. Washington DC: Pastoral Press, 1990.

Häussling, Angelus. *Moenchskonvent und Eucharistiefeier: eine Studie ueber die Messe in der Abendländischen Klosterliturgie des Fruehen Mittelalters und zur Geschichte der Messhäufigkeit.* Liturgiewissenschaftliche Quellen und Forschungen 58. Muenster: Westfalen, 1973.

———. "Motives for the Frequency of the Eucharist." *Concilium* 152 (1982): 25–30.

Häussling, Angelus, and Karl Rahner. *The Celebration of the Eucharist.* New York: Herder and Herder, 1967.

Heist, William W., ed. *Vitae Sanctorum Hiberniae e Codice olim Salmanticensi nunc Bruxellensi.* Subsidia Hagiographica 25. Brussels: Société des Bollandistes, 1965.

Hélène, Pétré, trans. and ed. *Éthérie: Journal de Voyage.* Sources Chrétiennes 21. Paris: Éditions du Cerf, 1948.

Hen, Yitzhak. "Introduction: The *Bobbio Missal*—from Mabillon Onwards." In *The Bobbio Missal*, edited by Hen and Meens, 1–7.

———. "The Liturgy of the *Bobbio Missal.*" In *The Bobbio Missal*, edited by Hen and Meens, 140–53.

———. "Rome, Anglo-Saxon England and the Formation of Frankish Liturgy." *Revue Bénédictine* 112, nos. 3–4 (2002): 301–22.

———. *The Royal Patronage of the Liturgy in Frankish Gaul: To the Death of Charles the Bald (877).* Woodbridge: Henry Bradshaw Society/Boydell Press, 2001.

Hen, Yitzhak, and Rob Meens, eds. *The Bobbio Missal: Liturgy and Religious Culture in Merovingian Gaul.* Cambridge: Cambridge University Press, 2004.

Hennig, John. "Old Ireland and Her Liturgy." In *Old Ireland*, edited by Robert E. McNally, 60–89. New York: Fordham University Press, 1965.

Herbert, Máire. *Iona, Kells and Derry: The History and Hagiography of the Familia of Columba.* Oxford: The Clarendon Press, 1988.

Herren, Michael W., trans. and ed. *The Hisperica Famina.* Vol. 1, *The A-Text: A New Critical Edition with English Translation and Philological Commentary.* Toronto: Pontifical Institute of Medieval Studies, 1974.

Herren, Michael W., and Shirley Ann Brown. *Christ in Celtic Christianity: Britain and Ireland from the Fifth to the Tenth Century.* Woodbridge: Boydell Press, 2002.

Higgins, J. G. *The Early Christian Cross Slabs, Pillar Stones and Related Monuments of County Galway.* BAR International Series 375, printed in 2 vols. Oxford: BAR, 1987.

Higham, Nicholas. *Rome, Britain and the Anglo-Saxons.* London: Seaby, 1992.

Hiley, David. *Western Plainchant: A Handbook.* Oxford: The Clarendon Press, 1993.

Hillgarth, J. N. "Modes of Evangelization of Western Europe in the Seventh Century." In *Ireland and Christendom,* edited by Ní Chatháin and Richter, 311–31.

Hogan, Edmund, trans. and ed. *The Irish Nennius from L. Na hUidre and Homilies and Legends from L. Breac: Alphabetical Index of Irish Neuter Substances.* Todd Lecture Series 6. Dublin: Academy House, 1895.

Holland, Martin. "On the Dating of the Corpus Irish Missal." *Peritia* 15 (2001): 280–301.

———. "The Synod of Dublin in 1080." In *Medieval Dublin III: Proceedings of the Friends of Medieval Dublin Symposium 2001,* edited by Seán Duffy, 81–94. Dublin: Four Courts Press, 2002.

Horn, Walter, and E. Born. *The Plan of St Gall.* 3 vols. Berkeley: University of California Press, 1979.

Hourihane, Colum, ed. *From Ireland Coming: Irish Art from the Early Christian to the Late Gothic Period and Its European Context.* Princeton: Princeton University Press, 2001.

Howlett, David R., trans. and ed. *The Book of Letters of Saint Patrick the Bishop.* Dublin: Four Courts Press, 1994.

Hudson, Benjamin T. "The Changing Economy of the Irish Sea Province: AD 900–1300." In *Britain and Ireland,* edited by Smith, 39–66.

Hughes, Kathleen. "The Celtic Church: Is This a Valid Concept?" *Cambridge Medieval Celtic Studies* 1 (1981): 1–20.

———. "The Changing Theory and Practice of Irish Pilgrimage." *Journal of Ecclesiastical History* 11 (1960): 143–51.

———. *The Church in Early Irish Society.* London: Methuen, 1966.

———. "Evidence for Contacts between the Churches of the Irish and English from the Synod of Whitby to the Viking Age." In *England Before the Conquest,* edited by Clemoes and Hughes, 49-67.

Hughes, Kathleen, and Ann Hamlin. *The Modern Traveller to the Early Irish Church.* 2nd ed. Dublin: Four Courts Press, 1997.

Hunwicke, J. W. "Kerry and Stowe Revisited." *Proceedings of the Royal Irish Academy* 102C (2002): 1–19.

Iñiguez Herrero, José Antonio. *El Altar Cristiano.* Vol. 1, *De los Origins a Carlomagno.* Pamplona: Eunsa, 1978.

———. *El Altar Cristiano.* Vol. 2, *De Carlomagno al Siglo XIII.* Pamplona: Eunsa, 1991.

James, Edward. "Archaeology and the Merovingian Monastery." In *Columbanus and Merovingian Monasticism,* edited by Clarke and Brennan, 33–58.

———. "Bede and the Tonsure Question." *Peritia* 3 (1984): 85–98.

Jaski, Bart. "The Vikings and the Kingship of Tara." *Peritia* 9 (1995): 310–51.

Jasper, R. C. D., and G. J. Cuming, trans. and ed. *Prayers of the Eucharist: Early and Reformed.* 3rd ed. Collegeville, MN: Liturgical Press, 1990.

Johnson, Maxwell E. "The Apostolic Tradition." In *The Oxford History of Christian Worship,* edited by Wainwright and Westerfield Tucker, 32–75.

———. *The Rites of Christian Initiation: Their Evolution and Interpretation.* 2nd ed. Collegeville, MN: Liturgical Press, 2007.

Joncas, Jan Michael. "Liturgy and Music." In *The Pontifical Liturgical Institute Handbook for Liturgical Studies.* Vol. 2, *Fundamental Liturgy,* edited by Anscar J. Chupungco, 281–321. Collegeville, MN: Liturgical Press, 1998.

Jones, Arnold H. M. *Constantine and the Conversion of Europe.* Toronto: University of Toronto Press, 1948.

Jungmann, Joseph A. *The Mass: An Historical, Theological, and Pastoral Survey.* Collegeville, MN: Liturgical Press, 1976.

———. *The Mass of the Roman Rite: Its Origins and Development (Missarum Sollemnia).* 2 vols. New York: Benziger Brothers, 1951.

———. *Pastoral Liturgy.* New York: Herder and Herder, 1962.

———. *The Place of Christ in Liturgical Prayer.* New York: Alba House, 1965.

Karkov, Catherine. "The Chalice and the Cross in Insular Art." In *The Age of Migrating Ideas,* edited by Spearman and Higgitt, 237–44.

Kelly, Fergus. *Early Irish Farming.* Early Irish Law Series 4. Dublin: Dublin Institute for Celtic Studies, 2000.

———. *A Guide to Early Irish Law.* Early Irish Law Series 3. Dublin: Dublin Institute for Celtic Studies, 1998.

Kelly, J. N. D. *Jerome: His Life, Writings, and Controversies.* Peabody, MA: Hendrickson, 1975.

Kennedy, Hugh P. "Tinkering Embellishment or Liturgical Fidelity? An Investigation into Liturgical Practice in Ireland before the Twelfth Century Reform Movement as Illustrated in the *Stowe Missal.*" DD thesis, St Patrick's College, Maynooth, 1994.

Kenney, James F. *The Sources for the Early History of Ireland I: Ecclesiastical.* New York: Columbia, 1929; repr. Dublin: Four Courts Press, 1993.

Kilmartin, Edward J. *The Eucharist in the West: History and Theology,* edited by Robert J. Daly. Collegeville, MN: Liturgical Press, 1998.

King, Archdale A. *Eucharistic Reservation in the Western Church.* New York: Sheed and Ward, 1965.

———. *Liturgies of the Past.* London: Longmans, 1959.

King, P. D., trans. and ed. *Charlemagne: Translated Sources.* Kendal: self-published, 1987.

Klauser, Theodore. *A Short History of the Western Liturgy: An Account and Some Reflections.* Translated by J. Halliburton. 2nd ed. New York: Oxford University Press, 1979.

Kodell, Jerome. *The Eucharist in the New Testament.* Collegeville, MN: Liturgical Press, 1988.

Lamb, H. H. *Climate, History and the Modern World.* London: Methuen, 1982.

Lambkin, Brian. "Blathmac and the Céli Dé: A Reappraisal." *Celtica* 23 (1999): 132–54.

Lapidge, Michael, ed. *Columbanus: Studies on the Latin Writings.* Studies in Celtic History 17. Woodbridge: Boydell Press, 1997.

Lawlor, Hugh Jackson, ed. *The Rosslyn Missal: An Irish Manuscript in the Advocates' Library, Edinburgh.* London: Henry Bradshaw Society, 1899.

Leask, Harold G. *Irish Churches and Monastic Buildings.* Vol. 1, *The First Phases and the Romanesque.* Dundalk: Dundalgan Press, 1955.

Leclercq, Jean. "Eucharistic Celebration without Priests in the Middle Ages." In *Living Bread, Saving Cup: Readings on the Eucharist,* edited by R. Kevin Seasoltz, 222–30. Collegeville, MN: Liturgical Press, 1987.

Leclercq, Jean, and H. M. Rochais, eds. *Sancti Bernardi Opera.* Vol. 3, *Tractatus et Opuscula.* Rome: Editiones Cisterciensis, 1963.

Leroy, F. J. "Proclus *De Traditione Divinae Missae:* Un Faux de C. Palaeocappa." *Orientalia Christiana Periodica* 28 (1962): 288–99.

Lewis, Suzanne. "Sacred Calligraphy: The Chi Rho Page in the *Book of Kells.*" *Traditio* 36 (1980): 139–59.

L'Huillier, Peter. *The Church of the Ancient Councils: The Disciplinary Work of the First Four Ecumenical Councils.* Crestwood, NY: St. Vladimir's Seminary Press, 1996.

Löwe, Heinz, ed. *Die Iren und Europa im Früheren Mittelalter.* 2 vols. Stuttgart: Klett-Cotta, 1982.

Macalister, R. A. S. *Corpus Inscriptionum Insularum Celticarum.* Vol. 2. Dublin: Stationery Office, 1949.

MacCathy, Bartholomew. "On the *Stowe Missal.*" *Transactions of the Royal Irish Academy* 27 (1886): 135–268.

MacDonald, Aidan. "Aspects of the Monastery and Monastic Life in Adomnán's *Life of Columba.*" *Peritia* 3 (1984): 271–302.

———. "Reiclés in the Irish Annals to AD 1200." *Peritia* 12 (1999): 259–75.

Mac Eclaise (pseudonym), trans. and ed. "The Rule of St Carthage." *Irish Ecclesiastical Record* 27 (1910): 495–517.

Mackey, James P., ed. *An Introduction to Celtic Christianity.* Edinburgh: T&T Clark, 1995.

MacIomhair, Diarmuid. "The History of Fir Rois." *County Louth Archaeological Journal* 15 (1964): 321–48.

———. *"The Poems of Blathmac."* Review of Carney, *The Poems of Blathmac. County Louth Archaeological Journal* 15 (1964): 358.

Macy, Gary. *The Banquet's Wisdom: A Short History of the Theologies of the Lord's Supper.* 2nd ed. Akron, OH: OSL Publications, 2005.

Maher, Michael. "Sunday in the Irish Church." *Irish Theological Quarterly* 60 (1994): 161–84.

Manning, Conleth. "Clonmacnoise Cathedral." In *Clonmacnoise Studies.* Vol. 1, *Seminar Papers 1994,* edited by Heather A. King, 57–86. Dublin: Dúchas—The Heritage Service, 1998.

———. "References to Church Buildings in the Annals." In *Seanchas,* edited by A. Smyth, 37–52.

Márkus, Gilbert. "The Sick and the Dying in the *Book of Deer.*" In *Studies on the Book of Deer,* edited by Katherine Forsyth, 67–97. Dublin: Four Courts Press, 2008.

Marshall, Jenny White, and Grellan D. Rourke. *High Island: An Irish Monastery in the Atlantic.* Dublin: Townhouse, 2000.

Marsilli, Salvatore, ed. *Anàmnesis: Introduzione Storico-Teologica della Liturgia.* Vol. 2, *La Liturgia: Panorma Storico Generale.* Casale Monoferrato: Marietti, 1978.

Martin, Francis Xavier. "Ireland in the Time of St Bernard, St Malachy and St Laurence O'Toole." *Seanchas Ard Mhacha: Journal of the Armagh Diocesan Historical Society* 15 (1992): 1–35.

———. "The Normans: Arrival and Settlement, 1169–c. 1300." In *The Course of Irish History,* edited by Moody and Martin, 95–112.

Mazza, Enrico. *The Celebration of the Eucharist: The Origins of the Rite and the Development of Its Interpretation.* Translated by Matthew J. O'Connell. Collegeville, MN: Liturgical Press, 1999.

———. "The Eucharist in the First Four Centuries." In *The Eucharist,* edited by Chupungco, 9–62.

McCarthy, Daniel P. *The Irish Annals: Their Genesis, Evolution and History.* Dublin: Four Courts Press, 2008.

McCarthy, Daniel P., and Aidan Breen. *The Ante-Nicene Christian Pasch,* De Ratione Paschali: *The Paschal Tract of Anatolius, Bishop of Laodicea.* Dublin: Four Courts Press, 2003.

McCormick, Michael. *Origins of the European Economy: Communications and Commerce, AD 300–900.* Cambridge: Cambridge University Press, 2001.

McKitterick, Rosamond. "The Scriptoria of Merovingian Gaul: A Survey of the Evidence." In *Columbanus and Merovingian Monasticism,* edited by Clarke and Brennan, 73–191.

McManus, Damian. "The So-Called *Cothrige* and *Pátraic* Strata of Latin Loan-Words in Early Irish." In *Die Kirche im Frühmittelalter,* edited by Ní Chatháin and Richter, 179–96.

McNally, Robert E., ed. *Scriptores Hiberniae Minores Pars I.* Corpus Christianorum Series Latina 108B, Scriptores Celtigenae. Turnhout: Brepols, 1973.

McNamara, Martin. "Apocalyptic and Eschatological Texts in Irish Literature: Oriental Connections?" In *Apocalyptic and Eschatological Heritage: The Middle East and Celtic Realms,* edited by Martin McNamara, 75–97. Dublin: Four Courts Press, 2003.

———. "The Inverted Eucharistic Formula *Conversio Corporis Christi in Panem et Sanguinis in Vinum:* The Exegetical and Liturgical Background in Irish Usage." *Proceedings of the Royal Irish Academy* 87C (1987): 573–93.

———. *Psalter Text and Psalter Study in the Early Irish Church, AD 600–1200.* Dublin: Royal Irish Academy, 1973.

Meeder, Sven. "The Early Irish *Stowe Missal*'s Destination and Function." *Early Medieval Europe* 13, no. 2 (2005): 179–94.

Meehan, Bernard. *The Book of Kells: An Illustrated Introduction to the Manuscript in Trinity College, Dublin.* New York: Thames and Hudson, 1994.

Meehan, Denis, trans. and ed. *Adamnán: De Locis Sanctis.* Scriptores Latini Hiberniae 3. Dublin: The Dublin Institute for Advanced Studies, 1983.

Meens, Rob. "The Frequency and Nature of Early European Penance." In *Handling Sin: Confession in the Middle Ages,* edited by Peter Biller and A. J. Minnis, 35–61. Woodbridge: York Medieval Press, 1998.

Metzger, Marcel. "The History of the Eucharistic Liturgy in Rome." In *The Eucharist,* edited by Chupungco, 103–31.

———, trans. and ed. *Les Constitutions Apostoliques III: Livres VII et VIII.* Sources Chrétiennes 336. Paris: Les Éditons du Cerf, 1987.

Meyer, Robert T., trans. and ed. *Bernard of Clairvaux: The Life and Death of Saint Malachy the Irishman.* Cistercian Fathers Series 10. Kalamazoo, MI: Cistercian Publications, 1978.

Meyvaert, Paul. "Diversity within Unity: A Gregorian Theme." In *Benedict, Gregory, Bede and Others,* edited by Paul Meyvaert, 141–62. London: Variorum, 1977.

Mitchell, Nathan. *Cult and Controversy: The Worship of the Eucharist outside Mass.* New York: Pueblo, 1982.

Mohrmann, Christine. "The Earliest Continental Irish Latin." *Vigiliae Christianae* 16, nos. 3/4 (1962): 216–33.

———. *Liturgical Latin: Its Origins and Character, Three Lectures.* London: Burns and Oates, 1957.

Moody, Theo W., and Francis X. Martin, eds. *The Course of Irish History.* 4th ed. Lanham, MD: Roberts Rinehart Publishers, 2001.

Moran, Josephine. "The Shattered Image: Archaeological Evidence for Painted and Stained Glass in Medieval Ireland." In *Art and Devotion in Late Medieval Ireland,* edited by Rachel Moss, Colmán Ó Clabaigh, and Salvador Ryan, 121–41. Dublin: Four Courts Press, 2006.

Murdoch, Brian. "Preaching in Medieval Ireland: The Irish Tradition." In *Irish Preaching,* edited by Fletcher and Gillespie, 40–55.

Murphy, G. Roland. *The Heliand: The Saxon Gospel.* New York: Oxford University Press, 1992.

———. *The Saxon Savior: The Transformation of the Gospel in the Ninth-Century Heliand.* New York: Oxford University Press, 1989.

Murphy, Gerard. "Eleventh or Twelfth Century Irish Doctrine Concerning the Real Presence." In *Medieval Studies Presented to Aubrey Gwynn,* edited by J. A. Watt, J. B. Morrall, and F. X. Martin, 19–28. Dublin: Colm O'Lochlainn, 1961.

Mytum, Harold. *The Origins of Early Christian Ireland.* New York: Routledge, 1992.

Nees, Lawrence. *Early Medieval Art.* Oxford History of Art. Oxford: Oxford University Press, 2002.

Neuman De Vegvar, Carol. "Romanitas and Realpolitik in Cogitosus' Description of the Church of St Brigit, Kildare." In *The Cross Goes North,* edited by Carver, 153–70.

Ní Chatháin, Próinséas. "Bede's *Ecclesiastical History* in Irish." *Peritia* 3 (1980): 115–30.

Ní Chatháin, Próinséas, and Michael Richter, eds. *Ireland and Christendom: The Bible and the Missions.* Stuttgart: Klett-Cotta, 1987.

———, eds. *Ireland and Europe in the Early Middle Ages: Learning and Literature.* Stuttgart: Klett-Cotta, 1996.

———, eds. *Irland und Europa: Die Kirche im Frühmittelalter.* Stuttgart: Klett-Cotta, 1984.

Ní Mheara, Róisín. *In Search of Irish Saints: The* Peregrinatio Pro Christo. Dublin: Four Courts Press, 1994.

Nocent, Adrien. "Questions about Specific Points." In *The Eucharist,* edited by Chupungco, 295–320.

Nodet, Étienne, and Justin Taylor. *The Origins of Christianity: An Exploration.* Collegeville, MN: Liturgical Press, 1998.

Nußbaum, Otto. *Die Aufbewahrung der Eucharistie.* Bonn: Hanstein, 1979.

Ó Carragáin, Éamonn. *The City of Rome and the World of Bede: The 1994 Jarrow Lecture.* N.p., 1994.

———. "The Meeting of Saint Paul and Saint Anthony: Visual and Literary Uses of a Eucharistic Motif." In *Keimelia: Studies in Medieval Archaeology and History in Memory of Tom Delaney,* edited by G. Mac Niocaill and P. F. Wallace, 1–58. Galway: Galway University Press, 1988.

———. *Ritual and the Rood: Liturgical Images and the Old English Poem of the* Dream of the Rood *Tradition.* London: The British Library, 2005.

———. "'*Traditio Evangeliorum*' and '*Sustenatio*': The Relevance of Liturgical Ceremonies to the Book of Kells." In *The Book of Kells: Proceedings of a Conference at Trinity College Dublin, 6–9 September 1992,* edited by Felicity O'Mahony, 398–436. Aldershot: Scolar Press, 1994.

Ó Carragáin, Tomás. "The Architectural Setting of the Cult of Relics in Early Medieval Ireland." *Journal of the Royal Society of Antiquaries of Ireland* 133 (2003): 130–76.

———. "The Architectural Setting of the Mass in Early-Medieval Ireland." *Medieval Archaeology* 53 (2009): 119–54.

———. "Church Buildings and Pastoral Care in Early Medieval Ireland." In *The Parish in Medieval and Early Modern Ireland,* edited by Gillespie and FitzPatrick, 91–123.

———. "Habitual Masonry Styles and the Local Organisation of Church Building in Early Medieval Ireland." *Proceedings of the Royal Irish Academy* 105C (2005): 99–145.

———. "A Landscape Converted: Archaeology and Early Church Organisation on Iveragh and Dingle, Ireland." In *The Cross Goes North,* edited by Carver, 127–52.

———. "Regional Variation in Irish Pre-Romanesque Architecture." *Antiquaries Journal* 85 (2005): 23–56.

———. "The Saint and the Sacred Centre: Characterising the Early Medieval Pilgrimage Landscape of Inishmurray, Co. Sligo." In *The Archaeology of the Early Medieval Celtic Churches,* edited by Nancy Edwards, 207–26. London: Maney Publishing, 2009.

———. "Skeuomorphs and Spolia: The Presence of the Past in Irish Pre-Romanesque Architecture." In *Making and Meaning in Insular Art,* edited by Rachel Moss, 95–109. Dublin: Four Courts Press, 2007.

Ó Clabaigh, Colmán. "The Benedictines in Medieval and Early Modern Ireland." In *The Irish Benedictines,* edited by Browne and Ó Clabaigh, 179–212.

Ó Corráin, Donnchadh. "Ireland *c.* 800: Aspects of Society." In *Prehistoric and Early Ireland,* edited by Ó Cróinín, 549–608.

———. "Irish Vernacular Law and the Old Testament." In *Ireland and Christendom,* edited by Ní Chatháin and Richter, 284–307.

———. "Mael Muire Ua Dúnáin (1040–1117), Reformer." In *Folia Gadelica: Essays Presented by Former Students to R. A. Breatnach, M.A., M.R.I.A.,* edited by Pádraig de Brún, Seán Ó Coileáin, and Pádraig Ó Riain, 47–53. Cork: Cork University Press, 1983.

Ó Cróinín, Dáibhí. *Early Medieval Ireland, 400–1200.* London: Longman, 1995.

———. "New Heresy for Old: Pelagianism in Ireland and the Papal Letter of 640." *Speculum* 60, no. 3 (1985): 505–16.

———, ed. *Prehistoric and Early Ireland.* Vol. 1 of *A New History of Ireland.* Oxford: Oxford University Press, 2005.

———. "A Tale of Two Rules: Benedict and Columbanus." In *The Irish Benedictines,* edited by Browne and Ó Clabaigh, 11–24.

Ó Duinn, Séan. *Where Three Streams Meet: Celtic Spirituality.* Dublin: Columba Press, 2002.

O'Dwyer, Barry W., trans. and ed. *Stephen of Lexington: Letters from Ireland 1228–1229.* Cistercian Fathers Series 28. Kalamazoo, MI: Cistercian Press, 1982.

O'Dwyer, Peter. *Céli Dé: Spiritual Reform in Ireland, 750–900.* 2nd ed. Dublin: Editions Tailliura, 1981.

Ó Fiaich, Tomás. "Irish Monks in Germany in the Late Middle Ages." In *The Churches, Ireland and the Irish: Papers Read at the 1987 Summer Meeting and the 1988 Winter Meeting of the Ecclesiastical History Society,* edited by W. J. Shiels and Dianna Wood, 89–104. Oxford: Basil Blackwell, 1989.

Ó Floinn, Raghnall. "The Bronze Strainer-Ladle." In *The Derrynaflan Hoard.* Vol. 1, *A Preliminary Account,* edited by Michael Ryan, 31–34. Dublin: National Museum of Ireland, 1983.

———. "*Insignia Columbae I.*" In *Studies in the Cult of Saint Columba,* edited by Cormac Bourke, 136–61. Dublin: Four Courts Press, 1997.

Ó hAodha, Donncha, trans. and ed. *Bethu Brigte.* Dublin: Dublin Institute for Advanced Studies, 1978.

O'Keeffe, J. G. "Cáin Domnaig I: The Epistle of Jesus." *Ériu* 2 (1905): 189–214.

———. "The Rule of Patrick." *Ériu* 1 (1905): 216–24.

O'Keeffe, Tadhg. *An Anglo-Norman Monastery: Bridgetown Priory and the Architecture of the Augustinian Canons Regular in Ireland.* Kinsale: Cork County Council/Grandon Editions, 1999.

———. "The Built Environment of Local Community Worship between the Late Eleventh and Early Thirteenth Centuries." In *The Parish in Medieval and Early Modern Ireland,* edited by Gillespie and FitzPatrick, 124–46.

———. "The Built Environment of Local Community Worship between the Late Eleventh and Early Thirteenth Centuries." Unpublished paper.

———. *Ireland's Round Towers.* Stroud: Tempus, 2004.

———. *Medieval Ireland: An Archaeology.* Stroud: Tempus, 2000.

———. "Romanesque as Metaphor: Architecture and Reform in Early Twelfth Century Ireland." In *Seanchas,* edited by A. Smyth, 313–22.

———. *Romanesque Ireland: Archaeology and Ideology in the Twelfth Century.* Dublin: Four Courts Press, 2003.

O'Loughlin, Thomas, ed. *Adomnán at Birr, AD 697: Essays in Commemoration of the Law of the Innocents.* Dublin: Four Courts Press, 2001.

———. "A Celtic Preface." *Furrow* 51 (2000): 34–38.

———. *Celtic Theology: Humanity, Word and God in Early Irish Writings.* New York: Continuum, 2000.

———, trans. and ed. *Discovering St. Patrick.* Mahwah, NJ: Paulist Press, 2005.

———. "Irish Preaching before the End of the Ninth Century: Assessing the Extent of Our Evidence." In *Irish Preaching,* edited by Fletcher and Gillespie, 18–39.

———. "Penitentials and Pastoral Care." In *A History of Pastoral Care,* edited by G. R. Evans, 93–111. London: Cassell, 2000.

———. "The Praxis and Explanation of Eucharistic Fraction in the Ninth Century: The Insular Evidence." *Archiv für Liturgiewissenschaft* 45 (2003): 1–20.

————. "The Significance of Sunday: Three Ninth-Century Catecheses." *Worship* 64 (1990): 533–44.

Ó Maidín, Uinseann, trans. and ed. *The Celtic Monk: Rules and Writings of Early Irish Monks.* Cistercian Studies Series 162. Kalamazoo, MI: Cistercian Publications, 1996.

O'Meara, John J., trans. and ed. *Gerald of Wales: The History and Topography of Ireland.* London: Penguin, 1982.

————. "Giraldus Cambrensis *In Topographia Hibernie:* Text of the First Recension." *Proceedings of the Royal Irish Academy* 50C (1949): 113–78.

Ó Néill, Pádraig. "The *Old-Irish Tract on the Mass* in the *Stowe Missal:* Some Observances on Its Origin and Textual History." In *Seanchas,* edited by A. Smyth, 199–204.

O'Rahilly, T. F. "The History of the *Stowe Missal.*" *Ériu* 10 (1926–28): 95–109.

O'Reilly, Jennifer. "The *Book of Kells:* Folio 114r, a Mystery Revealed Yet Concealed." In *The Age of Migrating Ideas,* edited by Spearman and Higgitt, 106–14.

Ó Riain, Pádraig. "The *Book of Glendalough* or Rawlinson B502." *Éigse* 18 (1981): 161–76.

————. "Rawlinson B502 alias *Lebar Glinne Dá Locha:* A Restatement of the Case." *Zeitschrift fur Celtische Philologie* 51 (2000): 130–47.

————. "The Shrine of the *Stowe Missal* Redated." *Proceedings of the Royal Irish Academy* 91C (1991): 285–95.

O'Sullivan, Ann, and John Sheehan. *The Iveragh Peninsula: An Archaeological Survey of South Kerry.* Cork: Cork University Press, 1996.

O'Sullivan, William. "Manuscripts and Palaeography." In *Prehistoric and Early Ireland,* edited by Ó Cróinín, 511–48.

Palazzo, Éric. *A History of Liturgical Books: From the Beginning to the Thirteenth Century.* Translated by Madeleine Beaumont. Collegeville, MN: Liturgical Press, 1998.

Panofsky, Erwin, trans. and ed. *Abbot Suger on the Abbey-Church of Saint-Denis and Its Art Treasures.* Princeton: Princeton University Press, 1946.

Parenti, Stefano. "The Eucharistic Celebration in the East: The Various Orders of Celebration." In *The Eucharist,* edited by Chupungco, 61–75.

Parry, Ken, and Archimandrite Ephrem. "Rhipidion." In *The Blackwell Dictionary of Eastern Christianity,* edited by Ken Parry et al. Malden, MA: Blackwell Publishing, 1999.

Parsons, David. *Liturgy and Architecture in the Middle Ages.* Deerhurst: Friends of Deerhurst Church, 1989.

————. "*Sacrarium:* Ablution Drains in Early Medieval Churches." In *The Anglo-Saxon Church,* edited by Butler and Morris, 105–20.

Paxton, Frederick S. *Christianizing Death.* Ithaca: Cornell University Press, 1990.

Pelikan, Jaroslav. *The Christian Tradition: A History of the Development of Doctrine.* Vol. 2, *The Growth of Medieval Theology (600–1300).* Chicago: University of Chicago Press, 1978.

Périn, Patrick, and Laurie-Charlotte Feffer. *La Neustrie: Les Pays au Nord de La Loire de Dagobert à Charles Le Chauve (VIIe–IXe Siècles).* Créteil: Museés et Monuments Départmentaux de Seine-Maritime, 1985.

Petrie, George. *Christian Inscriptions in the Irish Language.* Vol. 2. Dublin: Royal Historical and Archaeological Association of Ireland, 1878.

———. *The Ecclesiastical Architecture of Ireland: An Essay on the Origin and Uses of the Round Towers of Ireland.* 2nd ed. Dublin: Hodges & Smith, 1845.

Pfaff, Richard W. *The Liturgy in Medieval England: A History.* Cambridge: Cambridge University Press, 2009.

Piggott, Stuart. *The Druids.* 2nd ed. London: Thames & Hudson, 1985.

Pinell i Pons, Jordi. "History of the Liturgies in the Non-Roman West." In *The Pontifical Liturgical Institute Handbook for Liturgical Studies.* Vol. 1, *Introduction to the Liturgy,* edited by Anscar J. Chupungco, 179–95. Collegeville, MN: Liturgical Press, 1997.

———. "La Liturgia Gallicana." In *Anàmnesis,* edited by Marsilli, 62–66.

Plummer, Charles. *Bethada Náem nÉrenn: Lives of the Irish Saints Edited from Original Manuscripts.* Oxford: Oxford University Press, 1922.

———, trans and ed. *Vitae Sanctorum Hiberniae Partim Hactenus Ineditae: Ad Fidem Codicum Manuscriptorum Recognovit Prolegomenis Notis Indicibus Instruxit.* 2 vols. Oxford: Oxford University Press, 1910.

Porter, W. S. *The Gallican Rite.* London: Mowbray, 1958.

Preston, Sarah. "The Canons Regular of St Augustine: The Twelfth Century Reform in Action." In *Augustinians at Christ Church: The Canons Regular of the Cathedral Priory of the Holy Trinity Dublin,* edited by Stuart Kinsella, 23–40. Dublin: Christ Church Cathedral Publications, 2000.

Quasten, Johannes. *Music and Worship in Pagan and Christian Antiquity.* Translated by Boniface Ramsey. Washington DC: National Association of Pastoral Musicians, 1983.

———. "Oriental Influence in the Gallican Liturgy." *Traditio* 1 (1943): 55–79.

Rabe, Susan A. *Faith, Art and Politics at Saint-Riquier: The Symbolic Vision of Angilbert.* Philadelphia: University of Pennsylvania Press, 1995.

Ramis, Gabriel. "The Eucharistic Celebration in the Non-Roman West." In *The Eucharist,* edited by Chupungco, 245–62.

Reeves, William. "On the Céli Dé Commonly Called the Culdees." *Transactions of the Royal Irish Academy* 24, no. 3 (1873): 119–264.

Richardson, Hilary. "Celtic Art." In *An Introduction to Celtic Christianity,* edited by Mackey, 359–85.

———. "The Jewelled Cross and Its Canopy." In *From the Isles of the North: Early Medieval Art in Ireland and Britain,* edited by Cormac Bourke, 177–86. Belfast: H.M.S.O., 1995.

———. "Remarks on the Liturgical Fan, Flabellum or Rhipidion." In *The Age of Migrating Ideas,* edited by Spearman and Higgitt, 27–34.

———. "Visual Arts and Society." In *Prehistoric and Early Ireland,* edited by Ó Cróinín, 680–713.

Richardson, Hilary, and John Scarry. *An Introduction to Irish High Crosses.* Cork: Mercier Press, 1990.

Richter, Michael. *Bobbio in the Early Middle Ages: The Abiding Legacy of Columbanus.* Dublin: Four Courts Press, 2008.

———. "Das Irische erbe der Karolinger." In *Charlemagne and His Heritage,* edited by Butzer, Kerner and Oberschelp, 1:79–96.

———. *Ireland and Her Neighbours in the Seventh Century.* Dublin: Four Courts Press, 1999.

Rittmueller, Jean. "The Gospel Commentary of Máel Brigte Ua Maelruanaig and Its Hiberno-Latin Background." *Peritia* 2 (1983): 185–214.

———, ed. *Liber Questionum in Evangeliis.* Corpus Christianorum Series Latina 108F, Scriptores Celtigenae. Turnhout: Brepols, 2003.

Rouwhorst, G. "La Célébracion de l'Eucharistie selon les Actes de Thomas." In *Omnes Circumadstantes: Contributions towards a History of the Role of the People in the Liturgy,* edited by Charles Caspers and Marc Schneiders, 51–77. Kampen: J. H. Kok, 1990.

Russell, James C. *The Germanization of Early Medieval Christianity: A Sociohistorical Approach to Religious Transformation.* New York: Oxford University Press, 1994.

Ryan, John. *Irish Monasticism: Origins and Early Development.* 2nd ed. Dublin: Four Courts Press, 1972.

———. "The Mass in the Early Irish Church." *Studies* 50 (1961): 371–84.

Ryan, Michael. *Early Irish Communion Vessels.* The Irish Treasures Series. Dublin: Country House, Dublin, in association with The National Museum of Ireland, 2000.

———. *Studies in Early Irish Metalwork.* London: Pindar Press, 2002.

Ryan, Salvador. "'Reign of Blood': Aspects of Devotion to the Wounds of Christ in Late Medieval Ireland." In *Irish History: A Yearbook,* edited by Joost Augusteijn and Mary Ann Lyons, 137–49. Dublin: Four Courts Press, 2002.

Sayers, William. "Attitudes Towards Hair and Beards, Baldness and Tonsure." *Zeitschrift für Celtische Philologie* 44 (1991): 154–89.

Saxer, Victor. "L'utilisation par la Liturgie d'Espace Urbain et Suburbain: l'Exemple de Rome das l'Antiquité en le Haut Moyen Âge." In *Collection de l'École Française de Rome.* Vol. 123 printed in 2 vols., *Actes du XIᵉ Congrès International d'Archéologie Chrètienne,* 2:917–1033. Rome: Ecole Francaise de Rome, 1989.

Schneiders, Marc. "The Origins of the Early Irish Liturgy." In *Ireland and Europe,* edited by Ní Chatháin and Richter, 76–98.

Scully, Diarmuid. "The Portrayal of Ireland and the Irish in Bernard's *Life of Malachy:* Representation and Context." In *Ireland and Europe,* edited by Bracken and Ó Riain-Raedel, 239–58.

Selmer, Carl, ed. *Navigatio Sancti Brendani Abbatis.* Notre Dame, IN: University of Notre Dame Press, 1959.

Severin, Tim. *The Brendan Voyage: Across the Atlantic in a Leather Boat.* New York: Modern Library, 2000.

Sexton, Mary Regina. "Cereals and Cereal Foodstuffs in Early Historic Ireland." MA thesis, University College Cork, 1993.

Sharpe, Richard, trans. and ed. *Adomnán of Iona: Life of St Columba.* London: Penguin, 1995.

———. "Churches and Communities in Early Medieval Ireland: Towards a Pastoral Model." In *Pastoral Care Before the Parish,* edited by Blair and Sharpe, 81–109.

———. *Medieval Irish Saints' Lives: An Introduction to Vitae Sanctorum Hiberniae.* Oxford: The Clarendon Press, 1991.

———. "Some Problems Concerning the Organization of the Church in Early Medieval Ireland." *Peritia* 3 (1984): 230–70.

———. "St Patrick and the See of Armagh." *Cambridge Medieval Celtic Studies* 4 (1982): 33–59.

Sheehy, Maurice P., ed. *Pontifica Hibernica: Medieval Papal Chancery Documents Concerning Ireland 640–1261.* Dublin: Gill, 1962.

Sicard, Damien. *La Liturgie de la Mort dans l'Eglise Latine des Origiens à la Réforme Carolingienne.* Liturgiewissenschaftliche Quellen und Forschungen 63. Muenster Westfalen, 1978.

Simms, Katherine. "The Origins of the Diocese of Clogher." *Clogher Record* 10, no. 1 (1979): 180–98.

Smith, Brendan, ed. *Britain and Ireland 900–1300: Insular Responses to Medieval European Change.* Cambridge: Cambridge University Press, 1991.

Smyth, Alfred P. "The Effect of Scandinavian Raiders on the English and Irish Churches: A Preliminary Reassessment." In *Britain and Ireland,* edited by Smith, 1–38.

———. "The Golden Age of Early Irish Monasticism: Myth or Reality?" In *Christianity in Ireland,* edited by Bradshaw and Keogh, 21–29.

———, ed. *Seanchas: Studies in Early and Medieval Irish Archaeology, History and Literature in Honour of Francis J. Byrne.* Dublin: Four Courts Press, 2000.

Smyth, Matthieu. *La Liturgie Oubliée: La Prière Eucharistique en Gaule Antique et dans l'Occident non Romain.* Paris: Éditions du Cerf, 2003.

Snoek, G. J. C. *Medieval Piety from Relics to the Eucharist: A Process of Mutual Interaction.* Studies in the History of Christian Thought 63. Leiden: E. J. Brill, 1995.

Somerville, Robert. *Scotia Pontificia: Papal Letters to Scotland before the Pontificate of Innocent III*. Oxford: Clarendon Press, 1982.

Spearman, R. Michael, and John Higgitt, eds. *The Age of Migrating Ideas: Early Medieval Art in Northern Britain and Ireland*. Gloucester: Sutton, and Edinburgh: National Museum of Scotland, 1993.

Stalley, Roger. *The Cistercian Monasteries of Ireland: An Account of the History, Art, and Architecture of the White Monks in Ireland from 1142 to 1540*. New Haven: Yale University Press, 1987.

———. "Ecclesiastical Architecture before 1169." In *Prehistoric and Early Ireland*, edited by Ó Cróinín, 714–43.

———. *Irish High Crosses*. Dublin: Country House, 1996.

———. *Irish Round Towers*. Dublin: Country House, 2000.

———. "Sex, Symbol, and Myth: Some Observations on the Irish Round Towers." In *From Ireland Coming*, edited by Hourihane, 27–47.

Stancliffe, Claire. "Red, White and Blue Martyrdom." In *Ireland in Early Medieval Europe: Studies in Memory of Kathleen Hughes*, ed. Dorothy Whitelock, Rosamond McKitterick, and David Dumville (Cambridge: Cambridge University Press, 1982).

———. "The Thirteen Sermons Attributed to Columbanus and the Question of Their Authorship." In *Columbanus: Studies on the Latin Writings*, edited by Lapidge, 93–199.

Stern, Menahem. *Greek and Latin Authors on Jews and Judaism*. 2 vols. Jerusalem: The Israel Academy of Sciences and Humanities, 1974–80.

Stevenson, Jane. "The Antiphonary of Bangor." Review of Curran, *The Antiphonary of Bangor*. *Peritia* 5 (1986): 430–37.

———. "Hiberno-Latin Hymns: Learning and Literature." In *Ireland and Europe in the Middle Ages*, edited by Ní Chatháin and Richter, 99–135.

———. "Introduction." In F. E. Warren, *The Liturgy and Ritual of the Celtic Church*, 2nd fac. ed., 1987, xi–xcvi.

Stokes, Whitley. "The *Lebar Brecc* Tractate on the Consecration of a Church." In *Miscellanea Linguistica in Onore di Graziadio Ascoli*, 363–87. Turin: Case Editrice Ermanno Loescher, 1901.

Stokes, Whitley, and John Strachan, eds. *Thesaurus Palaeohibernicus*. 2 vols. Cambridge: Cambridge University Press, 1901–3.

Swan, Leo. "Monastic Proto-towns in Early Medieval Ireland: The Evidence of Aerial Photography, Plan Analysis and Survey." In *The Comparative History of Urban Origins*, edited by Clarke and Simms, 1:77–102.

Swanson, R. N., ed. *Continuity and Change in Christian Worship: Papers Read at the 1997 Summer Meeting and the 1998 Winter Meeting of the Ecclesiastical History Society*. Woodbridge: Boydell Press, 1999.

Swift, Catherine. "Forts and Fields: A Study of Monastic Towns in Seventh and Eighth Century Ireland." *Journal of Irish Archaeology* 9 (1998): 105–23.

―――. *Ogham Stones and the Earliest Irish Christians.* Maynooth: Cardinal Press, 1997.

Tachiaos, Anthony-Emil. *Cyril and Methodius of Thessalonica: The Acculturation of the Slavs.* Crestwood, NY: St. Vladimir's Seminary Press, 2001.

Taft, Robert F. *Beyond East and West: Problems in Liturgical Understanding.* 2nd ed. Rome: Edizioni Orientalia Christiana, 1997.

―――. *The Byzantine Rite: A Short History.* Collegeville, MN: Liturgical Press, 1992.

―――. *A History of the Liturgy of St John Chrysostom.* Vol. 5, *The Precommunion Rites.* Orientalia Christiana Analecta 261. Rome: Edizioni Orientalia Christiana, 2000.

―――. "Home-Communion in the Late Antique East." In *Ars Liturgiae: Worship, Aesthetics and Praxis. Essays in Honor of Nathan D. Mitchell,* edited by Clare V. Johnson, 1–25. Chicago: Liturgy Training Publications, 2003.

―――. "Is There Devotion to the Holy Eucharist in the Christian East? A Footnote to the October 2005 Synod of the Eucharist." *Worship* 80, no. 3 (2006): 213–33.

―――. *The Liturgy of the Hours in East and West: The Origins of the Divine Office and Its Meaning for Today.* 2nd ed. Collegeville, MN: Liturgical Press: 1993.

―――. "Mass Without the Consecration? The Historic Agreement on the Eucharist between the Catholic Church and the Assyrian Church of the East Promulgated 26 October 2001." *Worship* 77, no. 6 (2003): 482–509.

―――. "The Order and Place of Lay Communion in the Late Antique and Byzantine East." In *Studia Liturgica Diversa: Studies in Church Music and Liturgy; Essays in Honor of Paul F. Bradshaw,* edited by Maxwell E. Johnson and L. Edward Phillips, 129–49. Portland: Pastoral Press, 2004.

―――. *Through Their Own Eyes: Liturgy as the Byzantines Saw it.* Berkeley, CA: InterOrthodox Press, 2006.

―――. "Was the Eucharistic Anaphora Recited Secretly or Aloud? The Ancient Tradition and What Became of It." In *Worship Traditions in Armenia and the Neighboring Christian East: An International Symposium in Honor of the Fortieth Anniversary of St Nersess Armenian Seminary,* edited by Roberta R. Ervine, 15–57. Crestwood, NY: St. Vladimir's Seminary Press, 2006.

Tanner, Norman P., trans. and ed. *Decrees of the Ecumenical Councils.* Washington DC: Georgetown University Press, 1990.

Thibodeau, Timothy. "Western Christendom." In *The Oxford History of Christian Worship,* edited by Wainwright and Westerfield Tucker, 216–53.

Thomas, Charles. *Christianity in Roman Britain to AD 500.* Berkeley: University of California Press, 1981.

―――. "Imported Pottery in Dark-Age Western Britain." *Medieval Archaeology* 3 (1959): 89–111.

Tierney, J. J., trans. and ed. *Dicuili Liber de Mensura Orbis Terrae.* Dublin: Dublin Institute for Advanced Studies, 1967.

Triacca, Achille. "La Liturgia Ambrosiana." In *Anàmnesis,* edited by Marsilli, 88–110.

Van Dijk, Stephen J. P., and Joan Hazelden Walker. *The Origins of the Modern Roman Liturgy: The Liturgy of the Papal Court and the Franciscan Order in the Thirteenth Century.* Westminster, MD: Neuman Press, 1960.

van Hamel, A. G. "Poems from Brussels Ms. 5100–4." *Revue Celtique* 37 (1919): 345–49.

Verkerk, Dorothy Hoogland. "Pilgrimage *Ad Limina Apostolorum* in Rome: Irish Crosses and Early Christian Sarcophagi." In *From Ireland Coming,* edited by Hourihane, 9–26.

Vogel, Cyrille. "Les Échanges Liturgiques entre Rome et les Pays Francs jusqu'á l'Époque de Charlemagne." In *Le Chiese nei Regni dell'Europa Occidentale e i loro Rapporti con Roma fino all'800.* Settimana di Spoleto 7, 1:185–295. Spoleto: Centro Italiano di Studi sull'Alto Medioevo, 1960.

———. *Medieval Liturgy: An Introduction to the Sources,* revised and translated by William Storey and Niels Rasmussen. Portland: Pastoral Press, 1986.

———. "La Multiplication des Messes Solitaires au Moyen Âge." *Revue des Sciences Religieuses* 55 (1981): 206–13.

———. "L'Orientation vers l'Est du Célébrant et des Fidèles pendant la Célébration Eucharistique." *L'Orient Syrien* 9, no. 1 (1964): 3–38.

———. "La Vie Quotidienne du Moine en Occident a l'Époque de la Floraison des Messes Privées." In *Liturgie, Spiritualité, Cultures: Conferences Saint-Serge XXIXe,* edited by A. M. Triacca and A. Pistoia, 341–60. Rome: Centro Liturgico Vincenziano, 1983.

Wainwright, Geoffrey, and Karen B. Westerfield Tucker, eds. *The Oxford History of Christian Worship.* Oxford: Oxford University Press, 2006.

Walker, G. S. M., trans. and ed. *Sancti Columbami Opera.* Scriptores Latini Hiberniae 2. Dublin: School of Celtic Studies, Dublin Institute for Advanced Studies, 1957.

Wallace, Patrick. "Irish Early Christian 'Wooden' Oratories—A Suggestion." *North Munster Antiquities Journal* 24 (1982): 19–28.

Wamers, Egon. "Insular Finds in Viking Age Scandinavia and the State Formation of Norway." In *Ireland and Scandinavia in the Early Viking Age,* edited by Howard Clarke, Máire Ní Mhaonaigh, and Raghnall Ó Floinn, 37–72. Dublin: Four Courts Press, 1998.

———. "Some Ecclesiastical and Secular Insular Metalwork Found in Norwegian Viking Graves." *Peritia* 2 (1983): 277–306.

Ward, Benedicta, *High King of Heaven: Aspects of Early English Spirituality.* Cistercian Studies Series 181. Kalamazoo, MI: Cistercian Publications, 1999.

———. *The Venerable Bede.* Harrisburg, PA: Morehouse Publishing, 1990.

Ware, James. *The Whole Works of Sir James Ware Concerning Ireland,* edited and revised by Walter Harris. Dublin: Printed for R. Bell in Stephen-Street, Opposite Aungier Street; and John Fleming, in Sycamore-Alley, 1764.

Warner, George F., ed. *The Stowe Missal: MS. D. II.3 in the Library of the Royal Irish Academy, Dublin.* Suffolk: Henry Bradshaw Society/Boydell Press; orig. pub. 2 vols., 1906 and 1915; repr. 1 vol., 1989.

Warpole, A. S. *Early Latin Hymns with Introductions and Notes.* Cambridge: Cambridge University Press, 1922.

Warren, Fredrick Edward. ed. *The Antiphonary of Bangor.* 2 vols. London: Harrison & Sons, 1893–95.

———. *The Liturgy and Ritual of the Celtic Church,* with a monograph and updated bibliography by Jane Stevenson. Oxford: The Clarendon Press, 1881; 2nd fac. ed., Suffolk: Boydell Press, 1987.

———. *The Liturgy and Ritual of the Celtic Church,* with a new introduction by Neil Xavier O'Donoghue. Gorgias Liturgical Studies 64. Oxford: The Clarendon Press, 1881; 3rd fac. ed., Piscataway, NJ: Gorgias Press, 2010.

———. *The Manuscript Irish Missal Belonging to the President and Fellows of Corpus Christi College, Oxford.* London: Henry Bradshaw Society, 1879.

Watt, John. *The Church in Medieval Ireland.* 2nd ed. Dublin: University College Dublin Press, 1998.

———. "The Irish Church in the Middle Ages." In *Christianity in Ireland,* edited by Bradshaw and Keogh, 44–56.

Webb, J. F., trans. *The Age of Bede,* edited by D. H. Farmer. London: Penguin, 1988.

Webster, Leslie. "England and the Continent." In *The Making of England: Anglo-Saxon Art and Culture AD 600–900,* edited by Leslie Webster and Janet Backhouse, 167–84. London: British Museum Press, 1991.

Whitaker, E. C. *Documents of the Baptismal Liturgy.* 3rd ed. revised by Maxwell E. Johnson. Collegeville, MN: Liturgical Press, 2003.

White, James F. *Roman Catholic Worship: Trent to Today.* 2nd ed. Collegeville, MN: Liturgical Press, 2003.

Wilkinson, John, trans. and ed. *Egeria's Travels.* 3rd ed. Warminster: Aris and Phillip, 1999.

———. *Jerusalem Pilgrims Before the Crusades.* 2nd ed. Warminster: Aris and Phillips, 2002.

Wooley, Reginald Maxwell. *The Bread of the Eucharist.* Alcuin Club Tracts 10. London: Mowbray, 1913.

Woolfenden, Gregory. "The Medieval Western Rites." In *The Study of Liturgy,* edited by Cheslyn Jones et al., 264–85. 2nd ed. New York: Oxford University Press, 1992.

———. "Western Rite Orthodoxy: Some Reflections on a Liturgical Question." *St Vladimir's Theological Quarterly* 45, no. 2 (2001): 163–92.

INDEX

abuse, 15, 27, 159, 234n157
  liturgical, 95–96, 183
  in penitential, 93–95
  with *sacrificium*, 96, 250n324
Adomnán of Iona, 103, 170, 177,
  303n84. See also *De Locis*
  Sanctis; saints' lives
altars, 18, 21, 64, 175, 189, 253n351,
  296n3
  and abuse, 20, 94–95, 140, 273n148
  and eucharistic celebration, 18, 54,
    72, 101, 104–6, 109, 126, 136,
    140, 173–75, 249n310
  and eucharistic species, 60, 73,
    94–95, 106, 111, 165–66, 182,
    253nn349–50
  and laity, 31, 57, 92, 106, 129, 157,
    164, 168, 251n329
  and relics, 59–60, 140, 164
  of stone, 164–66, 168
  of wood, 164–66
  See also architecture: altars;
    iconography: altars
Amalarius of Metz, 51–52, 72, 137
Ambrose of Milan, 84, 239n214,
  242n244, 284n235
annals, 22, 28, 119–21, 149, 154, 161,
  163, 196, 232n128
  The Annals of Inisfallen, 28, 120
  The Annals of the Four Masters,
    159, 234n162

The Annals of Ulster, 22, 120, 131,
  154, 190
Anselm, 27, 29, 135
architecture
  altars, 54–55, 59–60, 101, 116, 119,
    136, 152–54, 159, 163, 170,
    301n58, 303n84, 304n90, figures
    16, 17
  church, 17, 47, 54–55, 101, 104,
    135–36, 138, 148–58, figures 1,
    15, 18
  Irish Cistercian style, 170, 202,
    250n318
  Irish Romanesque style, 157–61
  round tower, 160–63, 195, 302n73,
    303n84, figure 20
Armagh, 16, 153, 173
Augustine of Canterbury, 11–12,
  221n32, 224n56, 243n253,
  258n28
Augustine of Hippo, 30, 141–42,
  284n235
Augustinian Order, 7, 30, 50, 160,
  235n172, 236nn174, 176

barbarian tribes, 5–6, 8, 10, 50, 57, 59,
  232n136. *See also* paganism
Bede the Venerable, 8, 11–13, 16,
  149–50, 183, 187, 224n55,
  225n63, 276n173, 311n180
Benedict of Aniane, 48, 54

FATHER NEIL XAVIER O'DONOGHUE
is prefect of studies at Redemptoris Mater Seminary in Kearny, New Jersey.